Sports Economics

Books in the Sport Management Series
Sport Governance
Russell Hoye and Graham Cuskelly

Sport and the Media
Matthew Nicholson

Sport Funding and Finance
Bob Stewart

Managing People in Sport Organizations
Tracy Taylor, Alison J. Doherty and Peter McGraw

Introduction to Sport Marketing
Aaron Smith

More information on the series can be found online by visiting
www.elsevierdirect.com

Sport Management Series
Series editor
Russell Hoye

Sports Economics
Theory, Evidence and Policy

Paul Downward

Alistair Dawson

Trudo Dejonghe

AMSTERDAM • BOSTON • HEIDELBERG • LONDON • NEW YORK • OXFORD
• PARIS • SAN DIEGO • SAN FRANCISCO • SYDNEY • TOKYO
Butterworth-Heinemann is an imprint of Elsevier

Butterworth-Heinemann is an imprint of Elsevier
Linacre House, Jordan Hill, Oxford OX2 8DP, UK
30 Corporate Drive, Suite 400, Burlington, MA 01803, USA

British Library Cataloguing in Publication Data
A catalogue record for this book is available from the British Library

Library of Congress Cataloging-in-Publication Data
A catalog record for this book is available from the Library of Congress

ISBN: 978-0-7506-8354-8

For information on all Butterworth–Heinemann publications
visit our web site at www.elsevierdirect.com

Printed and bound in Great Britain

09 10 11 12 13 10 9 8 7 6 5 4 3 2 1

Contents

Series Editor

Dr. Russell Hoye is an Associate Professor in the School of Sport, Tourism and Hospitality Management, La Trobe University, Victoria, Australia. Russell has been involved in sport management education since 1993, working in Australia at La Trobe University, Griffith University, and Victoria University and in China with The University of Hong Kong and Tsinghua University. He is a board member of the Sport Management Association of Australia and New Zealand (SMAANZ). He was the Guest Editor for the inaugural special issue of *Sport Management Review* on professional sport in Australia and New Zealand published in 2005.

Russell's areas of expertise include corporate governance, organizational behaviour, volunteer management and public sector reform within the sport industry. He has acted as a consultant for the Australian Sports Commission, Sport and Recreation Victoria and a number of local government and non-profit organizations. His research interests focus on examining how governance is enacted with sport organizations and how volunteers engage with and are managed by sport organizations. He has published papers on these topics in journals such as *Nonprofit Management and Leadership, Sport Management Review, European Sport Management Quarterly, Society and Leisure, International Gambling Studies, Third Sector Review, Sporting Traditions, Managing Leisure, Football Studies, Annals of Leisure Research, and the Australian Journal on Volunteering.*

About the authors

Dr Paul Downward is Director of the Institute of Sport and Leisure Policy, University of Loughborough. Along with Alistair Dawson he is the author of the textbook *The Economics of Professional Team Sports* (Routledge, 2000). He is the editor of a book for the Office for National Statistics on the use of official data in understanding sports, leisure and tourism markets, and the author of numerous articles on the economics of sport. He has recently undertaken consultancy work for Sport England on participation, volunteering in sports clubs, and performance management, and for UK Sport on volunteering at the Manchester Commonwealth Games. He is a member of the International Association of Sports Economics, a founding member of the editorial board of the *Journal of Sports Economics*, and member of the British Philosophy of Sport Association. Outside of these areas Dr Downward has also published on the philosophy of economics, and pricing theory. As well as refereed papers he also has a book in each of these areas. He currently teaches a final year undergraduate module in Sports Economics, and contributes sports economics teaching to modules in Sports and the Leisure Industries, Managing Sports Organizations and Olympic Studies, at Loughborough University. Paul is currently playing veteran's rugby (and can be spotted on the cover) and coaches a junior side at his local club.

Alistair Dawson retired from Staffordshire University in 2000, but maintains an active research interest, particularly in the theoretical problems surrounding the measurement of uncertainty of outcome. Apart from *The Economics of Professional Team Sports*, with Paul Downward, Alistair has published articles in sports economics. Other fields in which Alistair has published include the econometrics of wage inflation, and the application of computer business and macroeconomic simulations to undergraduate learning and assessment. Alistair hopes to devote his remaining years to hill walking, photography, real ale and socializing with friends and family.

Dr Trudo Dejonghe is docent (professor) at the Lessius Business University Antwerpen and guest lecturer in VUB Brussels, Hogeschool Brugge and Copenhagen Business School. He is the author of *Sport en economie: een noodzaak tot symbiose* (sport and economics: a symbiotic necessity) (Arko Sports Media, 2004), *Sport en economie: een aftrap* (sport and economics: a kick off) (Arko Sports Media, 2007) and *Sport in de wereld: ontstaan, evolutie en verspreiding* (sport in the global space: evolution and diffusion) (Academia Press, 2001; 2004; 2007). He has researched the location-allocation problems of football clubs in Belgium (2001) and the Netherlands (2005).

Sport Management Series Preface

Many millions of people around the globe are employed in sport organizations in areas as diverse as event management, broadcasting, venue management, marketing, professional sport, and coaching as well as in allied industries such as sporting equipment manufacturing, sporting footwear and apparel, and retail. At the elite level, sport has moved from being an amateur pastime to a significant industry. The growth and professionalization of sport has driven changes in the consumption and production of sport and in the management of sporting organizations at all levels of sport. Managing sport organizations at the start of the twenty-first century involves the application of techniques and strategies evident in the majority of modern business, government and nonprofit organizations.

The **Sport Management Series** provides a superb range of texts for the common subjects in sport business and management courses. They provide essential resources for academics, students and managers and are international in scope. Supported by excellent case studies, useful study questions, further reading lists, lists of websites, and supplementary online materials such as case study questions and PowerPoint slides, the series represents a consistent, planned and targeted approach which:

- provides a high quality, accessible and affordable portfolio of titles which match management development needs through various stages;
- prioritises the publication of texts where there are current gaps in the market, or where current provision is unsatisfactory;
- develops a portfolio of both practical and stimulating texts in all areas of sport management.

The **Sport Management Series** is the first of its kind, and as such is recognised as being of consistent high quality and will quickly become the series of first choice for academics, students and managers.

Preface to Sports Economics

With the help of Trudo Dejonghe, this book radically extends and revises *The Economics of Professional Team Sports* by Paul Downward and Alistair Dawson. Not only has the coverage of professional team sports been radically updated, but the book also encompasses mass participation sport as well as aspects of sports events.

This has provided challenges. On the one hand mass participation sport has received relatively little research and textbook treatment in economics, although some notable contributions, cited within, stand out. In this respect, it is hoped that the book provides some innovative discussion. In contrast, professional sport and the economics of major events comprise burgeoning literatures, which provide challenges in summarizing its content. In this respect it is hoped that the book provides a good introduction to the main issues discussed in the literature.

A central reason for the combined treatment and coverage is that the different contexts of sport are now often integrated as economic activities in public policy discussion. As no previous economic literature exists that examines all of these contexts and their connections, we hope that the major contribution of the book is to show how this is possible, and that economics can contribute greatly to our understanding of sport.

In order to achieve this goal, core principles of economic theory coupled with specific conceptual innovations from economics in the context of sport are employed throughout the book, whilst recognizing that each aspect of sport has some distinctive characteristics. Relevant descriptive and inferential empirical evidence is cited, as well as the implications of the theoretical and empirical insights for policy. It should be emphasized that at no point are specific policy recommendations offered. Rather, the aim is to use theory and evidence to explore the underpinnings of alternative policy positions. Broadly speaking these include a choice of either allowing market forces to allocate resources in sport, or for policy makers to intervene in resource allocation to provide sport. The economic logic and trade-offs of each position is essentially compared.

A distinctive feature of the book is that its pedagogy aims to make sports economics accessible to those for whom economics is a relatively new area of study, or is not necessarily a major component of their studies, for example, for sports management students. In this respect, rather than using sports to exemplify a traditional economics curriculum, this book makes the contexts of sport the focus of analysis, and uses economics as and when it is needed to illuminate these areas.

Moreover, because the pedagogy of economics can be technical, drawing on mathematical and statistical analysis, most of each chapter, where possible, explores the issues at stake in verbal terms, providing historical and contextual commentary. Economic principles are presented in graphical format with the statement of, and commentary on, key equations. Derivations are kept to a minimum and developed most in appendices, for the more technically-minded reader. Reflection questions and boxes are also used in chapters to prompt the reader to think about specific points, as well as to provide the context for specific theoretical or empirical contributions that have been used to analyze sport.

The aim of the book was to be international in scope. However, partly as a result of language and partly as a result of the emphasis of the literature, it focuses primarily on comparisons between the US, the UK and mainland Europe. In this respect it is hoped that the book prompts research into sports economics in other contexts.

Chapters 1 and 2 provide overviews of key economic principles and methodology, and the definition and economic and political context of sport, respectively. Chapters 3 and 4 examine the demand for mass participation sport, introducing key theoretical features of consumption behaviour, as well as how economists analyze evidence. Evidence on participation is reviewed. Chapters 5 and 6 then examine the supply of mass participation sport, focusing on the policy rationale for public or private sector supply. The role of clubs and volunteers in sport are also discussed, as well as the growth of the private and informal sectors. In these chapters, the consumer–producer nature of the economic agent, and the activity of agents within "club goods" is emphasized.

Chapter 7 draws on this discussion to explain the origin and nature of professional sports competitions, as an evolution of club goods in which consumers and producers become specialized. Key aspects of the economics of competition – as detailed in contest theory – are discussed in connection with sport in general and then professional team sports. Themes in the economics of professional team sports are reviewed connected with the nature and objectives of the firm and the market structure of leagues. It is argued that sports leagues are cartels whose members' mutual interdependence needs to be managed.

Chapter 8 provides a detailed digression on the nature and measurement of "Uncertainty of Outcome" as a characteristic of this interdependence, as highlighted in contest theory. This is because uncertainty of outcome has assumed a central place in the literature examining the management and evolution of sports leagues. Chapter 9 then reviews the efficacy of policies that have been used by sports leagues with the purported intention of managing uncertainty of outcome. It is shown that, broadly speaking, the impact of policies will either be ineffective, or possible but difficult to implement, depending on the assumptions made.

Chapters 10 and 11 then examine the key sources of revenues and costs for professional sports; attendance and broadcast demand, and the labour market. In Chapter 10 it is identified that uncertainty of outcome is more likely to be important for broadcast audiences, and that market sizes and team qualities and possibly loyalty are key drivers of attendance demand, which is price inelastic. Chapter 11 argues that economic liberalization has produced rising player costs for teams, but the specific nature of the market structure is unclear. In this respect it is implied that league management policies have traditionally exploited players rather than affected uncertainty of outcome. The role of player–agents and the coach–manager are also discussed.

The book closes with a discussion of the economics of sports events and investment in infrastructure in Chapter 12. Here a number of themes corresponding to participation in, and provision of, sports events as distinct economic entities to sports leagues are discussed, drawing on contest theory. The chapter also examines in detail the economic case for investment in sports infrastructure that could apply to events or professional team sports. It is argued that the claim that benefits to society can be leveraged from public sector investment in professional team sports or sports events lacks a strong evidence base. Consequently, while a case can be made for such investment, considerable caution and planning is required to harness any spillover effects from the investments.

In concluding, it should be noted that sports economics is a growing area of study and a number of individuals and contributions have added to a vibrant development of ideas and research interests. It should become apparent on reading the book where the driving force of these ideas originates. This said it is clear that a book cannot do justice to all of the contributions that have been made. It is also clear that much remains to be done in research terms, and it is hoped that this book helps to stimulate some of this work. Readers should note that there is now an International Association of Sports Economists that hosts an annual conference dedicated to sports economics (see http://www.iasecon.net/), and also a dedicated journal, *The Journal of Sports Economics*, edited by Leo Kahane (see http://jse.sagepub.com/), that provide key forums for current work.

List of Figures

List of Tables

The Economics of Sport

- ■ To understand some main features of economics
- ■ To understand the relationship between sport and economics
- ■ To appreciate the main features of economic methodology
- ■ To understand how the perfectly competitive model of resource allocation could apply to sport
- ■ To appreciate why market failures are important in sport

1.1 INTRODUCTION

To understand how economics can be used to analyze sport requires an initial appreciation of some key tenets of economics on which to base subsequent, more detailed, discussion. To meet this need, this chapter begins by examining definitions of economics and shows, in the subsequent section, how these are related to the methodological emphasis of economic analysis. Section 1.4 illustrates the main emphasis of economics, and draws out the main policy thrust of economics, by outlining the key theory of the perfectly competitive model of resource allocation. A distinction is drawn between the production of predictions from theory, or "positive" economics, and the evaluation of the outcomes predicted, or normative economics. Section 1.5 presents elements of market failure that are invoked to provide a rationale for policy intervention. Each of the theoretical concepts, empirical approaches and policy implications discussed in this chapter are then referred to or elaborated on in subsequent chapters. Section 1.6 discusses the limits to policy action in sport, and a brief introduction to the empirical approach employed in economics to test predictions from theory is presented to conclude the chapter.

BOX 1.1 DEFINITIONS OF ECONOMICS

1. "Writers on political economy profess to teach, or to investigate, the nature of wealth, and the laws of its production and distribution, including, directly or remotely, the operation of all the causes by which the condition of mankind, or of any society of human beings, in respect of this universal object of human desire, is made prosperous or the reverse. Note that any treatize on political economy can discuss or even enumerate all these causes; but it undertakes to set forth as much as is known of the laws and principles according to which they operate."
   Mill, J.S. (1900) *Principles of Political Economy with Some of Their Applications to Social Philosophy*. London: George Routledge and Sons, p. 13.

2. "Political economy or economics is a study of mankind in the ordinary business of life; it examines that part of individual and social action which is most closely connected with the attainment and with the use of the material requisites of well-being. Thus, it is on the one side a study of wealth; and on the other, and more important side, a part of the study of man."
   Marshall, A. (1952) *Principles of Economics: An Introductory Volume*, 8th edn. London: Macmillan and Co., p. 1.

3. "Economics is the science which studies human behaviour as a relationship between ends and scarce means which have alternative uses"
   Robbins, L. (1940) *An Essay on the Nature and Significance of Economic Science*. London: Macmillan and Co., p. 16.

1.2 WHAT IS ECONOMICS?

Box 1.1 presents three historical definitions of economics that Lawson (2003) argues are widely acknowledged as foundations for the emphasis of economics. They are abstract and general, and have similarities and differences. Both Mill and Marshall, for example, emphasize the connection between individual human activity and society, particularly through the production and distribution of material that contributes to well-being. There is some implication that wealth is connected to measurable or tangible material that is, for example, exchanged on markets. It is this that tends to link the traditional study of economics with, for example, financial and industrial subject matter.

Clearly this could apply to professional team sports. In this context money changes hands in the production, distribution and consumption of sport. Money, of course, is the mechanism by which key sporting resources such as players are obtained and allocated between the various teams, to use in competition against their opponents on the field.[1] The purchase and sale of players, as well as payment to them to perform, requires financing decisions.

---

[1] In this book the words "player," "labour," "talent" and "athlete" are used interchangeably to refer to the competitors who, through their practise, produce sport. Note that this use of the term is different to "athlete" in common language, which is often identified specifically for those engaged in the disciplines of athletics.

Consequently, gate and television revenues need to be earned to pay players' salaries. Clubs and their amalgamated organizations, such as leagues and governing bodies, must coordinate match schedules since they cannot be produced in isolation, and potential spectators must be informed where and when matches are to occur. In turn, spectators need accommodation and a means by which payment can be made, while restricting access to the sport to non-payers. Historically, stadia were necessary features of commercial sports supply. Spectators could also pay to watch broadcast sport, although payment has not always been necessary.

Characteristics such as these indicate that, rather like the production, distribution and consumption of other goods and services, professional sport can be viewed as an economic process. Inputs, or *factors of production*, such as labour (the athletes and manager/coach) are combined with capital (the sporting field, equipment and so on) to produce, along with another team in the league, a product (the fixture) that is sold to consumers (spectators and supporters) typically in a stadium, or via broadcast media.

Yet Robbins' definition in Box 1.1, which has come to be embraced by economics, is broader in concept and consistent with recognizing that economic activity is not, of necessity, connected with the creation and redistribution of material wealth *per se*. In this regard there are similarities between professional team sports, as well as amateur sports and sport in general, as economic phenomena, if choices have to be made over the allocation of resources to supply and consume these activities. These issues are discussed in some detail, for example, in Chapters 3 and 6. If nothing else, participating or volunteering in sports activities "costs" time, which is a resource that is scarce to everybody. This is in addition to the resource allocation issues associated with the commercial provision of non-professional sports activities, as discussed in Chapter 5. Robbins has been one cornerstone of the development of economic methodology, which is now discussed.

1.3 ECONOMIC METHODOLOGY

Robbins' legacies for economics are two-fold. The first is that scientific propositions on economizing are associated with attempts to produce generalized understanding or "laws" of behaviour. The second is that economics becomes a tool for assessing rational choices between courses of action.

As far as testing economic theories is concerned, Friedman (1953) has been particularly important and emphasizes testing the predictions of theory regardless of the realism of its assumptions. Friedman's argument provides a link between theories that can be constructed on idealized conceptions of rational economic behaviour, that are literally false, for example motivated by the definition of Robbins, and the empirical relevance of theory as an aid to policy.

This broad method of analysis, in which rational economic behaviour is postulated for economic agents which is used to deduce predictions that are tested against data, is applied to all economic problems, including those associated with sport. Economics purports to offer "covering law" explanations of phenomena. The specific subject matter analyzed is understood in terms of a general theory of behaviour. In its core assumptions connected with rational behaviour, economic analysis does not make allowance for the analysis of different sports taking place in different countries or in different time periods. However, it does attempt to accommodate different institutional contexts. It is important to bear this issue in mind, as this approach is different to those of disciplines such as sociology, history and politics, which may be more familiar to, say, sports management students, and in which the specific context and character of sports is explored.

The economic approach can be understood more clearly, as well as highlighting some important economic concepts, by considering the core economic model of perfectly competitive market allocation of resources. Both its "positive" and "normative" characters are discussed. Although philosophically contentious these terms reflect, as distinguished by Friedman (1953), that statements about economic activity can have the aspiration of being value-free and concerned with testable theoretical propositions, or be concerned with prescription, for example policy, based on value judgements.

1.4 A CORE ECONOMIC MODEL: PERFECT COMPETITION AND EFFICIENT RESOURCE ALLOCATION

1.4.1 Positive economics

Although discussed in a more appropriate way in Chapter 9, the representation of a sports league is used to illustrate the model of perfect competition. The sports league can be viewed as the industry, or synonymously the market, producing the output of sporting contests, i.e., fixtures, with individual teams or clubs within the league being viewed as firms within the industry. The fans who pay to watch games are the consumers who demand sports fixtures. As implied earlier, it is assumed that economic agents in markets are rational. They have perfect information about the implications of their decisions, and they pursue clearly defined goals. It is assumed that clubs or firms seek to maximize their profit, while the fans seek to maximize their utility, which is enjoyment, from viewing fixtures from the league, made possible through the purchase of tickets.

While this might seem to be a reasonably plausible scenario, notwithstanding the assumption about the information possessed by clubs and spectators, the model also assumes that each club and fan is "atomistic," i.e., they are infinitesimally small relative to the total number of clubs or fans. In this regard, their individual decisions to buy and sell tickets to watch sports fixtures cannot affect industry-level activity as a whole. It is also assumed that there is freedom of entry and exit to the industry. This implies that unprofitable clubs can leave the market or league, while profitable clubs may attract the entry of other clubs looking to compete for their profits. Clubs may also offer more or less fixtures to the league as required. In this respect, resources in this sports market are free to come and go. It is also assumed that the product supplied by any set of teams – a sports fixture – is identical to all others,[2] and there are no differences assumed between the quality of sports fixtures or the identity of fans to particular teams. The only impetus to watching one particular fixture rather than another is the ticket price. However, because clubs cannot affect ticket prices, they cannot brand their fixture, and cannot draw on particular allegiances from fans. Everyone has to accept the ticket price as established in the market as a whole. Clubs are "price takers." These are clearly unrealistic assumptions.

To explore the implications of these assumptions in more detail requires exploring the demand side and supply side of the market in more detail. Figure 1.1 provides a diagrammatic representation of the league. On the right-hand side is a representation of the demand and supply of the league's fixtures as a whole. On the left-hand side is a representation of the costs and revenues facing an individual club within the league. As clubs are identical, this club is representative of all clubs. Prices and costs are measured on the vertical axis, and the number of club fixtures and the number of fixtures in the league as a whole are measured on the separate horizontal axes (Figure 1.1).

The full underpinnings of the demand side of the market are discussed in Chapter 3, consequently it is practical at this juncture simply to note that, for the market as a whole, i.e., the sports league, it is assumed that a rise or fall in ticket prices, will, in the absence of changes in other factors, reduce or increase the demand for sports matches. The demand curve represents planned purchases of tickets on the market for various prices. The inverse relationship implied by the curve is often referred to as the "law" of demand. The supply curve in a perfectly competitive market is the sum of the marginal costs (MC) of the many, identical, clubs that supply the market. Marginal costs are the

---

[2] The astute reader will note that, unlike manufactured goods, or say, gymnasium services offered by a sports facility, sports events need sporting competitors. This unique element of competitive sports is discussed at great length in Chapter 7.

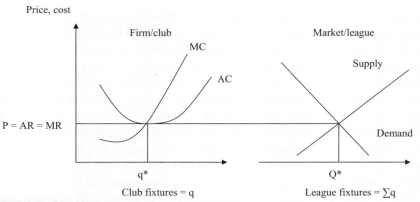

FIGURE 1.1 *A perfect competitive sports league.*
Key: P = price; MR = marginal revenue; AR = average revenue; MC = marginal cost; AC = average cost; q* = number of fixtures supplied by a club; Q* = number of fixtures in the league.

extra costs incurred from producing an extra item of output. In this context these will be the costs incurred from producing an extra fixture.

In this price-taking market, as discussed above, the coincidence of market demand and supply determines the market ticket price (P) and quantity (Q*). Here the intersection of these curves shows the mutually consistent set of plans for consumers to buy tickets to view fixtures and of clubs to supply fixtures in the aggregate. If demand and supply in the market set the price of the product, individual firms have to supply the product at this price. Consequently, the club's average ticket price for fixtures (average revenue, AR) and ticket price for any extra fixture supplied, marginal revenue (MR) are equal to the market ticket price (P). The intersection of the demand and supply curves also determines the number of fixtures in the league Q*.

> **Reflection Question 1.1**
> How many fixtures should each club provide to the league total?
> Hint: Think about the assumed objective of clubs.

The theory of perfect competition assumes that clubs wish to maximize profits. The maximum contribution to the firm's profit occurs where MC is equal to price or MR.[3] If the firm were to increase its output beyond q*, then

---

[3] This is a necessary condition for profit maximization. It is not a sufficient condition because one has to consider what happens to fixed costs.

the added cost, as indicated by the MC curve, exceeds the revenue received from the additional sale at market price P. Likewise, if the firm reduced its fixtures below q^*, then contribution to profit is missed, as $P = MR > MC$, which implies that profits are not maximized. Because the demand curve is given to the firm by the market, it should be clear that the MC curve is essential to understanding how much output competitive firms, and hence the market, supply.

What, then, are the extra costs that a firm incurs as it increases output by one unit? In economic terms, costs are broadly classified into fixed and variable costs. Examples of fixed costs would be the debt payments on investments for a new stadium. These debts have to be paid regardless of whether or not the team actively competed in their sport. Variable costs measure the costs that can be varied as the club commits resources to produce fixtures; consequently, they only need to be paid when varying the level of output of the firm, which is supplying sports fixtures.

Reflection Question 1.2

Consider a professional sports club. Which of its costs are likely to be viewed as variable, i.e., would vary directly with the number of fixtures offered?

Hint: Consider who actually produces the sports fixture on the playing field!

In economic theory labour costs are usually assumed to be the variable input to a firm's production in the short run, and clearly this is applicable to sports, if one considers who is actually required to produce a sports fixture and who would need to be paid to do so. The implication is that the firm can more easily adjust labour than capital. Labour markets are extremely important to the economics of professional sports, and are discussed more fully in Chapter 11. Intuitively, however, it is common to observe players being transfer-listed or sold when clubs face financial problems. In contrast, clubs tend to relinquish their stadium only under extreme financial pressure – when they effectively close. Of course, clubs also often build new stadia, to accommodate new capacity or to relocate to new cities, which is common in the United States (US). This issue is discussed more fully in Chapter 12. MC for clubs can be defined as in Equation 1.1:

$$\text{Marginal cost} \equiv \frac{\text{Wage rate of players}}{\text{Marginal product of players}} \qquad (1.1)$$

This relationship implies that the only reason that MC can rise for a given money wage rate is because the marginal product of labour (MPL) falls, as

BOX 1.2 WHAT IS MARGINAL COST?

In a competitive market, output such as fixtures can be sold at a specific price, this is marginal revenue. Each fixture also has a cost, its marginal cost. Equation 1.1 defines marginal cost as the money cost of producing the fixture, the wage rate, divided by the marginal productivity of the player producing the fixture. For example, if the wage rate that has to be paid to players to encourage them to be available for a fixture is €10 and the player performs over the whole fixture, then the marginal cost is €10. If the player only played for one-half of the fixture, perhaps because they were viewed as underperforming, then the marginal cost of the player would be €20. This higher marginal cost reflects the lower productivity of the player.

illustrated in Box 1.2. In the theory of competitive markets this is assumed to apply, reflecting a "law" of "diminishing marginal productivity." This implies that, in putting on more and more fixtures, clubs end up having to make use of less and less productive, i.e., skilful, players as the more skilful players are already being used, or need to be rested at times. This assumption is needed in the theory because without it there is no guarantee that MC would rise to equal price, which is constant, and hence the profit maximizing level of output for the firm identified where MR = MC at $q^\star$.

Reflection Question 1.3

Does this imply that teams could be of any size?
Hint: What is assumed about resource availability?

In principle, this means that the size of the team can vary according to profits. One could think of this as connected with variable squad sizes rather than actual players on the field. Better ways of viewing the employment of players in producing fixtures are discussed more fully in Chapter 9.

An important point to note from the above analysis is that actual profit for the club per fixture is indicated by the difference between the AR and AC curves. AC refers to both fixed and variable costs, and therefore describes the full, total cost per fixture. Note that, unlike with revenues, MC and AC are *not* the same. The former is the cost of producing the last fixture. The latter is the cost of producing each fixture on average. Consequently, as implied on the diagram, when MC is less that AC, AC falls. Conversely, when MC is greater than AC, AC rises. It follows that MC = AC at the lowest point of the AC curve. In Figure 1.1 the horizontal MR = AR curve was tangent to the AC curve at the point where MR = MC. This suggests that zero economic profit is earned. Technically this means that no supernormal profit is earned. In contrast, only the profit implied in the cost of capital, as incorporated in the AC curve, is received by the club. An important distinction to note here is that accountants refer to this as "profit," in economics it is viewed as the cost of keeping funds in the current line of economic activity. If this cost was not met, i.e., payment to the owner or investor in the club, they would invest their capital elsewhere. As discussed further in Chapter 12, economic costs reflect the opportunity costs of alternative uses of resources. It is clear from the above diagram that profit maximization in perfect competition ensures that costs are at their lowest possible level.

Predictions can be derived from the theory. Assume that interest in the sport rises from current levels. This can be illustrated on Figure 1.2 by drawing a new demand curve to the right of the existing demand curve, to show that spectators plan to view more fixtures for any given ticket price. This could occur if current spectators all wanted to see more fixtures or new spectators entered the market, or both. There is an important methodological point that needs to be noted at this juncture. In economics the effect of this change is considered *ceteris paribus*, that is holding other factors constant. This is not to suggest that economists view this as a description of the world as it operates. However, the focus of economic analysis is to examine the logical consequences of a change in one variable on another variable in isolation. This is a direct consequence of trying to establish causal links between variables as specified by various theories. It is these conditional or partial predictions that form the focus of testing in economics and why, in this particular case, a new demand curve is drawn as the only initial change taking place.

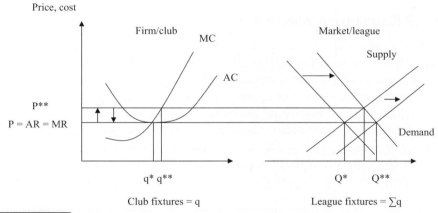

FIGURE 1.2   *Increased demand for sports fixtures.*
Key: P = price; MR = marginal revenue; AR = average revenue; MC = marginal cost; AC = average cost; q* = number of fixtures supplied by a club; Q* = number of fixtures in the league.

In the current context, Figure 1.2 illustrates that following the increased demand the consequent prediction is that the market initially establishes a new higher ticket price, P^{**}. For individual clubs this implies supernormal profits per fixture, as indicated by the fact that $P^{**} = AR > AC$ where profit maximizing behaviour predicts an increased number of fixtures at q^{**}, where $MR = MC$ in the short run. However, the assumption of free entry and exit to the market implies that new clubs will enter the league in the long run. In other words, capital can now vary and gets invested in this profitable industry. This suggests that the supply curve will now also move to the right, indicating that more fixtures can be supplied at any price. The consequent prediction is that ticket prices will fall.

Reflection Question 1.4
To what level will ticket prices fall?
Hint: Remember each club is assumed to be identical.

Because clubs are considered to be identical, the fall in prices will imply that supernormal profits will disappear and individual clubs will supply their original number of fixtures. The difference now is that more clubs will be in the league, which has expanded to Q^{**} fixtures overall. The "dynamic" process implied in the model is that prices act as a signal of profit opportunities for clubs to meet the utility or demands of fans. The league or market thus adjusts resources to ensure that more clubs emerge to meet this need.

1.4.2 Normative economics

Perfect competition also contains value judgements that are linked to economic policy prescription. The central normative proposition of the perfectly competitive model is that it represents the efficient allocation of resources.[4] Efficiency is concerned with the direction of scarce resources towards their best use, which produce maximum economic value or welfare. The current approach towards understanding this concept was introduced to economic discussion by Pareto (1906). The first and second fundamental theorems of welfare economics state that not only will a perfectly competitive equilibrium yield an optimal allocation of resources, for any given distribution of income,

---

[4] Other normative propositions are that decisions should be understood as deriving from individuals, and that the general value or welfare experienced by society is, in essence, a simple aggregation of the utility of individuals. This reflects the utilitarian ethical tradition of economics.

but also that every optimum allocation of resources is a perfectly competitive equilibrium. The precise demonstration of these theorems is beyond the scope of this book but, intuitively, it can be seen that the model discussed above involved scarce resources, because costs were assumed in production. Moreover, in the analysis of Figure 1.2, resources were attracted into the sports leagues in response to consumer demand. The consumer demand acted like a vote that was effective, because of the exercise of spending money on sports fixtures. How is this efficient though? To answer this question we can review two types of efficiency; productive and allocative efficiency. Each of these, although integrally connected, is best understood by considering the two sides of the market: supply and demand.

Production efficiency is connected to the idea of a production function, which conceptually describes how resources are employed in production or supply. Equation 1.2 describes a production function in which output "Y" is postulated to flow from the use of three factors of production: land (Ld); labour (L); and capital (K), terms that were referred to earlier. In economics all resources are associated with these generic categories, which are used to describe resources as inputs to economic activity.

$$Y = Y(Ld, L, K) \qquad (1.2)$$

A function is a shorthand description that indicates that a dependent variable, an object of analysis whose value can vary, is related to a set of independent variables, objects whose values can also vary. Equation 1.2 is a general function because no specific relationship is identified. In the case of sports fixtures above, we can say that the number of fixtures produced by a club will result from the employment of players as labour, a stadium as land and equipment, such as strips, and the relevant ball, etc., as capital.[5] But, of course, in this general sense nothing is said about in what way and by how much. The role of such functions is central in economic analysis and they are referred to in the appendix to this chapter, and throughout the book. Production efficiency then implies generating the maximum number of fixtures from the minimum amount of each resource.

Box 1.2 alluded to the concept of productivity. We can now understand this term more thoroughly by noting that marginal productivity is the additional output following the employment of an additional unit of a variable factor of production, or resource, combined with other factors of production, or

---

[5] At this point the astute reader should recall footnote 1, in which it was indicated that the presence of an opposing team is also required to produce a competitive sports fixture. For the moment, accept the proposition that all players fall under the remit of labour.

resources, being fixed. Average productivity relates the total level of output produced to the total level of resource inputs. In the context of the example of sports fixtures above, the marginal productivity of a player is essentially the amount of the fixture that they participate in every time that they are included in the team to produce the fixture (to play in the particular stadium, etc.). Average productivity is thus the total number of fixtures divided by the total number of players employed to produce them. Maximum productivity would thus imply that all players participated fully in every match and that players were selected in order of their abilities, and that in perfect competition the size of the team can be variable.[6]

The reason for this is connected to the second aspect of productive efficiency, and this is associated with "economy." The theory of perfect competition implies that clubs are price takers in the market for fixtures. Implicit in this discussion is that the purchase and sale of players and other resources is also facilitated on a perfectly competitive market. The wages of players are also given to the firm, as are the costs of land and capital, from their respective factor markets. As a result of this, the costs facing firms and the productivity of resources used by the firm are directly related. Indeed, costs are determined by the behaviour of productivity, as illustrated in Box 1.2. Maximum productivity, i.e., productive efficiency, must imply minimum cost, i.e., economy, as it is clear that the pressure of competition in the market will ensure that profit maximizing firms seek to minimize their costs by being as efficient as possible in production. As Figures 1.1 and 1.2 illustrate, under perfect competition the output of the club is determined at the lowest point on the AC curve. It can now be appreciated that this lowest point is determined by productivity being at the highest, so there are no better options for the employment of resources.

---

[6] As the astute reader should now be beginning to appreciate, there is a degree of difficulty of interpretation of these basic economic concepts in sports. These issues are discussed much more thoroughly in Chapters 7 and 11. This is because the nature of output is rather elusive. In the discussion above it is assumed that a fixture of appropriate duration is the relevant output of a sports club. Casual observation tells us that many professional athletes participate in most fixtures, and that clubs are not interested in producing fixtures *per se*, as these have been agreed in setting the scale of the league and number of times each team play. In this respect, teams may be interested in making profit and/or maximizing their relative performance in the league, recognizing that player performances and qualities can vary. Identifying and measuring this performance is difficult. In the case of the physical production of goods, however, one might more easily observe the same hours' work producing more or less units of output depending on effort, monitoring and incentives, etc.

An important corollary of the above discussion concerns the markets for factors of production, such as labour. Equation 1.1 indicated that profit maximizing output for a perfectly competitive sports club would be determined where marginal costs were equal to the wage rate divided by the marginal product of labour. Recalling that in a profit maximizing club, in perfect competition, MR equals MC, and that MR also equals P, then Equation 1.1 can be rewritten as Equation 1.3.

$$\text{Price} \equiv \frac{\text{Wage rate of players}}{\text{Marginal product of players}} \tag{1.3}$$

Multiplying both sides of this relationship by the marginal product of players per fixture gives Equation 1.4:

$$\text{Price} \times \text{Marginal product of players} \equiv \text{Wage rate of players} \tag{1.4}$$

or:

$$\text{Marginal revenue product of players} \equiv \text{Wage rate of players}$$

The marginal revenue product (MRP) of players is their contribution, in producing fixtures, to the club's revenues, as the fixtures are sold at their ticket price. Perfect competition suggests that player's wage rates should be equal to this contribution, which could then be viewed as a "just wage." This relationship is very important to the discussions in Chapter 11.

In contrast to the above conditions that suggest necessary, if not sufficient, conditions for the best use of scarce resources, because the focus is on the supply decision only, allocative efficiency is directly concerned with both demand and supply conditions. It occurs when prices reflect the true costs of production and benefits to consumers. The above discussion implies the former. So, also, while Chapter 3 covers the detail of the consumer decision, a utility maximizing rational consumer might be expected only to pay a price that represents their true individual subjective valuation, i.e., utility, placed on the service or product consumed, that is the fixture whose ticket is bought. However, care should be taken to note that it is logically possible that the prices paid by consumers, or received by clubs, do not reflect the true costs and benefits involved to society. This is discussed further below under the heading of market failure. Consequently, additional assumptions have to be met before one can guarantee that perfect competition is, indeed, an optimal allocation of resources.

To summarize this section, however, the main point is that a perfectly competitive allocation of resources in sports, and generally, is typically identified by economists as the most desirable situation, as it maximizes economic welfare. The core of conventional economic policy thinking, therefore, despite many conceptual concerns with the theory of perfect competition, is that policies that move towards the allocation of resources by a competitive market system are appropriate.

1.5 MARKET FAILURE AND THE RATIONALE FOR POLICY INTERVENTION

The desirability of a market allocation of resources in sport versus an alternative perspective in which active intervention is promoted in sports-related policy can be understood more clearly by reviewing what are traditionally referred to as market failures; these are defined as such because they stand in counterpoint to perfect competition. These failures, to a greater or lesser extent, relax the assumptions of the perfectly competitive model and suggest more realism. As a consequence, different predictions of behaviour become apparent.[7] This discussion also reveals that it may be conceivable that the economic logic of a competitive allocation of resources lies in direct conflict with the objectives of particular stakeholders in sport.

1.5.1 Monopoly

To begin discussion, perfect competition in markets has a polar opposite of monopoly, which, in the extreme theoretical sense, is when only one firm supplies the market. A league could be viewed as a monopoly. Theoretically this would mean, in comparison with perfect competition, that the supply curve of the market would represent the MC of the monopoly, and the equivalent sum of ACs would represent the monopoly league's AC. Likewise, the market demand curve would represent the monopolist's AR. Unlike the demand curve facing a perfectly competitive firm, this is not now horizontal. In contrast to the perfectly competitive club, in which AR and MR are equal, because the club cannot influence the ticket price on the market, the monopoly league can adjust its sales of tickets for fixtures by altering ticket prices. It faces the total market demand curve and is, therefore, a price maker.

---

[7] This generates something of a methodological conundrum in economics. By producing more realistic assumptions on a case-by-case basis, economic predictions become fully contingent. Consequently, tests of predictions do not necessarily refute the model, but could also reflect the inappropriate application of the model. Of course, analysis outside of experimental conditions and any use of statistical analysis cannot provide definitive tests.

To increase ticket sales the monopoly league can reduce ticket prices and *vice versa*.

Reflection Question 1.5

What will the monopoly league's marginal revenue curve look like?

Hint: Remember the discussion of average and marginal cost.

Note that if, in order to increase ticket sales, additional tickets are offered at a lower price than before, the MR earned by the league on these additional tickets will be lower than the AR earned on previous ticket sales. Consequently, in general, MR will be less than AR for a monopoly or, indeed, any other form of market that is not perfectly competitive and where firms can influence the market price. Appendix 1.1 illustrates that, with a straight line AR "curve," MR will be twice as steep. Figure 1.3 illustrates the situation of a monopoly league, using the same notation as previously.

Once again ticket prices and costs of production are measured on the vertical axis and the number of fixtures in the league on the horizontal axis. Profit maximizing behaviour implies that the number of fixtures supplied will be Q^* where MR is equal to MC. Because the monopoly firm faces the market demand curve, a ticket price of P^* can be set for each ticket, as this represents what consumers are prepared to pay to see Q^* fixtures. An important implication of monopoly supply is that even in the longer run, because of the lack of competition and inability of clubs to enter the league or rival leagues to be set up to supply the sport, supernormal profits can be earned. This is because, on each ticket sold, there is a mark-up above average costs (which, remember, includes normal profit) of $P^* - AC^*$.

From the normative perspective discussed earlier, this is viewed as problematic for economic welfare. Productive efficiency is not maximized, because the number of fixtures produced does not reflect the lowest AC. Even if demand fell, because of a reduction of spectator interest for the sport which could be indicated by a movement in the demand curve to the left such that ticket price mark-ups were squeezed to zero, and just normal profits were earned by the league, $P = AR = AC$ would have to take place, in the diagram, to the left of the lowest possible value of AC, where the demand curve was at a tangent to the AC curve.[8]

---

[8] It has also been argued that because monopolies do not face competition they become "slack" organizationally, i.e., exhibit x-inefficiency, consequently productive efficiency falls and costs rise (Leibenstein, 1966). The term "x-inefficiency" suggests that the inefficiency is neither due to productive nor allocative inefficiencies.

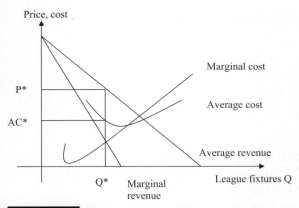

Price, cost

P*

AC*

Marginal cost

Average cost

Average revenue

Q*   Marginal
         revenue

League fixtures Q

FIGURE 1.3 *Monopoly supply of sports fixtures.*

Moreover, this suggests that the number of tickets sold will always be less than would have been the case under a perfectly competitive league. This produces an allocative inefficiency, which represents a deadweight loss of economic welfare. This can be illustrated with reference to Figure 1.4. Here, the profit maximizing ticket price and number of fixtures of the monopoly league, given by Q^* and P^*, are reproduced. However, these are compared to the profit maximizing ticket price and number of fixtures of a perfectly competitive organized league, given by Pc and Qc, respectively.

Reflection Question 1.6

What will be the profit maximizing price and output of a perfectly competitive sports league? Hint: Remember that the sports league represents the market as a whole for perfectly competitive sports clubs.

Recall from Figure 1.1 that, in a price-taking market, demand and supply set the market level ticket price and number of fixtures, and this is consistent with the profit maximizing behaviour of individual clubs. If it is assumed that the monopoly and perfectly competitive leagues face the same demand curve, and that the production functions are the same in the aggregate, then from the monopoly diagram the perfectly competitive equilibrium would be where demand equals supply (the MC curve).

Figure 1.4 illustrates that the monopoly price of tickets, P^*, is higher than the perfectly competitive price of tickets, Pc, and the number of fixtures supplied on the monopoly league, Q^*, is less than would be supplied in a perfectly competitive league, Qc. The welfare cost that results from having a monopoly league is indicated by the triangular area xyz. What is this welfare cost?

The total area xyz comprises two rectangles, wxy and wyz. The first of these refers to the lost

Price, cost

P*

Pc

Supply

x

y

w

z

Demand

Q*   Marginal   Qc   League fixtures
         revenue

FIGURE 1.4 *Monopoly versus perfectly competitive leagues.*

consumer surplus resulting from monopoly organization of the league. The second triangle shows the lost producer surplus. Conceptually speaking, the first of these is defined as the amount that consumers are willing to pay for a ticket above what they have to pay in a competitive market. Remembering that the demand curve represents what consumers are planning to purchase, any point on the demand curve represents willingness to pay. In a competitive market, consumers would actually pay Pc for tickets. Consequently, triangle wxy represents how much value is lost to consumers as a result of *not* having up to Qc number of tickets to purchase at a price of Pc, and which are valued more highly than Pc.

Likewise, producer surplus represents the difference between the price of tickets per fixture received by clubs under a competitive market, and the cost that clubs would incur but be willing to supply fixtures at. The supply curve represents the cost of producing each fixture. Consequently, by restricting the number of fixtures that could have been sold for ticket price Pc, a monopoly league loses the economic value of wyz, a series of fixtures for which Pc is greater than the cost of producing them.

It is important to indicate that these losses are viewed in terms of aggregate economic welfare. This is implied in comparing the alternative league outcomes of different economic organizations, or market structures. By construction, the perfectly competitive model represents the sum of values received by individual consumers and individual clubs. Yet each clubs share of, say, the forgone producer surplus, is by assumption miniscule. In contrast, the specific monopolist can make substantial extra profits by restricting output. A commercial organization may have objectives that do not correspond to those of maximizing the welfare of the broader economy more generally. This implies that there is always an economic incentive for organizations to look to establish monopoly power. It is for this reason that economic regulatory agencies often intervene in markets to reduce the monopoly power of specific organizations.

For example, they might look to tax away the supernormal profits in a lump sum form of the value $(P^\star - AC^\star) \times Q^\star$ in Figure 1.3. Such a policy would not affect the costs of production or productivity, and would thus be efficient. This policy would not, however, eradicate the deadweight loss. Alternatively, they might seek to force a change in the organization of the market, to encourage competition, or to enforce a greater supply of output, which will force price to fall. There are also other arguments for intervention in markets. However, these do not, of themselves, provide a rationale for trying to move towards a market allocation of resource, but in contrast, to rectify the problems of market allocation.

1.5.2 Equity

While the model of perfect competition offers an efficient use of resources, which can be identified with maximum social welfare, an implicit assumption in the model is access to the income required by consumers to express a demand for sports league tickets through purchases. The logic of the model is that economic agents can only be consumers because they have supplied their labour on the labour market to earn the requisite income to spend. The income earned, moreover, reflects their productivity. Likewise, those who own capital or land will only invest it in particular economic activities if the productivity of the investment is sufficiently high. Consequently, economic efficiency does not recognize the need to explore issues of the inequitable distribution of resources and the fact that those with higher incomes can demand more goods and services than others. A moment's reflection suggests examples where these issues may matter as indicated in the questions raised in Box 1.3.

Essentially answers to these questions hinge on the view that is taken of an unequal distribution of income, and if this biases outcomes in the market allocation of resources in favour of particular groups. In general, equity can be both understood, and addressed in policy, through vertical means, i.e., the "unequal treatment of unequals," or horizontally, through the "equal treatment of equals."

In the former case a sports club or league might have lower ticket prices for the unemployed, elderly or student fans, but charge a premium price for

---

BOX 1.3 DOES EQUITY MATTER IN SPORT?

Participation sport

1. Should local authorities subsidize/provide access to sports and leisure facilities?
2. Should students pay the same gym fees as university professors?
3. Should local authorities invest in a youth development funds?
4. Should the national government invest in sport facilities and participation programs in the short-term to reduce social security costs in the long-term?

Professional team sports

5. Are professional soccer players paid too much relative to nurses?

6. Are ticket prices too high for premiership soccer matches?
7. Should clubs share their gate revenues with smaller clubs?
8. Should local authorities subsidize professional team sports?
9. Should the government subsidize facilities for professional team sports?

Mega events

10. Should all tax payers contribute towards the costs of hosting the Olympic Games?
11. Should lottery funds only be directed towards athlete's development for those with a chance of winning gold medals?

executive boxes. This is an example of a policy of addressing vertical equity. One can argue that all are given opportunities to watch fixtures and are not discriminated against by income in this policy. Moreover, this (more) equal treatment of fans of a similar nature is an example of policy seeking horizontal equity. Consequently all students would pay the same ticket price according to the policy, as would all unemployed or elderly fans.

These policies may make economic sense for a profit oriented sports club, as discussed in Chapter 5, if these sets of fans represent distinct market segments. A policy dilemma only arises if all seats in a stadium could be sold at the executive price, then clearly equity and efficiency come into conflict as policies if one holds the value judgement that professional sport should be accessible to all fans. Rationing the allocation of tickets by price only would necessarily favour wealthy fans.

1.5.3 Externalities

A key assumption of the perfectly competitive model is that consumers and producers have property rights over the purchases and sales that they make. Clearly defined property rights, which are the legal rules that describe what people can do with their property, are essential for markets to be allocatively efficient as a form of voluntary exchange that takes place in the interests of both consumers and suppliers.

However, when property rights are not clearly defined, then markets can fail to produce an efficient allocation of resources. Externalities arise and can mean that the private benefits and costs received by or paid to a consumer or a supplier does not correspond to those of society. There will be spillover effects to third parties not formally engaged in the transaction. Positive externalities arise when the social benefits of consumption exceed those of the private individual, or the social costs of production are less than the private costs of production. Negative externalities occur in the opposite case. Here, the private benefits of consumption exceed the social benefits, or the social costs of production are greater than the private benefits. Box 1.4 gives some examples of externalities in sport.

What are the consequences of externalities? Positive externalities imply that the market undersupplies the amount of sport. Consequently, as with a monopoly, society experiences a welfare loss in the form of an opportunity cost. In contrast, negative externalities imply that the market oversupplies sport. Again, there is a welfare loss.

These two cases are illustrated below in Figure 1.5 for demand-based externalities associated with a sports league. Here, a competitive allocation of tickets is given by price Pc, and number of tickets, Qc, determined by the

BOX 1.4 EXTERNALITIES ASSOCIATED WITH SPORT

Positive externalities:
- Demand: fans that pay to watch professional sports fixtures are subsequently enticed to volunteer to provide sports opportunities for others.
- Supply: successful sports teams or events raise morale and encourage productivity in work efforts elsewhere.

Negative externalities:
- Demand: fans that pay to watch professional sports fixtures act as hooligans and vandalize localities.
- Supply: the growth of televised sport encourages "armchair" spectating, and reduces participation and health benefits.

intersection of the marginal private benefit (MPB) of fans and the marginal social cost (MSC) of their production. The presence of a demand externality means there is a true marginal social benefit (MSB), i.e., value, of the tickets that differs from the value associated with the actual purchases of tickets. This is because of the spillover effects of demand that are not actually accounted for in the market price. With supply-based externalities marginal social costs (MSC) would differ from marginal private costs (MPC).

In the case of positive demand externalities, the diagram on the left illustrates that the market under-provides tickets, as Qc < Qs, the competitive allocation of tickets is less than the socially optimal allocation of tickets. This is reflected in the market expressing a lower value than should be the case, as indicated by Pc < Ps, i.e., the actual price of tickets is lower than the socially optimal price. In the case of negative externalities, the opposite is true and the market over-provides tickets, as Qc > Qs and consequently Pc > Ps.

The presence of externalities provides a further direct rationale for active policy in the allocation of resources in sport. In the examples above this

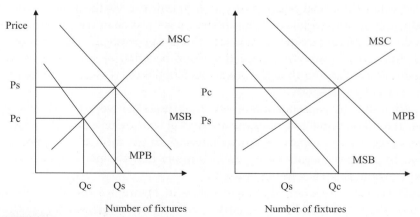

FIGURE 1.5 *Positive and negative externalities.*

implies providing a means of either increasing or decreasing demand to its socially optimal level. This reallocation of resources would involve internalizing the externality.

Increasing demand theoretically could involve providing direct benefits, such as grants to consumers to increase their demand. This is not an area of policy activity, however, in sport. Marketing and information campaigns may attempt to achieve these objectives, and recruitment campaigns for volunteers, for example, appeal to an underlying or latent demand. In the latter case restricting access to fixtures for hooligans at stadiums or restrictions on travelling to fixtures would reduce demand appropriately.

More generally, policy agencies can use taxes or subsidies to control externalities that emerge from the supply-side of the sports economy. Taxes act as an additional cost of production and thus shift the supply curve to the left, indicating that for any given price less matches, i.e., tickets, can be produced or equivalently, for any given level of tickets, the price will be higher. In contrast, subsidies act as a reduction in costs and shift the supply curve to the right. Unlike the case of monopoly such taxes or subsidies will not be lump sum but, rather, reflect either a fixed amount added or subtracted from each sale, known as a specific tax, or a fixed percentage of the value being added or subtracted to the proposed selling price, known as an *ad valorem* tax. Qualitatively the effects are the same. Of course, the actual costs or revenues that are imposed or generated from subsidies or taxes will vary, depending on the fiscal regime and the specific behaviour characterizing the sports market.

1.5.4 Public goods

If externalities are extremely severe, this implies that property rights cannot be allocated between those engaging in market transactions and those that do not. This leads to the free-rider problem, and means that markets fail completely in the presence of public goods. Public goods are both non-rival and non-exclusive. It is possible that goods and services may have one or both of these characteristics. The former characteristic implies that MC = 0. This might apply in sports contexts when an event or fixture takes place in a stadium in which there are spare seats. The costs of providing the event or fixture are not affected by the presence of additional consumers. In the examples of the competitive market above, it was assumed that spectators were rival, i.e., resources such as tickets were scarce. If one fan bought a ticket for a game, another could not see the same game. This is implied in the equalization of the demand and supply schedules in which all consumer and supplier plans were harmonized. Consequently, the competitive model assumes that fixtures are always sold out, a corollary being that clubs can easily adjust their stadium capacity to meet demand.

Non-exclusivity applies if consumers cannot be prevented from consuming the good, which they can be in the example above. One can speculate that early historic examples of sport, such as the early codes of football, were played on land which was open access. Under such circumstances, in principle, all fans that could physically fit onto the land could enjoy the spectacle. Of course, stadiums and dedicated sports facilities make sports potentially exclusive to avoid this scenario and to extract economic value from spectators. In the absence of such possibilities a direct rationale for policy makers to provide goods and services exists.

1.5.5 Imperfect information

Another form of market failure is connected with economic agents not possessing perfect information. There are degrees of lack of information discussed in economic analysis. Chapter 3 reviews some approaches that maintain that economic agents simply cannot optimize. Consequently, for example, they reject the idea that consumers maximize their utility and argue instead that agents exhibit "bounded rationality" and, as a consequence adopt rules of thumb, habits or decision heuristics to make decisions. There is a clear desire to conceptualize the processes by which decisions are made. This approach has its roots in psychology which is represented as relevant for understanding sports participation, for example from Sport England, in the UK.

A less radical approach that is often used to analyze employment or financial arrangements in economics, and has been used to understand aspects of professional sports, assumes that economic agents possess asymmetric information.

> *Information asymmetry occurs in transactions when one party possesses more or better information than the other party.*

Reflection Question 1.7
In what contexts might there be information asymmetry in sports transactions?
Hint: Think about the relationship between various stakeholders.

In the absence of being able to correct the information deficiency, for example, by monitoring, there are two main problems that can arise in economic transactions. Moral hazard might occur when agents behave differently than expected after a transaction has taken place. In contrast adverse selection may occur prior to a transaction taking place. The implication of these effects would be to promote market failure, because the quality of transactions falls.

Typically, and in professional sports, information asymmetry is important in a principal–agent context, where the principal may represent an employer, and the agent an employee or someone contracted to perform a function on behalf of the principal. Professional soccer players are thus "agents" to clubs, which are "principals." The club signs the player on a contract prior to their performance for the team. The player knows their own ability best and likely effort levels best, and thus the club is potentially at a disadvantage and, contrary to the result implied in Equation 1.4, pay the player more than they become worth in terms of their productivity. Likewise team managers are also agents, while club owners are principals. Managers might seek to target successes, while owners target profits, particularly if the team is publicly owned. While these may not be mutually exclusive objectives, there are still differences, as discussed in Chapter 7, which has implications for understanding the impact of policies on league management. Moreover, league and tournament organizers essentially contract teams and competitors to deliver certain outputs, a certain level of quality competition that the paying public wishes or expects to see. Such organizers need to ensure that the appropriate levels of competitive effort are elicited. Chapters 7 and 12 discuss these issues in some detail.

A variety of solutions to the problems of asymmetric information have been offered. Significantly, none of these, of necessity, requires the use of replacing the market with public policy agencies. For example, warranties act as signalling devices declaring the supply of appropriate quality goods and services. Screening devices allow the agent to choose between options in making a transaction. Product bundling and packages of tariffs, for example, in television or telecommunications are examples of screening. The nature of the customer is revealed and an appropriate "discriminatory" price is offered.

Screening is particularly prevalent in employment contracts. Instead of just receiving a fixed salary, incentive contracts, rewarding higher effort and performance, can be designed and will be attractive to those confident of their talents. Most professional sports have offered forms of incentive contracts to players, with win bonuses being an obvious example. The remuneration of tournaments, moreover, is predicated on providing enough high prizes to attract the best talent, while not undermining the incentives to participate by confining rewards for only the very best or winner.

Tournaments, as discussed in Chapter 7, are a form of incentive contract that is hierarchically structured, and in which performance is relative rather than absolute. Naturally, this coincides with a conceptual description of sporting contests, whether organized on a league or knockout basis.

However, there must be no incentive to focus only on the performance measure being directly rewarded. One can easily hypothesize that an incentive scheme rewarding the number of goals scored by a particular soccer player may promote undue selfish efforts, rather than concern with team performance, which might have been enhanced by other players' better scoring opportunities being continually overlooked. The general economic missive is that complex jobs should not be explicitly rewarded through such contracts. In team sports, then, team-based bonuses may also be appropriate.

1.6 LIMITATIONS TO POLICY MAKER INTERVENTION

With the exception of imperfect information, the above discussion of market failures arising from monopoly, equity, externalities and public goods are often presented as providing a direct rationale for policy maker intervention in the allocation of resources. However, there are also theoretical limitations to this possibility. In this regard there is no necessary presumption in favour of policy intervention.

1.6.1 The Coase theorem

As well as policy maker intervention, it is possible that when an externality affects few parties and if property rights are well-specified, economic efficiency can actually arise from the market through bargaining. In other words, gains from trade by internalizing the externality force a solution through the emergence of market trade. This proposition is the Coase theorem, which was developed by Coase (1960). There are varieties of the theorem in existence, but essentially it suggests that in the above circumstances the output and input configurations of resources will be independent of the allocation of property rights in the market. The Coase theorem has been particularly influential in the analysis of professional sports leagues in which, for example, the distribution of performances by teams, driven of course by the teams accruing playing talent resources i.e. labour, is independent of the contractual regime in the players' labour market.

1.6.2 Government failure

There are many reasons why government, or more broadly speaking, policy making intervention in sports may also fail. Naturally, these circumstances

undermine assumptions that non-market policy solutions to resource allocation in sport are automatically relevant. Philosophically speaking, one can
argue that elected government representatives may well have been chosen
initially to reflect the preferences and desires of the electorate or consumers.
However, over time electoral systems and political representation are not
flexible enough relative to markets to adjust to competing demands being
made on resources. Policy makers may also begin to pursue their own interests, as opposed to those of the electorate, which is known as regulatory
capture. This could shift focus onto the short-term benefits of policies, as
opposed to their longer-term legacies.

It is also possible that, over time, taxes and subsidies fundamentally distort
resource allocation and may impose their own externalities on society. For
example, taxes reduce consumer incomes which may reduce or crowd out the
social optimum levels of consumption of other goods and services, despite
apparently correcting a particular externality. Taxes may also provide disin-
centives to effort, which reduce productivity and raise costs. Of particular
relevance to sport is the role of the voluntary sector, as discussed in
Chapter 6. Inasmuch as both markets and governments do not meet the needs
of resource allocation in sport that is provided by voluntary organization, this
is an example of government, as well as market, failure.

1.7 EXPENDITURE-BASED RATIONALE FOR POLICY

The above discussion has hinged on the choice of having either active policy
or market allocations of resources in sport, in the context of a typical
concern for efficiency, i.e., an optimal allocation of resources. There has
been, however, another historical reason why policy agencies have intervened in economic decision-making. Unemployment can occur in situations when traditional industries are in decline, reflecting long-term
structural economic changes stemming from technological change, fundamental shifts in consumer tastes and changing global or political economic
conditions. Sport has been increasingly viewed as a means of offsetting the
implications of these changes in two major ways. The first is that the
advanced economies, such as Europe and the United States, have evolved
from being manufacturing providers to service-based economies. Sport is
part of this sector, as is discussed more in Chapters 2 and 12. Secondly,
investment in sport by policy agencies has been viewed as a means of
promoting this development. Importantly, the value of initial investment
need not be the full amount that is required to offset the structural problems
of long-term falls in income and unemployment, because of multiplier
effects. These are discussed further in Chapter 12 and Appendix 1.2.

1.8 AN EMPIRICAL FRAMEWORK

To close this chapter it is informative to outline, in broad terms, the empirical framework employed by economists that has been applied to the economic analysis of sports. The empirical approach is directly motivated by the methodological principle that economic analysis builds theories that yield predictions that can be tested against data. This section outlines the main elements of this process.

In the above discussion, economic relationships have been presented in equations and diagrams. The main reason for this is that they capture the logical relationships, and hence predictions, implied in economic theory. Diagrammatic analysis however only identifies qualitative predictions between two economic phenomena. Equations are central for the general quantitative analysis of these phenomena. To recap in the context of production efficiency, Equation 1.2 examined how output flows from the employment of resources described as land, labour and capital. There is a dependent variable and a set of independent variables in a general function. What lies behind this application to a particular context is a structure of functions. A specific form of functional relationship can be written as:

$$Y = \beta_1 + \beta_2 X_2 + \beta_3 X_3 + \ldots + \beta_k X_k \qquad (1.5)$$

Here, "Y" is the dependent variable and there are up to "k" independent variables, labelled as "X" with a subscript "1" to "k" that are viewed as contributing to the determination of "Y." Theory will specify the variables. In this general format the addition sign between each variable indicates that the independent variables affect "Y" separately or independently of the other variables. This is consistent with the desire to examine changes to "Y" following a change in a particular "X" *ceteris paribus*, or other things being equal, as discussed above. Convention specifies the presentation as positive, but in practice the sign could turn out to be positive or negative, depending on the actual behaviour being examined. The specification of independent positive or negative relationships between the variables means that the behaviour examined is hypothesized to be of a linear nature. This linearity is implied in a very specific sense. This is made clearer in considering the other terms in the equation.

While Y and each of the Xs are referred to as variables, precisely because their values can change as measurements of economic behaviour, the other "β" terms in the equation are referred to as parameters. These are viewed as fixed or unchanging, as they represent the structure or behavioural foundations that govern how the variables are related to each other, and consequently how

changes in one variable affect another. Each independent variable has its own parameter associated with it,
as indicated by the common subscripts 1 to k with the
variables, although clearly there is one major difference. The term β_1 does not appear to have a variable
X_1 associated with it, yet each of the other βs, 1 to k,
does. There is good reason for this: β_1 represents the
constant or intercept of the equation and is the value
taken by Y when each of the independent variables is
equal to zero. It provides the level of an economic
variable that is independent of the influence of other
variables. In practice, constant or intercept parameters
often have little empirical meaning. This is because,
while they may refer to a scenario which is logically possible, in practice this
logical possibility is a huge extrapolation away from typical relationships
observed in data. Figure 1.6 illustrates the constant or intercept, indicating
why the latter name is pertinent. Graphically it shows where the function
intercepts the Y-axis at a value where X_2 is zero.

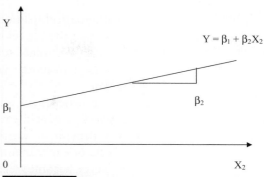

FIGURE 1.6 *The intercept and slope of a linear function.*

Naturally, in a graphical analysis only two variables are examined, Y and
X_2. Conveniently, however, the graph can also presents the logical nature of all
of the other parameters in the model simply by examining the parameter β_2
associated with X_2. β_2 is described as a partial slope coefficient or parameter. It
is partial in that it examines the relationship solely between Y and X_2. It is a
slope because it indicates how Y changes following a unit change in the value
of X_2. As drawn, it is implied that β_2 is positive. Specifically, the parameter
indicates that following a unit change of X_2, Y increases by β_2, *ceteris paribus*.
Each of the other βs would indicate the change in Y following a unit change in
the respective independent variable. Note that the graph is drawn in a straight
line. This reflects the fact that β_2 is fixed. Regardless of the values of X_2 from
which a change occurs, therefore, the subsequent change in Y will always be
the same. There is a hypothesized fixed relationship between changes in the
variables. It is important to note that this linear relationship applies regardless
of the units in which the variables are measured. Differences in these may
affect the economic interpretation of the relationship, but not the fact that
there is a constant degree of change implied in the relationship between the
variables.

It is the partial slope coefficients that are of direct interest to economists
because they describe how variables are related to one another. Assumptions or
hypotheses about these parameters thus form the basis of predictions that can
be tested against data. In testing these relationships, however, Equation 1.5
needs to be modified. As written, Equation 1.5 specifies a precise

mathematical relationship represented, for example, in Figure 1.6. This suggests that the behaviour of Y is fully understood. In the real world this cannot be. Theories might suggest which variables might be important in affecting Y, but not definitively. Economic research does not operate through experimentation.

An experiment engineers the isolation of intervening independent variables on a dependent variable. In a true laboratory experiment, the impact of independent variables is, essentially, fully understood. Translating the effects of experimental results to the real world outside of the experiment, however, becomes reminiscent of economic research as the impact of different variables needs to be isolated statistically. Because economic measurement and analysis takes place in the context of actual human activity, such as sport, assumptions have to be made about how factors other than those specified in a particular theory affect the dependent variable Y. In economic research statistical assumptions are made. To facilitate this, Equation 1.5 is rewritten as Equation 1.6. This is referred to as an econometric model.

$$Y_i = \beta_1 + \beta_2\, X_{2i} + \beta_3 X_{3i} + \ldots + \beta_k X_{ki} + \upsilon_i \qquad (1.6)$$

Two differences are noted. The first is that a subscript "i" is now attached to each variable. This is referred to as the index of observation, and will represent a particular set of observations or cases of the values of each economic variable. Thus, $i = 1, 2 \ldots 2000$ would indicate that 2000 observations on each variable were available to the researcher. The second difference is the final term in the equation, "υ_i." This is referred to as the stochastic or random error term of the equation. It represents the non-systematic effects on the dependent variable Y. Because it is a random variable, it makes Y, but not the independent variables, a random variable. Consequently, Equation 1.6 decomposes the behaviour of Y into a systematic component indicated by the independent variables and the random component, which cannot be predicted. The aim of economic research then becomes to use data on the variables to estimate the parameters using regression analysis, and to compare these with theoretical hypotheses about the sign and size of the parameters. Regression analysis helps to identify the effects of each independent variable on the dependent variable separately. Because the parameters are estimated from data on Y, which is random, and the independent variables, the parameters are also random variables. In this way statistical tests of the parameters can also be undertaken to make inferences about the applicability of the parameter values beyond the sample of data used in the analysis. Traditionally ordinary least squares (OLS) analysis has been used. Briefly, this approach estimates the parameters so as to minimize the sum of squared residuals in a regression, and thereby maximizes the

---

BOX 1.5 ASSUMPTIONS ABOUT THE RANDOM ERROR TERM IN OLS

1. The mean value of v_i is zero.
2. The variance of v_i is the same for all observations.
3. Each v_i is independent of the others (i.e. their probability distributions are independent).

4. Each v_i has a normal distribution.

"goodness of fit" of the regression. Residuals can be loosely viewed as an estimate of the values of v_i from the sample of data at the disposal of the researcher. A statistic, R^2, that lies between "0" and "1" indicates the proportion of explanation achieved, with "1" implying a perfect fit with the data, which is never achieved.

OLS assumes that v_i follows a normal distribution, and as a result so do both Y_i and the parameters. Because samples are used, tests of the parameters such as $H_0:\beta_i = 0$ against one of the following alternative hypotheses, $H_1:\beta_i \neq 0$ or $H_1:\beta_i > 0$ or $H_1:\beta_i < 0$ can be undertaken using the t-distribution, with a t-statistic being calculated by dividing the estimated parameter by the estimated standard error of the parameter. If the absolute value of the t-ratio is greater than 2, i.e., $|t| > 2$, then H_0 can be rejected at approximately a 5% significance level. This implies that a non-zero estimated coefficient can only have been a chance occurrence at most in 5% of occasions. OLS produces "best-linear-unbiased estimates," if the assumptions detailed in Box 1.5 are met.

This means that the estimated parameters are the best possible given the data available. The errors will be the lowest, and on average the parameter estimates will be correct. Much economic research thus involves correcting models to make these assumptions fit. In particular, assumptions 2 and 3 are addressed under the headings of heteroscedasticity and serial correlation. Solutions to these problems either involve adjusting the model (often referred to as generalized least squares) or the standard errors used to make the statistical claims.

There are an increasing number of regression estimators used in economic research resulting from the growth in computational power available to researchers, and increased sensitivity of researchers to more adequately capture the characteristics of the dependent variable being investigated. Examples of other techniques noted in the literature are given in Table 1.1

Regressions can be estimated for cross-section, time series or pooled/panel samples of data. These reflect observations across a sample of different economic units at a point in time, the same economic unit over a set of time periods, or a combination of these.

TABLE 1.1 Regression options

Type of estimator	Measurement of dependent variable	Typical application	Coefficient interpretation
1. Discrete choice			
Logit/probit	Binary values e.g., 1 or 0	Participation or not in an activity by an individual	The change in the odds of the possession of the characteristic scored 1 following a unit change in the independent variable
Poisson/negative binomial	Count data e.g., the number of occurrences of an event	The frequency of participation in an activity or the number of medals won by a country at the Olympic Games	The change in the conditional mean number of counts following a unit change in the independent variable
2. Limited dependent variable (censored)			
The Tobit model	Some values of the dependent variable are collapsed to one value	Attendance at sell out fixtures used to measure the demand for the fixture	As with ordinary least squares (OLS)
The Heckman model	Some values of the dependent variable are recorded only for sub-samples of the population	The frequency of participation in a sports activity depends on the prior choice to undertake the activity	Two equations are estimated: a logit/probit to estimate the likelihood of inclusion in the sample, with coefficients interpreted as above; and a regression that models the subsequent values of the dependent variable, with coefficients interpreted as with OLS
The hazard/survival model	The dependent variable measures a discrete and varying duration	The length of career of professional team sport managers	The proportional change in the duration of the hazard

1.9 CONCLUSION

This chapter has sought to revisit some basic economic tenets that are relevant to the study of sports economics. Consequently, it has been shown that the conventional economic scope of analysis is concerned with an optimal allocation of resources. The theory of perfect competition acts as a policy benchmark, which provides impetus to recommending the market-based provision of sports. It has also been indicated, however, that active policy intervention in sport can find a rationale through seeking to alleviate market failures, but also to promote economic development. A basic sketch of the empirical approach of economic research has also been given. Subsequent chapters employ these concepts in a more detailed analysis of participant sport, professional sports and sports events. The next chapter provides more detail on the definition of sport, its measurement and significance, and the alternative policy emphases of sports provision.

Appendix 1.1 The Relationship Between Average and Marginal Revenue in Monopoly

A straight line AR curve can be given by Equation A1.1.1. As described in the text, this is an example of a function in which the dependent variable, F (the number of fixtures), is related to the independent variable, P (the average revenue or ticket price). It is a specific rather than a general function, because the nature of the relationship between the two variables is specified. In this case, a straight line relationship is implied in which the number of fixtures equals "a" if the ticket price is zero, and reduces from that value as ticket prices increase according to the value of "b" (a and b are referred to as parameters of the function). The former is the intercept, or constant term, the latter is the slope coefficient.

$$F = a - bP \qquad \text{(A1.1.1)}$$

Where:

P is average revenue or ticket price;

F is the number of fixtures;

a is the constant or intercept and gives the number of fixtures when price is zero. This is the limit of demand.

b is the slope of the demand curve, and gives the number of the increase or decrease in fixtures following a unit decrease or increase in ticket prices. Mathematically, b is the derivative of the function F with respect to P, i.e., $-b = dF/dP$.

MR is the change in total revenue following a change in the number of fixtures supplied. To identify MR requires first finding total revenue (R). This can be obtained by multiplying Equation A1.1.1 by ticket price P to give Equation A1.1.2:

$$F \times P = R = aP - bP^2 \qquad \text{(A1.1.2)}$$

MR is then given as ∂R/∂P, which gives Equation A1.1.3:

$$dR/dP = MR = a - 2bP \qquad \text{(A1.1.3)}$$

Note that the slope of this marginal revenue relationship is given by Equation A1.1.4:

$$d(dR/dP)dP = dMR/dP = -2b \qquad \text{(A1.1.4)}$$

The slope is twice as steep as the demand curve.

Appendix 1.2 The Derivation of the Keynesian Expenditure Multiplier

Equation A1.2.1 describes consumption as a linear function of income, known as a consumption function, and Equation A1.2.2 shows that income is determined by consumption. In practice more complicated functions would be involved

$$C = a + bY \qquad \text{(A1.2.1)}$$

$$Y = C \qquad \text{(A1.2.2)}$$

Where:
Y is income
C is consumption
b is the marginal propensity to consume (mpc, i.e., 0.8)
a is the hypothetical minimum consumption required if income was zero.
To determine the overall level of income these equations are solved simultaneously. Thus:

$$Y = a + bY \qquad \text{(A.1.2.3)}$$

implying:

$$Y(1 - b) = a \qquad \text{(A1.2.4)}$$

implying:

$$Y = a/(1 - b) \qquad \text{(A1.2.5)}$$

Therefore, if the public authorities increased spending by €100m this would be equivalent to increasing a by this value, i.e. consumption that is not funded by current income. The multiplier is calculated as:

$$dY/da = 1/(1 - b) \qquad \text{(A1.2.6)}$$

or:

$$dY/da = 1/(1 - 0.8) = 5 \qquad \text{(A1.2.7)}$$

Consequently, multiplying the increase in expenditure "da" by the multiplier indicates the consequent rise in income:

$$(dY/da)\, da = €100/(1 - 0.8) = €500 \qquad \text{(A1.2.8)}$$

CHAPTER 2

The Nature, Organization and Economic Significance of Sport

OBJECTIVES

■ To appreciate the difficulties in defining sport as a distinct economic activity
■ To understand the main features of the policy and economic environment of sport
■ To appreciate the main research themes of mass participation sport, sports events and professional team sports

2.1 INTRODUCTION

The previous chapter provided an overview of economic analysis relevant to the study of sports. In this chapter an overview of the sports economy is attempted, so that the remainder of the book can provide a more detailed theoretical and empirical analysis of specific features and issues in sports economics.

This chapter addresses two main interrelated issues. The first is to explore what is meant by "sport" as an object of enquiry. In the next section some brief philosophical comments on the definition of sport are provided, before a concrete understanding of the contingent nature of sport is illustrated by addressing the second main theme of the chapter, which is to outline some key economic and policy characteristics of the sports environment. This discussion makes it clear why it is important to focus on the main subjects of this book; mass sports participation, professional team sports and sports events. Although they share common origins and elements of organization, there are also unique policy concerns and economic developments in each case that need to be understood. It is through a discussion of these segments of the sports environment that the main sports involved in each case are presented. The chapter closes with a brief review of the changing emphases of their policy and economic environment to set the scene for subsequent more detailed discussion.

2.2 WHAT IS SPORT?

In Chapter 1 it was argued that the most prevalent definition of economics was derived from Lionel Robbins as "the science which studies human behaviour as a relationship between ends and scarce means which have alternative uses." Robbins' definition is broad in conception and consistent with recognizing that economic activity is not, of necessity, connected with the creation and redistribution of material wealth. Consequently, it can apply directly to all activities that could be classified as sport, such as professional team sports, elite individual sports and, indeed, formal or casual mass participation in other activities. This is because individuals who participate in these activities need to make choices over their allocation of resources to supply and consume these activities. But this raises an extremely important question which is: what is sport? A moment's serious reflection reveals that, like many apparently tractable objects, sport appears easy to define at first hand. However, the boundaries that distinguish it from other activities are contentious and, indeed, can appear quite arbitrary. From a purely logical point of view, there is no simple list of activities that can be called "sport."

For example, at the outset of policy concerns with sports in Europe, the Council of Europe (1980) and Rodgers (1977, 1978) developed overlapping classifications of leisure, recreation and sport which have become accepted policy categories, and are still implied in the 1992 Council of Europe, European Sports Charter (Gratton and Taylor, 1985, 2000). The 1992 European Sports Charter argues that:

"Sport embraces much more than traditional team games and competition. Sport means all forms of physical activity which, through casual or organized participation, aim at expressing or improving physical fitness and mental well-being, forming social relationships or obtaining results in competition at all levels."[1]

And this definition is accepted by the policy makers of European countries. Within this definition, classifications essentially rely on differentiating activities according to their characteristics and organization, of which rules and governance are a central part. For example, Rodgers argues that sports have

---

[1] The charter was revised in 2001 but not the definition.

four essential elements present. Physical activity is undertaken, for a recreational (that is non-obligated) purpose and this takes place within a framework of organized competition that is regulated in an institutional setting.

However, despite the practical context, the boundaries between activities remains blurred. For example, many sports are undertaken as a professional activity, which implies that they are not recreational. Activities other than team sports, such as swimming and cycling, may take place under similar competitive and organized circumstances to team sports. However, these activities, and indeed many others such as team sports, may also take place in a noncompetitive and non-institutional environment. In this regard they could be viewed as "recreational" sports, inasmuch as formal rules of competition are not followed. Finally, leisure activities may embrace reading, watching the television, visiting a city, or indeed spectating at professional sports encounters. They are neither competitive, rule bound, nor physical activities. Walking and gardening are both physical activities, often undertaken for recreational purposes. Walking, as illustrated below, is often included in sports participation surveys by government and other agencies, but gardening is not. Sport England has recently classified darts as a sport, but not chess. However, the International Olympic Committee recognizes that chess is a sport. In this regard its governing body must ensure that its statutes, practice and activities conform to the Olympic Charter, as with the other recognized activities discussed below. It is clear then that, in practice, sport does not have a predetermined definition. It follows that one should always bear in mind the context in which the terms "sport," "recreation," "leisure" and "physical activity" are used.

This discussion illustrates the important point to grasp that the subject matter of this book essentially reflects definitions of sport that have come to be used within particular lines of enquiry, and advocated and discussed by various policy making bodies and, ultimately, to have come to be accepted by the wider public.

As Gratton and Taylor (2000) note, definitions of sport involve "the criterion of general acceptance that an activity is sporting, e.g., by the media and sports agencies" (p. 7). This implies that this book will inevitably show a degree of "bias" toward discussing sports and issues that are dominant in the academic literature, as a subset of popular and policy discussion. None of this is meant to imply that other issues or sports are of less significance *per se*.[2] To

---

[2] Consequently, for example, women's professional sports are emergent and reflect women's participation in sports traditionally associated with males. Historically, Negro leagues thrived in baseball in the US, and in the UK and in general, ethnicity and gender are important in consideration of patterns of participation in specific sports. Issues such as these are much more likely to be discussed in sociological literature. In economics, as indicated in the definitions discussed in Chapter 1, attention tends to focus on "agents" making optimal choices. These issues are discussed further in Chapter 4.

indicate what activities are defined as sport for policy and economic discussion, it is necessary first to address the economic organization of sports. This also indicates the various stakeholders that exist in the sports economy.

2.3 ECONOMIC ORGANIZATION

Figure 2.1 highlights a stylized sports environment which identifies the economic and policy relationships involved in sport, based on a modification of a schema presented in Gratton and Taylor (2000).

In Figure 2.1 the central triangular shape represents sports activity. Broadly speaking the horizontal dimensions measure the number of people involved in sport, the consumers and suppliers of sport. As one moves towards the apex the professional nature of sports participation and supply increases, and

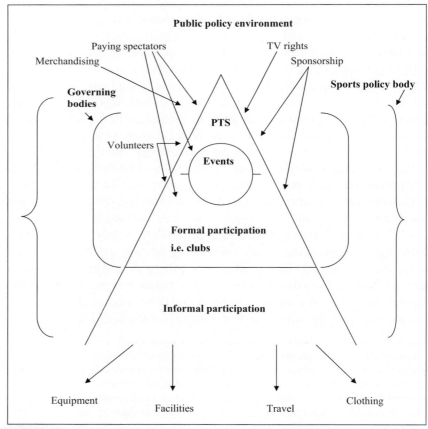

FIGURE 2.1   *The sports economy.*

consequently the numbers of people involved fall. At the apex, thus, is "elite" professional team sports (PTS). As one moves down the triangle one enters the domain of formal mass participation, facilitated through sports clubs or schools to informal and casual mass participation, in which consumers of sport and suppliers become more and more distant in their relationship. For example, as discussed in Chapter 5, traditionally sports can be viewed as being consumed and supplied through the formation of voluntary sports clubs; outside this domain participation can take place either through informal use of municipal or commercial facilities. The boundaries of this activity are, of course, difficult to establish, as reflected in the open-ended base of the pyramid. Sports events bridge the elite and mass participation boundaries because, as discussed further below, these are simply an episode of sports competition. Yet at one extreme, say the Olympic Games, professional athletes compete and are organized by economically powerful organizations. At the other, many formal amateur sports compete in events as voluntary clubs.

The diagram does allow for the possibility of participation at lower levels, feeding into higher level activity. A number of talent redistribution mechanisms might facilitate this. As discussed in Chapters 7 and 11 there are notable differences in the North American model of professional sports and some of the competitions in international sports, such as rugby union, where franchise systems operate as opposed to a system of vertical selection of clubs, which is common in European sports in general and soccer in particular. There are also sports policies that are put in place that seek to extract talent from lower levels of mass participation and to move this talent vertically.

The main commercial inputs to sport feed into the elite apex of the sports economy through merchandising, sponsorship, television rights deals and paying spectators, as discussed in Chapter 7. However, some sponsorship exists in amateur formal sports activity, and fee paying spectators are also possible. Non-commercial inputs are also very important. As discussed further in Chapter 6, volunteering is integral to all organized sport. The diagram also illustrates that flowing out of the direct involvement in sport are related derived demands, for equipment, facilities, etc.

> Derived demands express how interrelated economic activity is. For example, according to Alfred Marshall: "The demand for raw materials and other means of production is indirect and is derived from the direct demand for those directly serviceably products which they help to produce" (Marshall, 1952, p. 316, italics in original).

Once again extremes are possible. One may be the clothing and equipment required for an individual to participate in a casual activity. The other may reflect the need to create an Olympic village. The important point to note here is that sports are part of a set of interrelated markets.

All of this economic activity takes place within a regulatory framework. In sports there are three main tiers to this framework. The first is the public policy framework of national and supra-national policy-making agencies, which is illustrated by the rectangular shape which borders the diagram. In European countries, as implied earlier, the EU influences sports policy and markets, as well as national governments. However, most national governments, in connection with a form of local government, also have sports policy bodies which direct and implement policies. Often these have remits which embrace both mass participation and elite sports. This is implied in the open curly parentheses in the diagram. Finally, organized sport often takes place under the remit of governing bodies. This is discussed further in Chapter 6. However, and as discussed further in Chapter 7, governing bodies often face powerful counter-organizational pressures from professional sports. Moreover, almost by design they have no control over informal activity. This is why the curved brackets start at the juncture of formal and informal mass participation sport, but do not reach the apex of the pyramid.

Of course, the emphases of these relationships can change. Moreover, the comparability of the quantitative character of the sports environment between cases can be questionable, because of the potential differences in definitions of sport, but the qualitative structure of the sports environment, so defined, does have some reliability, as the following discussion reveals. This discussion draws on a wide variety of sources, but particularly useful overviews are provided in Carter (2005), Green and Houlihan (2005), and Houlihan (1997).

2.4 SOME INTERNATIONAL EVIDENCE ON THE SPORTS ENVIRONMENT

2.4.1 Public policy

Public policy involvement in sport has been steadily increasing. In part this is because of the growth in the globalization and commercialization of sport. As Green and Houlihan (2005) note, in Australia before World War II, federal government involvement in sport was *ad hoc*, and the same was true of Canada and the UK until the 1960s. As discussed in more detail later, the emphasis ebbed and flowed between developing mass participation sport and elite sport. Likewise, as Downward and Dawson (2000) argue, from an economic perspective regulation of professional sports fell within the broad remit of the Sherman Acts in the US and the Monopolies and Restrictive Practices Acts in the UK. Currently, within Europe, the Treaty of Rome provides the economic competition regulation framework. Box 2.1 illustrates issues that the European Commission has recently examined.

BOX 2.1 RECENT EU RULINGS ON SPORT

1. Media rights for the UEFA Champions League.
2. Multiple ownership of football clubs.
3. Football players' agents.
4. UEFA broadcasting rights.
5. Formula One – International Automobile Federation regulations.
6. Rules on the transfer of football players.
7. Grants to French professional football clubs.
8. The Mouscron case in relation to the UEFA home and away rule.
9. Doping case filed against the IOC by two swimmers who were banned for doping. The commission ruled that this fell outside the scope of community competition rules.

Source: http://www.euractiv.com

As can be seen, football provides a central focus for these regulatory initiatives, as it is the largest professional sport in Europe. However, more generally, sport is viewed as subject to the subsidiarity principle, which means that it is essentially a matter for member states. Box 2.2 indicates some important developments in the consideration of sport by the EU.

In addition to such supra-national policy making, the organization of sport in Europe has some common traits. Countries such as the UK and France have

BOX 2.2 SPORT AND THE EU

Sport is not dealt with separately as an EU policy area, neither are there permanent groups for addressing sports issues. These are dealt with in different committees, depending on the precise nature of the issue. The Committee on Culture, Youth, Education, the Media and Sport is one main forum for debate. There is also a Parliament Sports "Intergroup" which meets informally. Indirectly, sport is influenced by policy in a variety of areas, as detailed in the initiatives below.

- 1974: the Walgrave ruling established sport as an economic activity, and subject to the Treaty of Rome.
- 1992: the Maastricht Treaty referred to the social significance of sport.
- 1997: the Amsterdam Treaty stressed the importance of amateur sport, and the need for dialogue with sports associations, and emphasized the social significance of sport.
- 1999: the Helsinki Report stressed the need to safeguard sport structures and maintain the social function

of sport within the community framework. A sports unit was set up in the DG Education and Culture, to administer the European Year of Education through Sport 2004.

- In Nice in 2000, a council declaration again supported the need to preserve and promote the social functions of sport. It also noted the specific characteristics of sport, to intensify European cooperation in the area of doping and the UN Millenium Declaration on the promotion of peace and mutual comprehension by means of sport and the Olympic Truce.
- 2003: the council and parliament approved the establishment of the European Year of Education through Sport 2004.
- Article III–182 of the draft constitution refers to the educational and social role of sport. Sport is also listed in Article 16 as one of the areas where the EU may take supporting, coordinating or complementary action.

Source: http://www.euractiv.com

more generalized ministries as the first layer of state involvement, but some of these do have a sport remit. In the UK the relevant ministries are the Department for Culture, Media and Sport and the Department for Education and Science. In 2006, a new central government minister for Public Health was established to work in partnership with the Department for Culture, Media and Sport, the Department for Communities and Local Government, the Department for Transport, the Department for Education and Skills and sports delivery bodies to raise participation. Likewise, in France the Ministry for Youth and Sports, together with the Ministry of Education are involved in sports delivery. In Finland the Ministry of Education subsumes sports, whereas in Germany sport is devolved to its 16 constituent federal Länder (European Commission, 1999).

Some similar patterns exist elsewhere. In Japan sport lies within the remit of the Ministry of Education, Culture, Sport, Science and Technology, and in Canada, sport resides within the Federal Department of Canadian Heritage. In Australia there is much stronger direct federal support for sports agencies, in contrast to the US in which there is none. This is suggestive of a distinction between the US and other sports economies, a theme which is developed more later on in the book.

As well as central government, direct government involvement in sport is also mediated at local government levels. For example, in Germany and Finland, local authorities are the principle providers of funds for facilities and sports clubs. In Canada mass participation has tended to fall within the remit of the provinces (Green and Houlihan, 2005). As Houlihan (1997) notes, moreover, in the UK the distribution of responsibilities is complex at a local level. Historically in the US, by contrast, sport was supplied by the local, municipal and state authorities. However, there is a growing privatization of sport in the US, with facility redevelopment often being undertaken by private investment. In addition, the college system is uniquely placed in US sport in terms of bridging the gap between mass and elite participation.

2.4.2 Sports policy bodies

Lying below central government agencies, and in addition to local government, most countries have sports policy bodies which act as vehicles for delivering central and local government initiatives or allocating finances to sport. In the UK, UK Sport and four sports councils, Sport England, Sport Scotland and the Sports Councils for Wales and Northern Ireland perform these functions. However, as the Carter report (2005) indicates, there is a blurred distribution of functions and funding between the agencies.

In Germany, the German Sports Confederation (Deutscher Sportbund) and its regional offices perform the functions of public policy delivery and funding, and in Australia the Australian Sports Commission (ASC) embraces the delivery of elite sport via the Australian Institute of Sport. Policy associated with mass participation is administered via Active Australia. In addition, these agencies are partnered by the Australian Sports Foundation, which is a company governed by the ASC, whose role is to raise funds. Finally, in Canada, Sport Canada is directly responsible to the federal government and has three main divisions: Sports Programs; Sport Policy; and Major Games and Hosting Events.

2.4.3 Governing bodies and professional team sports

Once one moves away from the legislative and policy framework of sport, attention turns to the main organizational stakeholders in the provision of sport, the main elements of which are the participants and spectators, the clubs that organize sports competition and the governance of sport by clubs, along with other collective bodies. These stakeholders are related in a complex way that reflects historically and socially contingent formation, not least of which concerns the development of specific sports. It is significant to note that it is out of this complex evolution that professional sports leagues emerged, that large-scale events could develop, and that the structures that provide much mass provision of sport developed.

Downward and Jackson, for example, discuss the complex evolution of codes of football in the UK, its definition and governance. In brief, the important developments reflected the emergence from public schools of organized games of football. These were distinct from the informal traditional games played between villages, for example, versions of "Shrove Tuesday Football" such as are still played today in Ashbourne in Derbyshire, where two teams of unlimited size struggle to carry a ball to either ends of the village. The description as "football" reflected the fact not that a ball is kicked, but simply that it was distinct from pastimes such as hunting and riding which, being undertaken on horseback, were confined to the aristocracy (Houlihan, 1997).

Commensurate with a rise in voluntary associations, the Football Association (FA) was established in 1863 as the relevant governing body of the game of soccer. Rule changes led to association football encouraging a passing game using the feet (Williams, 1994, pp. 29–30). In contrast, Rugby School developed its own distinctive set of rules in 1862 to allow "old Rugbeians" to introduce an alternative to those interested in soccer. The Rugby Football Union (RFU) was established in 1871. At the outset the "Corinthian ideal" of amateur sport was embraced by both codes of football (Houlihan, 1997;

Downward and Jackson, 2003). In this regard, voluntary participation and organization was emphasized and remains today in mass participation sports clubs.

There was also, however, a growing concern to manage the increased popularity of both of the games. In large part this had been prompted by the development of cup competitions which provided incentives for clubs to codify their play according to particular sets of rules (Williams, 1994, p. 44); other than cup matches, fixtures tended to involve traditional or local rivalries.[3] Rapid expansion also carried with it the inevitable consequence of vertical segmentation and sporting differentiation. Alternative strategies evolved to cope with the expansion, particularly at the elite level. By 1888 soccer embraced professionalism at its highest level and the English Football League (EFL) was established to work with the FA to manage the competition between the top soccer clubs, while the FA was responsible for the management of the game as a whole, including its huge amateur base.

Leaving behind their amateur status, professional clubs began to incorporate themselves as limited companies. The rapidly-growing potential for earning money meant that enclosed stadiums were built, entrance fees for spectators extracted, and players paid and bought and sold. The need to pay to attract the best players existed even before the formation of the EFL, with evidence that paid professionals existed in 1876 (Vamplew, 1988).

As Dobson and Goddard (2001) note, the original 12 teams expanded to 16 in the top division. A further 12 clubs facilitated the creation of a second division before World War I. Movement between the divisions was based on merit, i.e., vertical selection. After the war, further expansion included a segmented third division for teams constituted on geographical lines for the north and south of England. This was achieved by incorporating elements of a previous southern league, which included some clubs from south Wales. By 1951, 92 league teams existed in the three divisions, and in 1959 the geographical basis of division three segmentation was replaced by a division three and four constituted on merit. During the 1970s and 1980s various changes took place. The most important of these included increasing the numbers of teams

---

[3] Such elements exist today in rugby union, the last sport to turn professional in the UK. Here the varsity match, between Oxford and Cambridge Universities, retains its social significance with the governing body and is played at Twickenham, which is the national stadium owned and managed by the Rugby Football Union. Outside of the County cup competitions also, amateur rugby union at a junior level is not organized by competitive leagues, unlike soccer. Likewise, invited "barbarian" teams are often put together to play international matches against national sides. The allegiance is to the game of rugby, with an implicit ethos being to play an expansive passing and attacking game for public enjoyment.

relegated and promoted, and the introduction of a play-off system to determine one of the promotion places. In 1993, the Premier League (PL) was formed by a breakaway of the division one sides, an issue discussed further in Chapter 7.

Coupled with domestic expansion in soccer, growth in international competitions promoted the need to develop supra-national governance. Procrastination by the English FA implied that in 1904, the Federation Internationale de Football Association (FIFA) was formed at a meeting of seven other European countries in Paris on 21 May, although the English FA soon joined. Initial competitions between countries took place at the Olympic Games before and immediately after World War I. Other countries, such as South Africa, Argentina and the US, joined FIFA, although England and Scotland refused to participate in competitions involving former wartime enemies. By 1930, under Jules Rimet's Presidency, the first world cup took place in Uruguay. With a break for World War II, the world cup has been contested every four years since. As can be noted below, a four-year cycle of international competition became a common basis of international competition, reflecting the time and travel costs associated with the expansion of competition. Competitions were of a knockout variety.

Reductions in travel costs generally meant that by the 1950s more regular international knockout competitions were held for both national sides and clubs. The Union of European Football Associations (UEFA) was established in June 1954 in Basel to oversee these developments in European football. Other continental associations have since formed. UEFA oversees the European Football Championship which started in 1958 between national teams, and a series of club-based international competitions. The European cup, for national league club champions was first contested in 1955, and this has subsequently evolved into the Champions league (CL), as discussed in Chapter 7. The Inter Cities Fairs Cup was established in 1955 to facilitate competition between national major knockout cup champions. This evolved into the UEFA cup in 1971. The UEFA cup also absorbed the Cup Winners Cup, which was started in 1961, in which lesser national knockout trophy winners competed.[4]

---

[4] FIFA recently launched an international World Club Championship, but it has met with mixed success. On one occasion Manchester United's participation in this cup, while withdrawing from the national FA Cup competition met with much protestations. The 2002 event was cancelled, but in 2005 a much reduced tournament took place. UEFA also oversees a number of other smaller competitions, including the Super Cup and the Intertoto Cup. In the former competition, Champions League winners play winners of the UEFA cup. The latter was originally a summer competition operated by some central European associations, but has expanded to become a qualifying tournament for the UEFA cup.

Over the same period, in which soccer developed, the rugby code was characterized by schism which was based on alternative approaches to "rejecting" professionalism. The divide occurred along broadly geographical, as well as class, lines. Many amateur rugby clubs were restricted to the professional classes. This was particularly the case in the south of England, but also in Liverpool, Sale and Manchester in the north of Britain. In contrast, in the north of England and south Wales the game was opened up to working men and artisans. Because of the length of the working week – including Saturday mornings until 1 pm – it was common for northern rugby union clubs to offer "broken time" payments to compensate for loss of earnings. The RFU in London were vehemently against this development and matters came to a head when, in the annual general meeting of the RFU in 1893, two coalitions of clubs – the Yorkshire branch and the remainder – debated the issue. The former argued that broken time would be the best means of avoiding professionalism, the latter not. The result was cast against broken time and the imposition of stringent rules against such payments instigated.

However, in 1895, 21 clubs of the Northern Rugby Union, based in York-shire and Lancashire, broke away to form their own league – the Northern Rugby Football League. Initially "professional players" receiving broken time payments were allowed, providing they were in full-time employment, and players could transfer between clubs if allowed by the Northern Union (Moorhouse, 1995, p. 61). By 1922 the game was relabelled as the Rugby Football League (RFL), to distinguish it from the RFU which managed the amateur game for the remaining teams. As with soccer, professionalism was embraced with the subsequent development of stadiums and incorporation of clubs.

Convoluted changes to both the structure of competition and rule changes followed the breakaway.[5] In the former case, traditionally struc-tured county championships were contested for five years following the first season. By 1902 two divisions were introduced with 18 sides each, and promotion and relegation again depending on merit. By 1905 the second division had contracted and the two divisions were scrapped again. A unique system was adopted within which approximately 31 teams competed for a single championship decided on the percentage of wins rather than the total number of points. From 1907 the top four teams contested the champion-ship by play-off. The next major changes were to come in 1962 in which eastern and western divisions were installed, only to be scrapped again in

---

[5] See Downward and Jackson (2003) and any *Rothman's Rugby League Yearbook* for a summary of key historical developments.

1964. In the new single division a play-off of the top 16 clubs decided the championship. This lasted until 1974, when two divisions were reinstated with play-off finals. The next major change was the creation of three divisions in 1995 making way for the creation of the super league (SL) in 1996 for the top sides, which will be discussed further in Chapter 13. From 1998 both the SL and the first division championships were to be decided from play-offs.

In the case of rule changes, attempts were made to speed up the game and encourage further handling of the ball. The main ones established a distinctive code of the northern rugby sides as opposed to the remainder of rugby union. From 1897 lineouts were abolished, because time-consuming scrummages tended to follow. In 1906 two of the forwards were removed, reducing team sizes to 13 men. A key rule change was the "play-of-the-ball" rule, which removed the need for a scrum following a tackle and an unplayable ball. Rewards for tries were increased – earning three points compared to the two from goals. This was subsequently increased to four points in 1983. In 1966 the number of tackles was limited to four, which was then extended up to six in 1972.

From an economic perspective, it is important to note that the above rule changes were not just directed at differentiation from rugby union. As professional sports, soccer and rugby league were in direct competition for both fans and playing talent. Consequently, teams such as Preston North End experimented with playing both codes. In general, being part of a well-organized football league with strongly professional aspirations, soccer teams flourished, as evidenced by the growth in scale of the EFL as opposed to the RFL (Williams, 1994, p. 82). Part of this expansion was at the expense of rugby league teams, such as Radcliffe and Walkden in Lancashire, which became unsustainable facing the competition for fans provided by the Bolton Wanderers and Bury FCs who were successful sides. Others, the most notable being Manningham, who had won the inaugural northern rugby union championship, converted to soccer in 1903 and re-emerged as Bradford City FC, who compete in the EFL today. Players also switched between codes. Part of the expansion of the EFL was, however, because it could monopolize the "vacant" midlands lying between the disputed geographical territories of rugby football. It was in direct response to the economic threat from soccer, thus, that rugby league struggled to adjust its form of competition and the rules of the game – to establish barriers to entry. It was also important that Yorkshire and Lancashire clubs played one another, because the initial competition with soccer was in the latter rather than the former county (Williams, 1994). Indeed the consolidation of talent in the former ensured that Yorkshire sides were dominant in the early years of rugby league. They won the county championship against their rivals in seven of the first eight seasons from 1889, and hence it was by no accident that they were the most vocal elements in the breakaway.

International rugby league, as with association football, developed out of early national competitions between members of the British Isles, however, competition with then colonial or near neighbours such as Australia, New Zealand and France soon took place. Its formal organization only developed with the formation of the Rugby League International Federation in France in 1948, as an attempt to preserve the game in France. France has struggled to recover from the political bans imposed on rugby league by the Vichy government. Other countries, particularly the pacific islands, subsequently played rugby league, as well as Russia and South Africa. In general, the strongest sides come from Great Britain, Australia and New Zealand, and currently these three countries compete in an annual tri-nations series.

In contrast to rugby league, rugby union remained staunchly amateur, although pressures towards becoming professional began in the 1960s. Essentially this was driven by gate-taking clubs wanting to increase resources through more regular competition. A national knockout cup was thus instigated in 1971 and national leagues finally established in 1976. In addition, the RFU and major clubs became increasingly dependent on gate money, sponsorship and media income. This was particularly fermented with the growth of interest in national team competition, ostensibly organized around the traditional annual competition including the home nations of the British Isles and France, the "five nations," which has recently been augmented to include Italy as the "six nations" in 2000. This international interest was galvanized around the instigation of a world cup, which was inaugurated in 1987 to promote more regular competition with southern hemisphere teams by separate national sides, in addition to traditional "British Lions" tours, on a four-year cycle, in which composite teams from the British Isles played other rugby union playing nations. Between 1900 and 1924 rugby union had been played at the Olympic Games, but with small numbers of participants.

By the 1990s English international players began using trust funds to get around professionalism rules, implying that earnings from sponsorship and appearances were not paid directly for playing, and there came public recognition that professionalism was more overt in other countries, particularly New Zealand and France. There was also concern that, coupled with the rise of the PL and the SL, media companies were seeking to develop a professional game, organized distinctly from traditional governing bodies. Consequently, by 1995 rugby union was declared an open game by the International Rugby Board (IRB).[6]

The IRB had been established in 1886 as the International Rugby Football Board (IRFB) by Scotland, Ireland and Wales, and subsequently England, following the resolution of concerns over representation and law-making powers. The current IRB comprises representatives from Scotland, Ireland, Wales, England, Australia, New Zealand, South Africa, France, Argentina, Canada, Italy and Japan, and actively seeks to develop the game internationally. It also controls international competition through the world cup and international seven-a-side tournaments.

Concern with the international games' development has also taken place against the backdrop of growing media incomes for sport and the desire not to lose players to rugby league deals. As with the development of the Premier league in association football, the Super league in rugby league and the Premiership in UK rugby union, the three main southern hemisphere rugby unions formed SANZAR (South African, New Zealand and Australian Rugby) which developed "Super" rugby in 1996. Growing out of earlier competitions between South Sea islands, this evolved into a league of originally 12 now 14 regional sides from these unions. A tri-nations series between the national sides of Australia, New Zealand and South Africa was also instigated in 1996.

A clear implication of the above discussion is that codes of football have evolved, reflecting both organizational and economic pressures, within an international setting. It is notable, thus, that alternative forms of football have also developed, for example in Ireland, Australia and North America. Links between these codes of football and those above are implicit, if not explicit, and reflect historical links between countries. Table 2.1 describes some characteristics of other professional sports.

2.4.4 Summary

These issues clearly demonstrate that team sports are organized in a complex way, with historically derived governing bodies managing mass participation of a formalized activity through clubs. Some of these clubs became professional, and leagues and other forms of competition emerged in both national and international contexts. Despite specific differences between sports, however,

---

[6] These pressures were also experienced in the southern hemisphere, with the establishment of a Super League in Australian rugby league. Fear over the potential loss of players led to the Super 12 competition being developed, as discussed below, to raise broadcasting revenue and to enable higher salaries to be paid.

TABLE 2.1 The origin and characteristics of other professional team sports

Sport	First club and rules	Countries played	Example of national governance	International governance	Examples of forms of competition
Cricket	Marylebone Cricket Club 1788	England, then initially Australia and South Africa, then the West Indies, New Zealand and India. Subsequently Pakistan, Sri Lanka and Zimbabwe	In England and Wales all competitions take place under the jurisdiction of the English and Wales cricket board (ECB)	The International Cricket Council (ICC), founded in 1989 from earlier bodies	International test cricket of five days duration plus various "limited over" one day games for full members of the ICC One day form world cup competition National games for county sides of four days duration plus various "limited over," one day games Amateur games of limited overs
Ice hockey	1877 McGill University students in Canada	Canada, US, Czech Republic, Finland, Russia, Slovakia, Sweden, UK	In the US (24 teams) and Canada (6 teams) the National Hockey League (NHL) prescribes the rules and governs the professional sport. Amateur sports in Hockey Canada and US Hockey compete with rules drawn from the NHL and the IIHF	International Ice Hockey Federation (IIHF)	The Stanley Cup is awarded to NHL league champions in a play-off system The annual world championships are competed for internationally by nations Ice hockey has been played at the Winter Olympic Games since 1924

| Basketball | 1891 Springfield College Massachusetts | The sport has global popularity. The US, South American, European, Asian and Australasian countries play basketball, as well as Russia, Scandinavia and the Baltic States | Most early competition in the US was between colleges and this led to the formation of the Intercollegiate Athletic Association (IAA) and subsequently the NCAA. Competition between numerous professional teams also took place. The National Basketball Association (NBA) was formed in 1946. The American Basketball Association (ABA) began in 1967 but merged with the NBA in 1976. The Womens National Basketball Association began in 1997 | US college varsity tournaments culminate in "March Madness" play-offs | The International Basketball Federation (IBF) was formed in 1932 for amateur players. Amateur and professional distinctions were dropped in 1989 | The NBA has a league structure | Basketball has been played at the Olympic Games since 1936, with women's basketball since 1976. The basketball world championships were first held in 1950 |

TABLE 2.1 *(Continued)*

Sport	First club and rules	Countries played	Example of national governance	International governance	Examples of forms of competition
Baseball	The New York Knickerbockers 1845	The US, Canada, Mexico, Caribbean countries, South America, Japan, Korea, Taiwan and European countries such as Italy, the Netherlands and some African countries, Australia and New Zealand.	In the US the National League (NL) has existed since 1875, despite rival leagues. It has 16 teams	The International Baseball Federation (IBAF) emerged in 2000 from earlier versions beginning in 1938	Each US league has a pennant race for the champion
			The American League (AL) has existed since 1900. It has 14 teams		The World Series set up in 1903 is played between the winners of the two main leagues
			The National Association of Professional Baseball Leagues was set up in 1901 and has become the basis of the minor leagues		World series were also played among Negro leagues
			Many amateur black players were forced to play in separate clubs and various "negro leagues" were formed, culminating in the Negro American League in 1937. This folded in 1960 as a result of the removal of race restrictions in 1947		The first official Olympic tournament took place in 1992, but the game has been removed from the 2012 games
					In 2006 a world baseball classic will take place replacing the previous irregular world cup that began in 1938. Mostly amateur players participate

as Arnout (2006) also confirms, it is argued that the above does illustrate that a pyramid structure of sports as represented in Figure 2.1 exists. There are distinctions in the US, where professional sports and amateur sports have developed more independently, but they are, of course, still inextricably linked in the sense that college sports and the minor leagues feed talent vertically into professional sports.

2.5 EVENTS AND MASS PARTICIPATION

Clearly, as described in Figure 2.1, mass participation activities provide the basis through which individuals or teams come forward to compete. Such competition then takes place according to an "event." However, this event can be organized by a league or knockout tournament, or a combination of these, as discussed further in Chapter 7, for a separate sport or for a collection of sports. In this regard what is meant by an "event" in this book has a specific meaning. It is essentially connected with a less-regular sports competition, in both the frequency of competition and the location in which it takes place compared to a league.

2.5.1 Events

The Olympic Games is the largest sporting event and, under the stewardship of Pierre Fredy (Baron de Coubertin), began formally in 1896 what we now understand as the summer games. The Winter Olympic Games commenced in 1924.[7] The International Olympic Committee (IOC) was established in 1894 to organize the first modern games, held in Athens in 1896. The Games have run up to the present day only being suspended in 1916, 1940 and 1944, because of the World Wars.

The organization of the games is controlled by the IOC in conjunction with partner agencies. These include international federations for specific sports, National Olympic Committees (NOC) within each country, who regulate the Olympic movement in that country, and specifically constituted organizing committees (OCOG) to stage the games. The latter are disbanded after each games. There are currently 202 NOCs and 35 international federations involved in the Olympic Games, and they are planned to supervise 26 sports scheduled for the 2012 London games. In the original games in 1896, nine sports were involved: athletics; cycling; fencing; gymnastics; weight lifting; shooting; swimming; rowing and wrestling. Current rules permit up to 28 sports. Individual sports require a two-thirds vote from the IOC to be

---

[7] In England versions of national "Olympic" competition preceded these dates.

BOX 2.3 2012 OLYMPIC SPORTS

Aquatics	Hockey	Cycling	Taekwondo
Archery	Judo	Equestrian	Tennis
Athletics	Modern pentathlon	Fencing	Triathlon
Badminton	Rowing	Football	Volleyball
Basketball	Sailing	Gymnastics	Weight lifting
Boxing	Shooting	Handball	Wrestling
Canoe/kayak	Table tennis		

considered as Olympic sports, and thereby become eligible for inclusion in a games. These include activities as wide in scope as climbing, bridge, chess (as noted earlier) golf, roller skating and surfing, and of course team sports such as cricket, baseball and rugby, which have been included in the past. Box 2.3 indicates the sports likely for the 2012 games, as baseball and softball have been dropped (http://www.olympic.org/uk).

For the Winter Olympic Games, cross-country skiing, figure skating, ice hockey, Nordic biathlon, ski jumping and speed skating have always been involved. In addition, the bobsleigh, curling, ice hockey and luge are very often included. Since 1960 in Rome, the Paralympic games for athletes with disabilities have been a part of the Olympic programme, with events taking place, for example, after the close of the summer games.[8] It is important to recognize, therefore, that the activities identified by the IOC as sport are also generated out of particular historical emphases and policy decision-making.

In this regard the other major events such as the Commonwealth Games (CWG), which is the second oldest multi-sport event, although lagging behind the scale of the Olympic Games, involves a different list of sports, as illustrated in Box 2.4.[9]

Since the Manchester Commonwealth Games in 2002, there have been athletics, swimming, table tennis and power lifting events for athletes with a disability.

---

[8] It should be noted that the "Special Olympic Games" and "Paralympic Games" are distinct organizations recognized by the IOC. Essentially the former is connected with the provision of year-round sports training and competition for individuals (age 8 and older) with intellectual disabilities. More than one million athletes in over 150 countries train and compete in more than 26 Olympic-type sports at local, state, national and World Games. The International Paralympic Committee, (IPC), in contrast, focuses on producing a games parallel to the Olympic Games, and other multi-disability competitions for elite athletes.

[9] For example, it is estimated that the 2006 games in Melbourne was about a third of the scale of the 2000 Sydney Olympic Games. http://www.minister.dcita.gov.au/kemp/media/ speeches/ Accessed on 21 June 2006.

BOX 2.4 COMMONWEALTH GAMES EVENTS

Current		Previous
Aquatics (swimming and diving)	Lawn bowls	Archery
Athletics	Netball	Cricket
Badminton	Rugby (sevens)	Fencing
Basketball	Shooting	Wrestling
Boxing	Squash	Judo
Cycling (road and track)	Table tennis	Rowing
Gymnastics	Triathlon	Ten-pin bowling
Field hockey	Weight lifting	

The Olympic Games and the Commonwealth Games are not the only major multi-sport events. There are also continental championships such as the European Games, the Asian, Pan American and African Games. As noted earlier, moreover, there are, of course, world championships in various specific sports, such as athletics. In this regard, only the world cup in soccer rivals the Olympic Games in terms of scale. The economics of these events is discussed more fully in Chapter 12. What is clear, however, is that these "events," as defined earlier, currently operate at the elite level, with participants that are now all professional in orientation. Significantly too, staging these events has become a competitive economic and political activity. Countries and cities now actively compete, through committing resources to bids, to host them. It is such developments which clearly merit economic analysis.

2.5.2 Mass Participation

Below the professional and elite level of sports is the mass participation sector. Care should be taken not to treat this sector as homogenous. One segment comprises formal club-based activities, for example operating under governing bodies that also govern elite team and individual sports and competition in leagues or events. In formal participation it is not uncommon practice to have elements of paid coaching and facilitation of sport, combined with huge levels of voluntary activity. In contrast, much participation now takes place by individual consumers who pay to participate in classes at health and fitness clubs or who participate in a highly informal and self-organized manner. The Carter Report (2005) estimates that up to 43% of sports participation in the UK operates on an informal basis.

> *Informal sport describes an activity that displays many of the characteristics of "formal sport," but does not involve structured competition governed by rules. Therefore, two people playing basketball on their local "Outdoor Basketball*

Initiative" site may be said to be engaging in informal sport, because the activity is very close to being what we understand basketball to be, but some of the defining characteristics of that sport have been compromised. Informal sports facilities can include skateparks, BMX tracks, basketball courts, kickabout areas and multi-use games areas. Associated facilities may include youth shelters or equipped play areas for younger children (Sport England, 2006).

Coalter (1999) charts the rise of this activity in the UK, and argues that it reflects more individualistic activity, flexibly organized on a non-competitive basis and showing more concern for fitness and health. In this regard, keep fit and yoga activities have recently increased very significantly for female participants, a trend also identified by the Australian Sports Commission (2004).

A detailed exploration of the reasons for participation in sports takes place in Chapters 3 and 4, along with a discussion of the supply structure of mass participation sports in Chapters 5 and 6. However, to indicate the types of activities that are conceptualized as sport outside the elite level of team and event sports, Table 2.2 presents examples on which different national public authorities collect data. It should be noted that these are not the only data sources for these particular countries, neither are they, in the light of informal sport, definitive. This said three issues are of particular interest concerning the definition of sport and its official measurement. The first is that there is some broad commonality over the activities investigated. Indeed, in Europe, the COMPASS project has been seeking to promote harmonization in the collection and reporting on official sport participation statistics.[10] The second issue is that some of the activities are unique to the country involved. This, of course, reflects the historical development of sports within the various countries, as discussed earlier. The final point to note is that the terminology varies according to context. Thus, soccer is used in North America and Australia for association football, which is referred to as football in the UK. Conversely, the term "football" is used for American football in the US, but qualified as such in the UK.

It is also important to note that the data collected on these activities does vary, reflecting differences in conception of participation. In Australia the Exercise, Recreation and Sport Survey (ERASS) commenced in 2001 and is conducted annually, commissioned by the ASC and state/territory departments of sport and recreation (see Australian Sports Commission, 2004). Participation is defined as active involvement, rather than coaching, officiating or spectating, and data is collected for those aged 15 years and older. Data

---

[10] See, for example, http://w3.uniroma1.it/compass/index.htm Accessed 13 June 2006.

TABLE 2.2 Examples of official data participation sports[1]

Australia	Canada	UK	USA
Aerobics/fitness	Badminton	Athletics	Aerobics/aerobic dance
Aquarobics	Baseball	American football	Baseball/softball
Athletics/track and field	Basketball	Angling	Basketball
Australian Rules football	Bowling	Badminton	Bicycle/exercise bike
Badminton	Curling	Basketball	Bowling
Baseball	Cycling	Bowls	Cross country skiing
Basketball	Ice hockey	Canoeing	Football
Billiards/snooker/pool	Rugby	Climbing	Gardening/yardwork
Boxing	Running	Cricket	Golf
Canoeing/kayaking	Skiing	Curling	Handball/racquetball/squash
Carpet bowls	Soccer	Cycling	Jogging/running
Cricket	Swimming	Football	Skiing
Cycling	Tennis	Gaelic sports	Soccer
Dancing	Track and field	Golf	Stair climbing
Darts		Gymnastics	Stretching exercises
Fishing		Hockey	Swimming
Golf		Horse riding	Tennis
Gymnastics		Jogging/running	Volleyball
Hockey		Keepfit/aerobics	Walking
Horseriding/equestrian		Martial arts	Water skiing
Ice/snow sports		Motor sports	Weight lifting/strength
Lawn bowls		Netball	
Martial arts		Rugby	
Motor sports		Sailing	
Netball		Skiing	
Orienteering		Shooting	
Rock climbing		Snooker	
Roller sports		Swimming	
Rowing		Squash	
Rugby league		Table tennis	
Rugby union		Tennis	
Running		Tenpin bowling	
Sailing		Volleyball	
Scuba diving		Walking	
Shooting sports		Weight lifting	
Soccer		Weight training	
Softball		Windsurfing	
Squash/racquetball			
Surf sports			
Swimming			
Table tennis			

TABLE 2.2 *(Continued)*

Australia	Canada	UK	USA
Tennis			
Tenpin bowling			
Touch football			
Triathlon			
Volleyball			
Walking (bush)			
Walking (other)			
Water polo			
Water skiing/powerboating			
Weight training			

are collected on participation during the 12 months prior to the interview. The sample size in, for example, 2004 was 13 662 persons.

In Canada, the activities above refer to those measured as part of the National Household Survey on Participation in Sport (NHSPS) conducted in 2004, of 2408 households, and commissioned by the Conference Board of Canada (see The Conference Board of Canada, 2005). Participation data are collected according to both active and non-active variants, such as volunteering and attendance at games or events, over a 12 month period, for those aged 16 years and above. Motorized sports are explicitly excluded, as well as activities that do not seek to improve personal sporting performance, such as jogging or cycling to work. In contrast in the US, the activities noted above are investigated in the National Health Interview Survey, which is a household survey conducted in 1985, 1990 and 1991 for individuals aged 18 years or older (see US Department of Health and Human Services, 1996). Participation is recorded for activity over the previous two weeks. In 1991, 43 732 households were surveyed.

In the UK, the activities refer to the General Household Survey (GHS) (see National Statistics, 2004). While the GHS is an annual survey of UK households, it only reports at various intervals on sports and leisure participation. The last two occasions, prior to the 2002 survey, on which the activities were derived were 1993 and 1996. The survey investigates participation primarily for those aged 16 or above in the four weeks before the interview with respondents took place, and for the 12 months before the interview took place. The activities noted above are categorized as "sports." Other activities that are categorized as "leisure" include watching television, listening to or playing music, reading, acting, dancing, attending leisure classes and other activities. It is clear that any empirical claims that are offered with respect to trends in mass participation sport should pay due regard to these definitional differences. More recently the Active People and Taking Part Surveys have been commissioned for England and the UK by Sport England and the DCMS respectively with more activites investigated. Chapter 4 gives some details of these surveys.

2.6 HISTORIC AND CURRENT POLICY IN SPORT: CHANGING EMPHASES AND VALUES

The above discussion has attempted to map out the broad structure of the meaning of sport as comprising a wide variety of activities being consumed and produced under different circumstances. The aim has been to provide an overview of the sport environment. Before closing this chapter, however, it is worth summarizing some of the main changes that have taken place in economic and policy emphasis within the sports environment as described above, as it is ultimately these changes that motivate issues of direct economic interest in sports.

To begin with, a general traditional tension identified in sports policy arises out of concerns for fostering mass participation and also elite sport success in the non-professional sports context, and particularly major events such as the Olympic Games. Houlihan (1997), Green (2004), and Green and Houlihan (2005) note, for example, that the traditional emphasis of sports policy in say Australia, Canada and the UK were aimed at raising general physical fitness and enhancing social welfare, but such initiatives have gradually been eroded in favour of the pursuit of elite success.

This suggests that one policy tension facing sport is the provision of public funds for the support of elite versus mass participation activities. As discussed in Chapter 1, there is an opportunity cost implied in supporting one rather than the other. From an economic perspective, however, this also raises the important prior questions of whether or not public funds should be used at all to promote mass participation and, further, to underpin elite sport activity, such as hosting and participating in sporting events which do not fund themselves. It has to be noted that economists are sceptical about the value of such initiatives.

Issues such as these have become important, because the scale of economic activity associated with elite sports at events has increased significantly. Blake (2005) estimates that the operating costs of staging the 2012 Olympic Games in London alone will be £1.010 billion, with further infrastructural investment costs of at least a further £642 million. Moreover, the 1972 Munich Olympic Games and 1976 Montreal Olympic Games made losses of £178 million and £692 million respectively, while the 1984 Los Angeles Olympic Games and the 1992 Barcelona Olympic Games made surpluses of £215 million and £2 million. Even as part of the process of bidding to host major events, cities now invest huge sums of money. For example, the London bid is estimated to have cost £17 million, while the 2010 winter games bid for Vancouver cost $35 million.[11] This competitive marketing of cities to hold events, as discussed in Chapter 12, is now often used to capture sports franchises, and has been described as a process of "glocalization" in which localities compete on global markets for sources of tourism and related expenditures (see, for example, Robertson, 1995). The economics underlying these issues need to be clearly understood.

The above discussion also hints at the internationalization, globalization and commercialization of sports generally.[12] Of course, in the case of professional team sports, as noted earlier, it has been argued that the spread and development of sports has occurred along increasingly commercial lines, developing and adjusting previous patterns of development. What is particularly significant in this regard, however, is the relatively recent but rapid growth of funds flowing between stakeholders in such sports.

To illustrate this point Dobson and Goddard (1995) note that in 1967 individual football clubs in England and Wales, in the most popular team sport, received £1300 from television sources for the showing of highlights. In 1978 the amount had only risen to £5800. In contrast, BSkyB paid over £600 million for the exclusive rights to broadcast live Premier league association football matches between 1997 and 2001, and £1.024 billion from 2002–2007.[13] Since 2006, as discussed in Chapter 10, exclusive rights for televising the Premiership do not exist. Table 2.3 also indicates the scale and variety of income for three top European football clubs for the 2003–2004 season. As well as the scale of funds involved, the table also reveals that revenue from television and commercial activities such as sponsorship and merchandising are now as important as attendances, the historical source of revenues, for the top clubs.

---

[11] See http://www.londontown.com/London/Timeline_of_the_Bid Accessed 14 June 2006 and http://thetyee.ca/Views/2004/05/24/Blame_It_on_Olympic_Fever/ Accessed 14 June 2006.

[12] Debates between theoretical notions of globalization and internationalization are beyond the scope of this book. Contrasting perspectives could be reviewed in Maguire (1999) and Houlihan (2005).

[13] See, for example, http://news.bbc.co.uk/1/hi/business/4949606.stm Accessed 14th June 2006.

TABLE 2.3 Scale and distribution of sources of European football club revenues

Club	Matchday		Broadcasting		Commercial		% Champions League
	£	€	£	€	£	€	
Manchester United	92.4	61.2	94.5	62.5	72.1	47.8	15
Real Madrid	62.0	41.1	88.1	58.3	85.9	56.9	13
AC Milan	27.9	18.5	134.4	89.0	60.0	39.7	10

Source: Deloitte (2005a).

Indeed, Deloitte (2005b) note that across Europe the major professional football leagues of the UK, France, Germany, Spain and Italy generated €5.8 billion in revenue in 2003–2004, of which the PL generated €2 billion. These revenues reflect growth from €1.95 billion in the period from 1995 to 1996. Coupled with this growth in revenue, wages and player salaries have also escalated from a total of approximately €1 billion in 1995 to approximately €3.6 billion in 2003–2004.

Similar developments have, of course, occurred in the US. Whereas $65 000 captured the rights to broadcast the World Series in baseball to fewer than 12% of US households in 1947, as Table 2.4 reveals, US professional sports are now million dollar industries employing million dollar athletes.

Understanding the main determinants of revenue and cost flows for professional sports, their changes and how, now justifiably viewed as large-scale industries, such sports are subject to the scrutiny of economic regulators in the light of claims made about the management of leagues is of direct interest to economists. Of course economic activity directly associated with sports is not just confined to the flows of revenues and costs within elite and professional team sports. Figure 2.1 shows that, flowing out of activity associated with sports are derived demands for related travel, equipment, facilities and

TABLE 2.4 US sports leagues

Sport	League revenue $ billion (2005)	Average player salary $ million (2005)
National Football League	4.8	1.25
National Basketball Association	3.1	4.92
Major League Baseball	4.1	2.5
National Hockey league	2.0	1.81
Major League Soccer	2.4	Not available

Source: Plunkett Research.[1]
[1] *See http://www.plunkettresearch.com/Industries/Sports/SportsStatistics/tabid/273/Default.aspx Accessed 15 June 2006.*

TABLE 2.5 Size of sports economy

Country	Spending € billion	% of GDP
France	25.4	1.7
Finland	1.7	0.9
Canada**	Not available	1.1–1.22
UK	20	2
US*	77.97	0.78

Source: Carter Report (2005).
* Plunkett research: only includes equipment, clothing and footwear $ values converted at an average 2005 rate $1.244: €1, US GDP in 2005 $12.36 trillion.
** Second figure from The Conference Board of Canada (2005).

clothing. In other words, economic activity directly associated with sports consumption and production "spills over" to the wider economy. Such effects are essential to understanding the full economic impact of sports, which are discussed in various forms throughout the book. Key to this are the multiplier effects discussed in Chapter 1. For now, however, it is worth noting that the increasing importance of sport to the wider economy has led to recent attempts to formalize the economic magnitude of sports through charting the value of spending as a share of the economy. While there are problems of measuring such values, Table 2.5 provides some examples of the relative importance of sport, as an indicator of the relative sizes of the sports economy, deriving from the sports environment as defined in Figure 2.1. A salutary point to note from the table is that while sport looms large in people's minds, in economics terms it is still a small proportion of overall economic activity, at least as measured. In this regard, it should be noted that it is the rapid changes in the economic profile of sports as discussed above, coupled with general interest in sport that, in essence, combine to make the study of the economics of sport both important and compelling.

2.7 CONCLUSION

This chapter has provided an overview of what is meant by sport, and how sport is organized internationally. It has been shown that "sport" is not a uniquely defined activity but, rather, reflects the historical development of particular activities that have come to be understood, provided and monitored in various guises. In this regard what is considered to be sport and, more importantly, how it is organized, can change. It has also been shown that there are three main segments in the sports economy, although they are integrally related, and these segments are the main subjects of this book: mass sports participation; professional team sports; and sports events. It has been shown that in many respects the latter two elite activities have grown out of mass participation activity and, corresponding with such evolution policy, tensions and shifts in the economics of the organization of the segments have occurred. In particular, this is connected with a growth in the commercial provision, or at least its logic, of sport and competition for public funds to supply sport. Having outlined the main tenets of economic theory relevant to examining sports, and having provided an overview of the sports economic environment, the remainder of this book probes each of these sections in more detail. The aim is to explore the relevant theory and evidence that yield a fuller understanding of these segments and their development.

CHAPTER 3

The Economics of Sports Participation[1]

[1] Elements of this chapter draw on Downward (2005).

OBJECTIVES

- ■ To understand economic theories of sports participation
- ■ To appreciate the policy implications of economic theories of sports participation
- ■ To appreciate why market failures could be important in sport

3.1 INTRODUCTION

This chapter begins an examination of mass sports participation as part of a broader process of sports consumption. Section 3.2 presents an initial "core" sports consumption model, by drawing on the hierarchical nature of the sports environment presented in Figure 2.1. Section 3.3 then presents how this model can be used to understand sport as a consumption of time, and as a consumption of goods. Section 3.4 presents an integrating framework for these theories, after which Sections 3.5 and 3.6 review alternative approaches to analyzing sports consumption, as well as considering the policy implications of the approaches.

3.2 A GENERAL ECONOMIC MODEL OF SPORTS CONSUMPTION

Figure 3.1 presents a core economic model of sports consumption. The figure shows that choice emerges from the interaction between the motives of consumers and the resources they have at their disposal. It is postulated that the sports consumer's motives will be influenced by their tastes or preferences, as

65

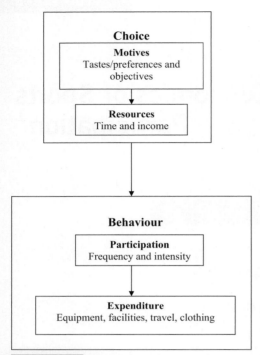

FIGURE 3.1 *Sports consumption.*

well as their objectives, which will imply a set of possible courses of action for the consumer. The resources at the consumer's disposal, i.e., their time and income, then identify feasible courses of action from which consumer behaviour emerges. Drawing on Figure 2.1, it is assumed that following choices about the frequency and intensity of participation, derived demands and expenditure on travel, equipment, facilities and clothing will follow. The next three sections outline these decision choices in more detail, by first of all identifying some basic features of economic decisions and then exploring situations in which the consumer allocates time to participate in sports, and then allocates financial resources to consume sports.

3.2.1 The dual decision hypothesis

A basic feature of economic analysis is that aggregate economic activity constitutes a flow of resources between economic agents. This is known as the "circular flow of income." In the simplest example, the flow of resources lies between "households" and "firms." Households comprise individuals who want to consume products and services, but who also provide work effort for firms to produce goods. In order to consume, the household needs to work to earn income. The household demands goods and services, but supplies labour effort to firms. Likewise, recalling Chapter 1, firms supply households with goods and services, but demand labour effort as a factor of production, in this case from households, to facilitate this. The expenditure of households will correspond to the income earned by firms and by households as employees of firms. Figure 3.2 illustrates the basic principle and the consequence that aggregate economic expenditure will correspond to aggregate economic income, or national income, in an economy.[2] The clockwise direction of the flows indicates the transfer of money payments. The anticlockwise flows indicate the real resources that correspond to the monetary transactions.

In practice, the circular flow of income is more complicated. There are leakages, in the form of savings by households, taxation by public authorities and imports of goods and services. Each of these, other things being

---

[2] An examination of Appendix 1.2 illustrates this proposition.

equal, will reduce the circular flow of income and the volume of national income.

Reflection Question 3.1 The circular flow of income
Why do imports, e.g., the purchase of overseas players by a football club or an overseas golfing holiday, reduce the circular flow of income?
Hint: Think about the destination of the expenditures.

The reason why savings and taxation reduce national income is because "expenditure" is being channelled away from firms, who cannot then use that income to employ labour from households. In the case of imports it reflects the fact that expenditures are being directed towards a different economy. Corresponding to these leakages is a series of injections to the circular flow. These comprise investment by firms, expenditure from public authorities, and exports. One of the key sources of investment funds for firms is savings, channelled to firms through the financial system. Thus, the banking system takes savings from households and lends this to firms to fund their investment decisions. Among other factors, therefore, the interest rate will make these activities interdependent.

The interest rate indicates the rate at which additional funds are received by savers for choosing not to consume their income now, but at some period in the future. It measures the time value of money. Clearly, as more individuals save it becomes difficult for financial businesses to pay the interest charges to savers, so they reduce the rate of interest they will pay. In turn, this will make the cost of borrowing money to invest less, and thus encourage less saving and more investment based on using borrowed money and vice versa.

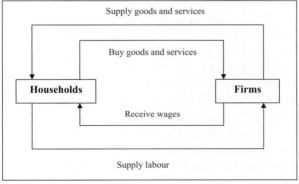

FIGURE 3.2   *A simple circular flow of income.*

Likewise, taxation is a source of income for public authorities to spend. In this regard injections to and leakages from the economy are closely related. Exports and imports, of course, are not directly related as decisions, but nonetheless their behaviour is related through, among other things, the exchange rate.

> *The exchange rate is the price of one country's currency in terms of another country's currency. Importing goods and services requires buying foreign currency and selling domestic currency to pay for the goods and services. Exporting goods and services implies receiving revenues in foreign currency which then needs to be sold and domestic currency bought. Consequently, the exchange rate will change according to the overall volume of importing and exporting that occurs. This affects the cost of the transactions, making imports or exports appear cheaper or more expensive depending on the circumstances, which, in turn, will affect importing and exporting behaviour.*

There has always been debate in economics about whether or not the circular flow of income automatically balances to ensure full employment and an efficient use of resources, as defined in Chapter 1. If all economic activity behaved according to the predictions of the model of "perfect competition" described there, then the economy as a whole would allocate resources efficiently. Key to this argument is the efficacy of prices, and the effectiveness of the market system, to channel resources to their appropriate uses. In this respect, the interest rate and exchange rate are considered to be important prices that coordinate the leakages and injections of savings–investment and imports–exports respectively. In turn, for many economists, it is recommended that governments should strive to ensure that the public finances balance and/or impose the smallest tax burden on the economy as possible. The latter point is justified by arguing that taxation reduces incentives to work. Such issues are of less direct interest for this book, although they are important in examining the impact of investment in sports infrastructure and events, as discussed in Chapter 12.

What is important to gain from this discussion is that it highlights that the sports consumer faces a "dual decision" dilemma. As a member of a household, if the consumer wants to purchase products and services, including sports goods and equipment, etc., then the individual will need to work to earn sufficient income to do so. However, work provides an obligation on the use of the consumer's time. Leisure, which is desirable, requires undertaking activities that do not place obligations on the consumer's time. However, because there is a time limit on the individual's capacity to work or to enjoy leisure (and indeed consumption generally) this implies a trade-off. The next section indicates how economists explore this trade-off in more detail, by examining a theory of rational individual choice.

3.2.2 The income–leisure trade-off

Economists have devised a relatively simple model to explore the dilemma faced by individuals between working to earn income, and not working and consuming time as leisure. It is called the income–leisure trade-off model. The main assumptions of the model follow.

3.2.2.1 Motives

1. Individuals seek to maximize their utility by consuming goods and services or enjoying leisure time. Utility, as discussed in Chapter 1, is simply defined as "satisfaction." In this respect, it describes the individual's preferences and tastes. It is considered to be a personal phenomenon and to be ordinal in nature. This means that individuals can compare two situations only for themselves, and express preferences over them, i.e., indicate which is associated with more utility, without being able to say anything about the extent of the difference in preferences or utility. Formally, this implies Equation 3.1, which indicates that utility, "U," depends on consumption through income "I," and the consumption of leisure time, "L."

$$U = U(I, L) \tag{3.1}$$

2. The individual always prefers more of both income and leisure to less of both. This implies that they are both "normal goods" and that the individual is willing, if necessary, to substitute more of one for less of the other. It follows that, if the individual gives up some leisure or income, then to leave the individual feeling as well off as previously, more income or leisure is required. It is also usually assumed that if, for example, the individual was currently consuming a lot of leisure, then it would take a smaller relative increment in income to persuade the individual to decrease their leisure by a certain amount, and *vice versa*. This is known as diminishing marginal utility,[3] and implies that relatively abundant goods or services are of less value to the individual compared with relatively scarce goods or services.

3.2.2.2 Constraints

1. Individuals are constrained in their activities by the rate of pay, "w" (per unit of time, e.g., hour, day or month, etc.) that can be earned from work, "W" and the finite amount of time available to them, "T." Formally, Equation 3.2 expresses the relationship that total time is equal to work plus leisure, and Equation 3.3 that income, "I," and hence consumption, is

---

[3] This is directly analogous to diminishing marginal productivity, discussed in Chapter 1.

work times the wage rate.

$$T = W + L \tag{3.2}$$

$$I = wW \tag{3.3}$$

2. Thus, if the rate of pay, w, is €10 per hour (and noting that there are 24 hours in a day, T), then this means that, in extreme cases, the individual could:

   (a) not work at all, W = 0, and hence receive no income, I = 0, for consumption of goods, but consume 24 hours of leisure, L = 24.
   (b) work for 24 hours, W = 24, and receive an income for consumption of I = €240, but consume no leisure, L = 0.

3. These are, of course, extreme cases and are referred to as corner solutions by economists. It follows that attention is focused on points in between these extremes. Thus, the individual could also consume 12 hours of leisure and receive €120 of income to consume goods, or consume 6 hours leisure and receive €180 income and so on. The time constraint acts to produce an income constraint, given a particular rate of pay. Equation 3.4 shows that the rate at which leisure can be substituted for income will reflect the wage rate. The equation indicates a negative relationship to imply the substitution of income by leisure.

$$\frac{-\text{Total income}}{\text{Total leisure}} = \frac{-€240}{€24} = -€10 \tag{3.4}$$

3.2.2.3 Leisure choice

To identify the choice of leisure that an individual makes requires examination of how the desire to consume more of both income and leisure becomes constrained by the time constraint. Formally, this implies that the consumer maximizes utility, as given by Equation 3.1, subject to the constraints given by Equations 3.2 and 3.3. Equation 3.5 illustrates the choice problem formally:

$$\text{Max } U(I, L) \text{ subject to } T = W + L \text{ and } I = wW \tag{3.5}$$

or:

$$I = w(T - L)$$

The choice decision is examined formally in Appendix 3.1. However, the intuition of the decision is demonstrated in Figure 3.3, which illustrates the time–income constraint facing consumers and their preferences, as well as the derivation of demands for leisure time and income.

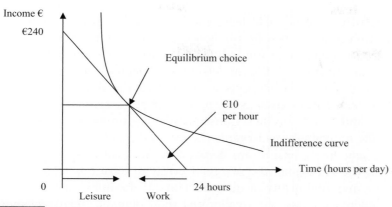

FIGURE 3.3 *The demand for leisure and income.*

In this figure, the vertical axis measures income. The horizontal axis measures the time period available for leisure, for example, 24 hours. The income constraint is represented by a straight line from 24 hours' leisure and zero income, to a maximum income of €240 and zero leisure at a wage rate of €10 per hour. The slope of this line is negative, as implied in Equation 3.1. Combinations of income and leisure along and below this line are feasible choices for the individual.

Preferences or tastes are represented by the indifference curve. Only one is drawn, but this should be thought of as one of a set which, just as contour lines represent sets of coordinates associated with a given altitude on a hill, represent combinations of income and leisure which yield the same level of utility. It was assumed above that individuals prefer more of both income and leisure, therefore indifference curves that are drawn out and to the right of the origin represent higher and higher levels of utility.

Reflection Question 3.2

Why does the indifference curve slope from left to right convex to the origin?
Hint: Examine assumption 2 of the motives for choice.

The indifference curves are drawn sloping from left to right, with a slope that is convex to the origin. In the first case this is because both leisure and income are normal goods. This means that one can be substituted for the other to leave the individual feeling the same level of satisfaction – as implied by the concept of an indifference curve. In the second case the slope of the indifference curve is known as the marginal rate of substitution (MRS) of leisure for income (or *vice versa*). The changing value of the slope is connected to the diminishing marginal utility received from consuming more and more of one good or service and less and less of another. Consequently, beginning from a situation in which the individual was towards the top of the indifference curve, higher income and lower leisure are demanded. As leisure is relatively scarce with respect to income, the marginal utility of leisure is relatively higher than the marginal utility of income. Thus, if the individual moved down the indifference curve, i.e., reallocated their demand, relatively more income could be given up than leisure time increased, but the individual would feel equally satisfied. As the individual moves further and further down the indifference curve, indicating greater and greater demand for leisure, the marginal utility of leisure time falls coupled with a rise in the marginal utility of income. Consequently, less and less income will be given up to compensate for increased leisure. More specifically, as indicated in Equation 3.6, this implies that the marginal rate of substitution of leisure for income is equivalent to the ratio of the marginal utility of income and the marginal utility of leisure. In general, the indifference curve summarizes the rational planned consumption possibilities of the individual.

$$\frac{\text{Marginal rate of substitution}}{\text{Marginal utility of leisure}} = \text{Marginal utility of income} \qquad (3.6)$$

3.2.2.4 Equilibrium choices of income and leisure

Combining the indifference curves and the income constraint enables us to identify conceptually, although qualitatively, the individual's rationally defined demands for income and leisure time. The logical point of utility maximization is where an indifference curve is tangent to the income–time constraint, as indicated on the figure. As indifference curves cannot cross – because they represent particular levels of utility – moving to the right or left of this point in reallocating leisure and income demands must force the individual onto a lower level of utility. Technically, this tangency implies that the consumer will be willing to substitute marginal increments in income against leisure at a rate equal to the wage rate. This is an important result, as it indicates that the wage rate measures how much value is placed on an hour of time by the individual. The wage rate is the opportunity cost of leisure. Equation 3.7 summarizes this relationship and shows that by equating Equations 3.6 and 3.3 an extra hour of leisure will reduce income by €10.

$$\frac{-\text{Marginal utility of income}}{\text{Marginal utility of leisure}} = -€10 \qquad (3.7)$$

3.2.2.5 Predictions from the model

The above analysis is clearly abstract and, perhaps, appears to have no obvious relevance to understanding the demand for leisure. This is certainly true of the model's description of decision making. However, recalling the discussion of economic methodology from Chapter 1, the model should be understood as a basis from which to make predictions. This theoretical objective lies at the core of much economic analysis. Let's assume that the wage rate increases. Wage rates have, for example, increased in most advanced economies over time. What are the implications for the demand for leisure? The income–leisure trade-off predicts that two effects will be set in motion.

3.2.2.6 The substitution effect

As wage rates increase, thinking about the idea of equilibrium, this suggests that the valuation placed on an hour of time has increased. This means that the price of leisure has increased. As a normal good, this must mean that the demand for leisure will fall and the demand for income through work rise correspondingly. Of course, the opposite will happen with a fall in the wage rate.

3.2.2.7 The income effect

On the other hand, as wage rates rise, it is now possible that undertaking the same level of work is still associated with a higher income. Consequently, more of both leisure and income can be achieved. It follows that, as a normal good, at least some more leisure time might be demanded. Once again, the opposite would apply with a fall in the wage rate. It is clear, therefore, that the net effect of these tendencies will produce the new demands for leisure and income. If the substitution effect dominates, less time for leisure will be demanded. If the income effect reflects a normal good then more leisure will be demanded. This can lead to the supply of labour becoming "backward bending," as wage increases lead to less and less labour being supplied. Ultimately what happens depends on the individual's preferences, and is an empirical question. The empirical support for such effects is discussed in the next chapter.

FIGURE 3.4

Income and substitution effects in leisure demand.

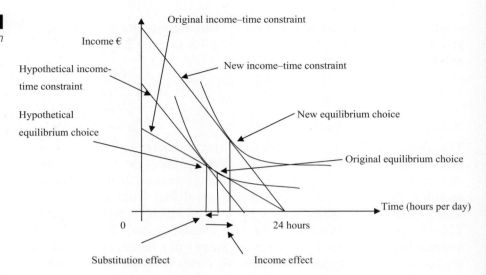

In terms of the graph, one way to illustrate the theoretical nature of the two effects is by establishing what the new equilibrium point would have been for a particular set of indifference curves, i.e. preferences. Figure 3.4 illustrates the changes in demand that occur, assuming that the income effect partially offsets the substitution effect.

An increase in the wage rate rotates the income constraint clockwise around its intercept with the horizontal axis. This is because, while the numbers of hours in the day remain constant, each hour's work now produces more income. This implies that the consumer's income–time constraint has relaxed, and higher utility can be achieved from reallocating their choices to new leisure and income demands. These will be identified by a new tangency on the highest indifference curve that is now possible. It is clear that in this case; overall more leisure is demanded, as well as some extra income. Arriving at the new leisure demand is, however, determined theoretically by the net outcome of the substitution and income effects.

Constructing a hypothetical income constraint tangent to the original indifference curve, but at a slope corresponding to the new wage rate, will establish a further hypothetical point of equilibrium on the original indifference curve. The movement from the original equilibrium to the hypothetical equilibrium identifies the substitution effect. The movement from the hypothetical equilibrium to the new actual equilibrium identifies the income effect. This makes it clear that the substitution effect is essentially a reallocation of demand purely as a result of a change in the relative price of leisure, whereas the income effect identifies the change in demand following the enhanced income from a price change.[4] The substitution effect measures the "Hicksian" demand, named after the economist John Hicks. The combined substitution and income effect measures the "Marshallian" demand, named after Alfred Marshall. Overall, the above analysis describes a simple general demand function for leisure time as implied in Equation 3.8:

$$D_L = D_L(w, P) \tag{3.8}$$

where leisure demand, (D_L), will depend on the opportunity cost of leisure, or wage rate (w) and the tastes and preferences of the individual (P). Theory suggests the broad prediction that a rise in the wage rate will normally lead to a fall in the demand for leisure, following the substitution effect, but produces an ambiguous overall effect when one allows for the income effect, assuming that leisure is a normal good. Figure 3.4 above implies that overall demand for leisure rises. It is possible that overall demand falls, if the income effect does not increase demand enough to offset the substitution effect or because the income effect actually reduces demand and reinforces the substitution effect.[5] This latter case would apply if leisure was an inferior good. The opposite effects could apply with a wage rate fall.[6]

---

[4] Indifference curves are not observable, because they are maps of individual preferences. This means that empirically measuring income and substitution effects, as described in theory, is impossible. However, to overcome this problem, economists often make use of the "Slutsky approximation." This implies viewing the income effect as the amount of income required not to place the individual at a point of tangency on the original indifference curve which cannot be observed but, rather, at the level of income that is required to make the previous choices affordable at the new relative prices. Comparing the choices made by the consumer would reveal the substitution effect. This would modify the diagram in Figure 3.4 by moving the hypothetical income–time constraint so that it passed through the original equilibrium choice. Logically, this would mean that the hypothetical point of tangency, which identified the new choices following the substitution effect, would also be on a new, slightly higher indifference curve. It is in this regard that the Slutsky analysis is an approximation. By comparing the value of choices at the original equilibrium, with regard to the original and subsequent prices, indicates the extent to which real income has changed.

[5] In the absence of the consumer having access to unearned income, it can be argued that the relationship between the decision to engage in leisure and the wage rate is likely to be unambiguous. Higher wages will unambiguously make leisure more costly. The ambiguity arises in the relationship between the hours of leisure and the wage rate, as it is here that a certain level of income can help to anchor consumption decisions.

[6] The astute reader will perhaps be aware that this suggests that preferences and tastes are clearly linked to the concept of goods being "normal" or not. As discussed later in the chapter, this raises issues about the role of tastes as independent influences on sports demand.

3.2.3 The derived demand for sports

As discussed above, it can be argued that the structure of sport demands is hierarchically linked. In this regard, while the demand for leisure does logically imply some reduction in available income for the consumption of other goods and services, nonetheless an element of the goods and services that are consumed will reflect the prior participation decision. For example, consumers' tastes and constraints determine a feasible desire to participate in a leisure activity, say, keep fit. The act of participation calls forth a set of derived demands for equipment, such as exercise mats, appropriate clothing, for example flexible Lycra wear, as well as facility demand such as room space, sound system and so on. Likewise, the demand to participate in hill walking as a leisure activity will involve a demand for travel to access the appropriate venue, such as a national park, as well as demands for clothing, footwear and possibly footpaths. Clearly, therefore this hierarchical structure of demands is a useful organizing schema.[7]

To understand the economic logic of the behaviour of such derived demand, and indeed the demand decision in economics generally, involves a straightforward modification of the principles already presented in the income–leisure trade-off model. Complications can be added, as discussed in Appendix 3.2, to reflect the durability and multiple uses of goods. However, for now, the main assumptions of that model are simply restated as follows:

3.2.3.1 Motives

1. Individuals seek to maximize their utility "U" by consuming goods and services, x_1 and x_2. Formally:

$$U = U(x_1, x_2) \tag{3.9}$$

---

[7] There are, of course, complications associated with this simple model. The main one is that it implicitly assumes a one-way causality from participation to demands for equipment, etc. This naturally follows from Marshall's original analysis. In the case of sport and leisure, however, it could be argued that matters are more complicated. For example, it is well known that sports clothing has fashion value. This means that the demand for sports clothing can be entirely unrelated to the level of participation in sports or leisure activities. Likewise, if one thinks of the leisure demands associated with tourism it may well be that travel is an integral part of the main "product," rather than a derived demand reflecting the need to travel to consume the tourism product. This, of course, does not necessarily undermine Marshall's analysis. The problem arises in the above examples because of the varying degrees by which demands are considered to be "separable" or "joint" respectively. These are issues of which Marshall was well aware and, in practice, show that the definition of specific markets and products will be of paramount importance.

2. The individual always prefers more of goods and services to less of both. This implies that they are "normal goods" and that the individual is willing, if necessary, to substitute more of one for less of the other. Diminishing marginal utility also applies, so that relatively abundant goods or services are of less value to the individual than relatively scarce goods or services.

3.2.3.2 Constraints

1. Individuals are constrained in their consumption activities by the income that they have earned, I, and the price of the goods and services that they wish to consume, p_1, p_2. This implies:

$$I = p_1 x_1 + p_2 x_2 \qquad (3.10)$$

2. Thus, if the consumer has earned I = €200 in the week and the cost of a pair of training shoes, x_1, is €40, i.e., p_1, this means that, in extreme cases, the individual could:

   (a) spend all of their income on five pairs of training shoes;
   (b) retain all of their income for consumption on other goods and services and spend nothing on training shoes.

3. Consider that sports vests, x_2, also cost €10, i.e., p_2. In this regard the consumer also has the choice to:

   (a) spend all of their income on 20 vests.
   (b) retain all of their income for consumption on other goods and services and spend nothing on vests.

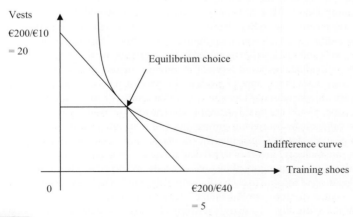

FIGURE 3.5 *Equilibrium demands for vests and training shoes.*

4. Consequently, if we restrict our attention to the consumption of vests and training shoes, to facilitate a graphical analysis, the consumer faces a budget constraint implying options to:[8]

   (a) spend all of their income on five pairs of training shoes and no vests.
   (b) spend all of their income on 20 vests and spend nothing on training shoes.

As implied in Equation 3.10. As with the income–leisure trade-off model, however, these are corner solutions to the consumer choice problem and, given the assumptions about utility, unlikely. Figure 3.5 illustrates a more appropriate equilibrium choice of vests and training shoes. An indifference curve is drawn to reflect preferences of the consumer over alternative consumption combinations of training shoes and vests. The slope and shape of the indifference curve reflects the assumptions made about preferences, as discussed above and in connection with the income–leisure trade-off model.

The budget line is drawn as a straight line connecting the extreme feasible choices facing the consumer, as identified in point 4 above. Each of these extreme possibilities of consumption are given by dividing the income available to the consumer, that is €200, by the price of vests or training shoes, that is €10 or €40. Consequently 20 vests or five pairs of training shoes could be purchased. It is important to recognize that the slope of the budget line is given by the ratio of these prices. The slope is negative, of course, as increases in income allocated to training shoes must be met be by a reduction in income allocated to vests. Equation 3.11 formally states this proposition.

---

[8] It is possible to consider the consumption of all other goods and services as the alternative to the consumption of either vests or training shoes. This would require treating the other goods as a composite commodity. Technically, this implies assuming that the relative prices of the commodities within the group remain fixed. If this is the case, then the quantities of each of the goods and services can be valued in the aggregate, using a price index in which the prices of the individual goods and services are proportionately related. This is an important concept as it suggests that groups of goods and services can be separated, that is preferences over them are independent of preferences for other groups of goods and services. In this regard, the goods would not be substitutable and the market would be segmented. Of course, the relative value of the composite commodity and vests and training shoes will change if prices change in the latter. Consequently, the decision process is more complex. Here consumers must allocate incomes to particular batches of goods and services, and then reallocate these subcomponents of income to goods and services within the segment. An optimal allocation of income to each subgroup of demands implies that the marginal utility of income is equal in each case. Appendix 3.1 outlines elements of the consumer choice problem more technically. The marginal utility of income is identified in this exposition as the Lagrange multiplier λ.

$$\frac{\text{Income allocated to vests}}{\text{Income allocated to training shoes}} = -\frac{200/10}{200/40} = -\frac{40}{10} \qquad (3.11)$$

This equation indicates that the rate at which income is transferred between vests and training shoes, as one is substituted for another, is governed by the prices of training shoes and vests. This is, of course, eminently logical, as training shoes cost four times as much as vests. So, each pair of training shoes is equivalent to four vests. As seen in the income–leisure trade-off model, the consumer will maximize utility where the indifference curve is tangent to the income constraint. Formally this implies:

$$\text{Max U} = U(x_1 x_2) \text{ subject to } I = p_1 x_1 + p_2 x_2 \qquad (3.12)$$

As the slope of the indifference curve, the marginal rate of substitution, is equal to the ratio of the marginal utilities of vests and training shoes, this implies that in equilibrium the consumer chooses to purchase vests and training shoes up to the point at which the ratio of marginal utilities is equal to the ratio of prices. This is an important result as it suggests that, in general, the subjective utilities attached to goods and services are measured by their market prices.

3.2.3.3 Predictions from the model

As with the income–leisure trade-off model, predictions of demand can be made. If, for example, the consumer decides to reduce the amount of leisure that they wish to consume and consequently increase their income, then this would shift the budget constraint to the right, as implied in Figure 3.6. The intuition of this change is given by considering that that numerator of the extreme possibilities both increase, meaning that more vests or training shoes could be purchased. A higher indifference curve is now attainable for the consumer, so, assuming that vests and training shoes are normal goods, more of both goods are likely to be purchased, as indicated by the arrows that indicate an increase in the demand of both goods following a move to a new equilibrium position.

This suggests that demand for sports equipment, facilities and so on, is expected to vary directly with consumer income. If the price of one of the goods changes, then for analogous reasons to the price of leisure, i.e., the wage rate changing in the income–leisure trade-off model, an income and substitution effect will take place. Figure 3.7 illustrates this possibility for a decrease in the price of a pair of training shoes. Note here that, following the price reduction, the budget line pivots out to the right around the extreme value of possible vest consumption. This is because the fall in

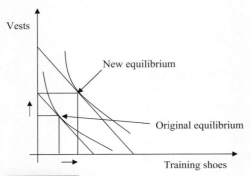

FIGURE 3.6   *The effects of higher income on consumer demand.*

price of training shoes makes it possible to consume more pairs, but if no training shoes were purchased then only the same maximum number of vests could be purchased. The income and substitution effects are once again identified by constructing a hypothetical budget line, with the same slope as the new price ratio, but tangent to the original indifference curve. The movement between equilibrium points on the original indifference curve identifies the substitution effect, that is to say, the change in demand purely following from a change in prices. The slope of the indifference curve implies that demand increases with a price fall and *vice versa*. The income effect is then identified by examining the move from the hypothetical equilibrium on the original indifference curve implied by the result of the substitution effect, to the new equilibrium on the new indifference curve. Analogous to Figure 3.6, the shift between equilibrium points is identified by the parallel shift in the budget constraint, indicating that incomes have risen but prices remain constant. Conceptually, this identifies the income that is gifted to the consumer simply because the price of one of the goods has fallen. Because the same number of pairs of training shoes could be bought now for less income, this leaves additional income for the consumer to allocate between other purchases, as well as training shoes. The figure is drawn consistent with the assumption that vests and training shoes are normal goods, to indicate that both the substitution effect and the income effect reinforce one another to generate extra demand for training shoes following their fall in price.

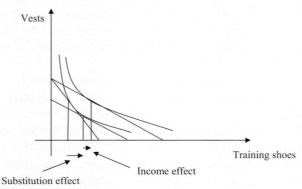

FIGURE 3.7   *The effects of a price change on consumer demand.*

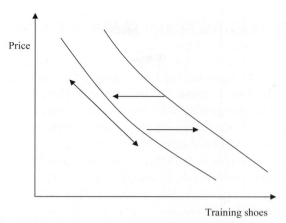

FIGURE 3.8 *A theoretical demand curve for training shoes.*

The above analysis suggests that the demand for sports equipment, clothes and facilities (x) can be summarized in Equation 3.13:

$$x = x(p, p^\star, I, P) \qquad (3.13)$$

Demand is likely to increase or decrease with decreases or increases in the price of the good or service, i.e., p; increase or decrease with an increase or decrease in the price of other goods or services, $p^\star$ because of substitution, and increase or decrease with increases or decreases in consumer incomes, I.[9] Such predictions are dependent on consumer tastes and preferences, P, remaining constant.

The basic predictions from this analysis are illustrated in Figure 3.8, where a demand curve for training shoes is drawn. Changes in the price of training shoes, other things being equal, will cause demand to increase or decrease by movements along the curve, whereas changes in income or preferences, or the price of other goods will, for each change other things being equal, cause the demand curve to shift to the left or right as fewer or more training shoes are demanded at any given price respectively.

---

[9] This assumes that goods are essentially gross substitutes. Goods could be complementary, in which case changes in the price of one of these goods will have the opposite effect on the level of demand for other goods. One might argue that tennis racquets and tennis shoes are complementary, as both are required to play tennis and changes in the price of one item will affect the demand for tennis and thus the demand for the other product. The substitution or complementarity of equipment demands is thus likely to be mediated by a change in activities, or adjustment to the level of the activity respectively.

3.3 AN INTEGRATING FRAMEWORK FOR CONSUMER CHOICE

The above analyses provide the traditional economic analysis of choice. However, there are a number of limitations with these models, as made transparent by the economist Gary Becker in what has become known as "New Household Economics." As Downward and Riordan (2007) note, in Becker (1965) the allocation of time is explicitly integrated into the consumption decisions of individuals. The individual, in turn, is explicitly theorized to be part of a household. This results in the distinction between consumption and production being removed. In contrast, the resources of "time" and "market goods" combine in "household production" to generate the basic commodities that yield utility from consumption. As all economic activities involve time and other goods, purchased via markets, economic agents essentially make choices involving the relative intensity of these inputs in both producing and consuming commodities. The basic commodities that are consumed, Z, are thus functions of goods bought on markets, x, and time, t. Formally household production is implied in the following production function:

$$Z = Z(x, t) \tag{3.14}$$

Utility, moreover, is then a function of the consumption of these produced goods and services:

$$U = U(Z_1, Z_2 \ldots) \tag{3.15}$$

Consequently, Equation 3.14 is an additional constraint that the individual faces when consuming goods and services along with Equations 3.2 and 3.10. Appendix 3.1 illustrates the implication of these changes more specifically, but the logic of the changes is to make the choice problem one of maximizing utility, which depends on the "basic" goods and services, subject to a resource constraint also based on these.

$$\text{Max } U = U(Z_1, Z_2 \ldots) \text{ subject to } G(Z_1, Z_2) \tag{3.16}$$

Figure 3.9 illustrates the main implications of Becker's analysis. If Z_1 is a relatively time intensive activity, say golf, and Z_2 a relatively goods intensive activity, say weight training, then an increase in the wage rate "w" would make the cost of golf relatively more expensive and generate a substitution of more weight training for golf, because the resource constraint would change slope. The resource constraint depends, in part, on the relative price of the commodities and also on the relative cost of time used to produce the commodities. A significant aspect of Becker's work is that in the main it confines analysis

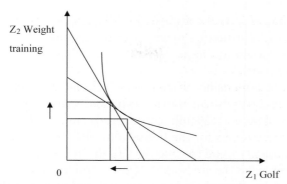

FIGURE 3.9 *A change in the relative price of good- and time-intensive commodities.*

to "substitution" effects resulting from the change in the relative price of resources, including time. If the consumer experienced an increase in unearned income, then a parallel shift in the resource constraint, analogous to Figure 3.6, would take place, but this would be due to exogenous changes to the resources at the consumer's disposal.

Reflection Question 3.3

Does the New Household Economics approach imply an income–leisure trade-off?
Hint: Think about what the cost of leisure must be.

Becker, specifically, explores the relationship between this analysis and the traditional approach. He writes:

"What, then, is the relation between our analysis, which treats all commodities symmetrically and stresses only their differences in relative time and earning intensities, and the usual analysis, which distinguishes a commodity having special properties called "leisure" from other more commonplace commodities? It is easily shown that the usual labour–leisure analysis can be looked upon as a special case of ours in which the cost of the commodity called leisure consists entirely of foregone earnings and the cost of other commodities entirely of goods." (Becker, 1965, p. 98)

More generally Becker (1976, 1992) emphasizes that his approach is not defined by the specific nature of the material under investigation, but rather its method – the optimizing behaviour of individuals. Consequently, economic agents maximize welfare, as perceived by them, subject to income, time, information and other limiting resource constraints. It is assumed that economic agents exhibit stable preferences, which therefore should not be used to explain demand changes, as implied in Equation 3.13, and that in addition to markets or arenas of formal contractual exchange, as typically identified in economics, the social structures in which agents operate, such as households, act as if they are markets to allocate resources according to their shadow prices, i.e., opportunity costs.[10]

An important dimension of this approach is that, as elaborated in Becker (1974), individuals can allocate time and market goods to invest in personal capital, skills and capabilities, or social capital and reputation which provide the greatest return for the household. This implies that individuals invest in their human capital (see Box 3.1). In this regard, preferences become partially endogenous to the analysis. As Downward and Riordan (2007) note, this has obvious implications for the demand for sport. On the one hand, participation in sports activities requires the acquisition of consumption skills. This suggests that previous consumption in the same activity can increase current consumption of the same activity. Likewise, consumption of one sports activity may increase the consumption of another sports activity because of, for example, implicit skill transfer, such as agility, timing, hand-eye coordination, etc. There is an obvious rationale, therefore, for expecting the demand for any one sport to be positively related to the demand for other sports in the context of personal consumption capital investment (Appendix 3.1 illustrates these propositions).

In summary, therefore, this new economic framework suggests that utility maximization can embrace a variety of specific objectives, not simply the consumption of physical resources, and can easily apply to sports participation and expenditure on sports goods and equipment. While equipment demand may be derived from participation, it is also essentially maintained that both of these are derived from investment in the stock of personal, social or health capital of individuals. The price of resources is likely to be the main influence on demand, as socio-economic factors such as income levels, health and education are also, at least partially, the outcomes of decisions by consumers.

---

[10] In this sense, naive views that economics is concerned only with material objects or formal exchange and contract are rejected. Moreover, as far as interpreting empirical work is concerned, there are a number of interrelated points to note regarding Becker's analysis. Results from econometric work on any given sample need to be interpreted carefully. On the one hand, the measured income and price effects may mask the true resource allocation issues at stake. This is because they only crudely capture the true shadow prices of economic allocation. On the other hand, the usual proxy variables for tastes, such as socio-economic characteristics, should be viewed at least partially as the results of agents' decisions. It follows that variations in their impact should not necessarily be seen as evidence of unstable preferences, but potentially resource adjustment over time in line with decision making based on stable preferences.

BOX 3.1 FORMS OF CAPITAL

A number of versions of "capital" and investment in capital are important for understanding sports participation. Gary Becker has been instrumental in developing the concept of human capital in economics, distinguishing it from traditional economic concepts. He writes:

"To most people capital means a bank account, a hundred shares of IBM stock, assembly lines or steel plants in the Chicago area. These are all forms of capital in the sense that they are assets that yield income and other useful outputs over long periods of time.

But these tangible forms of capital are not the only ones. Schooling, a computer training course, expenditures of medical care, and lectures on the virtues of punctuality and honesty also are capital. That is because they raise earnings, improve health, or add to a person's good habits over much of his lifetime. Therefore, economists regard expenditures on education, training, medical care and so on as investments in human capital. They are called human capital because people cannot be separated from their knowledge, skills, health or values in the way they can be separated from their financial and physical assets."

Gary Becker *The Concise Encyclopaedia of Economics*, http://www.econlib.org/library/Enc/HumanCapital.html Accessed 7 January 2007.

From a broader intellectual perspective other forms of capital exist. Pierre Bourdieu has been particularly influential. Bourdieu (1986) distinguishes between:

■ economic capital, which is the traditional resources explored by economists, such as land and other assets;
■ cultural capital, which reflects the knowledge and skills possessed, typically, endowed by parents and education. It might comprise, linguistic acumen, understanding or possession of works of art or academic attainments;

■ social capital, which reflects relationships and networks of influence of either a formal institutionalized or informal mutual acquaintance nature.

Social capital has also been explored by Putnam (2000) as the value associated with being a member of a social network. A distinction is made between bonding and bridging social capital:

■ bonding social capital refers to social networks of relatively homogenous individuals;
■ bridging social capital refers to social networks of relatively heterogenous individuals.

Significantly, also, consumers may invest in characteristics that make them more similar or less similar to other persons. This is suggestive of the establishment of "lifestyles" and distinct consumer groupings – reflecting social capital formation. This suggests that socio-economic characteristics may reflect the outcome of choices, which is important in interpreting the empirical evidence on participation, discussed in the next chapter. For current purposes, however, what is important to note is that once utility depends on previous consumption or the consumption of others, through interdependent preferences, then it is possible to explain why participation takes place in particular groups of activities and by particular groups of individuals. Significantly, it is possible to extend this analysis to cover investment in health. Grossman (1972a, b), provides a seminal analysis that augments the analysis of Becker to show that the demand for healthcare is derived from an investment in the stock of health. Viewing the demand for sports or sports participation as a demand for healthcare naturally sees it as deriving from a broader concern to accumulate health. It is likely that, empirically-speaking, health will affect sports participation, although care needs to be exercised in interpreting cause and effect.

3.4 POLICY IMPLICATIONS

Chapter 1 indicated that the main economic policy proposition is that the market allocation of resources in sport is considered to be, in a normative sense. Consequently, mass participation should be derived from the exercise of freely choosing individuals, and provided for by the private sector. From this theoretical perspective, the only possible grounds for active policy seeking to promote participation or to provide facilities for participation might lie in arguments that the market will fail because of the presence of monopoly, an overt ethical concern with the equity of access to participation opportunities or the presence of externalities or public goods that need to be corrected, or accounted for.

The analysis of the decision to participate above is predicated on these not being central problems and this raises problems for policy makers who might, as discussed in Chapter 2, want a theoretical rationale for actively seeking to intervene in the economy to raise participation levels. To begin with, and discussed in detail in Chapter 5, it is difficult to argue that monopoly supply of mass sports participation opportunities exists. While the history of mass sports provision has been, for example in the UK, one of public sector provision and subsidy, this has recently shifted towards a more commercial basis, with a lesser monopolistic character. Inevitably this carries with it an argument that the costs of participation have increased rather than fallen, reflecting a degree of public subsidy for sports provision being removed. From a policy perspective this is a *de facto* indication that current policy thinking is not as concerned with equity, or that externalities or public goods are viewed as general characteristics of sport.

Moreover, the theories discussed above broadly assume away concerns with equity, externalities and public goods. On the one hand, the utility maximizing choices made reflect the individual's preferences and desires, which are assumed to be fixed (by the agent). This suggests that policy aimed at directly manipulating preferences is unethical and inconsistent with an individual's right to choose. On the other hand, while policy could target "income constraints" on participation, there are subtle but compelling theoretical arguments against such an initiative. The analysis above has presented the equilibrium choice of the consumer in isolation. This might be referred to as a partial equilibrium approach. Yet, as Section 3.2.1 indicates, such decisions are really part of an interconnected set of decisions in a general equilibrium. Here, the logic of free choice carries over to the individual simultaneously determining their income levels through the choice to work more or less hours. Indeed, the logic of the New Household Economic approach suggests that other socio-economic characteristics are also, at least partially, chosen by the agent, and in this sense do not, of necessity, provide a basis on which active policy promoting participation should be pursued.

In addition to these normative concerns, the practical impact of policy is challenged by the New Household Economics approach. This is because Becker (1974) presents a version of the Coase theorem, which was discussed in Chapter 1. The Coase theorem states that when an externality affects few parties, and if property rights are well-defined, then bargaining can promote economic efficiency because externalities become internalized, thus forcing a market solution to the resource allocation problem. This theorem can apply in the New Household Economic approach under the heading of the "Rotten Kid" theorem as part of the framework in which investment in characteristics, i.e., personal or social capital, is analyzed. Here consumption decisions are interdependent because of interdependent preferences.

The Rotten Kid theorem suggests that any interdependency of utilities between consumers will not affect the consumption patterns or welfare of either in the face of a redistribution of resources between them. It essentially argues that policy will have an invariant outcome. In the context of sport, this situation might arise when a policy maker's utility depends on the utility of policy recipients. Consequently, a policy maker might receive benefit, i.e., political satisfaction, for raising participation levels of policy recipients. However, any transfers of income between the policy maker and the recipient, for example to facilitate sports participation, will not affect the consumption or welfare of either. This is even if the policy maker intends to enhance the welfare of the recipient and the latter does not share this desire.

The reasoning behind such a conclusion is as follows. If the transfers of income to recipients require tax revenue to fund them, the future tax burden on recipients would be rationally taken account of by utility maximizing individuals. Consequently, their current behaviour would account for this possibility already. Hence, the current situation cannot be improved on. Likewise, even if transfers were made conditional on the consumption of specific activities, for example, to promote consumption of sport because it was felt to be a merit good, incentives exist to undermine this policy.

> *A merit good exhibits positive externalities, but will be under-consumed because the individual's decision does not take account the benefits that further consumption would have for society. The positive externalities thus need to be internalized to increase efficiency.*

If the recipient did not want to spend the transfers on the targeted activity, the transfers would clearly be worth less to them than to the policy maker. This might result in further reductions in consumption of what is perceived to be an inferior good. This might in turn undermine the incentive to give transfers.

The upshot of these discussions is that there can be no strong rationale for active sports policy other than ensuring equal access to information about sports for the population to allow agents to make free choices. If these choices are deemed undesirable to policy makers then, so be it! A theoretical motivation for policy activism, therefore, requires an alternative theoretical analysis.

This could be found in heterodox economics, which challenges elements of the methodological and theoretical basis of the approaches discussed above. Downward (2007) and Downward and Riordan (2007) provide an overview of these approaches and argue that three main contributions are relevant: psychological theories of consumption; post-Keynesian theory; and sociological theory. An important feature of these approaches is that they focus more on a descriptive elaboration of the processes by which participation decisions are made, rejecting rational choice under perfect information. Theoretically, a direct interdependence between preferences that is the basis of agent choice, and consumption activity of both the agent and other agents is also suggested as opposed to relying on stable preferences that are in essence independent of the choices made. These are important distinctions to note because they provide a rationale for policy activism.

If one views consumption activity as emerging from processes under which preferences can actually change as a result of a new opportunity to participate in previously unfamiliar activity, and that constraints face voluntary action, for example because agents do not possess optimizing capability or particular characteristics and social circumstances, such as income differentials, act to exclude consumption opportunities, then active policy becomes an option. It could target both the constraints and agent choice in seeking to promote greater participation. Obvious examples would be to ensure that facilities are available to all, preventing exclusion on personal or social criteria through legislation, coupled with the flow of resources to support areas in which choices are desired but not attainable, for example because of economic underdevelopment or cultural restraint. It is important to be aware of these alternative perspectives, as discussed in the next chapter. The empirical evidence does not present a clear arbiter on these issues, although common general factors associated with participation do emerge. Policy prediliction can thus be rationalized, to some extent, by a prior theoretical predilection.

3.5 CONCLUSION

This chapter has begun an examination of mass participation in sports by discussing various economic theories of choice. Sports participation has been rationalized as part of a broader process of sports consumption in which time is allocated to participation in activities and then expenditures. Following this discussion various critiques of, and complications with, the basic model have been reviewed. These include: a review of theories that challenge the motives and choice constraints implied in the model; the implied direction of influences on choices; and, consequentially, the implications of the choices that are made. Based on this discussion it is argued that support for policies that promote mass participation can be found. Consequently, it is argued that awareness of the alternative approaches to mass participation is important for suppliers of sport in both commercial and non-commercial settings. The next chapter examines these issues further by exploring the empirical evidence on sports participation.

Appendix 3.1 Utility-Maximizing Behaviour

In this appendix the basic elements of solving constrained optimizing problems, as implied in the choice problem of neoclassical economics, are presented. The Lagrange multiplier method is most often used to solve these problems. It is named after Joseph Lagrange, the French mathematician who developed the method. The method implies taking a constrained optimization problem and converting it into an unconstrained optimization problem. This is achieved by producing a linear combination of both the objective function and the constraint, such that their values are equal, for a given value of the constraint λ, which is known as the Lagrange multiplier (LM). For any given value of the LM, differentiating the optimization problem and solving for the value of the variables when the differential is equal to zero will identify the optimal solution, i.e., when infinitesimally small changes in the variables will not affect the value of the function being optimized. Technically speaking, this produces "first order conditions" (FOC) for the optimum. Therefore, a maximum or minimum solution might be identified. In utility maximization, however, assuming that the utility function exhibits diminishing marginal utility, i.e., the utility function is quasi concave, is sufficient to produce a maximum solution. Diminishing marginal productivity would imply maximum profits in the case of the constrained optimization problem in the case of firms' profit maximizing. Therefore, in the case of the income–leisure model the choice problem implied in:

$$\text{Max } U(I, L) \text{ subject to } T = W + L \text{ and } I = wW \tag{A3.1.1}$$

or:

$$I = w(T - L)$$

Would become:

$$Z = U(I, L) - \lambda(I - w(T - L)) \tag{A3.1.2}$$

FOCs would be:

$$\partial Z/\partial L = \partial U/\partial L - \lambda w = 0 \text{ or } \partial U/\partial L = w$$
$$\partial Z/\partial I = \partial U/\partial I - \lambda = 0 \text{ or } \partial U/\partial I = \lambda \qquad \text{(A3.1.3)}$$
$$\partial Z/\partial \lambda = I - w(T - L) = 0 \text{ or } I = w(T - L)$$

The first equation shows that the marginal utility of leisure is equal to the wage rate, as discussed in the text. This means that the value of leisure is implied by the wage rate. The second equation shows that the marginal utility of income is implied in the LM. This is the "shadow price" of income, reflecting how utility would change following a change in the budget constraint implied in the final equation. The optimal conditions are thus conditional on a value of the LM. In the more general case of the consumer choice problem:

$$\text{Max } U = U(x_1, x_2) \text{subject to } I = p_1 x_1 + p_2 x_2 \qquad \text{(A3.1.4)}$$

Would become:

$$Z = U(x_1, x_2) - \lambda(I - p_1 x_1 - p_2 x_2) \qquad \text{(A3.1.5)}$$

FOCs would be:

$$\partial Z/\partial x_1 = \partial U/\partial x_1 + \lambda p_1 = 0$$
$$\partial Z/\partial x_2 = \partial U/\partial x_2 + \lambda p_2 = 0 \qquad \text{(A3.1.6)}$$
$$\partial Z/\partial \lambda = -(I - p_1 x_1 + p_2 x_2) = 0$$

An important feature of this solution is that the first two FOCs imply:

$$\partial U/\partial x_1 / \partial U/\partial x_2 = -p_1/p_2 \qquad \text{(A3.1.7)}$$

This shows that the ratio of marginal utilities of consumption of goods and services is equal to the ratio of their prices, as implied in Figure 3.5.

Solving for the specific demand functions associated with a utility maximizing problem requires a specific form of utility function. A common function that is often used is the Cobb–Douglas function, where utilities are increased through consumption of goods and services according to parameters which appear as exponents. Other forms of utility functions are often used. They impose particular restrictions on the patterns of demand that can be derived, which can then be tested. In general, however, they all retain the essential property that utility increases at a diminishing rate following the consumption of goods and services. Equation A3.1.5 can be written using a Cobb–Douglas utility function as:

$$Z = x_1^\alpha x_2^\beta - \lambda(I - p_1 x_1 - p_2 x_2) \qquad \text{(A3.1.8)}$$

and the following derived:

$$x_1 = (\alpha/\alpha + \beta)I/p_1 \qquad (A3.1.9)$$

This equation, known as a Marshallian demand curve after Alfred Marshall, shows that the demand for x_1 will rise with consumer income "I" and fall with the price of x_1, i.e., p_1. An analogous solution procedure would produce a demand for x_2 as:

$$x_2 = (\beta/\alpha + \beta)I/p_2 \qquad (A3.1.10)$$

The New Household model of consumer demand can be analyzed using the tools of constrained optimization. A more specific form of Equation 3.16 may be written as a utility function of the basic commodities that are dependent on time, "t" and goods x_1 and x_2, as implied by Equation 3.14. In turn, the constraint facing households then becomes one of the cost of goods from the market, which will depend on their relative price, and the cost of time, as implied by the wage rate. Specifically one has to recognize that the consumer, as a producer, has to commit time or goods to produce either Z_1 or Z_2 so that total money income will be equivalent to either expenditure on goods or forgone income from allocating time to the production of goods as opposed to work. Equation A3.1.11 presents the LM formulation of the optimization problem. The first term on the right-hand side is the utility function. The term in brackets is the modified constraint. Here b_1 and b_2 represent the proportions of Z_1 or Z_2 that are derived from x_1 or x_2 respectively; t_1 and t_2 likewise represent the proportions of time committed per unit of Z_1 or Z_2, which has a price of w. In this regard, the production functions are assumed to be of a simple proportionate form. S is "full income" which can either be spent on market goods or represents forgone money income.

$$L = U(Z_1, Z_2) - \lambda(p_1 b_1 Z_1 + p_2 b_2 Z_2 + wt_1 Z_1 + wt_2 Z_2 - S) \qquad (A3.1.11)$$

FOCs for this problem imply:

$$\partial U/\partial Z_1 / \partial U/\partial Z_2 = -(p_1 b_1 + wt_1)/(p_2 b_2 + wt_2) \qquad (A3.1.12)$$

which implies that the price of the commodities Z_1 and Z_2 depend on the prices of x_1 and x_2, as well as the wage rate as the opportunity cost of time. The prices also depend on the coefficients b_1 and b_2 and t_1 and t_2. A goods-intensive activity such as weight training, Z_1, would thus have a lower value of "t" and a higher value of "b" compared to a time intensive activity such as golf, Z_2. The slope of the constraint in Figure 3.7 is given by A3.1.12. It follows that an increase in "w" will increase the cost of the time-intensive activity more, i.e., the denominator of the equation, showing that the marginal utility of Z_2 will now be greater than for Z_1 in equilibrium. This must imply substitution away from Z_2 towards Z_1, because of diminishing marginal utility substitution towards more goods intensive activities.

Investment in human or social capital implied in Gary Becker's analysis can be illustrated. For a Cobb–Douglas utility function Downward and Riordan (2007) derive:

$$C_2 = \left(\frac{\beta}{\alpha + \beta}\right)\frac{M}{p_2} + \left(\frac{\beta}{\alpha + \beta}\right)c_1^0 \qquad \text{(A3.1.13)}$$

which is the Marshallian demand for a commodity, "C," augmented by the last term on the right. The interpretation of this term suggests that consumption is higher than it would have been, because of the presence of previous consumption, i.e., investment in consumption skills, or the acquisition of social characteristics. In this respect, previous consumption of the same or similar activities is predicted to increase current consumption of them, and predicts that sets of consumer characteristics are likely to be associated with distinct groupings over time as social capital accumulation.

Appendix 3.2 Durable Goods, the Time Value of Money and Investment Demand

Durable goods

Durable goods yield a flow of services or utility over time, rather than being used up with one consumption act. It is clear that both training shoes and running vests are durable goods that are "stocks" or assets, from which flows of utility can be derived through their repeated use. This makes the purchase of these goods "investments." The analysis of the chapter should be seen as a long-run equilibrium set of choices in which the stock of assets is adjusted. More specifically, however, the investment "Iv" in each asset, "A" for each time period "t" can be represented as:

$$Iv_t = A_t - (1 - \theta)A_{t-1} \qquad \text{(A3.2.1)}$$

Or:

$$Iv_t = dA_t + \theta A_{t-1} \qquad \text{(A3.2.2)}$$

This means that investment is equal to the change in the capital stock or net investment, plus replacement investment. The term "θ" represents the amount of depreciation of the asset for the last period's use. To retain the current stock of the asset would require compensating for this depreciation by adding a proportion of the last period's asset stock. In non-industrial contexts such depreciation may not be explicitly accounted for, but it is present nonetheless. This analysis shows that time matters for investment. However, because time is passing, the effects of interest rates on the value of flows of income and expenditure should really be accounted for. To do this one needs to understand the time value of money.

The time value of money

As discussed above in the chapter, the rate of interest measures the time value of money. It should not be confused with the rate of inflation, which measures the change in the purchasing power of money because of a change in the general level of prices. Even if inflation were zero, the rate of interest would be positive. The nominal rate of interest is the rate of interest excluding the rate of inflation. The real rate of interest is the nominal rate of interest minus the rate of inflation. Because the value of money varies over time, it would be wrong to simply compare the flows of incomes and expenditures across different time periods, as one would not be comparing like with like. In contrast, it is usual to convert flows of expenditures and incomes into present values, i.e., their values expressed in the current time period.

To give an example, suppose €10 is saved in a bank, and the current rate of interest is 10% per annum. At the end of this year this will produce €$10(1 + 0.1) = $€11. What about the end of year two? If the savings are left in the in the bank, interest would compound with earnings $(€10(1 + 0.1))(1 + 0.1) = €10(1 + 0.1)^2 = €12.10$. In principle, this process can continue and in general the future value of any amount "A" saved at interest rate "r" over "t" periods will be:

$$\text{Future value} = A(1 + r)^t \tag{A3.2.3}$$

Now, it follows that the present value of any amount "A" saved at interest rate "r" over "t" periods will be:

$$\text{Present value} = A/(1 + r)^t \tag{A3.2.4}$$

Consequently, €12.10 received in two years time at a market rate of interest of 10% is equivalent to €$12.10/(1 + 0.1)^2 = $€10 today.

This means that, if a consumer was consuming goods and services over time, say two periods, with x_1 referring to the current period's consumption and x_2 to the next period's consumption, the utility maximizing problem would become:

$$\text{Max } U = U(x_1, x_2) \text{subject to } W = p_1 x_1 + (p_2/1 + r)x_2 \tag{A.3.2.5}$$

Note that the price of "next" period's consumption, x_2, is discounted into present values. Technically, too, as the sum of two different periods' flows of consumption, the constraint is now labelled "W," to represent wealth. As should be clear now from the discussion of these appendices, wealth is a stock and the sum of a series of income flows. Once this complication is allowed for, the analysis of consumer choice can proceed as before. Figure A3.1.1 reproduces Figure 3.3, but translates it into consumption over time, i.e., use, of training shoes.

The slope of the budget line is now a wealth constraint with a slope determined by the present value of future prices and the current price. Based on these relative prices the consumer chooses to "buy," i.e., use, combinations of training shoes over time. In this case, the training shoes or assets constitute wealth that finance a certain use of them. In this case, the prices of p_1 and p_2 are really implied from the use of the training shoes rather than simply by their actual market prices. Nonetheless, it follows that the values of I_t and p_1 and p_2 in Equation A3.3.7 should really be discounted to period $t - 1$ to make the analysis more robust. Chapter 12 discusses investment decisions in sport in more detail. There are further complications, however, when considering the consumption of investment goods.

Investment demand

The above analysis suggests that consumption over time can undergo smooth transitions. This might be reasonable with non-durable goods, for example substituting a visit to the gym next period for one this period if p_1 falls relative to p_2. In Figure A3.3.1 this would make the budget line steeper, pivoting around the horizontal intercept, to recognize that more current consumption could be undertaken for any amount of future consumption. As detailed in the chapter, income and substitution effects (over time) would take place with the prediction that with normal goods more current consumption than before would take place.

However, with durable goods, the substitution is unlikely to be a smooth transition. This is because the asset can essentially "fund" a number of particular incidences of consumption. For example, if training shoes last approximately six months and are used to run three times a week, then the single purchase of training shoes can fund 72 different runs. As Gratton and Taylor (2000) recognize, sports goods consumption is likely to be unstable and volatile. A simple model of accelerator effects is used to illustrate this purpose[11].

If "Ivx" represents investment in a sports good, such as training shoes, and the change in demand "dD" represents the change in use of the shoes, which will be a certain number of

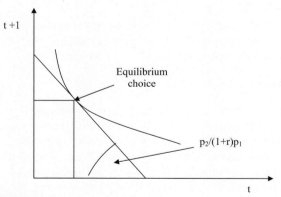

FIGURE A3.1.1 *Consumption of training shoes over time.*

---

[11] A variety of economists proposed an accelerator mechanism to link changes in the trade cycle to investment decisions. See, for example, Clark (1913), Samuelson (1939) and Hicks (1950).

times per given period, then if the accelerator coefficient "a" is the number of times a pair of shoes can be used to support an activity (which is the capital/output ratio) over the same period, the accelerator model is:

$$Ivx = adD \qquad (A3.2.6)$$

Thus if $a = €2$, because say the shoes cost €100 and could be used 50 times before depreciating beyond use, and is currently stable, there will be no investment. If demand increases, say, from currently 20 runs to 36 runs (dD = 16) over the period, then Ivx will rise "suddenly" to €32. If the number of runs increases further, to 48 from 36 (dD = 12), then Ivx will actually fall to €24. Note that, despite the additional increase in runs, investment value has actually fallen, but is still positive. To retain the current level of demand for training shoes would have required the number of runs to increase from 36 to 52 (dD = 16, again), i.e., a constant growth of demand would be required. It follows that, if the growth of demand is successively larger, investment will increase, if growth reduces, even though it does not become negative, investment will fall. If demand stabilizes, then once dD = 0, investment will also return to zero.

It should be noted that the model assumes that product differentiation is constant. It follows that technological improvement or marketing activity may increase Ivx through adjustments in "depreciation" of a substantive or perceived kind. Indeed, given the relatively stable participation rates in sport, which are noted in the next chapters, marketing behaviour may explain the growing expenditures in these industries as sports equipment, particularly clothing and footwear, are presented as general fashion items.

CHAPTER 4

The Economics of Sports Participation: Evidence

- To understand how economists model the demand for sports participation and consumption
- To understand how sports participation is measured by official sources
- To appreciate some of the main empirical patterns of international sports participation and consumption

4.1 INTRODUCTION

In the previous chapter various economic theories of choice were presented. The aim was to indicate how participation decisions in sport are fundamentally linked to expenditure decisions, and to explore the likely efficacy of policies aimed at promoting sports participation. In this chapter attention turns towards the evidence associated with sports participation and expenditure and, consequently, to explore the potential targets for policy intervention.

Section 4.2 discusses the main sources of official and widely-used unofficial data on sports participation and expenditures, and presents some descriptive statistics from these sources. Section 4.3 then identifies how these data have been modelled using econometric methods, with reference to the theories of sports demand discussed in Chapter 3. Section 4.5 reviews the implications of the findings from the literature for sports policy, before the chapter concludes.

4.2 EMPIRICAL EVIDENCE ON PARTICIPATION AND EXPENDITURE IN SPORTS

4.2.1 Mass sports participation: Sources of official and unofficial data

As discussed in Chapter 2, there are a variety of official data sources internationally investigating mass sports participation. This reflects the nature of the agency collecting the statistics, the policy purpose to which the statistics might be put, and convention. Different activities might be investigated because of their heritage or the particular collective definition of sport employed. There may also be some terminological ambiguities connected with the activities associated with country-specific nomenclature, for example over definitions of "football." How participation is measured may also vary. This not only concerns the type of activities that are investigated, but the frequency of participation, the standard period scrutinized, and measures of the intensity or duration of the activity. Finally, the periodicity of data collection also varies. In part this reflects the sources of data. Traditionally, data may have been collected as part of a particular module appended to a regular social survey or alternatively it may reflect a specifically commissioned piece of work.

Table 4.1 illustrates some international official data sources. They are considered official data because they are either produced directly by government agencies or through policy bodies funded by them. The first column indicates the country in which the data applies; the second column includes both the name of the survey and the sponsoring agent. The subsequent columns indicate how the data were collected, some dates over which the survey was carried out, the age used to define an adult, the approximate sample size and, finally, how participation was measured. It is clear that some variety is evident across these characteristics.

There have been some attempts to produce a greater degree of commonality of data collected, particularly within the European Union. van Bottenburg et al. (2005) note three main initiatives for the promotion of harmonized statistics through standardized questionnaires: COMPASS (Coordinated Monitoring of Participation in Sports); HETUS (Harmonized European Time Use Studies); and IPAQ (International Physical Activity Questionnaires). However, it should be noted in the context of Chapter 2, that as sports have figured much more prominently in recent policy discourse, and because policy initiatives require targets to be met for participation, more dedicated context-specific data collection is also apparent. For example, while in many respects the General Household Survey monitors participation for an accepted list of activities described as sport or leisure in Britain, the survey "Active People," commissioned by Sport England in 2005, represents a significant investment of £6 million aimed at producing data that are representative at local authority level, hence its very large sample size. The motivation for such data is clear, which is to provide the means to monitor how the specific policy agency meets its targets and policy priorities by delivering sport through community sport networks.

In addition to the official data, various other "unofficial" data sources on participation and expenditure exist. In the UK, Mintel market intelligence reports are available on a wide range of specific sports and the sports sector as a

TABLE 4.1 Some official sports participation data

Country	Survey (1) and sponsor (2)	Type	Typical dates	Adult age	Approximate sample size	Activity measure
USA	National Health Interview Survey (NHIS) National Statistics Centers for Disease Control and Prevention	Household interview	1957–current	18 years	36 000–44 000	Type, frequency, intensity over two weeks
	1. Behavioural risk factor surveillance system (BRFSS) 2. National Center for Chronic Disease Prevention and Health Promotion	Telephone interview	1984–current	18 years	35 000–107 000	Type, frequency, intensity over past month
Canada	1. National household survey on participation in sport[1] 2. The conference board of Canada	Telephone interview	2004	16 years	2408	Type, frequency, duration over the past 12 months
	1. General Social Survey 2. Statistics Canada		1985–2005			Type
Australia	1. Exercise, Recreation and Sport Survey (ERASS) 2. Australian Sports Commission	Telephone interview	2001–2005	15 years	13 726	Type, frequency, duration over the past 12 months
	1. Population Survey Monitor 2. Australian Bureau of Statistics	Household interview	1993–2000	18 years	3000	Any sport over the past 12 months
Great Britain	1. General Household Survey (GHS) 2. National Statistics	Household interview	1987, 1990, 1993, 1996, 2002	16 years	19 529–14 819	Type over the past 12 months
	1. Active People 2. Sport England	Telephone interview	2005	16 years	363 724	Type, frequency over past four weeks
	1. Taking Part 2. Department of Culture Media and Sport	Household interview	2005	16 years	28 117	Type, intensity over the past four weeks Type over the past 12 months

TABLE 4.1 *(Continued)*

Country	Survey (1) and sponsor (2)	Type	Typical dates	Adult age	Approximate sample size	Activity measure
European Union	1. Various European Barometers (EB)		1983 (EB19), 1987 (EBs 28, 28.1), 1990 (EBs 33, 34.2), 1997 (EB47.2), 1998 (EB50.1), 1999 (EB52.1), 2001 (EB55.1), 2003 (EBs 58.2, 2003.1, 60) 2004 (EB62.0)	15 years	varies	Type, frequency and duration over 12 months
	2. European Commission					

¹ *This survey also measures the economic expenditure of households on sport.*

TABLE 4.2 Top ten and team sport participation rates[1]

USA activity		Canada activity		Australia activity		Great Britain activity	
NHIS 1991	**%**	**NHSPS 2004**	**%**	**ERASS 2005**	**%**	**GHS 2002**	**%**
Walking	44.1	Ice hockey	6.6	Walking (other)	37.3	Walking	35.0
Gardening	29.4	Golf	6.5	Aerobics	18.5	Swimming (indoor)	12.0
Stretching	25.5	Baseball	4.7	Swimming	14.4	Keep-fit	12.0
Cycling	15.4	Skiing	4.0	Cycling	10.3	Snooker	9.0
Weight lifting	14.1	Soccer	3.8	Tennis	7.8	Cycling	9.0
Stair climbing	10.8	Volleyball	3.1	Running	7.7	Weight training	6.0
Running	9.1	Basketball	2.8	Golf	7.1	Running	5.0
Swimming	6.5	Tennis	2.6	Walking (bush)	5.7	Golf	5.0
Basketball	5.8	Curling	2.6	Football (outdoor)	3.8	Soccer (outdoor)	4.0
Golf	4.9	Bowling	2.4	Basketball	3.5	Bowls	3.0
Baseball	3.5	Included above		Rugby league	1.2	Basketball	1.0
Football	1.5			Rugby union	1.0	Cricket	1.0
Soccer	0.9			Cricket	1.0	Rugby	0

[1] *Data are taken from the following sources: U.S. Department of Health and Human Services, Centers for Disease Control and Prevention, National Center for Chronic Disease Prevention and Health Promotion, (1996); The Conference Board of Canada (2005); Australian Sports Commission (2005), Fox and Rickards (2004). Zero figures correspond to participation rates less than 0.5% of the population.*

whole. The Sports Industry Research Centre (SIRC), based at Sheffield Hallam University, also produces market reports and forecasts for the sports market. In the US and Australia SMGA International and Sweeney Research, respectively, are commercial agencies which provide such data.

4.2.2 Mass sports participation: Descriptive evidence

To give an overview of participation, Table 4.2 presents some statistics from a selection of the data sets described above for the top ten activities in each country, plus the rates for the team sports that dominate the professional industry.

Notwithstanding the different sampling periods and questions, the data reveal a number of interesting points. The first is that participation rates are greatest for leisure and/or recreational activities and then they rapidly decline

TABLE 4.3 Overall participation rates[1]

Country	%
Finland	85
Sweden	82
Denmark	69
Ireland	60
Netherlands	59
UK	55
France	54
Belgium	51
Luxembourg	48
Germany	47
Austria	45
Spain	43
Italy	33
Greece	32
Portugal	27
Australia	69
US	76
Canada	31

[1] *Data are taken from Van Bottenberg et al (2005) for the European countries. The same data sources are used for Australia, US and Canada.*

through various forms of keep fit activity to more passive activities, such as golf. The second point is that traditional team sports appear as relatively small-scale activities. As discussed further in the next chapter, this has potential implications for sports policy. Table 4.3 presents participation at least once per month for European countries in 2004, Australia and Canada in 2005, and the US for at least some activity over the year.

It is clear that, in spite of comparative measurement issues, participation rates vary quite widely by geographical dispersion. This hints at broader structural differences in participation. Such structural differences are also evident within countries. Table 4.4 highlights how overall participation varies according to key socio-economic criteria, depending on its availability in published form. Despite the variation in measurement, some general patterns are clear. Males tend to participate more than females, and participation falls with increasing age, but rises with higher incomes and better education. There is also some evidence of ethnic differences in participation, and that household status and the presence of children can affect participation.

Policy makers have suggested reasons for such differences. It is argued by van Bottenburg et al. (2005) that differences in gross domestic product (GDP) can account for the variation in participation rates across Europe, in other words that income is a key "driver." Various other drivers are identified.

TABLE 4.4 Socio-economic determinants of participation

Socio-economic indicator	US % NHIS 1991	Canada % NHSPS 2004	Australia % ERASS 2005	Great Britain % GHS 2002[1]	Europe[2]%
Male	78.6	39.0	83.5	65	41
Female	73.1	23.4	83.1	53	35
Age	(18–29) 78.3	(<20) 67.2	(15–24) 93.4	(16–19) 77	(15–24) 60
	(30–44) 76.6	(20–29) 53.7	(25–34) 89.9	(20–24) 69	(25–39) 41
	(45–64) 74.2	(30–39) 42.5	(35–44) 88.9	(25–29) 70	(40–54) 34
	(65–74) 74.3	(40–49) 33.3	(45–54) 88.8	(30–44) 67	(55+) 28
	(75+) 66.3	(50–59) 29.6	(55–64) 90.7	(45–59) 59	
		(60+) 26.1	(65+) 90.1	(60–69) 50	
				(70+) 30	
Ethnicity	White 78.5			White 67.9	
	Black 71.6			Non-white 65.5	
	Hispanic 66.4				
Annual household income (weekly income for Great Britain)	(<$10k) 69.7	(<$20k) 21.7		(<£200) 9.3	
	($10k–$20k) 69.8	($20k–$40k) 26.1		(£200–£400) 11.9	
	($20k–$35k) 75.7	($40k–$60k) 35.5		(£400–£600) 14.5	
	($35k–$50k) 80.5	($60k–$80k) 41.9		(£600–£800) 11.4	
	(≥$50k) 85.6	($80k–$100k) 46.3		(£800–£1000) 7.1	
		(≥$100k) 55.1		(≥£1000) 13.7	
Marital status				married) 38.4	
				(other) 29.5	
Children in the household		Children 37.6		Children 22.0	
		No child 37.0		No child 45.8	
Highest education	College (16+) 85.8	<High school 16.7		Degree 22.9	(16–19) 32
		High school 34.7		A Levels 9.3	(20+) 50
		University 46.7		O Levels 15.9	

[1] Ethnicity and income figures are based on the authors' own calculations from the raw data and refer to rates against each group total and the total sample size respectively.
[2] Data are taken from Van Bottenberg et al (2005) for the European countries.

Sport England (2004a) suggests that "ageing" affects participation by reducing the physical ability to participate and, moreover, raises the concentration of any sport "illiteracy" among the population at large. Time pressures associated with increased work hours for employees in the UK arguably reduce participation. These time constraints in turn affect the capability of volunteers and professionals to support and to develop sport. Well-being and obesity are identified as alternative scenarios associated with increasingly sedentary lifestyles which would affect participation. The levels of investment connected with the provision of facilities in the locality can affect participation, as does education, which has the potential to shape the tastes and provide opportunities for sport. These opportunities may be through the provision of facilities directly or indirectly through education's potential to raise employment and income. Variations in access to sport are thus important, and this will also depend on any additional constraints implied by any sex and ethnic discrimination.

Similar drivers are identified elsewhere. The Conference Board of Canada (2005) identifies age, gender, income and education as key drivers of change, but in addition to this find household composition significant. Similarly, the Australian Sports Commission (2005) found that age, sex, labour force status and education level affect participation. They also identify the importance of regional status in affecting participation. For example, participation rates are higher in state capitals than in other areas. The identification of these drivers appears to have occurred only indirectly with reference to theory. Sport England (2004b) documents how consultation with academic research and data scrutiny led to the development of their drivers of participation. In contrast, van Bottenburg et al. (2005) argue that European patterns of participation could be accounted for by social-psychological and sociological theory, accounting for the interaction between personal, interpersonal and environmental factors, such as:

"...age, gender, education, socio-economic status, perceived advantages and barriers, perceived health/fitness, intention, self-efficacy, self motivation, social support and the subjective experience of the living environment and everyday surrounds." (van Bottenburg et al., 2005, p. 187)

However, in both cases, it is notable that no reference to economic theory is made, despite the discussions in Chapter 3 in which it is clear that many of the variables mentioned can be interpreted through the lens of economic theory.

4.2.3 Expenditure on mass sports participation

With respect to analyses of expenditure on sport, the main official sources of data tend to be expenditure surveys that are used for monitoring national economies and, for example, to underpin such data as presented in Table

TABLE 4.5 Consumer spending on sport

Great Britain £ million (2001)			Australia $ million (2003)		
Item	1999	2004	Item	1998	2003
Sport clothing and footwear	2817	4054	Bicycles	40.4	52.4
Sport equipment	900	1386	Boats	406.9	395.3
Health and Fitness	1339	1531	Camping equipment	111.0	133.1
Boats	701	850	Fishing equipment	141.2	185.5
Participant sports	2036	1923	Golf equipment	80.7	80.7
Spectator sports	801	750	Sports footwear	380.7	459.8
Sport gambling	2025	3404	Swimming pools	611.5	1375.4
Sport TV and video	1345	1852	Other sports equipment	363.1	818.8
Sport related publications	633	551	Hire of sports equipment	60.4	24.2
Sport related travel	1013	965	Health and fitness charges	276.9	580.8
Other expenditure	428	418	Sports club subscriptions	483.1	419.5
Total	14 036	17 684	Spectator admission fees	349.3	294.4
			Sports facility hire	1041.8	927.7
			Sports lessons	437.8	423.5
			Total	4784.9	6172.2

2.4 concerning the overall scale of sport in the economy. Disaggregation is, therefore, constrained to reflect the categories investigated by particular surveys. There are, of course, some exceptions. Taks and Kesenne (2000) combined data from a survey of 512 households in Flanders with government expenditure data, private expenditure and investment, to identify a Gross Regional Sport Product of US$4.3 billion, noting a rise of 4.7 times the level of 15 years previously.

More generally, rising sports expenditure is identified by the available research from official surveys. In the UK SIRC (2005) estimates, based on the family expenditure survey, that the value of sports expenditure increased from £14 036 million in 1999 to £17 684 million in 2004, allowing for inflation. Similarly, in Australia, the Australian Bureau of Statistics argue that the household expenditure survey of 2003 reveals an increase in expenditure from 1998 of AUS$4,784.9 million to AUS$6,172.2 million allowing for inflation. Some indication of the dispersion of these expenditures is given in Table 4.5.

In Great Britain it is clear that the main components of increased expenditure are clothing and footwear, sports gambling, which has emerged as a dynamic market, and sport television and video. Coupled with the static expenditure from participants, these changes in expenditure patterns are indicative of relatively autonomous changes in demand. Such claims receive support from unofficial sources of data. Mintel (2005), for example, indicates that leisurewear for general, as opposed to sporting, use is a growing market, and that satellite television spectatorship has affected participation levels in sport. It is also argued that the growth in expenditure on sports equipment is indicative of purchases of items, such as bicycles, golf and keep fit equipment. Such developments, coupled with the growth of expenditure on health and fitness, are suggestive of a more individualistic and informal participation in sports than through organized clubs. Similar patterns appear to be the case in Australia, with expenditure on hire charges falling but equipment purchases rising, along with swimming payments and increases in expenditure on footwear and bicycles. These issues are discussed further in the next chapter as they indicate how supply may well have changed to meet changing demands, particularly as there has been growth in the private sector provision of sports facilities.

In terms of the general drivers of expenditure, rather than its distribution, The Conference Board of Canada (2005) reports that in 2004 households spent approximately $15.8 billion on sports compared to $8.9 billion in 1994. This represents a rise in the proportion of GDP spent on sport from 0.9% of GDP to 1.2% of GDP. It is argued that rising incomes, coupled with participation in sports contribute towards the higher spending. In contrast, family size can increase spending, but this reaches a plateau with more than two children in the household. Likewise, SIRC (2005) argues that increases in GDP have helped to increase the spending on sports in Britain. Results such as these suggest that sport is either a normal or a luxury good.

> *In economics, and as implied in Chapter 3, a normal good is one whose consumption rises with increases in income. A superior good will experience a greater proportionate increase in consumption than the increase in income. This means that the share of household budgets spent on the superior good will increase.*

While an economic interpretation can be placed on such data, none of the official or commercial reports specifically test economic theories in connection with their claims. The next section concludes the chapter by discussing the evidence of sports participation and expenditure that has this objective.

4.3 MASS SPORTS PARTICIPATION: THEORETICAL AND EMPIRICAL ANALYSIS

In this section, analyses of data directly concerned with testing hypotheses about sports consumer behaviour in the mass participation context are discussed. Drawing on the results shown in Figure 3.1 concerned with the allocation of leisure time, participation in sport and subsequent expenditures are discussed.

4.3.1 Leisure time

There is a voluminous amount of economic literature that examines, indirectly, the demand for leisure time, as the counterpoint to the supply of labour in the labour economics literature. As discussed in Chapter 3, in the traditional income–leisure trade-off model leisure is seen as the residual of work and the wage rate as the opportunity cost of leisure. In this section for brevity, therefore, attention turns to studies that were directly motivated by a concern for leisure as the prime unit of analysis. The direct concern for the demand for leisure time can be noted as corresponding with the growing acceptance of the New Household Economics of Gary Becker, discussed in Chapter 3. For example, Gronau (1973) analyzes the intrafamily allocation of time and argues that:

"... the classical dichotomy of 'work in the market' versus 'leisure' may serve as a good approximation to the role the husband plays in the production activity of the household, but does gross injustice to the wife. To call the whole of the time spent by the wife outside the market sector 'leisure' is to overlook the production activities she engages in at home ... and the wife's allocation of time should therefore be analyzed in terms of a three way division of work in the market, work at home and leisure." (Gronau, 1973, p. 634)

Notwithstanding the presumption about gender roles implied in this research, it is also noted that:

"... (a)n empirical estimation of the demand for leisure and supply of work at home calls for detailed data concerning the time budgets of the various family members. The existing data are too crude to provide conclusive results." (Gronau, 1973, p. 641)

Consequently, the value of housewives' time is estimated on US census data for 1960 by predicting the potential wage rate of females who do not work for given income, and the age and education characteristics of those who do work, controlling for the probability of the individual working by imputation from the normal distribution. This potential wage is then regressed on income and the probability of working. It is identified that income increases the value of time for white females, and more so generally in the presence of children.

More directly, Abbott and Ashenfelter (1976) and Phlips (1978) make use of utility functions including leisure time directly and a "full income" constraint to explicitly derive the demand for leisure, defined as hours not spent working,

BOX 4.1 LINEAR EXPENDITURE MODELS

It was shown in the last chapter that the typical demand for sports equipment, clothes and facilities (x) can be presented as dependent on the price, p, the price of other goods or services, p*, consumer incomes, I and preferences P.

$$x = x(p, p^*, I, P)$$

It follows logically that demand can also be represented in terms of expenditure, i.e.:

$$px = px(p^*, I, P)$$

Two common specific forms of analysis of expenditures that are often employed in economics, or implicitly underpin the econometric analysis of expenditures are:

1. the Engel curve: $px = \beta_1 + \beta_2 I$
2. the linear expenditure system: $p_i x_i = p_i y + \beta_i (I - \sum p_j x_j)$

The Engel curve models the impact of income, and possibly other factors, on expenditure on a good. The linear expenditure system is similar, but accounts for the fact that expenditure on good "i" can only be funded out of income minus the expenditure on all other goods "j." In this equation, "y" represents some minimum amount of consumption of good "i" that is required.

as part of a system of equations including the demand for other goods and, in Phlips (1978), the demand for money also.[1] Based on the same US data ranging from 1938 to 1967, linear expenditure systems, as discussed in Box 4.1, are estimated to reveal that the demand for leisure time rises with income.

Two consequences of the theoretical and modelling strategy are that first, specific restrictions are imposed on the demand functions. Leisure and all other goods or money are treated as gross substitutes, because they account for elements of a full income constraint. The second point is that goods and leisure demands are not derived in a hierarchical way, as they reflect the joint allocation of resources by the consumer. This is a direct consequence of the New Household Economic approach.

Since these earlier studies, research has probed the specific factors that affect the use of time. For example, Gronau (1977) used the 1972 panel of the Michigan Study of Income Dynamics to analyze the determinants of hours at work in the market, work at home and hours' leisure. Using OLS analysis, it was identified that females' leisure time increased with age, education, and her husband's income and education, but declined with the presence of children aged 0–17 in the household, the presence of children at school, the number of

---

[1] The estimated model is referred to as "seemingly unrelated regression" (SUR) because a series of regressions for each element of expenditure is estimated with no expectation that dependent variables for one equation appear in other equations. The correlation between the equations occurs through the random error terms and, in this case, arises because the budget constraint must equal the sum of expenditures on the different elements.

rooms in the house (proxying the need for housework) and her previous employment experience.

Similar analysis was undertaken by Kooreman and Kapteyn (1987), who also made use of US University of Michigan Survey Data, but undertook an improvement in the analysis by formally controlling for sample selection by using a Heckman model to first impute the (shadow) wage of nonworking and working women, recognizing that wage data only applies to those who work. In this respect, the probability of working being conditional on a set of the individual's characteristics is used to impute the wage rate, in contrast to Gronau (1973).

It is identified that the presence of children affects female participation in leisure, unlike males. Male leisure demand falls and then rises after 50 years of age. Education can lead to some substitution of passive activities like reading, watching television, etc., for males, but the reverse is the case for females. As wage rates rise, it can be shown that demand for leisure increases for males, but falls for males in sports-related activities. The opposite is the case for females, whose demand for leisure falls. Interestingly, such findings are synonymous with the descriptive results presented in Table 4.4 and indeed more recent research. Table 4.6 summarizes the results of more recent literature on the demand for leisure time, where the sign indicates the influence on leisure time by variables in the analysis.

In summary, it appears that males tend to have more leisure time than females, and that education and income can raise the time spent on leisure, although work time and the constraints of family can reduce this. The former

TABLE 4.6 The determinants of leisure time

Author	Influences on leisure time
Zuzanek (1978)	Male (+); female employment (−); education (+); age (+ then −)
Solberg and Wong (1991)	Male (+ with wage, wife's wage, − with travel, wife's travel); female (+ with husbands wage, − with travel, wife's travel)
Altergot and McCreedy (1993)	Children (−); married male (+) for passive leisure
Dardis, Soberon-Ferrer and Patro (1994)	Age (− active leisure; + passive leisure); education (+); male (+)
Robinson and Godbey (1997)	Age (+ then −); education (+); children (−)
Bittman and Wajcman (2000)	Male (+)
Thrane (2000)	Male (+); full-time employment (−); age (+ then −); children (−)
Lee and Bhargava (2004)	Married (−); children (−); full-time or part-time work (−); male (+); black (−)

is the case particularly for males and the latter is the case for females. Interestingly, it should be noted that by no means are all of the studies above directly motivated by the New Household Economic approach. Most of the studies in Table 4.6, in fact, adopt a more sociological approach consistent with an heterodox economic perspective (for example, Thrane, 2000; Bittman and Wajcman, 2000; Robinson and Godbey, 1997; Altergot and McCreedy, 1993; Zuzanek, 1978), consequently the commonality of results is actually coupled with a variety of theoretical explanations, which is important in considering policy options. Similar results also apply to analyses of the decision to participate or not in specific activities.

4.3.2 Participation in sport

Table 4.7 presents the results of a survey of studies that have all used official data to examine the choice to participate in various activities for a variety of countries. A number of general findings appear from the research, although naturally there is some variation reported in the detail of the studies. Once again, it is evident that males tend to participate more in sport and more frequently than females, but in particular activities, such as aesthetics, and sports such as skiing and skating, this is not the case. It is also evident that lower age, income and socio-economic status, for example being at a professional or managerial level or being a skilled worker, raise the participation rate in sports. The same is true of better health, and higher levels of education, as well as having access to vehicular transport. This is also the case where there is participation in other activities or other family members are active.

Notably, drinking alcohol is associated with higher participation in sport as opposed to smoking. More generally there is evidence that increased work hours can reduce participation rates, as can being of non-white ethnicity. A variety of household characteristics also reduce participation in sport. These include being married or a couple and, particularly, the presence of children in the household.

A number of the studies also investigate the frequency of participation. It is not uncommon for the signs on the variables noted above to be reversed in this case. Thus age, being married, unemployed, part-time employed or retired, raise the frequency of participation, while education and being in full-time employment reduce it. There are also some common features, for example, the number of activities participated in raises the frequency of participation for given activities. In short, it appears to be the case that the decision to participate and its frequency are relatively discrete choices.

TABLE 4.7 Results of a survey of studies using official data into the choice to participate in various activities

Country	Author	Sample characteristics	Theory and estimator	Findings
US	Cicchetti et al. (1969)	1960 National Recreation Survey; n = 16 000; combined with 1965 Bureau of Outdoor Recreation; n = 7200; 24 activities	Neoclassical demand OLS on participation or not OLS on days participated in 1959	Age (−); non-white (−); male (+); income (+); education (+); facility supply (+) Age (+); non-white (−)
US	Adams et al (1966)	University of Michigan Survey Research; n = 1352; 3 activities	Neoclassical demand OLS on participation or not OLS on days participated in 12 months	Age (−); income (+); male (+); education (+); white (+) Age (−); male (+); white (−)
US	Stemple (2005)	1998 NHIS; n = 32 240–22 500; 25–80 years old; 21 sport and physical activities	Heterodox (Bourdieu) Logit on participation or not in last two weeks	Income (+); education (+) [variance according to combinations of economic and cultural capital; dominant classes have broad range]
US	Humphreys and Ruseski (2006)	2000 BRFSS n = 175 246, >18 years; 56 activities	Becker Heckman model Participate or not in *some* activity in the past month Frequency Heterodox	Age (+); married (+); income (−); employed (−); education (−); female (−); white (−); urban (−) Age (−); married (−); children (−); income (+); employed (−); retired (+); education (+); female (−); white (+); urban (+); health (+)
Great Britain	Gratton and Tice (1991)	1985 Health and Lifestyle Survey; n = 9003; GHS 1997, 1980, 1983, 1986, 1987	Logit on participation or not in the last two weeks in any sport OLS on frequency × energy expended Logit on participation or not in last four weeks OLS on frequency in last weeks	Male (+); age (−); socio-economic status (+); income (+); illness (−); number of activities (+) Male (+); number of activities (+); unemployed (+); retired (+) Age (+); male (+); education (+); socio-economic group (+); full-time employment (−); number of activities (+) Age (+); male (+); number of activities (+); part-time employed (+); illness (+); student (+); keep house (+); separated (−); married (−); children (−); unskilled (−)
Great Britain	Farrell and Shields (2002)	1997 Health Survey of England; n = 3811 households = 6467 individuals; 16–65 years; 7 activities	(Implicit Becker household preferences) Random effects probit on participation in the last four weeks for >15 minutes in all sports plus the top seven	Male (+); age (−); married (−); children for males (+); infant (−); ethnic minority (−); education (+); drinking (+); smoking (−); health (+); income (+); unemployment (+); household membership (+)
Great Britain	Sturgis and Jackson (2003)	2000 Time Use Survey; ≥8 years; 42 sports activities	Logit on membership of activity groups Active aerobic Non-active competitive Outdoor competitive Outdoor non-competitive	Age (−); number of adults in the household (−); income (+); male (+); London/SE (+); own house (+); education (+) Age (−); income (+); male (+); car ownership (+); north (−); education (−); married (−); co-habitation (−) Number of adults in the household (−); income (+); male (+); car ownership (+); separated (+) Age (+ then −); number of adults in household (−); children (−); income (−); male (−); managerial (+); intermediate mangaerial (+); car ownership (+); east (−); carer (+); own house (+); education (+)
Great Britain	Downward (2007)	2002 GHS n = 14 819; >16 years; top 10 sports activities	Neoclassical and heterodox Logit on participation in any sport, walking and individual activitites in the last four weeks	Working (+); skills/professional (+); education (+); married (+); regions not SE (+); male (+); white (+); health (+); smoking (−); drinking (+); access to vehicle (+); age (−); children (−); number of adults in the household (−); income (+); work hours (−); unpaid work hours (−); volunteering (+); number of leisure activities (+)

TABLE 4.7 (*Continued*)

Country	Author	Sample characteristics	Theory and estimator	Findings
Great Britain	Downward and Riordan (2007)**	2002 GHS; n = 14 819; >16 years	Becker and heterodox	Age (−); skills/professional (+); drinking (+); regions not SE (−); access to a vehicle (+); sports, other club membership (+); volunteer (−); number of sports (+); sport lifestyle (−)
			Heckman model Participate or not	Education (−); number of males in the household (+); health (+); employment (−); north (+); access to a vehicle (−); income (−); unpaid work (+); number of sports (+); sport lifestyle (+); recreation lifestyle (+); leisure lifestyle (−); volunteer in sport (−)
			Frequency of participation in any sport, recreational sports and specialized sports	
Flanders	Scheerder et al (2005a)*	1979 Leuven growth study; Flemish girls; 1989/199 study on movement activities in Flanders; n = 38 376; 19–77 years	Heterodox (Bourdieu)	Age (−); female (−); class (+); family size (+); urban (+)
			Logit on Participation in the year membership of activity groups; participation in the year	
			Solo sports	Female (+)
			Competitive and outdoor sports	Male (+); class (+)
			Duo/team sports	Female (−); age (−); class (+)
			Club sport	Age (−); female (−); class (+)
			Non-organized sport Heterodox (Bourdieu)	Age (+); female (+); family size (−)
Flanders	Scheerder et al (2005b)*	1969 Leuven growth study of Belgian boys; 1979 Leuven growth study of Flemish girls 1989/99 university survey; n = 22 424	Logit on membership of activity groups; participation in the year	
			Traditional Aesthetic	Humanities school (−); parents participating in sport (+) Female (+); age (−); humanities school (+); socio-geographical (+); parents participating in sport (+)
			Family Glide	Female (+); socio-economic (+); parents participating in sport (+) Female (+); age (−); humanities school (+); parents participating in sport (+)
			Exclusive Heterodox (Bourdieu) market segmentation	Female (+); age (+); family size (−); socio-economic (+)
Flanders	Taks and Scheerder (2006)*	1999-2001 Study on Movement Activities in Flanders; n = 5172; 6–18 years	Logit on membership of activity groups; participation in the year	
			Traditional	Female (−); age (+); socio-economic (+); parents participating in sport (+)
			Family Aesthetic	Female (+); socio-economic (+); parents participating in sport (+) Female (+); age (−); humanities school (−); parents participating in sport (+)
			Exclusive/glide	Females (+); age (+); family size (+); socio-economic(+); parents participating in sport (+)
			Popular action And numbers of sports	Age (−); socio-economic (+); parents participating in sport (+)
			One – univores	Female (−); age (−)
			Two – bivores	Age (+); parents participating in sport (+)
			More than two – omnivores	Female (+); socio-economic (+); parents participating in sport (+)

Country	Study	Data	Theory / Method	Results
Australia	Stratton et al. (2005)	2002 General Social Survey; n = 15 500	No explicit theory; Logit on participation in the last 12 months (Could include non-activity involvement in sport)	Age (−); male (+); state (+); suburb (+); professional (+); income (+); socio-economic (+); couple no children (+); single (+); education (+); english speaker (+); health (+); easy transport (−); not safe environment (−); weekly contact family friends (−)
Norway	Skille (2005)	Primary data from author n = 566	Heterodox [Bourdieu]; Logit on participation or not in Sport city program activities	Female (−); academic school (+); active family members (+); volunteer family members (+); peer and media information (+)
			Conventional activities	Female (−); academic school (+); active family members (+); active friends (−); volunteer family members (+); peer and media information (+)
			Sport city program versus conventional activities Becker	Academic school (−); peer and media information (+)
Germany	Breuer (2006)	1984–2003 Socio-economic panel; n = 98 772	Logit on participation once a week	Income (+); working time (−); education (+); age (−); immigrant (−);
Germany	Lechner (2008)	1984–2006 Socio-economic panel n = 6751	No explicit theory; Probit on participation at least monthly	Males: German (+); education (+); year (−); technical occupation (−); autonomy at work (+); never smoked (+); high life satisfaction (+); unemployment (+)
				Females: year (−); German (+); children <3 years (−); children >10 years (+); family income (+); office work (−); low autonomy at work (−); autonomy at work (+); illness (+); unemployment (+); inhabitants per km² (+); city centre (−)

Studies used either factor analysis of cluster analysis to group activities.

**Study used cluster analysis to identify lifestyles. See Box 4.2 for a discussion of these techniques.*

BOX 4.2 FACTOR AND CLUSTER ANALYSIS

Section 4.2 outlined the main elements of econometric research. Implicit in this discussion is that theory identifies specific independent variables that affect the dependent variable, and that the sample of data on which analysis is based is fully transparent. However, in practice, independent variables may be related, and data sets might comprise sub sets or strata. Techniques of analysis derived from psychology, the behavioural sciences and biology have been developed to address such issues further, and are now becoming commonly used in economics.

Factor analysis: this is a statistical technique that identifies linear combinations of variables, known as factors, which account for the variance in the individual variables allowing for "errors." As a result, the factors can be thought of as latent variables and included in the analysis instead of the original variables. The number of factors will be less than the number of original variables.

Cluster analysis: this is a statistical technique that classifies cases in a data set into subsets, known as clusters. The clusters will be measured as similar or dissimilar to one another according to a measurement criterion being applied to the values of the variables used to characterize the cases. Cluster membership is thus an indicator of a subsample in the data.

4.3.3 Expenditure

The empirical analysis of expenditure in sport is much less developed in the literature. As a result, the findings are also less consistent. For example, Lera-Lopez and Rapun-Garate (2005) review a sparse literature and note that studies have shown that males tended to spend more money than females on sports. Spending also appears to be linked to rising income. However, the effects of age and education are less clear-cut. While Lamb et al. (1992) report that younger people spent more on sport in the UK, in Japan and Belgium Oga (1998) and Taks et al. (1999) suggest the opposite applies, respectively. Taks et al. (1999) also suggest that spending might fall with education.

Lera-Lopez and Rapun-Garate (2005) undertook their own survey in Navarra, Spain, to examine the links between participation and expenditure, although no explicit theoretical orientation is noted. Based on a sample of 700 respondents, they estimated an ordered-probit model to identify the frequency of sports participation in the previous year, based on categories of participation. They then estimated a Tobit model to examine consumer expenditure in euros per year. The Tobit model was used because expenditure is bounded below by 0. It was identified that participation frequency echoed the results of the research surveyed above. Thus, the frequency fell for females and the employed, but increased with age. Spending also fell for females, but increased with education and income. This suggests that there is a direct relationship between participation and sport but, naturally, facilitated by access to income.

4.3.4 Summary

The above review suggests that consumption in facets of sport, the allocation of time, the decision to participate and the frequency of participation and subsequent expenditure on sport are indeed linked, as implied in outline in Figure 3.1. Significantly, there is some broad qualitative consensus as to the determinants of these features of activity. Significantly, however, a variety of theoretical positions has motivated the research and could explain the broad findings including, therefore, the nature of these inter-relationships.

Consequently, the research is consistent with the income–leisure trade-off model in viewing the results on the effects of income and work hours on leisure time or participation or with New Household Economics, in which such findings coupled with the significance of socio-economic characteristics to participation are viewed as indicative of investment in personal consumption capital and human/social capital, and specialization in the division of labour in the household, with child-care being substituted for participation by females, and particular activities appealing to the different sexes according to the development of lifestyles.

In contrast, one could view these latter characteristics as products of social constraints at work which help to shape preferences, as emphasized in heterodox accounts. As discussed in the previous chapter, these provide alternative perspectives for deliberations over policies being aimed at influencing participation in sport. On the one hand, if the observed patterns are indicative of the exercise of given stable preferences then active policy becomes a distortion to price signals and indicative of a welfare loss, as discussed in Chapter 1. This is because economic inefficiency is implied because the marginal benefits and costs of transaction are not being taken into account.

On the other hand, if it is argued that choices are not, at least in part, freely made, either through informational or social opportunity deficiencies, then policy that seeks to educate about the benefits of sports participation and/or to alleviate the resource and social constraints that affect it become relevant. Significantly, as discussed above in the consideration of policy drivers of participation, and in the next chapter, there is a current rhetorical sweep towards advocating policies to promote participation in sport and physical activities. This suggests that in practice, if not explicitly, policy makers embrace the latter theoretical perspective more. This provides a counterpoint to the main discussion in the next two chapters that examine the changing supply conditions in mass participation sport. Paradoxically, there is a movement towards a greater market-oriented supply of leisure, and it is not entirely clear that policy intervention will have the desired effects on the voluntary sector, which is hugely important in the supply of mass participation sport.

4.4 CONCLUSION

In the previous chapter, various economic theories of choice were presented to suggest how the use of time can influence the decision to participate in sport and, in turn, undertake expenditure. In this chapter attention turned towards the evidence associated with sports participation and expenditure and, consequently, exploration of the potential targets for policy intervention. After presenting the main empirical framework used by economists to examine economic relationships, the main sources of official and widely used unofficial data on sports participation and expenditures were presented, along with some descriptive statistics from these sources, and subsequent policy discussion. The chapter then examined a variety of empirical evidence on the demand for leisure time, the decision to participate in sport and its frequency, as well as expenditures that have been motivated by a direct desire to test various theories of choice. It has been shown that common qualitative understanding of the influences on sports consumption are identified, but alternative theoretical explanations can support these results. Consequently, there are possible tensions implied in promoting policies to affect sports participation.

CHAPTER 5

The Supply of Participant Sport: The Public and Private Sector

OBJECTIVES

- To understand the economic rationale for the public and private sector provision of sport
- To appreciate the empirical evidence on the provision of sport
- To assess the rationale for public policy on the provision of sport

5.1 INTRODUCTION

In this chapter, and the next, attention turns towards providing an appreciation of the supply of mass participation sport. This is a very difficult task to undertake, because the supply structure is complex and there is a shortage of detailed theoretical and empirical work, with most literature comprising policy-related documentation and investigation. There is also some commercial research available. There has also been rapid growth in the private sector provision of sport, particularly in the UK, facilitated by political initiative and following market opportunity.

This chapter aims to outline these developments. Section 5.2 briefly charts the structure of supply in both the UK and a number of other countries. Section 5.3 explores some general policy initiatives that have been promoted to raise sports participation, and the motives for these policy initiatives. Section 5.4 then outlines the economic rationale for public policy intervention and, by implication, to explain why private sector provision and informal participation can be understood as alternative supply structures. The economic logic underpinning public policy recommendations to promote sports participation is discussed.

Section 5.5 then provides an indication of the growth and economic nature of private sector provision of sports in the UK. Section 5.6 discusses informal sports participation and Section 5.7 the supply of sports equipment. The main conclusion is that careful reflection is required to make a case that the market is not providing adequate supply either in the private sector or by informal activity.

5.2 THE STRUCTURE OF SUPPLY

As discussed in Chapter 2 the economic regulation of sport falls within the remit of the Federal Sherman Acts in the US and currently, throughout Europe, the Treaty of Rome. However, notwithstanding such federal or supranational policy making, the organization of sport has some common traits, although it is not granted any special or distinct status compared to other activities. Various central/federal ministries contribute to the organization and development of sports policy, some with specific sports remits and others as part of broader portfolios. Likewise, direct government involvement in sport is also mediated at local government levels and, in some countries such as Germany and Finland, local government involvement dominates. The delivery of sports policy, moreover, is undertaken by various policy bodies which, either jointly or distinctly with concerns to promote elite sport, directly seek to promote and fund mass participation sport. Traditionally this has comprised working with educational institutions, governing bodies and their clubs, but as discussed further below, increasingly recognizes that much participation now takes place by individual consumers who pay to participate in classes at leisure clubs or who participate in a highly informal and self-organized manner. It is clear, therefore, that there is a mixed economy in the supply of mass participation sport.

Table 5.1 provides evidence of the relative mix of the sectors supplying sport by indicating the location of participation, for a number of countries and varieties of dates. It should be noted that blank cells indicate a lack of data rather than the sector being of no importance and that in the final column participation that takes place in sports clubs is, of course, another form of public-sector provision, supported by large numbers of volunteer activity.

While there is considerable variability in the data, not least of which concerns the period of reporting, the data does show that informal sports participation is the largest sector of activity, followed closely by sports clubs. Each of these elements of mass participation supply is now investigated in turn.

TABLE 5.1   Location of sports participation

Country	Public (including education and local authority)	Private	Informal	Sports club
*England (2002)[1]	15%	16%	49%	20%
*Germany (1994)	3%	6%	64%	27%
*Austria (2000)		5%	74%	21%
Finland (2001)	6%	10%	75%	16%
Denmark (1998)	9%	38%	84%	49%
Ireland (1987–2002)				33%
Netherlands (2001)				52%
Belgium (1999)			68%	49%
Portugal (1998)	36%	24%	15%	43%
Spain (2000)			66%	25%
Lithuania (2001)	49%	29%		23%

Source: [1]Carter (2005); others van Bottenburg et al. (2005).

* *Percentage of total.*

5.3 THE PUBLIC SECTOR

Table 5.2 indicates some comparative data on the current scale of the public sector's involvement and financing of sport. While the numbers in Table 5.2 look large, they should be seen in perspective. For example, the Sky television deal for broadcasting premiership matches between 2002 and 2007 comprised £1.024 billion. An important feature of Table 5.2 is that both investment in mass participation sport and elite sport development is included in the public sector figures. The allocation of funds to these sectors reflects a potential policy trade-off as is now discussed.

TABLE 5.2   International comparisons of sport funding

Country	Central/federal £ billion	Regional/local £ billion	Lottery/gaming £ billion	Total £ billion	Per capita £
*England	0.044	1.914	0.242	2.2	42
Germany	0.08	2.37	0.01	2.46	30
France	1.60	4.85	0.15	6.60	110
Finland	0.12	0.26	0.06	0.44	84
Canada	0.20	1.92	0	2.12	66
Japan	2.23	3.26	0.06	5.55	44
Australia	0.08	0.74	0	0.82	43

Source: Carter (2005) except * DCMS/Strategy Unit (2002).

5.3.1 UK sports policy and provision

Current sports policy and provision in the UK underwent a significant overhaul following the publication of *Game plan, a strategy for delivering Government's sport and physical activity objectives in 2002* (DCMS/Strategy Unit, 2002). This document identified two main objectives for government policy (p. 12) which have recently been reaffirmed in *Playing to win: A new era for sport* (DCMS, 2008):

1. a major increase in participation in sport and physical activity, primarily because of the significant health benefits and to reduce the growing costs of inactivity;
2. a sustainable improvement in success in international competition, particularly in the sports which matter most to the public, primarily because of the "feel-good factor" associated with winning.

5.3.1.1 Participation

A number of potential interacting benefits are noted that arise from the public provision of mass sport and physical activity. These include enhancing:

- personal satisfaction and social life, by promoting subjective well-being, citizenship and productive economic behaviour;
- health, by directly tackling issues such as obesity and diabetes, as well as psychological well-being;
- education, by using sport to improve cognitive, emotional and motivational impacts on academic performance;
- crime reduction, by displacing time, reducing boredom, enhancing self-esteem, improving cognitive skills, providing alternative peer groups and creating positive relationships with "significant others;"
- social inclusion, by developing communities, reducing deprivation and building social capital;
- the environment, through urban and community regeneration.

5.3.1.2 Elite sport

A number of interrelated benefits are also proposed to follow from the public provision of elite sport. As far as international sporting success is concerned, a number of impacts are identified:

- feel-good factor, raising well-being, productivity and social capital;
- economic performance, reflected in greater consumer confidence, productivity and share prices, at least temporarily;
- improving the image of the UK to promote tourism and inward investment.

These impacts could also be, of course, connected with the hosting of elite sports events as opposed to merely competing in these events, which is discussed at length in Chapter 12. Suffice it is to say at this point that, as a result of these potential impacts (referred to as legacies in the case of the Olympic Games), it is argued that there is positive feedback between such investment and participation in sport, thus:

"... it is not possible to say that increasing mass participation will automatically improve international success, or that international success will necessarily drive mass participation. Both issues need to be tackled separately, leading to a twin track approach." (DCMS/Strategy Unit, 2002 p. 84)

As Box 5.1 illustrates, however, there is the presumption of positive feedback.

5.3.2 Other sports policy and provision

The approach adopted in the UK is contrasted with three other current approaches in DCMS/Strategy Unit (2002). These include:

- a laissez-faire approach in the US in which sport is not considered to be a federal government concern, consequently, no state support is offered;
- Finland, in which sport is seen as central to social policy and active recreation encouraged; and
- Australia in which elite sporting success is presented as central to national identity.

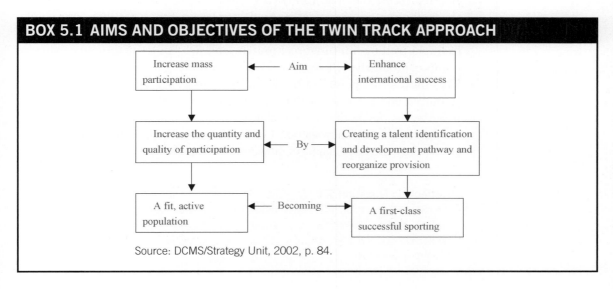

BOX 5.1 AIMS AND OBJECTIVES OF THE TWIN TRACK APPROACH

Source: DCMS/Strategy Unit, 2002, p. 84.

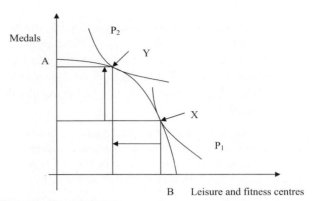

FIGURE 5.1 *Sports policy trade-off.*

This is not to suggest that the benefits of mass participation, as recognized above, are not perceived to be important in the US and Australia (see also the Conference Board of Canada, 2005), but that the balance of emphasis is clearly different, which ultimately depends on the different assumptions made about the responsibility of the individual or state to produce these benefits, and indeed, this balance has changed over time as with the UK.

Figure 5.1 illustrates the economic tension involved, making use of a modified version of the consumer choice framework developed in Chapter 3. For illustration here, the vertical axis represents the number of medals earned at the Olympic Games as a direct consequence of funding, while the horizontal axis represents the number of leisure and fitness facilities provided. The curved line A–B represents the opportunity cost frontier for the use of public funds, when the maximum number of either medals or leisure fitness facilities, or a combination of both, is identified for a given total value of investment, as indicated for example, by the penultimate column in Table 5.2. Points on the curve represent points of productive efficiency in the use of resources, as discussed in Chapter 1. This means that points to the left of the curve indicate an inefficient use of resources, and points to the right of the curve are unattainable. The curve is thus described as the production possibilities frontier. It acts as a budget constraint facing the public policy agency. Unlike the linear budget line facing the consumer presented in Chapter 3, however, the frontier is curved.

Reflection Question 5.1

Why will the production possibilities frontier be curved concave to the origin?

Hint: Each of the alternatives, medals or leisure and fitness centres, are outputs from a production function. Each output will be produced, in theory, according to diminishing marginal productivity.

The curved slope reflects the diminishing marginal productivity of resources being increasingly invested in either the accumulation of medals or the building of new leisure and fitness centres. As discussed in Chapter 1, each of the two alternatives of medals or leisure and fitness centres can be viewed as the outputs of a production function in which the resources of land, labour and capital are committed by the policy maker. As more of each resource is applied to produce either, it is assumed that their output increases at a decreasing rate. Consequently, if one begins from a point such as "X," reduces the building of leisure and fitness centres and reallocates the resources to producing medals, the resources will have a larger effect in the latter case. The opposite would occur if beginning at a point such as "Y," where more resources were initially invested in winning medals, and then some resources were reallocated to building leisure and fitness centres. The slope of the curve thus represents the marginal rate of transformation of resources.

The marginal rate of transformation is the rate at which one good can be transformed into the other. The slope thus represents the opportunity cost of one good, compared to another.

The indifference curves, P_1 and P_2, drawn on the figure, represent policy makers' preferences for combinations of the use of resources. They can be viewed as representing a social welfare function, which is discussed further in the next section. The slope of the indifference curves or marginal rate of substitution will reflect the relative subjective utilities received by the policy maker as they switch from one policy objective to another. Any point of tangency between the indifference curves and the production possibilities frontier thus represents the optimal choice for the government. As drawn, they indicate either a change in preferences over time towards medal accumulation rather than leisure and fitness centres from points "X" to "Y" respectively, or the difference between Finland and Australia's policy priorities.

5.4 THE ECONOMIC RATIONALE FOR PUBLIC POLICY

While the above discussion has charted the extent of public sector intervention in the sports market, and indeed presented some of the specific reasons used to justify why this is the case, the general economic logic and issues underlying these presumptions or interpretations of evidence has not been made clear, but it resides in some of the issues discussed in Chapter 1 under the heading of normative economics. This is, in fact, an issue explicitly identified in DCMS/ Strategy Unit (2002) in which economic efficiency and equity are identified as possible reasons for intervention. Each of these concepts is now discussed in more detail.

5.4.1 Economic efficiency

It was argued in Chapter 1 that economic theory presents maximum economic welfare for society, or efficiency, as consistent with a competitive market allocation of resources where both productive and allocative efficiency are implied. Outputs are produced at lowest possible cost and the prices at which resources are traded reflect the true benefits and costs to society. Key to facilitating these results is that property rights to resources can be allocated clearly to those engaging in market transactions and those that do not. Property rights can now be more formally defined as:

"... the rules (whether formal and legal or informal custom) which specify which individuals are allowed to do what with resources and the outputs of those resources. Property rights define which of the technologically feasible economic decisions individuals are *permitted* to make." (Gravelle and Rees, 2004 p. 9, italics in original).

It should be added here that the permissibility of property rights to facilitate transactions logically depends on their being defined or measurable. If they are, then they define private goods which can be bought and sold on markets. Chapter 1 suggested two contexts in which this was not possible. This is when consumption decisions are non-rival and when they are non-exclusive. As presented in Figure 5.2, a variety of economic goods exist.

This suggests that, in practice, according to degrees of non-rivalry or excludability, a variety of types of goods exist with some spillovers to other parties than those engaged in a transaction. Externalities, as discussed in Chapter 1, are the key spillovers. On this basis Table 5.3 indicates the nature of the externalities involved according to the suggested benefits of increasing mass participation noted earlier, and how public sector provision of sport may correct the impacts.

What mechanisms could be used to achieve these adjustments, to harmonize marginal private and marginal social costs and benefits? It is clear now that three main policy tools could be used. As discussed in Chapter 1, taxes or subsidies could be employed to adjust the market price either up or down to correct for the overprovision or underprovision, respectively. Underprovision could be directly corrected for by the public sector supply of the activity directly or through incentives and subsidy from the public sector. Finally, information

Characteristic	Rival	Non-rival
Excludable	Private good.	Club goods
Non-excludable	Common property resource	Public goods

FIGURE 5.2 *Types of economic good.*

TABLE 5.3 Externalities and participation in sport

Benefit of participation	State of externalities	Corrective impact of sport
Personal satisfaction and social life	MSB > MPB	Enhance personal and social capital
Health	MSC > MPC	Increase human capital/productivity Decrease healthcare costs
Education	MSC > MPC	Increase human capital/productivity Increase social capital
Crime reduction	MSC > MPC	Increase social capital Decrease policing costs
Social inclusion	MSC > MPC	Increase social capital

deficiencies can also be targeted to allow better informed decisions to be made and to help in establishing property rights.

5.4.2 Equity

Equity in sport has traditionally been promoted in policies of "sport for all," such as the explicit commitment to this aim in the 1975 Council of Europe Charter and implicitly in the European Sports Charter (DaCosta and Miragaya, 2002). In the context of the discussions of Chapter 1, to maintain that equity provides a rationale for public policy in sport, therefore, requires a presumption that the current combination of resources available to consumers is first, not adequate for them to consume the amount of sport that they would otherwise wish to or secondly, that they should consume a different amount than they currently do. In the former case, concerns about equity overlap directly with concerns for social exclusion, as emphasized by Collins (2003, 2004), inasmuch as a lack of income can constrain participation in sport. It is clear, however, that while income is important, the New Household Economic approach of Chapter 3 directly recognizes that access to market goods and time also matter, because they form the inputs to the household production function. It follows that equity is connected more generally to the presence of constraints on individual choice and, in this regard, the policies required to correct for inequity can be the same. Consequently, while taxation or subsidy can be used to adjust the prices paid for access to the good or service, a direct focus on changing income differentials might target both horizontal and vertical equity. Willingness to pay is thus balanced against ability to pay.

Equity is linked to the concept of merit goods, which are goods judged by an individual or society to be more appropriate than those that would have been chosen according to consumer preferences, which are measured by willingess to pay. It is on this basis that it has often been argued that the direct provision of such goods is more acceptable than a reallocation of income (Musgrave and Musgrave, 1973; Musgrave, 1987). As Cicchetti et al. (1969) note, merit goods are essentially a redistribution of income in specific commodity forms.

Notwithstanding these distinctions, however, the above discussion suggests that equity and economic efficiency are to an extent, in conflict, if willingness to pay is not also an expression of ability to pay. However, the forms in which this applies are quite complex and depend, to an extent, on what is implied by equity. The point can be illustrated by examining alternative concepts of the maximization of social welfare other than the outcomes of a market allocation of resources, which have been described as efficient. Box 5.2 indicates some alternative social welfare functions that are discussed in the economic literature.

> *A social welfare function ranks alternative social states, as a utility function for individuals ranks alternative uses of resources.*

It is significant to note that they have different implications for both vertical and horizontal equity. They also refer either to resources or to the utility experienced from the consumption of resources. Ultimately, policy makers implicitly or explicitly adopt such a function in making resourcing decisions. A market-based approach, emphasizing efficiency, could therefore be identified with a utilitarian approach.

Technically, however, the utilitarian approach had its theoretical origin in the addition of measurable cardinal utility. Consequently, Bergson (1938) and Samuelson (1947) proposed a general social welfare function comprising the ordinal utility of all members of society. The Pareto criterion then argues that if one individual's utility increases, other things equal then so must social welfare. But this is simply one ethical judgement, and as Samuelson (1947) argues, the function is consistent with other ethical beliefs. It should be noted that the social welfare function is always specified with respect to a given income distribution. Significantly, therefore, complications apply to any attempt to evaluate redistribution policies, discussed

BOX 5.2 CONCEPTS OF SOCIAL WELFARE

Egalitarian: all members of society receive equal goods and services;

Utilitarian: maximizes the sum of individual utilities;
Rawlsian: maximizes the utility of the least well-off.

for example by Kaldor (1939), Hicks (1939) and Scitovsky (1941).[1] Perhaps more seriously, Arrow (1950, 1963) has shown that there is no social welfare function derived from individual preferences that satisfies four relatively uncontroversial conditions including: that the social welfare function can apply to any pattern of preferences; that the social welfare function is consistent with the Pareto principle; that the social welfare function ranks states consistently regardless of how states are presented as choices to individuals; and non-dictatorship. Dictatorship implies that a particular individual's choices become decisive.

It follows that attempts to derive a policy preference based on the aggregation of individual preferences cannot be achieved without compromising at least one of these conditions. Consequently, Figure 5.1 can perhaps best be seen as indicative of the policy makers' preferences and beliefs as opposed to individual's in society in as much that they reflect choices made by elected representatives.

5.4.3 UK policy revisited: Mechanisms to promote participation

Having explored the economic logic for public sector intervention in the sports market, an examination of the mechanisms proposed in the UK is now undertaken to reveal the logic of typical policy mechanisms that have been used or could be used to boost participation. Figure 5.3 reveals that the DCMS/ Strategy Unit (2002) seeks to target both the demand- and supply-side factors that affect sports participation, also in the context of both human and physical capital.[2]

In the context of demand it is clear that one option is to enhance the information set by which individuals make choices. While this enhancement

---

[1] Kaldor (1939) and Hicks (1939) suggested "compensation" criteria to try to rectify the compromise to Pareto efficiency implied in a redistribution of resources, which will inevitably imply that different individuals in society gain and lose as incomes are reallocated. The criteria imply examining the potential for gainers to compensate losers, or *vice versa* to facilitate or avoid changes in resource allocation respectively. The idea has analogies with the income effect discussed in consumer choice in Chapter 3. However, the criteria developed were not invariant to the direction of the change in resource allocation, prompting Scitovsky (1941) to develop a criterion in which potential gainers can compensate the potential losers and still remain better off, and potential losers could not offer incentives to gainers to forego the change.

[2] The emphasis here is on adults aged 16 years or over. Separate strategies for school children aged 11 years or under and between 11 and 16 years of age are proposed as part of the curriculum. The real strategic issue is considered to arise once compulsory schooling finishes, when the constraints on participation begin to emerge which seek to build on previous experience of sports at school.

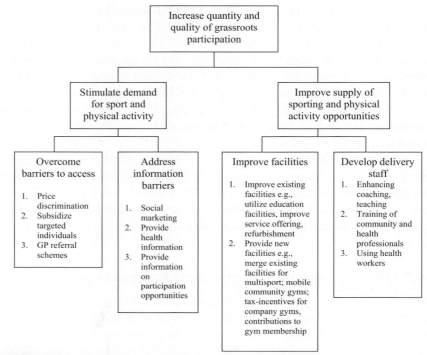

FIGURE 5.3 *UK sports participation policy options.*

of information can be undertaken through social marketing, that is direct campaigning, it is also implied that this could take place directly through the supply side. In this case, those who do not participate in sport might also be those who have direct contacts with community groups and health professionals who might be dealing with the consequences of social exclusion, criminality and poor health. This would provide opportunities to promote sports participation.

The enhanced training of such staff, and others at various sports facilities might also send the signal (as discussed in Chapter 1) that enhanced quality of provision is available, and thereby increase participation. As detailed in Section 5.3.1, and revealed in Figure 5.3, moreover, there is a general focus on the need for increased efficiency in the supply of sports in policy discussion. This is manifest in a number of ways. In part it is proposed that efficiency gains could be achieved by making greater use of existing educational public facilities in the community that have previously been solely for use in education. However, the growth in concern for increasing efficiency has also developed commensurate with a decline in the emphasis on supplying sports facilities directly by the public sector. This reflects a policy view that the private sector may provide services more efficiently than the public sector or at least that the basis of its decision making, with clear commitment to accountable targets, has relevance to the supply of sport. This perspective gained momentum in the 1980s in the UK as part of a broad policy sweep towards privatization and the deregulation of markets that were dominated by monopoly government agencies. In the UK this emphasis has been manifest in policies such as compulsory competitive tendering (CCT) for local authority services so that the provision of sports and leisure services could only be retained by the public authorities if they had competed for the right to provide such services with other private sector companies according to a sealed bid auction. The only exceptions were facilities provided solely for educational and community group establishments. As Henry (2001, p. 140) notes, the current policy emphasis is on "best value"(BV) to remove the excessive emphasis on costs that had occurred with CCT and:

"... to secure continuous improvement in the way in which its functions are exercised, having regard to a combination of economy, efficiency and effectiveness." (Sport England,
1999b, p. 3)

Reflection Question 5.2

How are efficiency, economy and effectiveness related to economic efficiency?
Hint: Think about resource, use, costs and objectives, say, in perfect competition.

It should be noted that all three of these terms are subsumed in the economic concept of efficiency. If one believes that Pareto efficiency currently exists because of the presence of a competitive market, then it follows that the production function describing the use of resources to produce outputs must describe maximum technical efficiency, i.e., the minimum level of inputs are being used to produce the maximum level of outputs. If the markets for factors of production are perfectly competitive then the nominal value of the resources expressed as wages, interest rates and rents will be at their lowest possible level. These two conditions in turn mean that economic costs, which are the nominal values of factors of production divided by their marginal productivities (see Chapter 1, Equation 1.1), will be at their lowest level. Finally, the objective of suppliers, i.e., profit maximization, is achieved under the conditions where marginal revenue is equal to marginal cost.

It should also be noted, however, that this does not mean that BV automatically proposes a competitive allocation of resources or the aspiration to profit maximization. The welfare reorientation of BV does not necessarily target the Paretian ideal. A different objective might be set that does not target profits and that may involve trading-off the interests of particular stakeholders in society, for example, because of equity criteria. If this objective is achieved, then effectiveness is achieved. This is consistent with striving for the "efficiency" and "economy" of supply provision as far as achieving that particular target would allow. In this regard BV can be seen as a compromise between seeking economic efficiency, as defined in technical economic terms, and achieving policy goals, perhaps associated with the access issues that are not likely to be of interest to purely commercial facilities.

Figure 5.4 illustrates the main principles involved in which two types of customers are presented as applicable to a sports centre, those able to pay a higher price and those able to pay a lower price. This might apply in situations where there are socially advantaged and disadvantaged potential participants or customers. The price that they each pay for the use of the facility could give them access to a particular activity or any bundle of activities and is considered essentially the same for individuals belonging to either of these groups. It is assumed that there is a constant AC for the supply of these facilities. In this case the equivalence of the AC and MC implies that only average variable costs (AVC) are considered. This would correspond to the required comparison in which a local authority owned facility was being run either by a private company or by local authority employees. The implication is that the fixed costs of the facility are not being treated as part of the comparative profit or loss calculations concerned.

Recalling the discussions of Chapter 1, it was noted that profit maximizing behaviour, as might be expected of a private company, would imply targeting the provision of output where MR = MC. This must occur at the point indicated "private" in Figure 5.4. The implication is that further use of the facilities would require making them accessible to those not able to pay the relevant price, which would not be in the interests of the company. In contrast, a public sector or welfare ethos might have as its goal increasing access to sport, for the reasons discussed earlier. In this respect the facility might be used up to full potential capacity, to the point indicated "public."

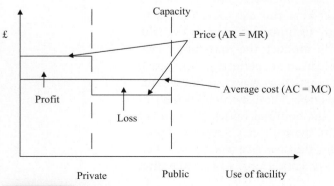

FIGURE 5.4   *BV and policy outcomes.*

It is clear, however, that in order to achieve this target prices would have to be lower to attract such participants. However, this situation would lead to MR < MC, with the consequence of not maximizing profits. The facility would make an overall profit or loss depending on the relevant size of the areas marked "profit" or "loss" if two levels of price were established (see the discussion of price discrimination below). A larger loss would be made if the same lower price were charged to all consumers.

Reflection Question 5.3

What would be the extent of loss if one price were charged?
Hint: Consider the difference between AR = MR and AC = MC.

In the latter case, if the lower price were charged all users would pay less than AC = MC and as a consequence the loss would correspond to this difference times the number of activities participants. Significantly, BV suggests that loss in itself is not a problem. On the contrary, what matters is being effective, i.e., achieving objectives. In this regard, if the objective is to maximize participation in sport, such a loss is of no concern. Moreover, it is clear that regardless of which objective is sought, economy and efficiency will help to achieve this, because if AC = MC is at its lowest possible value consistent with the policy target, then either profits are maximized or any losses that occur are kept at a minimum. The latter case would reduce the scale of any subsidy required to maintain the use of the facilities and reduce the opportunity cost of investing resources elsewhere.[3]

A significant implication of this approach is that the ownership of the asset is not considered to be important *per se*, and this explains the shift in policy emphasis away from the provision of facilities. The key issue for policy is access to facilities as a policy objective. This has helped to reinforce the growth of private sector provision in the UK, as discussed in the next section. The use of the price mechanism to promote participation is also emphasized in the

---

[3] In the current case, because MC = AC there is an assumption that factors of production exhibit constant marginal productivity, so the efficiency and economy of profit maximization and participant maximization would be equivalent. However, this would not be the case if diminishing marginal productivity applied. Here, MC rises with increases in output, so it follows that output levels above the MR = MC level will be supplied at higher MC and AC. Losses will be higher than the diagrammatic case for the facility and implied by perfect competition. So, in economic efficiency terms, any equivalence between productive efficiency, cost minimization (economy) and allocative efficiency (prices reflecting opportunity costs) is compromised.

other options to promote participation in DCMS/Strategy Unit (2002, p. 108). These include:

1. part funding participation in activities through employer subsidies or directly subsidizing employees;
2. encouraging firms to be flexible on work times to help promote participation;
3. subsidizing individuals directly through the use of GP referrals, swipe cards and vouchers for use at sports facilities.

Each of these mechanisms either reduces the cost of participation directly or indirectly, for example, by allowing individuals to reallocate work and household work time. They target specific individuals to whom a price reduction should apply. If the target for policy is to promote more participation, then it can be shown that this will be the most effective tool. Consider Figure 5.5; it presents the consumer choice framework developed in Chapter 3. Here, the two economic goods being considered are visits to sports facilities and other, non-sport, consumption goods. To respect individual preferences, a general government payment might be made to a disadvantaged individual who does not currently participate much in sport. Alternatively, the price of access to sports facilities only might be subsidized as implied above. It can be shown that the latter will promote more use of sports facilities.

    The first of the two policies is consistent with the income effect discussed in Chapter 3 and moves the budget constraint out from the origin in a parallel fashion. It is possible that some extra sports participation might follow, but also the consumption of other goods will increase as the income is distributed across consumption decisions. In principle, less sport might even be chosen, which is the case drawn for those having weak preferences for sport, as is likely for disadvantaged groups (see DCMS/Strategy Unit, 2002, p. 105). In this case, participation is considered to be an inferior good by the individual. In contrast, if only visits to sports facilities are subsidized, then this is equivalent to a substitution effect. The income constraint pivots through the initial equilibrium to indicate that resources have increased if further visits to sports facilities are undertaken.[4] Here more sports participation must follow.

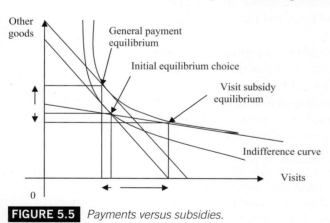

FIGURE 5.5 *Payments versus subsidies.*

---

[4] Resources fall if fewer visits are undertaken. This implies additional opportunity costs from not increasing visits to sports facilities.

There are a number of caveats that should be added in closing this discussion. The first, and most obvious, is that if such subsidies were applied to all visits to sports facilities, this might compromise equity objectives and reinforce benefits to those already participating in sport, despite targeting lower participating groups. It is clear, therefore, that only those viewed as disadvantaged should receive the subsidy. Vouchers would require clear property rights and not be transferable.[5] GP referral schemes would automatically imply this with named individuals being "prescribed" opportunities to engage in sports activity. The second qualification is that, just as with equity objectives, such subsidies place policy priority above consumer preferences generally. This is because they distort the market prices or values on the use of resources from those that would have occurred. Despite the policy objectives being seen as necessary by policy makers or their supporters, there is a direct sense in which individual preferences are compromised. It is clear that the DCMS/Strategy Unit (2000) recognizes these issues and argues that:

> "We do not suggest that equality of outcomes should be a goal, because people have different tastes, but we do argue that equality of opportunity should be a goal." (DCMS/Strategy Unit, 2002 p. 78)

The general point, however, is that a legitimate case for public policy to promote sports participation is possible, but its logical underpinnings and justification should involve making explicit arguments about the nature of market functioning. In particular, informational problems need to be presented which provide a basis for the presence of externalities, which might then be consistent with, resulting from, or resulting in, other constraints on efficient economic behaviour. An explicit concept of equity might also need to be made clear. In general, policy solutions that target equity or efficiency concerns through subsidies to price signals require recognizing that policy makers preferences are promoted, as opposed to those of all consumers as would be presented in a market allocation of resources.

5.5 THE PRIVATE SECTOR

It has been noted that there has been growth in private sector provision of mass participation. This finding, coupled with the concern that there is no evidence of any major longitudinal growth in mass sports participation in the UK, suggests a changing composition of demand over time as much as any sustained secular change. Table 5.4 presents some comparable time-series data for

---

[5] If vouchers were transferable then the Coase theorem would predict that recipients would allocate them to others with a greater wish to engage in sport in return for some other benefit, perhaps cash or goods in kind.

TABLE 5.4 Sports participation 1987–2002 (%)

Activity	1987	1990	1993	1996	2002
Swimming	13	15	15	15	14
Keep fit/yoga	9	12	12	12	12
Weight training*	5	5	5	6	5
Soccer	5	5	4	5	5
Golf	4	5	5	5	5
Tennis	2	2	2	2	2
Badminton	3	3	3	2	2
Lawn/carpet bowls	2	2	2	2	1
Squash	3	3	2	1	1
Table tennis	2	2	2	2	1
At least one activity (excluding walking)	45	48	47	46	43

Source: Fox and Rickards (2004).
* *Combined with weight lifting until 1996.*

mass participation, for adults aged 16 years or above in the four weeks before the interview for the GHS, for a number of activities that might be associated with public or private sector facilities provision. The data indicate a general stagnant level of participation, with some apparent structural shifts of interest, for example, away from squash.

This would suggest that any growth in the private sector supply of this market has arisen largely from changes in a previously public sector industry to the mixed economy noted earlier, commensurate with the emphasis on compulsory competitive tendering and best value, producing market segmentation across suppliers reallocating the derived demand for facilities.

It is difficult to identify general supporting evidence for this proposition, but it appears to be the case for health and fitness clubs, leisure centres and swimming pools in the UK (Mintel, 2005a, 2006). The commercial evidence that is publicly available suggests that private health and fitness clubs operate at the "top end of the market," while local authority centres, evolving primarily from swimming pool provision and the earlier policy desires of the 1970s to provide public sector facilities, are supplying the other elements of the market. Significantly, there is evidence that it is in this sector that participation demand is weak. Such inferences are borne out by an examination of the supply provision indicated in Table 5.5, in which participation in the last 12 months by adults aged 15 years or over at various locations is reported.

While participation is undertaken at multiple locations, consistent with more than one sport being undertaken by individuals, it is noticeable that participation at local authority centres has actually fallen in relative terms since the time when BV was introduced, and this is also the case in other

TABLE 5.5   Location of sport provision

Location	1998 %	2000 %	2003 %	2005 %
Local authority sports centre	50	48	46	38
Private club or gym	32	33	34	32
Local park	23	22	22	24
Home	24	23	21	22
School/college/university	17	16	14	13
Local authority sports ground	12	9	11	8
Place of employment	8	7	6	4
Elsewhere	31	25	25	26
Sample size	1126	1187	1062	971

Source: Mintel (2005a).

locations. The exceptions are participation in parks, home and private sector provision *per se*, which appears to account for a constant share of demand usage. The stable market sectors appear to be informal participation, discussed further below, and the private sector. It is important to note, in this regard, that the declines are not necessarily commensurate with reduction in supply opportunities in the local authority sector. Mintel (2005b) estimates that there were 2596 local authority centres in 2004, with an expected additional 128 in 2005. Moreover, 165, 124, 91, 42 and 79 were each added in the previous years, suggesting investment and rising supply capacity. Significantly, it is reported that this additional capacity is being operated by private sector management. While 616 of the centres were run under contract in 2003, 129 were run by in house "Direct Service Organizations," 332 by private leisure management contractors and 155 by trusts or volunteers.

These patterns would suggest that this sector is attempting to compete with the private sector with the suspicion from the data that such hybrid organizations are struggling to cope with the aims of "sport for all" as a social and welfare policy, while seeking to operate on commercial principles. In contrast, a buoyant but consolidating private sector segment of supply has emerged, as detailed in Table 5.6. There is a market leader, Fitness First, and a core of multiclub suppliers each offering clubs of similar size and operating on a membership basis. The economic principles that can describe both of these market characteristics are now discussed.

5.5.1 Market structure

The characteristics of the market presented in Table 5.6 are common across many industries and can be described as an oligopoly.

TABLE 5.6   Private sector health and fitness clubs 2007

Company/owner	Brand(s)	Clubs	Members	Average members/club
Fitness First Holdings Ltd	Fitness First/Fitness First for Women/Kaizen	183	452 000	2470
Whitbread plc	David Lloyd	59	325 000	5508
Virgin Active Ltd	Virgin Active	72	288 301	4004
LA Fitness plc	LA Fitness/Promise	87	261 000	3000
Esporta Group Ltd	Esporta	53	220 000	4151
Bannatyne Fitness Ltd	Bannatyne Health Club/Just Fitness	61	180 000	2951
Cannons Health & Fitness Ltd	Cannons	52	177 000	3404
JJB Sports plc	JJB Health Clubs	39	175 000	4487

Source: Mintel (2007).

An oligopoly is a market dominated by a small number of sellers, each referred to as oligopolists. This contrasts with monopoly in which the market is dominated by one seller. The Greek prefix (oligo or mono) thus distinguishes the market.

Box 5.3 briefly outlines some alternative theoretical models of oligopoly that have been used in economics to analyze their behaviour. Unlike the largely hypothetical models of perfect competition and pure monopoly presented in Chapter 1, oligopoly models try to capture elements of realism through their descriptions of markets, while retaining the assumptions that rational economic agents both have perfect information and optimize their decisions. A further key difference is that, because oligopoly models focus on competition between a relatively small numbers of suppliers, the reactions of suppliers to the actions of other "known" suppliers have to be directly accounted for in the analysis. In the case of perfect competition, suppliers have no discretion to act different from the market, but take the market price as given. In monopoly the firm is the market, and can set the price according to the level of possible demand. In

BOX 5.3 TYPICAL OLIGOPOLY MODELS

Cournot model: named after Augustin Cournot, this model originally addressed competition between two firms, and concerns competition over output levels in the industry.

Bertrand model: named after Joseph Bertrand, this model is concerned with competition over prices.

Stackelberg model: named after H. von Stackelberg, this model is concerned with competition over output in the industry when one of the firms is a market leader.

BOX 5.4 ELEMENTS OF GAME THEORY

Some key elements of game theory include the following:

1. Non-cooperative versus cooperative games
   A game is cooperative if binding contracts can be written as a solution between conflicting objectives. If the cost of a private fitness instructor's services are, say, 10 per hour, but the instructor was seeking a fee of 20 per hour, in practice any agreed fee between 10 and 20 with customers is possible as both parties could be better off. Essentially a bargain over consumer surplus and profit takes place.
   In contrast, in non-cooperative games this is not possible.

2. Dominant strategies
   To analyze non-cooperative games, the game's outcome will depend on the strategy adopted by economic agents. A dominant strategy is an optimal strategy regardless of what other agents choose to do.

3. Nash equilibrium
   Named after the famous mathematician, John Nash, a Nash equilibrium is a dominant strategy in which agents are doing the best that they can given the actions of the other agents. A Nash equilibrium does not have to exist for games and there can be multiple equilibria.

4. Repeated games
   Many economic transactions are undertaken repeatedly. To account for this, rather than viewing the situation as a "one-off" game, a repeated game can be modelled. If this is the case then reputations for behaviour emerge. Different behaviour can be predicted if a finite or infinite horizon for the game is proposed.

5. Sequential games
   If agents make decisions and act simultaneously, then the game is different than if agents make decisions in sequence.

oligopoly situations it is theorized that large firms have a degree of monopoly power only. It follows that different models will yield different specific predictions.

To understand the interaction between suppliers, or indeed any agents, economists make use of game theory. Box 5.4 indicates some general characteristics of game theory, with some more detail presented in Appendix 5.1. For the purposes of this book, the broad point that matters is that oligopoly markets can generate competing incentives. On the one hand, profitable opportunities exist for the suppliers to collude, tacitly if not formally, to act as a monopoly to raise the profits of the set of firms. The profit can then be distributed. It remains, however, that there will always be counter incentives for competitive innovation. An individual firm could, say, cut prices to capture more of the market and thus attempt to make higher individual profits than previously, at the expense of the other firms. This can make such collusive behaviour unstable and coordination in a cartel difficult to manage.[6] It should also be noted that explicit coordination is contrary to economic competition regulations. There is no evidence of such behaviour in the UK fitness market.

---

[6] The stability of cartel behaviour in professional sports is discussed more generally in Chapter 7.

In the light of such competing tensions it is often argued that oligopoly markets will be characterized by product differentiation and non-price competition to avoid "Bertrand" price competition, and to compete over market shares and to defend market segments as implied in "Cournot" competition. First mover advantages do exist, however, such that market leaders can emerge as suggested by Stackelberg.

5.5.2 Pricing

The tariff structure operated by most sports facilities is evidence of a lack of simple price competition in private sector sports facilities. Typically, a two-part tariff structure is employed, which can be viewed as a form of price discrimination. This form of tariff structure implies making a membership payment and then some subsequent payment for the use of facilities, rather than just paying a fee for use, which is more prominent in the previously or current public sector facilities (Mintel, 2005b). Such a system of payment can be viewed as a mechanism to promote loyalty in the use of facilities through being a member of the club. As discussed in Chapter 3, the consumer can be viewed as investing through the purchase of a durable good.

Durable goods yield a flow of services or utility over time rather than being used up with one consumption act.

> **Reflection Question 5.4**
> Why is a sports club membership like a durable good?
> Hint: How does the membership yield utility?

The investment nature of the membership fee is implied via a payment being required to make use of facilities. This payment is written off, i.e., the value of the membership depreciates over time, regardless of whether or not the facilities are actually used. Under such conditions the consumer faces a modified budget constraint in which they first of all make a decision to join a club or not and then, subsequent to this, make a decision on how many times to use the facilities based on the usage fee. It is clear, however, that if the facilities are used the fixed membership charge can be spread over the subsequent usage.

The economic problem facing sports facilities suppliers, therefore, is to attempt to forecast such behaviour and, in seeking profits, to set a high membership fee and lower usage cost, or *vice versa*. There is no simple formula that indicates how profits would be maximized under such circumstances, but there is clearly a trade-off involved. It seems logical to argue that lower membership fees and lower usage fees might generate a large degree of market penetration, but this might compromise a supplier's identity with the "top end of the market." The discussion of social interactions in Chapter 3, for example, indicated how consumer prestige might be affected by such behaviour, as consumers identify with particular characteristics of membership. Table 5.7 indicates how in the UK target markets are defined in terms of membership segments.

To summarize the above discussions, in the UK context the private sector supply of sports participation can be understood as an oligopoly, competing for members. It is clear that this segment of the industry has, to an extent, captured the willingness to pay for sports participation, as evidenced by the membership structure of such facilities. There is, therefore, clear evidence of the market internalization of consumer surpluses that existed with purely subsidized public provision. In contrast, previous public sector facilities, or those still in the public sector, now face a more challenging market segment, comprising those that participate less or lack

TABLE 5.7   Evolving marketing strategies

Company	Change in strategy
Fitness First	Fitness First Platinum: upmarket with a pool Fitness First Express: pay-as-you-go with no benefits Fitness First for Women: women-only clubs Kaizen: older and non-familiar clients
David Lloyd Leisure	More emphasis on the health and fitness plus racquets facilities: upmarket and the emphasis of current expansion
Virgin Active	Rebranding and refurbishing facilities bought from Esporta and Holmes Place
LA Fitness	Competing in value-for-money segment; low membership fees, plans for brand promotion
Esporta	Plans to consolidate around racquet clubs, which combine with health and fitness facilities
Cannons Health and Fitness	Consolidate existing sites
JJB Health	Aggressive promotion of new and some indoor football facilities
Total Fitness	Promotion as exercise, hydrotherapy and rehabilitation facilities, patient referral, as well as general health and fitness
De Vere	Promotion and investment in Village Leisure Clubs brand, others remaining stable

Source: Mintel (2007).

the commitment for membership schemes. While the degree of private sector supply may vary between countries, it seems likely that similar potential challenges for promoting and facilitating greater overall sports participation will apply, unless policy can both attract participation and also match requisite facilities for participants. The key to achieving this policy balance will be the management of any segments that exist in the market.

5.6 INFORMAL PARTICIPATION

All of the descriptive data above suggests that informal sports activity is one of the most stable and largest segments of the market. This form of participation is the most difficult to classify and to understand because it lies outside the official governance of organized sport. Box 5.5 provides a definition of informal sport.

Consequently, the informal sector is one of changing emphases in which forms of current, officially recognized sports can take place informally or even new "sports" can develop. This is an important point to note because, as discussed in Chapter 2, current formalized sport has its origins in informal activity and such developments continue to occur. For example, in recent years in the UK "five-a-side football" as well as being played in an entirely self-organized manner, has also emerged into a branch of commercially organized activity, facilitated by companies such as PowerLeague Ltd. This has prompted the existing governing body, the FA, to seek to work with such providers, which it has recognized as being the source of much of the investment and growth in participation. The aim is to provide governance and standardization of the "small-sided" game. Similar patterns of development have occurred with other activities.

BOX 5.5 INFORMAL SPORT

Informal sport: this term describes an activity that displays many of the characteristics of "formal sport," but does not involve structured competition governed by rules. So two people playing basketball on their local Outdoor Basketball Initiative site may be said to be engaging in informal sport, because the activity is very close to being what we under-stand basketball to be, but some of the defining characteristics of that sport have been compromised.

Informal sports facilities: these can include skateparks, BMX tracks, basketball courts, kickabout areas and multi-use games areas. Associated facilities may include youth shelters or equipped play areas for younger children.

Source: Sport England, South West (2006)

Bicycle motocross (BMX) began as a non-motorized form of motocross in California in the 1960s, and is still regarded as a street activity associated with youth culture. However, it became an Olympic sport for Beijing 2008 (http:// www.olympic.org). Since January 1993, BMX has been fully integrated into the International Cycling Union (UCI). A similar pattern of development has been experienced in snowboarding, growing again out of "sub-cultural" activity to become an official sport in 1985, with the staging of the first world cup in Austria. To harmonize contests, the International Snowboard Association was founded in 1994. Snowboarding is also now an Olympic sport and stages its own international events.

Examples such as these suggest that the supply of informal sports is potentially quite fluid, but that some movement towards formal organization appears with the desire to hold competitions. This issue is discussed further in the next chapter, when the economic logic underlying the origins of sports clubs and their governance is presented. As far as activity of a purely informal and non-competitive form is concerned, supply will either be facilitated by the public or private sectors, as described above in which many activities, such as swimming, cycling and keep fit, take place either through the newly-developed organizations just described or simply at home or other convenient locations such as parkland and the local neighbourhood.

Under such circumstances, as Chapter 3 discussed in detail, inasmuch as the consumer of sport can also be presented as the producer of sport, through combining time and market goods, then the distinction between a discrete supplier and the consumer disappears. To encourage such participation then, in part at least, is to also encourage its simultaneous supply. Significantly, this might not necessarily involve working through the organized structures of sport. By definition, their formality does not apply. As implied in Section 5.4, therefore, any policy aimed at relaxing the socio-economic constraints on individuals will at least, indirectly, also potentially alleviate the constraints on the supply of informal sport. However, it is noted in DCMS/Strategy Unit (2002) that targeting preferences would be required for individuals that have already shown a reluctance to participate in sports.

It follows also that other policy interventions might be necessary, such as providing appropriate open spaces in which to engage in the relevant activities, such as skate parks, exercise trails, etc., (Sport England, SouthWest, 2006) or providing cycle tracks or lanes. It is clear in this context that "sport" becomes subsumed within the domain of broader social policy in which transport and urban development play a role. This raises some interesting economic issues, connected with the "externalities" that are being used to justify the promotion of sports participation, discussed in Section

5.3. Unless the relevant sport and transport agencies work towards common objectives then a valuable opportunity for progress will be missed. This provides a rationale for the recent changes in sports policy governance in the UK, noted in Chapter 2.

Opportunity costs do arise, however. Table 5.8 below reports the sports club participation rates for a number of activities, including the most widely participated-in activities and traditional team sport activities. The second column provides rates of participation across the population. The last column reports the participation rates of these participants in sports clubs.

It is clear that sports club activity increases most with more specialized competitive sports, yet these involve low proportions of the population. The two largest participation activities, other than walking, are swimming and cycling yet, relatively speaking, there is very little formal sports club activity involving these pursuits. While swimming is catered for in leisure centre provision generally, where activities such as keep fit and even jogging may also be provided, as discussed above these may be more available through private sector provision, which limits opportunities to those able and willing to pay for access to the facilities. In contrast, for the majority of those cycling and others engaging in keep fit and jogging, formal supply opportunities may be limited. While Figure 5.1 described a policy trade-off between elite and mass participation sports, it may well be that a similar trade-off applies between formal, club-based activity and informal activity.

TABLE 5.8   Sports club participation

Sport	Overall participation rate	Sports club participation rate
Swim indoors	13.2	3.0
Swim outdoors	3.0	1.7
Keep-fit	12.8	3.5
Cycling	9.5	1.3
Weight training	5.9	3.8
Football indoors	2.0	12.0
Football outdoors	3.8	21.7
Jogging	5.2	3.6
Cricket	0.6	42.4
Rugby	0.5	61.8
Netball	0.3	24.2

Source: General Household Survey 2002 Own Analysis.

5.7 SPORTS EQUIPMENT

Implicitly the discussion above has centred on facilities provision. As discussed in Chapter 2, however, the derived demand for equipment will also reflect current participation rates and, in turn, be connected to the ability of individuals to supply sports activity. As discussed in Chapter 3 and above, as market goods, along with time, equipment can facilitate sports participation/production. It goes without saying that generally speaking, access to equipment to play golf, sail or mountain bike will be limited according to the ability to pay. In this respect, the private sector market for equipment is a highly diverse and global industry in which multinational brands, such as Nike, Adidas, Trek, etc., compete alongside other more rudimentary brands, such as Dunlop, Hi Tech and unbranded items. Table 4.8, in Chapter 4, provided some comparative data on sports expenditure. Suffice it is to say here that in terms of the UK, Mintel (2005c) suggests that a complex supply chain provides for such expenditure with channels of distribution as indicated in Table 5.9.

It is clear that the majority of sales are made through sports specialists. Mintel (2005c) estimates that 35 multi-outlet groups dominate the market, which also comprises a large number of independent traders. It should be recognized, however, as discussed in Chapter 4, that despite the location of the purchases, many of the purchases are unconnected with participation, particularly in terms of clothing and footwear. Training shoes are often seen as casual wear and the replica kit market is unconnected with participation *per se*. It is more likely that club shops for golf and other team sports and at fitness centres are important suppliers of equipment for participants. This is also more likely with non-club-based activity such as cycling and home gym equipment. As discussed in Chapter 4, however, in general the sports equipment market seems to be one, in the UK at least, which is probably connected with a

TABLE 5.9   Sports good sales

Channel of distribution	% of sales
Sports specialists	74
Club shops	6
Department stores	6
Home shopping	5
Clothing specialists	4
Footwear specialists	3
Others	2

Source: Mintel (2005b).

more individualistic and informal participation in sports than through organized clubs.

5.8 CONCLUSION

In this chapter the supply structure of mass participation sport has been presented as a counterpoint to the previous two chapters, which explored participation in mass participation sport as a consumer demand decision. It is argued that the supply structure is complex, comprising interrelated and also distinct sectors that have changed over time. Because of the lack of international research, primary policy and market research documentation has been used to discuss the UK context as a basis for examining the economics of the supply of mass participation sport. The logic of public sector involvement in sports provision has been discussed as being grounded in externalities. An exploration of the oligopolistic market structure of private sector provision has also been provided. The informal sports sector has been discussed, along with the market for sports equipment.

Despite the obvious differences in emphasis that will apply in other countries, the chapter has highlighted that, in economic terms, policy intervention requires making the case that property rights are incompletely allocated. If this is not the case then the private sector, either through the provision of facilities or individuals engaging informally in sport and purchasing relevant equipment as consumer/producers, will allocate appropriate resources to sport. In the former case pricing and competitive strategies will emerge as with other markets. In such a case, regulation of the market would simply require the usual economic regulation required to ensure that the oligopoly behaviour of the private sector does not become anti-competitive.

If one argues that property rights are incompletely allocated, then a case for policy intervention can be made and presented as based on either efficiency or equity grounds. This is the current policy stance in the UK. In such circumstances, the chapter has examined how policy options might correct for the misallocation of resources by targeting both the demand side and supply side of the market, with a particular focus on facilities. It has been implied in the chapter that the current balance between public and private sector facilities provision leaves the former sector in the potentially difficult role of trying to match competition from the private sector and to meet social welfare objectives.

The chapter has also hinted at another policy tension which is connected to the scale of informal activity unconnected to sports clubs, and which may or may not be met by existing facilities provision. Inasmuch as sports clubs and facilities are the traditional focus of sports policy makers and policy funding, it may be that this simply subsidizes multi-sport participants who are able to access market provision for activities at the cost of other activities that equally could meet the rationale put forward for intervention in sport, such as health, but that because of their less specialized nature may also be more accessible to the currently less active.

Appendix 5.1 Some Elements of Game Theory

Some basic elements of game theory can be illustrated using a hypothetical example of sports clubs. Consider a market in which there are two main suppliers "Health" and "Fitness" who seek to maximize their profits. They have to decide whether or not to increase their profits by attempting to increase their competitiveness, "compete" or remaining as they are "don't compete." This might be through increased marketing activities or price reductions. They recognize, however, that if they undertake such action, then similar competitive retaliation is likely. The "payoff" matrix, which summarizes the impact on profits for each course of action is presented below. The columns summarize "Health's" options and the rows "Fitness" options. Each cell describes the impacts on profits for Fitness and Health, respectively.

		Health	
	Strategies	Compete	Don't compete
Fitness	Compete	−10/−10	+100/−20
	Don't Compete	−20/+100	+20/+20

Now if Health doesn't increase competition, Fitness stands to receive either 20 if it doesn't increase competition or 100 if it increases competition. The same applies for Health. There are strong incentives, then, for both suppliers to increase competitive activity. However, this means that both suppliers end up losing 10. This is a Nash equilibrium. In this case the outcome is suboptimal. It is a well-established result called the "Prisoners Dilemma" and arises because each supplier acts non-cooperatively with the other, but individual incentives dominate collective interests.

Should the game be played iteratively, rather than simultaneously, then clearly in a one-shot context, the firm able to set their strategy first would benefit. This is known as first mover advantage. The above example also indicates another feature of supplier behaviour, which is the existence of incentives to collude rather than to be competitive. If suppliers did agree for example, not to compete, then both would end up better off than the Nash equilibrium. While this seems unlikely in a "one-shot" context, because of the Nash and first mover scenarios, if the decisions were made repeatedly over an infinite horizon, then cooperation, not competition, becomes the rational response. This is because agents realize that any initial competitive advantage would automatically be removed by sustained retaliatory behaviour in the next periods. This is known as a "tit-for-tat" strategy. It follows, then, that collusion is always possible in oligopoly markets, but this may break down with any perceived first mover advantages becoming apparent. As is discussed in the case of professional sports leagues, these scenarios have some credibility.

CHAPTER 6

The Supply of Participant Sport: Volunteers and Sports Clubs

OBJECTIVES

■ To appreciate the structure and diversity of the sports club system
■ To appreciate the motivation, profile and value of volunteers in sport
■ To understand the economic rationale for volunteering and the origins of sports clubs
■ To appreciate policy debate on the organization and financing of voluntary sports clubs

6.1 INTRODUCTION

In the previous chapter various mass participation sport supply opportunities were discussed. One key component of organized sport is the sports club sector which, as was implied in Chapter 2 (see, for example, Figure 2.1), is where much of the formal demand and supply of mass participation sport is located and which acts as a conduit for elite support development. In Section 6.2, although the literature is relatively sparse and dated, some comparative insights are provided on the system in various European countries. It is suggested that there is typically a hierarchical structure to sports club systems in Europe. Section 6.3 then explores the economic logic of the systems, their hierarchical nature and their general economic rationale. Some comment is made on their contribution to social welfare. As volunteers are extremely important to sports club systems, Section 6.4 presents some comparative insight into the motivation for and scale of volunteering. Following this descriptive overview of the sector, Section 6.5 explores the economic logic

147

underlying volunteer activity and its value. The chapter concludes with a discussion of the policy issues concerning sports club systems.

6.2 THE SPORTS CLUB SECTOR

As implied in Chapter 2, Szymanski (2006a) has argued that sports clubs in the UK grew out of "associativity," that is "the tendency of individuals to create social networks and organizations outside of the family" (p. 1) that became possible during the enlightenment of the eighteenth century.

The emphasis of the clubs was on competition. In contrast to the UK, Szymanski (2006a) argues that European sports clubs tended to emphasize individual mental and bodily health through German *Turnen* and Swedish Gymnastics, often overseen by the state with military training as an objective. Heinemann (1999) argues that these three influences gained momentum over traditional folk games and pastimes in various European countries, but ultimately a common form of hierarchical organization emerged based on the English model, often reflecting the promotion of "English" sports. In the US, similar associativity developed through sports clubs, and either evolved into professional activity or remained a community activity with little formal link between them. In the US, therefore, college sports became the link between amateur and professional status for athletes, with local government the agent for overseeing community sport. What follows, then, is primarily a discussion of a European model of development carried over to many other countries. However, elements of the model will apply ubiquitously, such as the links between clubs and their organizing bodies and links to local government.[1]

6.2.1 European hierarchical sports organization

Table 6.1 summarizes some (historical) comparisons between country sports club systems. The main elements of sports governance are listed in the third column and the number of clubs in the sports club system in the fourth column. The resources of the clubs are then indicated in subsequent columns. These are shown to include the providers of facilities, the volunteer base in aggregate and typically per club, together with the sources of monetary funds.

---

[1] An interesting point to note, that is not pursued further in this book, is that current emergent professional sports in countries like China, Korea and Japan adopted elements of the US system of closed leagues and franchises to pool talent, raise competitive levels and have more commercial viability. This model is increasingly the case with developments in European sports, as discussed further in Chapter 7.

TABLE 6.1 European sports structure

Country	Source	Sport governance	Clubs	Facilities provision	Volunteers	Members	Typical funding (approximate)
Italy	Parro et al. (1999)	CONI 39 competitive federations; 16 associated activities; 13 multi-sport networks	CONI – 70 535; Others – 4788	local authorities	701 795		CONI; 90% from betting; sports federations; CONI and 30% from sponsorship
Spain	Puig et al. (1999)	54 sports federations; 600 regional federations	44 509			male predominance (up to 75%); average 200 members	federations; 65% from public sources; clubs; 32%–59% fees; 68%–32.8% sponsorship, lotteries
France	Le Roux and Camy (1999); Carter (2005)	CNOSF; 120 federations; 84 federations	160000; 170 000	municipal	>1 million	average; 60 members	federations; 36% public finance; clubs; 60% public finance
Switzerland	Stamm and Lamprecht (1999)	SOV; 81 sports	28 000			male predominance; 1.5-2 million; average; 60 members; (up to 800 on average)	SOV and federations; lottery and sponsorship
Germany	Horch (1974); Heinemann and Schubert (1999); Carter (2005); Breuer (2007)	DSB; Länder sport associations	80 000; 66 500; (pre-unification); 88 531; >90 000	60% municipal; 68% municipal;	2.6 million; 2.8 million	younger male predominance; average; 300 members; average; 300 members	public finance
Belgium	Taks et al. (1999)	Belgian Olympic and Interfederal Committee (BOIC); 106 sports federations (1999); 80 sports federations (1990)	19 000 [Flanders 1999]; 14 002[a]	56% local authority; 14% private		male predominance (60%); average; 67 members[a]	public finance; clubs; public finance, membership, sponsorship, etc.

TABLE 6.1 (*Continued*)

Country	Source	Sport governance	Clubs	Facilities provision	Volunteers	Members	Typical funding (approximate)
Denmark	Ibsen (1999)	Denmark Sports Federation; Danish Gymnastic and Sports Association; Danish Companies' Sports Federation; Team Denmark	14 000; and 7000 company clubs				95% lottery and pools
Norway	Skirstad (1999)	norwegian olympic committee/norwegian confederation of sports 56 sports federations/committees approx 500 regional sports federations sports clubs	13 113	government (37%) clubs (45%)		male predominance (61%); typically 101–500 members	confederations, etc. gambling revenues clubs facilities 37% income generation 18% fees 14.1% grants
Finland	Koski (1999); Carter (2005)	Finnish Olympic Committee/Finish Sport Federation National district federations sports clubs	7800			male predominance (58%); average 330 members	lottery funding federations 13%–74% public funds clubs facilities municipal funds
UK	Carter (2005)	British Olympic Committee/UK Sport regional sports councils national/regional governing bodies sports clubs	106 423	local authority or private		average 77 members	lottery/public funds lottery/public funds/ commercial grants and commercial income fees
USA	Carter (2005); Slack (1999)	United States Olympic Committee state organization educational-based					sponsorship and donation

a Excludes soccer and cycling.

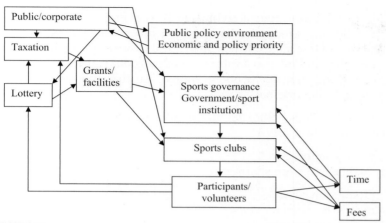

FIGURE 6.1 *The traditional (English) model of European mass sports organization.*

The table reveals that resources in sport are essentially threefold. The first is voluntary labour provided by the members of the clubs in accordance the origins of the club systems. Naturally, fees may be paid by volunteers and/or members. There will be commercial activity by clubs and organizations, embracing hospitality, sponsorship and the commercial use of any assets owned. Finally, there will be public sector payments, such as grants or subsidies, typically funding sport via indirect taxation in the form of lotteries and gambling.

Figure 6.1 provides a stylized model of the system of sport that has emerged in Europe, which shows that even with a relatively small set of stakeholders, a complex set of interactions exists. The vertical structure in the figure indicates the typical governance of sport, while the arrows indicate flows of resources.

From an economic perspective this discussion promotes questions concerning why voluntary sports club systems exist and why they have the broad hierarchical features that are described above.

6.3 THE ECONOMIC FOUNDATION OF SPORTS CLUB SYSTEMS

6.3.1 Club goods

The economic rationale for sports clubs was presented in the previous chapter, where it was argued that the allocation of property rights was important for defining the character of goods in economics, and Figure 5.2 indicated that club goods would exist in situations where consumption was excludable, but non-rival. More formally:

"A club is a voluntary group deriving mutual benefit from sharing one or more of the following: production costs, the member's characteristics, or a good characterized by excludable benefits . . . thus, the utility *jointly* derived from membership and the consumption of other goods must exceed the utility associated with non-membership status." (Cornes and Sandler, 1986 p. 159, italics in original)

Cornes and Sandler's (1986) definition indicates essentially two key elements of club goods. These are:

1. Voluntary action.
2. Mutual benefit from sharing:

    a. production costs
    b. members characteristics
    c. excludable benefits.

These two characteristics distinguish club goods from public goods. In the case of public goods, it would be impossible for individuals to exclude themselves from consumption.[2] However, with club goods, individuals choose to become part of a group to consume the good. Significantly, this suggests that membership enhances the individual's utility. Yet, as the good is consumable collectively and, as choice is involved, this must imply a degree of excludability or, synonymously, that shared consumption can impose costs on the individual.

Reflection Question 6.1

How can sports clubs share production costs, member's characteristics or a good characterized by excludable benefits?

Hint: Think about how competitive sports need to be supplied, why some memberships are not simply connected with paying a membership fee and if sports are public goods.

Consider 2c first: it is clear that excludable benefits could apply to any sports club. Access to facilities and equipment can be controlled by the club through the prior need to become a member. Members can then share their use. Membership might also convey less tangible benefits. In the context of point 2b, it was discussed in Chapter 3 that consumer–producers of sport might invest in personal consumption capital, and social capital and reputation, as part of their choices to participate in sport. Clearly, sports clubs provide an obvious example of this opportunity, in which membership might

---

[2] For example, even if you were a pacifist, you could not avoid "consumption" of a national defence strategy.

reflect a desire to be associated with other members' characteristics, perhaps at the expense of non-members, or between particular sports or clubs within sports. Finally, in the case of 2a it is clear that in sport, competition against other competitors of necessity implies shared production costs. Sports are an example of joint production. Of course, individuals might compete against their own benchmarks, but comparison against other athletes requires, literally, the production of a competition in which other athletes are directly involved. Team sports simply extend this basic principle so that athletes need to work together to produce their own team efforts, to be set against those of another team. It is clear, also, that these elements of club goods might be closely interconnected. Consequently, both 2a and 2b imply that memberships can affect production costs and also the character of memberships.

In club theory, "congestion" can arise, which acts as an exclusion criterion by raising the costs of being a member either through having to ration memberships by paying fees, and/or perhaps reducing the "exclusivity" of the club, and thus potential membership, as discussed in the previous chapter. In summary, therefore, club goods require voluntary choice being undertaken in the context of achieving partially rival benefits with memberships limited because of congestion. It follows that, in terms of social welfare, clubs are efficient if the marginal benefits of membership are equal to the marginal costs of "exclusion."

The basic principles of club theory, and its social welfare implications, can be illustrated in Figure 6.2. In this simple example the assumptions are:

1. membership comprises homogenous individuals maximizing their utility;
2. the population is partitioned into a set of clubs so that all belong to one club supplying the good, but not to other clubs supplying that club;
3. all of the supply of the club good is utilized by members;
4. the club good is partially substitutable by a private good.[3]

Under these circumstances one can present the consumption of club goods for a "representative" individual and club. In Figure 6.2 private goods, for example activities provided by a private sector

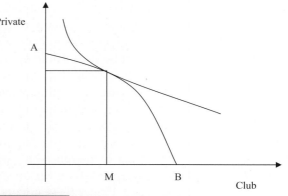

FIGURE 6.2   *The demand and supply of club goods.*

---

[3] The substitutability that underpins these costs may vary. For example in participating in a team sport, such as rugby, one might pay to use a gym in the private sector or use gym facilities provided by the voluntary club in which the team is based, to increase strength.

club, are indicated on the vertical axis, and the club good, for example, activities of a voluntary sports club, on the horizontal axis. The curved line A–B is the production possibilities frontier defined by reallocating resources between the private or club good. The slope of the curve will represent the MRT of the club good with respect to the private good, as discussed in Chapter 5. It represents the opportunity costs of providing a private good or a club good by reallocating resources between the alternative supply opportunities. In this respect, taking the perspective of the sports participant as a consumer–supplier, the resources committed to consume–supply a sports activity might be income and time. The balance between these will differ, depending on whether or not one primarily purchases the activity and simply supplies consumption time to the private sector activity or, in contrast, primarily supplies time to the voluntary club, with minor financial expense.

The indifference curve indicates the preferences of the individual between the goods. Its slope will represent the marginal rate of substitution (MRS) between the alternatives. The point of tangency between the indifference curve and the production possibilities frontier will be the consumer–producers optimum choice. The equilibrium condition will be:

$$\text{MRS}_{\text{(Club-Private)}} = \text{MRT}_{\text{(Club-Private)}}. \tag{6.1}$$

Nested within this condition are two outcomes, reflecting the fact the individual is both a consumer and producer of sports in clubs. The first is that point "M" represents the membership of the club, i.e., the demand. However, it also represents the provision of the club, i.e., its supply. In this respect the demand and supply of the club good is simultaneously determined. If the entire population can be represented by such behaviour, then Equation 6.1 must imply a Pareto optimum.[4]

It is clear that the above representation is extremely abstract, notwithstanding the methodological emphasis of economics described in Chapter 1. It is likely that sports clubs will operate with some spare capacity, that the population will not be completely decomposable into a set of clubs providing that particular activity, and that clubs are also likely to be discriminatory in terms of membership, with some form of hierarchical structure for their governance both within specific clubs and across the sport as a whole as a club good. Under these circumstances, as argued in detail by Cornes and Sandler

---

[4] This proposition is often described as the "integer problem" in club theory (see Cornes and Sandler, 1986). Pareto optimality requires that the entire homogenous population can be a multiple of the representative club, with no one left out. No reallocation of members can then increase efficiency.

(1986) and Sandler and Tschirhart (1997) one cannot make a case *a priori* that clubs are Pareto optimal.

6.3.2 Provision of club goods

While the above discussion explains why clubs might exist, a natural question to ask is why doesn't the public sector provide clubs *per se*?[5] Weisbrod (1978, 1988, 1998) argues that this is because the voluntary, i.e., club sector acts to correct government failure as much as market failure, because of an inability of the government or market to supply sports for heterogeneous activities on a relatively small scale. The public sector will tend to supply goods according to a political rule. Under these circumstances it is likely that some consumers will be left dissatisfied, as simple rules are unlikely to cope with the required variation of preferences. Figure 6.3, derived from Weisbrod (1978), illustrates this situation.

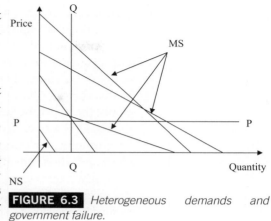

FIGURE 6.3   *Heterogeneous   demands   and government failure.*

In this figure the vertical axis indicates the price of sports and the horizontal axis their quantity. The series of sloped lines, from left to right, represent the demand curves for sports for a series of consumers. With public sector provision each consumer would pay a (tax-based) price of P. Under this rule it is clear that the majority of consumers would like supply to be at least equal to Q. However, this is not the case for the demand by consumers, "NS" who, by having a small demand both receive and pay too much for sport. Likewise, of those whose demands are partially met, a number indicated by MS, would prefer more sport to be supplied at price P. Only the remaining consumer receives their precisely desired amount. The implication is that the MPB and MPC faced by consumers are not, in general, equivalent and consequently are non-Pareto optimal choices.

Consequently, unsatisfied consumers will have an incentive to voluntarily adjust towards an optimum. In a mixed economy NS might have no option but to contribute towards sport provision. However, MS will have an incentive either to enter the market and use the private sector to meet their demands, to form voluntary clubs to do likewise, or to engage in informal activity.

But which of these might it be? This is not a straightforward question to answer. For example, under the conditions of the representation of clubs in Figure 6.2 there is no necessary reason for members of clubs to own the club.

---

[5] Support here is defined generally to include full financing regardless of who actually provides the good, such as contracted agents.

"Under ideal circumstances, any of a number of institutional forms can operate the club efficiently" (Cornes and Sandler, 1986, p.188).

One can argue that the preferences of individuals and the technical conditions of supply seem to be important, coupled with the informational requirements of decisions. It follows that the more homogeneous the demand the greater the possibility that both government and the private sector could supply the sport, because the general ability to meet consumer preferences increases. However, to the extent that individuals prefer control over their consumption, for example, as their incomes rise and they prefer to specify where and when consumption takes place, according to their preferences, then one might expect the private sector to meet such demands increasingly and this might explain the current growth of private sector provision of sports as implied by Weisbrod. This tendency may then be reinforced with excludability in consumption facilitated by supply conditions. Health and fitness clubs, golf clubs and tennis clubs might fit this characteristic, with more opportunities to engage in the activity individually. Synonymously also, the growth in informal sport, which by its nature is extremely heterogeneous in character, i.e., not formally circumscribed, may be understood as a shift in demand away from public sector provision and even that which was previously met by clubs, towards more minority, i.e., highly specific, activities, which also cannot be met by the public sector.[6] However, where joint production is involved, i.e., some form of organized opposition is required, such as in team sports, then voluntary clubs may remain important.

This discussion highlights a complex policy dilemma. It might be argued as is the logic of neoclassical economics that preferences are given to consumers. Under such a perspective it might also be argued that there is inevitability towards any change in supply observed given the technical conditions of the production of the sport, and information problems in public sector provision. On the other hand, if preferences can be viewed as partially endogenous to the economic system, then policy may help to form preferences, and this might subsequently affect choices and supply-side evolution (in the absence of public sector supply of facilities). Yet, as discussed in the previous chapter, in a policy environment in which individual choice and accountability have been championed, then to the extent that this focuses sports participation around individual choice this may, inadvertently, squeeze the resources currently invested in sport through consumer–producers acting as volunteers in the sports system. Significantly, also, to the extent that such a mixed economy prevails, the

---

[6] While characteristics of the activity might be common, e.g. using a skateboard or kicking a football, the context of the activity might be unique and flexible.

welfare implications of changes are not entirely self-evident *a priori*, as with club theory.

An interesting feature of Weisbrod's (1978, 1988) work is the suggestion that one could measure the extent to which an organization can be characterized as supplying club goods. This is through the calculation of the "degree of collectiveness" of an organization's income streams (Weisbrod, 1978, p. 173). The assumption here is that the forms of income for an organization are related to the character of their outputs. In this respect, an index of zero would suggest that the revenue streams are all private sales, and consequently a pure private good is supplied. If the index was 100, then all of the income would be donations, and a club good supplied.

6.3.3 Hierarchical form

The above discussion, while addressing the origin and provision of club goods, does not, of itself, address the question of why a hierarchical governance structure is ubiquitous in sports club systems. It seems reasonable to argue that the overall scale of a sports club system will be decided by the limits of demand from consumer–producers of mass sport, or constraints on supply imposed from current governance. Thus, the regulation of a sport requires definition of the characteristics of the sport and its activities to potential suppliers, as well as control over access to the sports club system. However, while the "English" model of sport requires the rank ordering of competitors, which suggests that the organization of competitions will need to be hierarchical; this does not of itself imply a need for a hierarchical governance structure. An explanation for this must depend on other factors.

Economic theory predicts that hierarchies can be an efficient form of organization relative to voluntary associations or peer groups and market-based economic activity involving contractual relations between all parties. This argument has been developed in a number of seminal contributions by Williamson (1969, 1975, 1981, 1985), and builds on the idea that relevant organizations emerge to minimize the transaction costs required to undertake economic activity. The implication is that resource allocation is essentially facilitated by different forms of "transactions."

Reflection Question 6.2

What are transaction costs?

Hint: There are no transaction costs suggested by the economic model of competition and market exchange discussed in Chapter 1. This is why the "firms" are presented as very small. How might costs arise if the assumptions of this model are relaxed?

BOX 6.1 THE ORGANIZATIONAL FAILURES FRAMEWORK

1. Human attributes:

   a. bounded rationality: implies that economic agents act rationally to pursue their goals, but lack information and ability to fully formulate and solve problems;

   b. opportunism: "extends the assumption of self interest seeking to make allowances to self interest seeking with guile" (Williamson, 1981, p. 1545).

2. Environmental attributes:

   a. uncertainty and complexity of transactions;

   b. frequency of transactions;

   c. the number of transactors;

   d. asset specificity, which concerns the nature of the investment required to undertake transactions and can refer to:

      i. human asset specificity, that key individuals with tacit knowledge or on-the-job training are essential for the transactions;

      ii. physical asset specificity, that key equipment or sites are required for a transaction;

   e. atmosphere, which concerns the perception of the environment in which transactions take place.

Transaction costs are said to arise in economic activity because of the interaction of certain human and environmental characteristics in the organizational failures framework proposed by Williamson to examine the efficiency of economic organizations. Box 6.1 outlines the human and environmental activities considered as central to Williamson's analysis. The approach argues that under certain conditions inefficient transactions can take place, because of inappropriate organizational arrangements. In general, this follows from economic agents acting "opportunistically" to pursue their own self-interest at the expense of others, hence compromising social welfare. This provides incentives, therefore, for new organizational arrangements to be developed to correct this inefficiency. It is suggested, for example, that if the number of parties to a transaction is low, and there is a low frequency of transactions between the parties and that the asset associated with the transaction is highly specific, then market exchange may be inefficient. This is because opportunism creates the possibility of either adverse selection or moral hazard. Examples of these were discussed briefly in Chapter 1.

The organizational failures framework can suggest why hierarchical organization has emerged for sport generally. Figure 6.4 illustrates the case.

Given four parties to a transaction, A, B, C and D, the left-hand side diagram indicates the complexity of transactions that would be required in a system of market exchange, when each party has to trade with each other, or a pure peer-group system of voluntary activity, in which communication

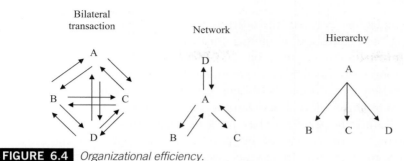

FIGURE 6.4 *Organizational efficiency.*

between all parties is required to organize activities.[7] There are a total number of 12 lines of communication involved in this option. These might be considered to be the range of possibilities in which opportunistic behaviour, i.e., transaction costs and organizational failure can occur.

A limited form of organization, i.e., a network with a coordinator A, is presented in the middle diagram. Here it is clear that the number of lines of communication are halved compared with bilateral transactions. The coordinator role may, of course, rotate in a democratic way, but may require some learning by the relevant party to undertake their coordination activity. In contrast, on the right-hand side diagram is an example of a hierarchy, with an authorized party, A, coordinating activities between B, C and D. Here, the lines of communication are halved once again, from a network down to three. This example indicates the situation in which transaction costs, and the possibility of organizational failure, are minimized. It is this general principle that may help to explain why:

1. sports clubs have hierarchical membership structures and management structures to organize and deliver sport;
2. competition is organized between clubs through governing bodies;
3. different sports, or competitions, are organized by different governing bodies.[8]

The latter case can be said to extend the simple hierarchy of Figure 6.4 and suggests that relative to, say, government funding agencies, different sports

---

[7] This resonates with the earlier discussion in which the market versus voluntary organization can be seen, in logic, as potentially equal alternatives in the absence of further, more detailed discussion of the nature of the economic activity undertaken.

[8] Consequently, the International Olympic Committee may work with different national Olympic committees to oversee governance of the "sport" within different countries. In turn, the national committees work with discrete sport governing bodies.

governing bodies represent the different "divisions" of a multidivisional enterprise. The organizational failures framework argues that such multidivisional structures help to economize on the bounded rationality and information costs faced by strategic managers when seeking to govern complex conglomerate businesses (Williamson, 1971). Economic welfare is thus enhanced by this evolution of organizations.

Significantly, however, this may not be the case with sport *a priori*. It may be the case that, in the absence of the "pure" commercial pressure and financial objectives in sport, the "economic case" being made by policy makers, as opposed to genuine commercial pressure for organizational change, can be limited or muted. This might explain the current hybrid form adopted in the UK in which clearer higher level strategic accountability has been put in place with reorganization, but lower level delivery retains a network structure through county sports partnerships. It may also explain the relative differential emphasis of the hierarchical structures in the European countries discussed in Section 6.2.1.

6.3.4 Economic evaluation

The above discussion has revealed that sports clubs have evolved historically as part of sports systems. In economic terms, their rationale can be understood as meeting the relatively small-scale and heterogeneous demands of consumer–suppliers of goods which are partially excludable but non-rival. The growth of organized sport has brought with it pressure to organize in a hierarchical way; pressures that have increased with a more strategic orientation for sports policy. However, at the same time divergent patterns of demand have emerged which has led to a growth in the private sector consumption of sport and also a growth in informal sports activity. Inasmuch as individual choice is being exercised by consumer–suppliers of sport in these contexts, i.e., either to consume sport informally or through voluntary clubs, or through private sector provision, then it might be argued that the current systems of sports supply is efficient in a Pareto sense. The organizational failures framework reinforces this view inasmuch as it proposes that efficient organizations emerge to provide efficient supply opportunities. However, it has been argued above that the economic efficiency properties of club goods, and particularly those of a complex hierarchical form, as is the case with sport, cannot be presupposed. This is particularly the case in the political economy environment of sports systems, and it seems likely that, in economic terms, sports systems operate in a second best economic sense.

The second best theorem suggests that the welfare implications of policy shifts, in a world not characterized by Paretian optima, require case-by-case consideration and comparison. This is despite a tendency in the economic literature to assume that piecemeal movements toward a more market-oriented supply organization necessarily increase social welfare. In this respect, policy movements towards a more competitive market allocation of resources cannot be presupposed to represent Pareto improvements.

The practical importance of this for policy evaluation is that focus should be on the question of whether or not any new supply arrangements prevent participation in sport that previously used to take place but is not now possible, without a reduction in the welfare of the individuals. It is clear that income redistribution matters in this regard, and this is why equity of access is an important issue in sport. More generally, this discussion implies that there is a real sense in which the policy priorities of public authorities matter and need to be evaluated.[9] Appendix 6.1 outlines the second best theorem.

6.4 VOLUNTEERING IN SPORT

The above discussion has made it clear that voluntary association has been an essential element of mass sport supply through sports clubs. In this section some of the main ideas connected with volunteer motivation, its scale and value is addressed, building on some of the material discussed in Section 6.2. Subsequent sections then indicate how economic theory can be used to explain the choice to volunteer, as well as to calibrate its value. To begin with, the definition of volunteering is discussed.

6.4.1 Defining volunteering

Volunteering is an elusive concept to define as it embraces different kinds of activity in varying degrees and across a variety of sectors of society. Cultural and political contexts also clearly affect volunteering traditions (Lukka and Ellis, 2002; Salamon and Anheier, 1997; UN, 2001). Drawing on Cnaan et al. (1996), it can be argued that four main elements are associated with various definitions of volunteerism. These include: the degree of free will involved in volunteering; the degree of remuneration involved; the structure of

---

[9] Perhaps indirect evidence of this is the tolerance of different societies for different forms of sports system. Of course, none of this precludes that more general tendencies are evident in sports systems. The point is that despite these tendencies, say, towards market-based supply, economic efficiency does not necessarily increase. The exclusion of previous participants in sport because of, say, price changes that follow a regime change in supply, may thus imply a welfare loss rather that be indicative of an optimal reallocation of resources by the consumer–supplier.

volunteering; and the intended beneficiaries of the volunteer act (see Cuskelly et al., 2006). From the point of view of the limited formal analysis and empirical research that exists, a variety of specific definitions are used. In Australia, the Australian Bureau of Statistics (2005) defines a volunteer as:

". . . someone who willingly gave unpaid help, in the form of time, services or skills, through an organization or group within Australia. People who did voluntary work overseas only are excluded. The reimbursement of expenses in full or part (e.g., token payments) or small gifts (e.g., sports club t-shirts or caps) are not regarded as payment of salary, and people who received these are still included as volunteers. However, people who received payment in kind for the work that did . . . are excluded." (Australian Bureau of Statistics, 2005, p. 4)

In Canada a volunteer is:

". . . any individual who volunteered, i.e., who willingly performed a service without pay, through a group or organization during the 12-month reference period preceding the survey." (Research Centre or Sport in Canadian Society/Centre for Sport Policy Studies, 2005, p. 10)

The latter study argues that the UK has been at the forefront of volunteer research in sport. In this regard, as indicated by Nicholls (2004), two definitions are potentially relevant. The first reflects the 1997 National Survey of Volunteering. Here, volunteering is defined as:

". . . any activity which involves spending time, unpaid, doing something that aims to benefit (individuals or groups) other than or in addition to, close relatives, or the benefit of the environment." (Institute for Volunteer Research, http://www.ivr.org.uk/researchbulletins/bulletins/1997-national-survey-of-volunteering-in-the-uk.htm Accessed December, 2007)

The second is specifically concerned with sport as proposed by Gratton et al. (1997). Here volunteering reflects:

". . . individual volunteers helping others in sport, in a formal organization such as clubs or governing bodies, and receiving either no remuneration or only expenses." (Gratton et al., 1997 p. i)

It is clear that, with the exception of the Institute for Volunteer Research definition, the emphasis has been on formal volunteering. In contrast, LIRC (2003) redefined sports volunteering for the UK to be:

". . . individual volunteers helping others in sport and receiving either no remuneration or only expenses." (LIRC, 2003 p. 6)

The shift in emphasis of the UK definition was to recognize the importance of informal contributions to sport. It should be noted, however, that given the relatively small amount of research on sports volunteering, in general the common emphasis is to emphasize free choice, with volunteers only receiving reimbursement of expenses at most, and activity taking place within a formal organization.

6.4.2 Motivation and constraints on volunteering

In descriptive empirical research the specific reasons individuals give for why they volunteer their time and skills are quite varied. Table 6.2 indicates some of these reasons according to reviews undertaken by the sources indicated in the first row of the table.[10] Both motivations to volunteer and the benefits from volunteering are noted. It is possible to review statements such as those in Table 6.2 and to argue that, while some distinctions in the motivations and benefits for volunteering exist, they also include common reasons such as: contributing to the sport and the community, particularly in the context of family connections; generating friendship, as well as experiencing new things; and developing new skills. The enhancement of personal development and employment prospects are also commonly cited. Interestingly, such a perspective implies a degree of altruism, but also self-interest, in the sense of enhancing the individuals's own identity and social standing, and generating skills for employment prospects (see also Cuskelly et al., 2006). This has implications for the economic analysis of volunteering discussed later.

Much of the research on volunteering also suggests that the voluntary sector is facing increasing constraints. This was mentioned earlier in Section 6.2, when discussing sports clubs. To begin with, Weed et al. (2005) note that the changes to the sports club sector have led to tensions, because of the need to operate in an increasingly commercial environment with the consequent individualization of sport activity, and because of a focus on professionalism in supply coupled with the incorporation of sports into public policy, with the consequent focus on accountability and service provision in the light of receiving public funds. These tensions particularly centre on a conflict between the traditional, but informal, associativity facilitated by volunteering, which might enhance social capital and citizenship as well as support sport, and the pressures for more formal management and organization, which run counter to this ethos. The latter may, thus, lead to a reduction in volunteer commitment and recruitment. Table 6.3 presents the types of constraints on volunteering stated in the descriptive empirical literature. The interpretation of such constraints in economic terms is considered below, after the patterns and scale of volunteering are discussed.

---

[10] It should be noted that these motivations may be associated with countries other than the source of the claim.

TABLE 6.2 Volunteer motivations and benefits

LIRC (2003)	Australian Bureau of Statistics (2005)	Research Centre or Sport in Canadian Society/Centre for Sport Policy Studies (2005)
Motivations		
Shared enthusiasm for the sport	Learning new skills	The opportunity to help others
Affiliation to their club	Gaining training	Contributing to a valuable area
Social rewards from volunteering	Helping others	Having fun
Giving something back/duty	Increasing enthusiasm and energy	Promoting and maintaining sports
Involvement with own children	Sharing talents, abilities and experience	Contributing where a family participates
Enjoyment	Fighting boredom	Contributing to the community
Wanting the club to do well:	Making new friends	Using skills
■ *No replacement/no one else*		
■ *Fear club will collapse*		
Love of the club/sport:	Building self-confidence	Learning new skills
■ *Grew up with the club*		
■ *Progression of involvement*		
Wanting to keep the club going	Exploring career opportunities	Companionship and friendship
Wanting to see youngsters/team get better	Feeling needed, useful and appreciated	
Using time while children participate	Gaining a new direction in life	
Wanting a challenge	Giving something back to the community	
Maintaining involvement after playing	Being a team member	
Personal development	Getting closer to the sport or activity an organization represents	
To find out about the club	Contributing to the sport or activity	
To do something in retirement	Having fun and enjoying themselves	
Benefits		
Social benefits		Gained fundraising skills
Enjoyment		Learned coaching, judging, refereeing and officiating techniques
Fulfilment from helping others		Acquired organizational and managerial skills
Satisfaction		Increased knowledge
Pride in helping the club and its participants do well		Helped to succeed in paid job
Satisfaction from keeping the club going		Helped chances of finding a job
Achievement, rewarding, challenge		Helped to find employment
Satisfaction from seeing youngsters succeed/get better		Made new friends, contacts
Sense of belonging to the club and wider community		Promoted services and business
Opportunity to gain new skills and personal development		Developed network of influence
Uses time while children participate		

TABLE 6.3 Volunteer constraints

LIRC (2003)	Australian Bureau of Statistics (2005)	Research Centre or Sport in Canadian Society/Centre for Sport Policy Studies (2005)
Lack of time	Lack of skills, training and experience	Lack of time
Too old	Lack of understanding of volunteering	Lack of interest
Demands of job	Low income levels	Not aware of volunteering opportunities
Family commitments	Limited life experience	Not asked
Children grew up	Lack of acceptance	Did not know how to get involved
Help no longer wanted	Lack of child care	Financial costs
Not enough other volunteers	Lack of time	Concern over being sued
The work is left to fewer people	Cost and availability of transport	Unwilling to make a commitment
Requires specialist skills	Geographic isolation	Contributions not recognised
The club is asking more, because of governing body organizational pressure	Language and cultural barriers	Family obligations
Feel that efforts are wasted	A need for higher levels of formal education and training	Dissatisfaction with experience
No appreciation or thanks for your efforts for the club		No supervision
Stopped playing the sport		

6.4.3 The profile and scale of volunteering

Table 6.4 presents some broadly comparative results on sport volunteers. It is clear that sports' volunteering is dominated by males between the ages of 20 and 50 years, predominantly in full-time work and, with the exception of the UK, with children in the household. Significantly and perhaps related to the latter point, the weekly hours of volunteering are much higher in the UK. There is some evidence that other sports activity is more important to sports volunteers than other activities and volunteering. In fact, the Research Centre for Sport in Canadian Society/Centre for Sport Policy Studies (2005) identifies that male volunteering tends to be associated directly with the sport, for example, coaching, training and officiating, whereas female activities are more diverse. There is also indirect evidence of this for the UK, according to LIRC (2005) in which the preponderance of activities are dominated by coaching, administration, officiating and fund raising, and males make up the majority of volunteers.

In the light of earlier expressed concerns about constraints in volunteering, the changing significance of volunteering activity to the sports economy can be revealed when considering some comparative data on trends in volunteering.

TABLE 6.4 Volunteer profiles[a]

LIRC (2003)	Australian Bureau of Statistics (2005)	Research Centre or Sport in Canadian Society/Centre for Sport Policy Studies (2005), Cuskelly et al. (2006) [b]
Gender	Gender	Gender
■ Male 67%	■ Male 62%	■ Male 86 % (64%)
■ Female 33%	■ Female 38%	■ Female 14 % (36%)
Age	Age	Age
■ 16–24 28%	■ 18–24 12%	■ < 25 4% (<24 19%)
■ 25–34 22%	■ 25–34 18 %	■ 25–34 6% (13%)
■ 35–44 21%	■ 35–44 29 %	■ 35–44 52% (41%)
■ 45–59 19%	■ 45–59 28%	■ 45 + 39% (27%)
■ 60–69 10%	■ 60–69 8%	
	■ 70 + 4%	
Children	Children	Children
■ Yes 32%	■ Yes 64%	■ Yes 94%
■ (22% 5–15 years old)	■ (53 % 5–15 years' old)	
■ No 68%	■ No 36%	■ No 6%
Employment	Employment	Employment
■ Full time 56%	■ Full time 59%	■ Full time 65% (Full or part-time 84%)
■ Part-time 14%	■ Part-time 22%	■ Education 16%
■ Retired 9%	■ Unemployed 2%	■ Retired 3%
■ Full time education 10%	■ Not in labour	■ Non working 13% (16%)
■ Non working 11%	■ Force 17%	
Hours volunteered per week		Hours volunteered per year
■ Formal and informal 4 hours		■ < 12 hours 15%
■ Formal 5.3 hours		■ 10–25 hours 54%
Non-sport volunteers as well	Non-sport volunteering activity	■ 26–50 hours 22%
■ Formal and informal 15%	■ Participate in sport 69%	■ > 51 hours 9%
■ Formal 14%	■ Participate in non- organized activity 14%	
	■ Attended sports events 77%	

[a] Percentages are rounded
[b] The data for Canada from the primary source focus on team sports and are based on a relatively small-scale pilot study. More general data are provided in the source in parenthesis.

Cuskelly et al. (2006) argue that in Canada volunteering fell by 13% (from 7.7 million to 6.2 million) between 1997 and 2000, although average volunteer hours rose by almost 9% (from 149 hours per year to 162 hours per year). In contrast in Australia, while there was a 24% increase in volunteer numbers between 1995 and 2000, volunteer hours fell by 20% in sports volunteering. Finally, Gratton et al. (1997) and LIRC (2003) argue that volunteering hours increased by approximately 45% (from 183 million to 266 million) between

1995 and 2002, while the number of volunteers increased by approximately 35% (from 1.49 million to 2.01 million).[11] However, it should be recognized that this comparison includes volunteering in education and events. Focusing purely on sports clubs and national governing bodies, volunteer hours increased by approximately 40% (from 170 million to 237 million) and volunteers by 33% (from 1.19 million to 1.6 million) (LIRC, 2003, p. 22). The implication is that volunteering is essential to the supply of sports and "remains the bedrock of opportunity in many sports" (LIRC, 2003, p. 33).

One of the key findings from the comparative data is it would appear that for the UK, more hours per volunteer are being required to support sport. However, in Canada total volunteer hours fell from 1147.3 million to 1053 million, while in Australia they increased from 517.7 million to 704.1 million hours. The broader implication of these trends is that, in the absence of new volunteers, existing volunteers have to work harder. More generally, more volunteer effort, if not volunteers, might be required to support at best, as was discussed in Chapter 4, static participation in sport. It is clear, therefore, that a "supply-side constraint" is tightening in sports systems.

6.5 AN ECONOMIC ANALYSIS OF VOLUNTEERING

The economic analysis of volunteering can proceed readily from the theory of the consumer–producer developed in Chapter 3, although this brings with it some interesting issues for debate. To begin with the general motivation implied in consumer theory is utility maximization. This implies self-interested behaviour in consuming as many goods and services that are possible. Is this reconcilable with voluntary and altruistic motives? Becker (1976, 1992) emphasizes that utility is the welfare of the individual as defined by them and is not tied, neither is economic analysis generally, to the specific nature of the material under investigation. In this respect, drawing on Becker (1974), one can identify that charity or altruism, which is implied in voluntary acts of giving donations of goods or time to other individuals or organizations, can be examples of utility maximization, as individuals optimize on the use of resources that raise their well-being. This might help to explain why, as noted earlier, both self-interest and altruism arise as common motives stated by volunteers.[12]

---

[11] This is just for formal volunteers, to control for the definitional change of volunteering between the two pieces of research.

[12] This is not to suggest that such an analysis is without criticism. For example, Becker's analysis is a form of meta ethics, in which morality or virtuous or envious behaviour is treated as a special case of a broader, but nonetheless specific, utilitarian approach.

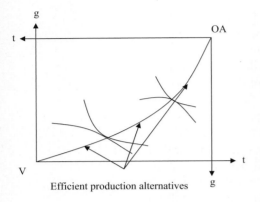

Efficient production alternatives

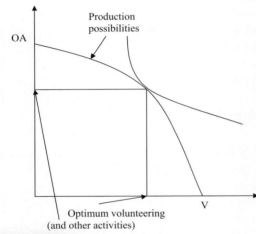

FIGURE 6.5 *The volunteer decision.*

In this framework, the resources that the individual has at their disposal are goods bought on markets, x, and time, t. It is clear that volunteering will be a time- rather than goods-intensive activity. Therefore, it is not surprising, as described above, for time to be identified as a fundamental constraint by volunteers on their level of activity.

The other major constraints identified by volunteers are connected with organizational experiences, such as lack of appreciation or supervision, or poor relationships with other organizations. While recognized as constraints by volunteers, lack of appreciation can be connected with a reduction of individual welfare identified by volunteers. This might arise directly from reductions in the benefits received from an activity in which tacit or literal appreciation was expressed, or indirectly from the failure to receive benefit transfers from others, through their allocation of resources to the individual concerned. This naturally also applies to lack of supervision, or poor relationships with other organizations which also may imply a need, on behalf of the volunteer, to commit more of their own time or goods to activities to overcome these problems.

Consequently, volunteering can be understood from the economic perspective of the consumer–producer discussed in Chapter 3. This approach also implies how the value of volunteering can be inferred. To illustrate this Figure 6.5 is derived, based on a number of assumptions described below.[13]

1. The individual has two basic commodities that can be consumed–produced: volunteering "V" and other activities "OA."
2. Both volunteering and other activities are produced from the commitment of time, "t," and market goods, "g," which are given in supply.
3. The production functions are:

$$V = V(g, t)$$

---

[13] This is an example of the optimizing behaviour outlined in Chapter 3, Section 3.2.4.

and:

$$OA = OA(g, t)$$

4. The consumer's utility is a function of V and OA so that:

$$U = U(V, OA)$$

In this analysis the consumer's marginal utility with respect to V and OA are assumed to be positive but diminishing. Further, in an analogous manner, the level of output of V and OA can be described by a set of isoquants which indicate equal levels of output of each commodity, given the use of resources of time and market goods to produce them. The shape and slope of the iso-quant reflects that the production function exhibits positive but diminishing marginal productivity associated with each of the inputs to the production function. The slope of the isoquant is referred to as the marginal rate of technical substitution (MRTS) between the inputs.

The box at the top of Figure 6.5 illustrates the production functions for each of the basic commodities, volunteering (V) and other activities (OA). The production of V begins at the origin in the bottom left-hand corner of the box, and increases in a northeasterly direction as more time and goods are committed to production. The isoquants measuring equal levels of output for different combinations of input are drawn convex to this origin and slope down from left to right. In contrast, OA begins at the origin in the top right-hand corner of the box, and increases in a southwesterly direction as more time and goods are committed to production. The isoquants measuring equal levels of output for different combinations of input are drawn convex to this origin and also slope down from left to right.

Reflection Question 6.3

Which points in the box will indicate productive efficiency?

Hint: Think about the use of inputs to produce a given level of output.

Note that the box implies that the fixed endowments of goods "g" and time "t" can be allocated either to the production of V or of OA. An efficient allocation of these inputs to the production of either V or OA must, therefore, ensure that all of the resources are employed and that the outputs of either of the basic commodities are as high as possible. Points in the box that satisfy this property are on the curved line joining the origins. These are where the MRTS of time and goods are equal in the production of both V and OA for the individual. In each of these cases it would be impossible to reallocate goods and time to increase production of V or OA without reducing the output of OA or V, respectively.

This curve can thus be used to derive the production possibilities for V and OA, which is drawn in the lower part of Figure 6.5. Conceptually, it maps out the alternative combinations of V and OA implied for alternative efficient allocations of "g" and "t" for the production of alternative levels of V and OA. The slope of the curve is the marginal rate of transformation (MRT) of V and OA, and is the rate at which each good can be substituted by reorganizing the production activity of the individual, while being efficient. The indifference curve of the individual is then drawn to indicate that the optimal choice between V and OA is where the MRT and MRS of V and OA are equal. Analogous to the discussion of club goods, this is where the marginal benefits of consuming V and OA are equal to the opportunity costs of producing V and OA. Indeed, it should be clear that the amounts of V and OA consumed and produced become equivalent where:

$$MRSV_{,OA} = MRTV_{,OA} = MRTSV_{,OA} \tag{6.2}$$

It follows that the marginal value of volunteering can be implied as the opportunity cost of OA foregone. This suggests a substantial difficulty in valuing volunteer activity in practice. It might be tempting to use the opportunity cost of time only as an approach. This is to directly apply the income–leisure approach of Chapter 3, illustrated in Figure 3.3, where it is identified that the wage rate is equivalent to the opportunity cost of time in leisure. In this regard, by analogy, one might argue that voluntary time – as a form of leisure – has the same opportunity cost. Indeed, this is the approach often adopted in practice in empirical work in which a volunteer hour is multiplied by an appropriate wage rate, or volunteers are asked to impute a value of compensation for their time, if not working. These individual valuations can then be aggregated. Table 6.5 presents some examples from sport.[14]

In this respect LIRC (2003) note that:

"The valuation of the hours of volunteering is at the average hourly
earnings for all industries for 2002 of £11.69 ... It is the value of the
hypothetical cost of replacing ... the sports volunteers with paid labour."
(LIRC, 2003 p. 14)

---

[14] Other examples apply outside sport, such as Wolff et al. (1993). Davies (2004) discusses some other examples from sport.

TABLE 6.5   The value of volunteering

Author	Country	Value
Taks et al. (1999)	Belgium	10 billion (Belgian francs)
Heinemann (1999)	(West) Germany	6 billion (Deutschmarks)
LIRC (2003)	England	14.1 billion (£)

The assumption here is that while the individual may not necessarily substitute work and volunteering, one must identify what the alternative might be if the volunteer did not offer their time, i.e., having to pay the opportunity cost for someone else with equivalent skills. As Freeman (1997) argues, however:

"*A priori*, one might expect that volunteers would consist largely of people with low opportunity cost of time – low-wage workers or the jobless . . . But . . . few . . . demographic contrasts between volunteers and non-volunteers are consistent with a simple opportunity cost explanation of volunteering." (Freeman, 1997 p. 146, italics in original)

This suggests that a more sophisticated "average cost" based on the volunteers' socio-economic profiles and the industrial sectors in which they work is appropriate. The reason for this is because of the skill differences and the fact that not all volunteers work (Brown, 1999). However, this raises the important conceptual point that once human capital is considered then the opportunity cost of time *per se* is not an adequate representation of the value of volunteering (leisure in this context). To repeat a discussion was raised in Chapter 3:

"It is easily shown that the usual labour–leisure analysis can be looked on as a special case . . . in which the cost of the commodity called leisure consists entirely of foregone earnings and the cost of other commodities entirely of goods." (Becker, 1965 p. 98)

Consequently, unless an attempt is made to estimate the opportunity costs of volunteering in terms of not just the allocation of work time, but also contingent on human and social capital investments, then the estimates are likely to be biased.

Conceptually, a model should be specified to analyze the set of decisions to consume other goods, to go to work or not, and to volunteer within the context of a household. On the basis of this model one could, in principle, identify a properly weighted monetary equivalent to volunteer hours. Freeman (1997) provides an analysis of volunteering generally in which utility depends on goods, leisure time and charity which, in itself, is produced by the inputs of volunteer time and donations. Based on data from the US from the 1989 Current Population Survey, and the 1990 Gallup Survey of Giving and Volunteering in the US, regression analysis suggests that including a "charitable production function" is more consistent with the evidence than an approach in which all volunteer hours are treated as equivalent.

No such work has been undertaken in sport. The very limited multivariate work that exists focuses less on the value of volunteer time and more on the choice to undertake volunteer activity. It is also based on small sample sizes, consistent with the difficulties in data collection. Wilson (2004) examines the choice of 112 volunteers in Athletic clubs in the southeast of England to enter a coach education programme. Broadly it is shown that time constraints and household patterns of activity matter, but these are different for the genders. For example, with participation in sport females have to trade-off coaching opportunities. In general, however, as noted above, working is positively associated with volunteering, which challenges a simple opportunity cost of time analysis.

Burgham and Downward (2005) analyzed data on 126 individuals (63 males and 60 females) including swimming volunteers, as well as non-volunteers, at facilities in which swimming clubs were operating. It was identified that increasing age, having previously been a swimmer and having children swimming were the main factors that promoted the likelihood of becoming a volunteer. There was some indication that full-time work reduced this likelihood. Based on the subsample of 58 volunteers, it was shown that being female, in full-time work, with a higher salary increased hours per week volunteered. The same was the case for having previously been a swimmer and having children currently swimming. However, the hours worked per week and having children not connected with swimming reduced the hours volunteering. The upshot is that, as implied with the participation literature reviewed in Chapter 4, personal consumption capital is generally also important to promoting volunteering. The obvious recruitment pool for volunteers is participants, as implied by the consumer–producer model.

There is some evidence, also, that the decision to volunteer is not the same decision as committing hours to volunteering in sports participation, i.e., the duration of the activity, as also argued in Downward and Riordan (2007). In this respect there is some evidence that the income–leisure trade-off is important for volunteering. While higher incomes and full-time work can promote volunteering, the hours worked constrain this opportunity. Not surprisingly, females volunteer more as they were less likely to be in full-time work. This suggests that household allocation of time is important in volunteering, as also implied by the consumer–producer model.

As the above analyses are small-scale, although their basic descriptive characteristics are in line with larger descriptive studies, the implication is that volunteering provides a fertile area for future research.

6.6 POLICY IMPLICATIONS

The previous section suggests that economics would support the view that if the benefits of volunteering were falling and the opportunity costs increasing, it is likely that individuals will reallocate time and market goods to the consumption and production of other activities. The discussions above indicated that there is some evidence of the substitutability of sports volunteering with sports participation and other consumption activities, but also that a potentially increasing supply constraint in volunteering is evident in the sense that more total hours are being required to support static participation levels. Inasmuch as the age profiles of volunteers are concentrated around the middle aged and that there is a growth in informal and commercialized forms of sport consumption, then this supply constraint may or may not be a problem.

If one adopts the perspective that the consumer–producer always allocates resources optimally then, notwithstanding the discussion of second best earlier, one might argue that the various sectors of mass sports supply could be said to be adjusted to an optimum level. However, the analysis above suggested that the sports club system is based on the supply of older volunteers. Chapter 4 indicated that the demand for sports club activities is more likely for younger participants. Traditionally, therefore, an "intertemporal" supply chain could be said to have existed in which consumer–producers shift more from participation in, to provision of, sport. This suggests a possibility of potential disequilibrium that might persist as participants' age. Over time, it might be the case that volunteering and participation in non-club sports activities become more substitutable, because of the growth in emphasis of individual consumption. In this sense, there is likely to be excess demand from newer generations of sports participants, because the supply of volunteering shrinks. If the sports club system is considered to be important to social welfare, then active support may be required from the public sector to prevent its reduction. Sports clubs also need to ensure that participants remain involved as volunteers. However, as discussed earlier, it is not entirely clear that the public sector can adequately supply club goods, or that volunteers welcome more formal systems of management as they are required to be accountable for funding. The outcome may be, then, that a welfare judgement needs to be made that increased inefficiency in supply, either through informational problems of matching supply to demands or a lack of monitoring and reduced formal accountability, is a price worth paying for overall higher participation levels. Such decisions seem to be inevitable in a second best economic scenario.

6.7 CONCLUSION

In this chapter, elements of the broadly hierarchical sports systems typical in Europe, and, by implication components of hierarchical sports systems else-where, have been presented. It is noted that sports clubs and voluntary labour are a central feature of these systems. It is argued that the traditional English concept of sport lends itself to hierarchical sports competitions but, of itself, this does not account for the hierarchical governance structures in sport. It is argued that voluntary sports clubs emerge as a result of both government and market failures, but in theory they can only be efficient in a second best welfare sense because of the restrictive assumptions implied by efficiency with club goods. It is argued that hierarchical governance structures can be explained in terms of the organizational requirements of sport and the need to govern sport strategically. In this respect, policy initiatives that seek to increase the accountability of sports organizations can add to this impetus and efficiency gains can be made.

However, there is a potential shortfall in volunteer activity for sports club systems. This may be exacerbated by the increased time costs imposed on volunteers in more formal systems of accountability. Furthermore, if the public sector promotion and support of sports club participation becomes increasingly required this will involve potential inefficiencies. In this regard, contrary to the claim stressed that the public sector in the UK should provide efficiency, economy and effectiveness; these may best be viewed as partially contradictory objectives.

Appendix 6.1 The General Theory of Second-Best

"The general theorem for the second best optimum states that . . . in a situation in which there exist many constraints which prevent the fulfilment of the Paretian optimum conditions, the removal of any one constraint may affect welfare or efficiency either by raising it, by lowering it, or by leaving it unchanged." (Lipsey and Lancaster, 1956–1957, pp. 11–12)

To illustrate this proposition, reconsider Equation 6.1. If there are two individuals in an economy with different tastes then two different club memberships would be derived in each case. Consider now that person A consumes–supplies more of the club good than person B. Assume that the government imposes a sales tax on the club and private sector supply of sports to raise revenue. An optimum tax-raising strategy would be to tax the club good at a greater rate than the private good for person A and *vice versa* for person B. Suppose that the government decides to employ a uniform tax rate to ensure that Paretian conditions are met, that both consumers face the same set of prices, and that the same amount of revenue be raised. In this case, both consumers would be forced onto lower indifference curves, reducing welfare. Figure A6.1.1 illustrates the proposition in which it is possible to show that the equilibrium situation for each person while paying a uniform price, indicated by the diagonal constraint linking the axes, suggests a lower indifference curve than could be possible for less consumption of the preferred good at a differential, i.e., higher tax price for each of them, as illustrated by the constraints of different slopes.

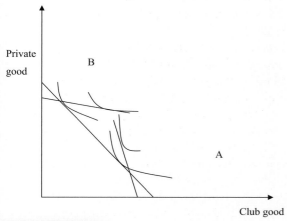

FIGURE A6.1.1   *The second-best theorem.*

CHAPTER 7

The Market for Professional Sports: General Themes

- To understand the origin of professional sports
- To analyze sports as economic contests
- To explore and understand the peculiar economics of professional sports
- To compare and contrast European and US leagues and their sources of finance
- To consider sports leagues as monopolies or cartels
- To consider the evolution of sports leagues

7.1 INTRODUCTION

In this chapter attention turns towards the analysis of professional team sports, with Section 7.2 discussing briefly the transition of sports from an amateur to professional status. Section 7.3 then outlines a more general set of principles that underpin the nature of sports competition as an economic contest and links this discussion to the design of sporting competitions, particularly league and cup competitions, and other forms of tournaments. Drawing on this discussion, Section 7.4 outlines key concepts that have been applied in the analysis of professional team sports, and provides a sketch of the development of more recent forms of competitions. The discussion indicates the importance of the underlying economic components of sports leagues and their potential need to coordinate results, as well as their sources of revenues and costs. Section 7.5 closes the discussion with a comparison of European and US sports leagues.

7.2 THE TRANSITION TO PROFESSIONALISM

7.2.1 Sports clubs: Key concepts revisited

Chapter 6 argued that sports clubs evolved historically along with sports systems to meet the relatively small-scale and heterogeneous demands of consumer–suppliers of goods which are partially excludable but non-rival. Sports clubs are examples of club goods, with individuals choosing (in practice subject to exclusion criteria) to become part of the collective group to consume–produce both the sports activity and membership to enhance their utility. In this respect, the club acts to internalize the externality of non-rival benefits by controlling access to the sport, facilities, equipment and reputation benefits provided by the club.[1]

Of specific importance to sports clubs is that the consumption–production of the sports activity requires the sharing of production costs in supply, not only with regard to the running or administration of the club but, more fundamentally, sport is a prime example of joint production, when individuals are competing against others. Here, competitors need to cooperate to facilitate sport, either within the club or across clubs as part of a sports system. In this regard, team sports simply extend this basic principle to the case in which opponents operate as groups rather than as individuals. Equations 7.1 and 7.2 summarize this relationship in the form of a production function which, as detailed in Chapter 1, describes the production of output from the use of inputs. Equation 7.1 recognizes that a sports contest within a club (subscript "wc") requires the club's land and capital and the efforts of two competitor members, A and B.

$$\text{Contest}_{wc} = \text{Contest}_{wc}(\text{Land}, \text{Capital}, \text{Competitor}_A, \text{Competitor}_B) \quad (7.1)$$

$$\text{Contest}_{12} = \text{Contest}_{12}(\text{Land}_{c1}, \text{Capital}_{c1}, \text{Competitor}_{c1}, \text{Competitor}_{c2}) \quad (7.2)$$

Equation 7.2 shows that in a sports contest between clubs 1 and 2 with subscript "12", signifying that club 1 is the "home" club and club 2 the "away" club that competition emerges from the use of the labour efforts of competitors from each club, c_1 and c_2 respectively, and the land and capital of one of the clubs, in this case c_1.

As the discussion above reveals some general conceptual features of sports club competition, it follows that changes in the form of consumption and production of contests will occur with a move from voluntary to professional sports. The following sections address these issues in more detail; the discussion begins with an examination of the transition of clubs to professionalism through a process of formalization.

---

[1] As discussed earlier, externalities arise whenever the consumption or production acts of individuals directly affect the utility or objectives of other economic agents, rather than being mediated by the market system.

7.2.2 Formalization

In amateur sports participants can be viewed as consumer–producers, because they combine voluntary time plus membership fees and other donations and expenses to fund the supply of the sports activity in which they typically participate. Szymanski and Zimbalist (2005) confirm this in connection with baseball in the US. In their original format the typical form of contest in clubs occurred between relatively close communities and, in many respects, the specific event was significant as a relatively infrequent gathering between communities. In early baseball games large social events coincided with the games. In order for the sports to grow and to develop, however, formalization was required in terms of defining the nature of the sport, i.e., the rules of the contest, and in deciding how contests could be organized. In economic terms this meant that the product needed to be defined and made sufficiently homogenous so that (a potential) large-scale demand could develop and supply become organized to meet it.

As discussed in Chapter 2, the emergence of the Football Association (FA) in 1863 began the formalization of association football, and likewise the Rugby Football Union (RFU) was established in 1871. Much earlier, in 1858, the National Association of Baseball Players (NABBP) had emerged in the US, initially:

"... to preserve the social values that they believed in and had little interest in fostering the expansion of the game ..." (Szymanski and Zimbalist, 2005, p. 19)

However, three subsequent and interrelated developments can be said to have eroded this perspective, which heralded the onset of professionalism and brought about the formation of hierarchical and commercial governance. The first was the development of organized competition. Commensurate with the establishment of governing bodies of sport, in England, knockout cup competitions soon developed, as discussed in Chapter 2. A key function was to formally amalgamate the informal growth in the supply of clubs in England that had taken place typically through county-based organizations. Local rivalries became popular spectacles and, not surprisingly, gave rise to payment to watch the games. Similar developments arose in the US with the widespread growth of baseball, although in a less structured way. As Szymanski and Zimbalist (2005) note, by the 1860s most US states had baseball clubs and "barnstorming" competitions including touring clubs with crowds in excess of 5000 spectators. In general, teams could organize their own fixtures.[2]

---

[2] Prior to the Civil War, English cricket sides (not representative) had fairly regularly toured the US, playing local teams on a relatively informal basis.

However, a growing demand for a more homogenous sports' contest raises both the incentive for, and the possibility of, organizing a team for commercial motives, to access payment by spectators. This naturally carried with it the need to build stadiums and venues to extract revenue.[3] In turn, accessing paying spectators for commercial gain raised the second stimulus towards professionalism, which was that it provided an incentive to pay players, i.e., to attract the best talent to a team to enhance the prospects of success.

For example, while the FA was initially founded on amateurism, by 1888 the English Football League (EFL) was established and accepted by the FA to prevent schism, consequently the payment of players was accepted in soccer for those residing within a six mile radius of a club in 1885.[4] By 1895 it had become the case that players could only be transferred between clubs for the payment of a fee agreeable to the existing employer as part of the "retain and transfer system," while in the face of rising wage rates a maximum wage was established in 1900.[5] In contrast, differences occurred in rugby football because of the northern rugby union clubs offering "broken-time" payments to compensate for loss of earnings. This led to a split in the RFU and the formation of the Rugby Football League (RFL) in 1895. The game soon became fully professional, because it was in direct competition for both players and spectators from association football.[6]

Similar schism occurred in the organization of baseball in the US. As Szymanski and Zimbalist (2005) argue, the first fully professional baseball team, the Cincinnati Red Stockings, was established in 1869. Naturally, this team had to leave the NABBP, which was founded on amateurism, but it prompted other teams to leave also. As a consequence, the National Association of Amateur Baseball Players (NAABBP) and the National Association of

---

[3] The commercial imperative in organization was not overt. Indeed, in football it has been argued by Russell (1997) that the FA deliberately raised prices to try to maintain football's appeal to the skilled working and lower middle classes. Likewise, Syzmanski and Zimbalist (2005, p. 33) note initial resistance to admission price cutting in the NL in response to the formation of the IL to avoid the "patronage of the degraded" but "recognition by the respectable."

[4] An amateur football association emerged in 1907, but this rejoined the Football Association in 1914.

[5] Both the maximum wage and retains and transfer systems are discussed in more detail in Chapters 9 and 12.

[6] Indeed, amateur rugby league only developed some separate administrative status in 1973 under the auspices of BARLA, the British Amateur Rugby League Association, reflecting a critical fall in amateur activity under the governance of the professional clubs who, as discussed in Chapter 2, were also experiencing huge declines in attendance.

Professional Baseball Players (NAPBBP) were established to govern the alternative dimensions of the game in 1871.

The final development towards professionalism occurred with the formation of leagues with the need to pay professional players prompting a requirement to extract more regular gate money and to utilize facilities more fully. In the case of the EFL, the FA retained overall control of football in terms of the development and interpretation of rules and, indeed, the parameters of commercial activity. As well as the movement of players between clubs and their salaries, as discussed above, ticket prices were agreed on, limitations on dividend payments to shareholders were agreed and directors could not be paid for their efforts. The league soon developed, flourished and expanded, principally organized on vertical selection by merit and some geographic boundaries for the less successful teams, to allow for the problem of travel costs.[7] Likewise, in professional rugby, while traditionally structured county championships were contested initially a league of two divisions was introduced by 1902, with 18 sides each and promotion and relegation again depending on merit. Further variations in league format then followed.

According to Szymanski and Zimbalist (2005), a major impetus to the development of leagues in English sport was the formation of the National League (NL) for baseball in the US in 1875, which English administrators were familiar with. However, its defining characteristics were different. The league emerged as a direct challenge to the NAPBBP over disputes concerning the signing of players and threats to the longevity of the game emerging from match fixing, and betting corruption, undermining public confidence in the sport. The NL was primarily concentrated in the northeastern US, the traditional home of baseball, and had the following characteristics:

1. a league board of team owners with authority to make all decisions and to enforce rules;
2. players bound to their contracts with no managerial powers;
3. a closed league of teams granted a territorial monopoly with limitation of franchise numbers and eligibility of the size of a city to host a franchise;
4. teams paid annual dues;
5. teams play a balanced list of home and away fixtures;
6. imposed ticket prices;
7. alcohol, gambling and Sunday fixtures banned;
8. independent umpires.

---

[7] It is notable that the growth of mass railway transport made football clubs tend to locate near railway stations to facilitate access to competitors, as well as to provide access for spectators (http://www.spartacus.schoolnet.co.uk/Fhistory.htm Accessed 31 March 2008).

The strictures of such a league, its relatively small scale initially of six and then up to 12 teams in the 1890s, coupled with its exclusivity, meant that rivals developed, such as the International League (IL) in 1877, stemming from the NAPBBP, in which player cooperatives were common. The NL adopted policies to make it as popular as possible to avoid threats to its existence. Consequently, the IL collapsed in 1880, to be replaced by the American Association (AA) in 1883, which made agreements about territorial exclusivities and player reserve systems.

The AA folded by the 1890s, but player reserve systems had become a central part of the competitive process between the NL and any future rival leagues. These systems recognized the property rights of teams over their players and led to compensation payments to teams when other larger and more successful teams sought to buy their better talent, in much the same way as the retain and transfer system in football. The concentration of talent helped to develop the distinction between the Major League, i.e., the NL, and other "Minor League" teams.[8] By 1901 one of the minor leagues, the Western League, had redeveloped into a Major League, the American League (AL), by capturing the new potential markets in the southwestern US and offering franchises to cities that lost franchises with the NL. Since 1903 the winners of each of the major leagues have competed in a "World Series."

7.2.3 Review

There are clearly distinct similarities in the shift towards professionalism in these oldest team sports. Consumer–producers operating in a world in which clubs were essentially self-financing from members, in the manner of mutual societies, developed into hierarchical organizations, governing activities in which both professional producers and distinct gate-paying spectators existed. Drawing on Weisbrod (1978), it can be argued that the degree of collectiveness of income streams to the outputs of the organization shifted from being close to 100, as a club good, towards being much closer to zero, as a private good.

Despite these similarities, however, it is also clear that the specific approaches to professionalism had distinct characteristics. In baseball, organization developed from commercially-minded owners who, in many respects, looked to protect the economic viability of their activities. In England, soccer and rugby league developed under the governance of one structure, each with aspirations to cover both the amateur and professional levels of the

---

[8] An important facet of the reserve clause was the option to draw on the talent as needed. This meant that the larger teams could hoard talent off their "active" team roster in the lower leagues and not have to pay major league salaries.

TABLE 7.1   Comparison of voluntary and emergent professional sports

	Members	Private investors
Ownership		
Governance	▪ Club: members ▪ Sport: governing body	▪ US: team owners ▪ Europe: team owners and governing body Europe: team owners and governing body
Club objectives	Non-profit	▪ US: profit ▪ Europe: success and financial survival
Consumption	Consumer–producer members	Gate paying spectators
Production	Consumer–producer members	▪ Professional athletes ▪ Professional management Europe: non-remunerated directors
Form of competition	Cup competitions Traditional fixtures Ad-hoc tournaments	Cup competitions League fixtures

game and, in contrast to a closed league format, retain the vertical structure of competition that has come to symbolize European sports. This included access to professional status and the possibility of success at that level being governed by merit, with no obvious institutional recognition that making a profit was central to activities. This is despite the fact that professional clubs now had an entirely different financial structure to the amateur clubs. Indeed, throughout the history of soccer and rugby league, the absence of profit seems to be accepted as a facet of business reality (Jackson, 1899; Szymanski and Kuypers, 1999; Downward and Jackson, 2003). In contrast, despite the stated claims of club owners, it is argued that US sports have tended to make profits, even if these are not declared (Fort, 2000; Szymanski and Zimbalist, 2005). Table 7.1 summarizes the typical main economic differences between voluntary and professional sports, as implied by the historical emergence of the latter from the former.

Some more detailed differences between the US and European models of professional team sports are discussed later in this chapter. At this juncture, however, attention turns towards more formally outlining some key economic principles associated with the economic nature of contests. They provide a basis for understanding some general themes in the economic analysis of professional team sports, and indicate how they relate to other forms of sport, such as events. Moreover, the incentives that led towards formalization and professionalism discussed above can be highlighted.

7.3 SPORTS COMPETITIONS AS ECONOMIC CONTESTS

In two insightful papers (and other contributions) Szymanski (2003a, b) has proposed that sports contests can be understood as economic tournaments (or synonymously contests). As defined in Chapter 1, tournaments are concerned with economic activity whose output is assessed in relative rather than absolute terms. It is because tournaments produce a rank ordering of outcomes that they are directly applicable to sports.

> **Reflection Question 7.1**
> Why do the rank order outcomes of a contest make tournament theory relevant to sports? Hint: Think about how the winner of a cup competition, athletic race or league champion is defined.

It is quite clear that in sporting contests of any type the winners, whether of a knockout cup competition, a league championship, an athletic race, a high jump or whatever, win that event by finishing above their opponents according to some ranking rule that links the performance of the competitor to their assigned rank order. In the case of some sporting competitions the ranking rule may carry with it an absolute yardstick. World records for the times of various races, distances of various throwing events, heights and distances of various jumping events or weights lifted are examples of absolute yardsticks. In many cases, however, the performance of competitors is measured purely in a relative sense, i.e., how they performed against one another in a specific context. The precise way in which this takes place can vary and, as indicated in Table 7.2, follow either the knockout form of traditional cup competitions, round robin leagues or some hybrid version. The reason why the former arrangement and its hybrids are more likely can be understood to be a direct result of economic incentives. These will include pooling together the better talent, i.e., restricting the scale of competition, attracting better quality competitors and rewarding genuine effort more than luck (which is more likely to affect a knockout competition with randomly matched competitors and each match being crucial). The details of these incentives are now discussed.

7.3.1 Contest/tournament theory

As Szymanski (2003a, b) argues, tournament or contest theory has its roots in the seminal work of Tullock (1980), which explores "rent-seeking" behaviour by "contestants" for public funds. The analysis has subsequently been used in labour market analysis and other forms of economic activity.

TABLE 7.2 Typical forms of tournament in sport

Form of tournament	Description	Example
Single rank order tournament	Individuals/teams meet for a single specific contest	Stroke play golf, marathon running, time-trial cycling
Single elimination knockout tournament	A hierarchical series of rounds of competition between contestants, with the top ranked in each case only progressing	FA Cup, Wimbledon
Double elimination tournament	As above, but subsets of the best losers are given another chance to compete	Athletics (heats) Rowing
Round robin tournament	All contestants meet an equal number of times	Sports leagues (some)
Multi-stage tournaments	Contestants meet initially in groups then either progress to:	
	An elimination tournament	World cup, Super-bowl, play-offs, e.g., divisional promotion in English football, Heineken Cup in rugby, Champions League in football
	Further round robin tournament	World series
	Match play golf	Contestants meet in a series of contests each decided by holes won, not strokes played
Challenge	Champions taken on by the right to challenge, based in other tournaments	Boxing

The concept of economic rent has its origins in the work of David Ricardo regarding the differential return to more productive land relative to unproductive land. More generally, it represents the difference in the return to a factor of production and the amount that would be required to prevent that factor of production being reallocated to an alternative use. This latter value is referred to as the transfer earnings (or the reservation wage in the case of labour).

Rent-seeking behaviour refers to the activities of economic agents extracting a return as a factor of production that is not directly connected with their productivity, but is more a reflection of their control over resources as a result of regulation or other constraints, such as asymmetric information, on mutually beneficial exchange as defined in the theory of competitive markets.[9] In this respect, monopoly power can be viewed as rent seeking, especially if the monopoly exists as the result of regulation. As discussed above and further in Chapter 11, it is possible to identify the traditional forms of labour market in sports, in which maximum wages and reserve clauses have existed, as forms of rent-seeking behaviour, because they use regulations either to restrict the mobility of players or the level of their wages, in contrast to what voluntary exchange would produce. The principal–agent problem also provides opportunities for rent-seeking behaviour. Rent-seeking is inefficient, therefore, as it is connected with the transfer of incomes between economic agents at the expense of possible welfare gains. From a purely economic point of view, as Frick argues, one of the primary objectives of tournaments is that they act:

"... as devices ... (that) ... can be very helpful in eliciting the effort levels that are necessary to give the principal the highest expected net profit ... and subject to the constraint that the agents must be given a remuneration package attractive enough to enter the competition." (Frick, 2000, p. 512)

From a sporting point of view, therefore, tournament theory can indicate how hard a contestant is likely to work relative to their opponents, which adds to the potential for their success and the overall quality of the competition as this effort is balanced against opponents. It also highlights that this process entails an economic trade-off between the competitor, the agent, who needs to be enticed to take part in the contest, and the principal or organizer of the contest, who is seeking an economic return from organizing the activity, but who needs to employ the competing agents. Furthermore, tournament theory indicates that a balance needs to be struck between relative contestant effort and

---

[9] Profit in this sense is seen as a result of mutually beneficial exchange. Marxist theory would argue that profit is connected with the regulations governing the private ownership of property, and is also rent-seeking. Consequently, there is some ambiguity about these distinctions.

TABLE 7.3   Assumptions and implications of tournament theory

Assumption	Commentary
1. Athlete's output depends on their own deterministic efforts, plus random influences beyond their control but may be common to all competitors, such as weather, the state of equipment or facilities, or design of tournament	1. This identifies that each competitor can influence the outcome by their own endeavour, but subject to their competitors' actions and also other factors
2. The strategies of contestants can be analyzed using game theory and, in particular, Nash (non-cooperative) Equilibrium	2. Recall from Chapter 5 that game theory is used to examine interacting economic agents. Nash Equilibrium reflects economic agents optimizing, given the actions of their competitors
3. The stability of the Nash Equilibrium requires some uncertainty over the outcomes	3. If this is not the case, the contest would become predictable and undermine its own existence. This is discussed further in the text
4. The rewards from any competition should be predetermined and increase with rank to provide incentive to compete	4. Without a differential return to performance, competitors would not increase the effort put into competition[a]
5. With equally talented competitors and with equal economic endowments, athletes will choose the same level of effort and the probability of winning is equal	5. This situation comprises a case of pure competitive balance
6. If contestants are heterogeneous more able competitors are more likely to win the contest. If competitors do not know their relative abilities, no effects on effort are likely. If they do, then effort levels will fall	6. In a case of unbalanced competition, both weaker and stronger competitors would economize on their efforts, recognizing their likely performance

[a]There is an important point to emphasize here, which is that the reward structure, which need not be monetary, aims to increase efforts (reduce rent seeking) rather than generate effort *per se*. This means that competition is not impossible without inducement, but that higher level competition is.

randomness in affecting outcomes because of joint production. Frick (2000) outlines the main assumptions and implications of tournament theory, which are briefly summarized in Table 7.3.

Drawing on these assumptions, a simple version of the theory provided in Szymanski (2003b) can be presented to illustrate the main predictions. Assume that there are two competitors, 1 and 2. It can be argued that their success in a competition "S" can be produced by their effort "Π,"[10] as detailed in Assumption 1 of Table 7.3. In this way, Equations 7.3 and 7.4 provide a production function for success in a competition. The equations are written in Cobb–Douglas form, as presented in Appendix 3.1, because it is recognized that the productivity of the effort is captured in the exponential parameter "γ."

The parameter γ can be viewed as reflecting the tournament's design and consequently its ability to convert the competitor's efforts into success. It is the same in both cases, to reflect a lack of bias in the tournament as indicated in Assumption 5 of Table 7.3.

$$S_1 = \Pi_1{}^\gamma \tag{7.3}$$

$$S_2 = \Pi_2{}^\gamma \tag{7.4}$$

The probability, P, of success then becomes:

$$P_1 = \frac{\Pi_1{}^\gamma}{\Pi_1{}^\gamma + \Pi_2{}^\gamma} \tag{7.5}$$

$$P_2 = \frac{\Pi_2{}^\gamma}{\Pi_1{}^\gamma + \Pi_2{}^\gamma} \tag{7.6}$$

Equations 7.5 and 7.6 describe a logit form of contest success function for the competitor. This specifies that their individual probability of success depends on the exercise of their effort relative to the total effort in the contest, i.e., that provided by both contestants, as given in the denominator of the two equations. An important feature of these two equations is that they capture the externality essential to sporting competitions through joint production (as discussed earlier with Equations 7.1 and 7.2).

Two further important results can be demonstrated from these equations, and they concern the tournament design parameter γ. As shown in Appendix 7.1, if this parameter is set equal to zero, the tournament cannot discriminate between the efforts of the contestant and each competitor ends up with the same, equal, chance of success. The tournament becomes a pure lottery. Equations 7.5 and 7.6 would reduce to:

$$P_1 = P_2 = \frac{1}{2} \tag{7.7}$$

---

[10] The random impact "z" on success could be introduced explicitly by a function such as $S_1 = \Pi_1{}^\gamma \exp^z$, where exp is the base of natural logarithms. If the effect of random elements on success on average is 0, then exp becomes 1 and average success becomes equivalent to the expression in the text.

If, on the other hand, the tournament could perfectly discriminate effort from random chance, then γ would tend toward infinity. In this case, however, should any competitor exhibit more effort, then this competitor would have a probability of:

$$P11 \qquad\qquad (7.8)$$

That is tending towards "1," or complete certainty. The tournament becomes "an auction in which the largest contributor of effort is certain to win" (Szymanski, 2003b, p. 469). This actually applies for sufficiently large finite values of γ. This highlights, as emphasized earlier, that effective tournaments require balancing the systematic efforts of competitors with random influences, as also stated in Assumption 3 in Table 7.3. This is because Equations 7.7 and 7.8 provide scenarios in which competitors have no incentive to participate in the tournament. Appendix 7.1 shows that, in general, increases in the value of γ impair (improve) the success probabilities of lower (higher) effort teams. An exception is where each competitor exerts the same effort. The probabilities of success are then invariant to γ and equal.

Reflection Question 7.2

Why would complete certainty or complete uncertainty undermine the existence of tournaments?

Hint: What is the motive for athletes to compete in sport?

There are two potential reasons why complete certainty or uncertainty could lead to market failure for a tournament, and this is connected with the motives of competitors in sport. If athletes viewed their efforts as not having an impact on the outcome of the tournament, then clearly the incentive to participate with all but minimal effort would apply, which ultimately would undermine the tournament. Likewise, as indicated in Assumption 6 of Table 7.3, if it became known that one competitor had a disproportionately greater prospect of winning the tournament, then overall effort in the tournament would fall, again undermining it. The tournament would fail because of declining quality, caused by moral hazard.

Assumption 2 in Table 7.3 suggests that the solution to the contest can be identified as a Nash equilibrium (see Chapter 5). This requires specifying the payoff, R, to each contestant, recognizing the efforts of the other contestants, and then finding the optimal effort levels of each contestant, given the efforts of the other contestants. Equations 7.9 and 7.10 describe the payoffs to each contestant, where V is the value of winning the tournament, which can be described in monetary or non-monetary terms, and c is the marginal costs of the effort, which are assumed to be identical according to Assumption 5 in Table 7.3.[11]

$$R_1 = P_1V - c_1\Pi_1 \tag{7.9}$$

$$R_2 = P_2V - c_2\Pi \tag{7.10}$$

As Appendix 7.2 shows, the Nash equilibrium effort level for the contest for each contestant, Π^e, will be as implied in Assumption 5 in Table 7.3:

$$\Pi^e = \frac{\gamma V}{4c} \tag{7.11}$$

Recognizing this, a tournament with "n" contestants would produce an equilibrium level effort of:

$$\Pi^e = \frac{\gamma V(n-1)}{n^2 c} \tag{7.12}$$

This equation summarizes a number of important interrelated features about tournaments that can help to understand the economics of sports. If the quality of the tournament, "Q," is likely to be a function of the equilibrium effort of competitors:

$$Q = Q(\Pi^e) \tag{7.13}$$

and, in particular, quality rises with effort such that:

$$\frac{\delta Q}{\delta \Pi^e} > 0 \tag{7.14}$$

Equation 7.14 provides a formal basis for suggesting that, *ceteris paribus*:

1. The fewer the contestants are in number, n, the greater the effort that will be exerted by them. This will subsequently raise the economic value of the contest as it will be more attractive to spectators. This highlights that broader participation and economic viability are likely to be negatively related. As discussed earlier, this can explain why the US model of a smaller closed league has been directly associated with profits, in contrast to larger European leagues, particularly with football in the UK, where profits have

---

[11] As Szymanski (2003b) notes, "If contestants have different marginal costs of effort functions, then the contest will be asymmetric – some players will achieve a higher probability of success for any given level of effort ... the alternative is to assume that individual effort contributions of a given amount produce different probabilities in the contest success function ... From an economic perspective these are essentially equivalent problems..."

been less common but greater numbers participate. It also suggests that the largest economic value in individual sport tournaments is likely to be where smaller numbers of better competitors meet.

2. If the value of the tournament "V," is higher, the greater will be the effort invested by competitors. Other things being equal, this indicates that tournaments funded at a higher level are more likely to be of a higher quality. This means that there is a greater chance of sporting records or higher levels of achievement occurring. Likewise, there is greater chance of positive feedback between sporting performance and economic returns.

3. In contrast, the level of effort, and quality of competition is likely to fall as the general MC of effort, "c" rises, other things being equal. This is a sensible economic result, which draws on Equations 7.9 and 7.10, and indicates that if increased effort has no effect on the chance of winning a competition, an increase in the cost of effort would be balanced by a reduction in effort to ensure that payoffs remain the same. This suggests that the quality of competition would fall and, as a result, its economic attractiveness would decrease. This result is equivalent, therefore, to having a tournament with lower quality participants.

4. The greater the value of the tournament parameter, "γ," the greater the effort of contestants will be and consequently, the higher the quality of the tournament and the potential economic return. Recalling that this parameter measures the ability of the tournament to distinguish between the efforts of the contestants and luck, it follows that a tournament such as a round-robin league will be of a greater overall quality than a knockout cup competition, with corresponding greater economic value. The same would be the case for multi-stage tournaments.

Point 4 reveals that the parameter γ measures the rate at which effort can be converted into probable success. Other things equal, a stronger effect (greater value) of γ means a stronger incentive for competitors to exert effort, increasing the competition's quality and likely economic value. When the league is perfectly balanced, only the incentive effect operates, therefore in a perfectly balanced league γ will deliver most effort, quality and value. In an unbalanced league the incentive effect can be offset by a reduction in the balance of competition.

This point is interesting for three reasons. Broadly it suggests a basis for understanding why professional leagues evolved out of knockout competitions or became multi-stage tournaments with elements of leagues. The intuition is that in a pure knockout tournament, the random matching of opponents and the fact that every game can eliminate a team from competing further means that the element of chance in the teams' success is relatively large. League fixtures and "repeated trials" are more likely to reveal systematic and genuine efforts, and underpin commercial viability.

It also suggests why balance in competition is seen to be potentially important to sports leagues. For example, in their design home and away games are typically played to reduce home advantage or bias, as is evident from a variety of sources such as the influence of crowds on officials (see Downward and Jones, 2007; Sutter and Kocher, 2004; Neville and Holder, 1999). Historically, as discussed in Chapter 9, it can indicate why revenue sharing and labour market restrictions have been justified in leagues to reallocate the ability to buy labour efforts in a more balanced way.

Finally it suggests why the "calibration" of tournaments changes to seek to elicit greater efforts. In soccer in 1981, in England and Wales, and subsequently embraced by FIFA in 1995 and most other soccer leagues, the metric for ranking results shifted from two points for a win to three. The aim was to raise attacking play, the quality of the contest and thereby spectator interest. More recently, in rugby union competitions such as the Premiership, the Heineken Cup or the Super 14 competitions, bonus points are awarded for scoring four or more tries or for maintaining losses to within seven points. Once again, the aim is to raise the quality of competition through rewarding attacking play, but also to encourage efforts to attack even if the team is losing.[12]

What drives these broad predictions is the joint production of sports contests which, in turn, can be understood as having two key dimensions, the quality and uncertainty (together with its counterpart, success) of a contest. As such they can provide the basis for the economic analysis of sporting contests, particularly as they will also affect the value of competitions. This is now illustrated in connection with a discussion of some specific themes associated with the analysis of professional team sports.[13]

7.4 FOUNDATIONS OF THE ANALYSIS OF PROFESSIONAL TEAM SPORTS

This section begins with a discussion on the basis of the joint production of sports contests in professional team sports. This requires investigating if the sports "league," i.e., the clubs, owners and governing bodies that organize the competition, can best be understood as a monopoly firm or a cartel of firms in an oligopoly market. The objectives of the firm are then

---

[12] This is because the numerical aggregation of results to define a rank is arbitrary overall, but can induce sporting incentives as the significance of a specific result can vary the overall set of possible results.

[13] These concepts are also drawn on in a discussion of sports events in Chapter 12.

discussed. The chapter closes with a review of league structures in the US and Europe.

7.4.1 The production of professional team sports

Professional team sports can be analyzed from an economic perspective in which labour (mainly players), capital and land (stadiums and other facilities) are combined by clubs who supply teams to produce a saleable product – the game or contest.[14] To obtain revenue to pay for inputs it is necessary to exclude non-paying spectators, hence the universal use of stadiums and a traditional suspicion of live broadcasting of sports. For teams to cover their costs, each must be guaranteed a minimum number of home games for which tickets can be sold, which suggests league or round robin tournaments rather than knock-out competitions. As an organizational structure, leagues comprise sets of individual clubs that fall within the broader governance structures outlined in Chapter 2. There are potential divisions of interests between league and club, because of the existence of externalities in production noted earlier in the chapter. Indeed, it was a result of this difference that prompted one of the seminal contributors to the literature, Neale (1964), to coin the phrase "the peculiar economics of sport."

7.4.2 The peculiar economics of sport

Early contributors to the economics of professional team sports, Rottenberg (1956) and Neale (1964) stressed the importance of a key externality known as the uncertainty of outcome (UO) hypothesis:

"... that a more or less equal distribution of talent is necessary if there is to be uncertainty of outcome; and that uncertainty of outcome is necessary if the consumer is going to be willing to pay admission to the game." (Rottenberg, 1956, p. 246)

Consequently:

"... consider the position of the heavyweight champion ... He wants to earn more money, to maximize his profits. What does he need in order to do so? Obviously a contender, and the stronger the contender the larger the profits from fighting him ... since doubt about the competition is what arouses interest ... Pure monopoly is disaster: Joe Louis would have no one to fight and therefore no income." (Neale, 1964, pp. 1–2)

---

[14] While the emphasis in discussion earlier in this book has been on clubs, consistent with the literature "teams" are now referred to as the key facet of clubs.

These quotations illustrate the joint production element of sports discussed above, in which contests depend on the exercise of efforts and economic value is likely to be linked to cases where greater joint effort occurs, with comparable skills. The upshot is that public interest in sport (and hence attendance and revenue) increases, other things being equal, when teams are as closely competitive as possible. Domination of the league by Team A is liable to reduce interest in and attendance at games involving the remaining teams, e.g., B versus C and C versus D, even if attendance at games involving Team A does increase. In the longer run, even Team A would suffer if the standard of competition declines.

Neale (1964) identified another externality associated with sports, which he termed the "fourth estate" or "league standing" effect. Inasmuch as interest in the sport is not just confined to spectators observing the actual contest, but spills over to the general public, a positive externality exists from the sport. This permits the media to earn revenue by reporting sport results without any contribution to the cost of producing sport. Consequently, the sale of rights to broadcast its matches represents a sport league internalizing some of the media benefits created by its operations.

> The term is derived from a two-centuries-old notion that the press was the "fourth estate," being preceded by the aristocracy, the church and the common people. Aristocracy and church were represented in the upper chambers of national legislatures, the people in the lower chamber. The press was seen as sufficiently important, even then, to constitute a distinct interest group in society rivalling the others in importance. The name of the pre-revolutionary French legislature translates into English as "the Estates General." Some of the terminology survives – e.g., "the House of Commons."

A similar positive externality exists for the betting industry. The sale of programmes and "fanzines" exemplify clubs' internalization of a portion of the league standing benefit inasmuch as they capture elements of interest associated with their specific club and specific opponents. The presence of unofficial material, however, reveals that property rights are not fully allocated.

7.4.3 The league as a natural monopoly or as a cartel

Because of UO, Neale (1964) argued that the market for professional team sports differs significantly from most industries. In Chapter 1, the standard competitive model of markets suggests that the firm chooses its level of output to maximize profit. In contrast, the sports team's level of output is determined by the league, which determines both its membership and the number of games each plays in the season. This led Neale to consider that the league constituted a natural monopoly firm, with clubs acting as plants. Natural monopolies can be said to exist if one firm can produce output at a lower (social) cost than two or more firms, or if only one firm seems able to survive competition. Both of these criteria appeared to exist for Neale, with joint production allowing the first condition to occur, and the fact that most sports seemed to be organized in national leagues or that play-offs or subsequent tournaments existed to produce a national champion, consistent with the latter condition because it is most profitable. Thus, as noted earlier, separate leagues for baseball exist in the US but they have always, since becoming major leagues, organized play-offs in the World Series. Likewise, while boxing has always had several governing bodies and world titles, most kudos attaches to the fighter who manages to unify the titles. Neale's analysis depends crucially on the assumption that the individual team cannot determine its output. The extent to which one is willing to accept this proposition depends on how one defines output, which he took to be the number of games played. This assumes that playing qualities are the same. If they are not then this offers opportunites to market a different product by some of the "plants."

That the team has discretion over its output relative to the league was an important factor in the view, put forward by Sloane (1971), that the league is a cartel, as defined in Chapter 5. In the cartel model the club behaves as a firm rather than as a plant, although it is still subject to UO and still unable to offer saleable output in the absence of the league. The cartel model has the advantage over the natural monopoly model, however, in that it highlights the relationships between clubs and leagues and the implied need to manage these. While cooperation between clubs is essential (hence the relatively light-handed treatment of sports leagues by competition policy) there will be times when some clubs will perceive that private advantage can be had by breaking ranks with the membership as a whole, as indicated earlier in the formation of the first leagues. The cartel model seems to have explanatory power as far as recent developments in leagues are concerned. Box 7.1 illustrates some recent changes to leagues in the UK, in which traditional competitions have evolved separate administration for higher level domestic competition which provides access (potential in the case of cricket) into international competition.

As well as internal threats to its existence, a cartel's continued existence also depends on its ability to protect its business from independent entry, which is most evident in the US. In the closed-league US sports, the geographic spread of franchises can be managed to create a latent demand for a franchise. One implication of this scarcity is that it can be used to leverage public investment for sports facilities (see Chapter 12), although rivals can emerge. For example, Fort and Quirk (1995) note that between 1920 and 1994 seven leagues had existed in football, not counting the black American leagues that

BOX 7.1 RECENT EVOLUTIONARY CHANGES TO LEAGUES

Soccer

Premier League (PL): the largest clubs broke away from the English Football League, financed by the largest share of the new media income from promotion. Relegation to the remaining league, the championship, is possible.

Champions League (CL): the European Cup in soccer evolves into a multi-stage tournament with a pool stage and a knockout element.

Rugby League

Super League (SL): an equivalent development to the premier league in rugby league. Initially a closed league was proposed, but promotion and relegation was retained with exceptions for development clubs. Currently "franchises" for three year membership will commence in 2009.

Rugby Union

Premiership: an equivalent development to the premier league in rugby union. Promotion and relegation to the National League is possible.

Magners League: a league for the "Celtic" nations of Ireland, Scotland and Wales comprising "franchises" from regional sides. No promotion or relegation.

Heineken Cup: a champions' league for teams from the Premiership and French First Division which qualify and Magners League teams, together with Italian teams.

Cricket

County Championship: reformed to include promotion and relegation.

Limited over games: development of 20-Twenty Cricket will be influenced by the development of the Indian Premier League.

---

disappeared or were absorbed as racial integration progressed, and that fourteen of the then extant NFL teams had begun in rival leagues. New US football leagues have continued to appear and disappear. In major league baseball, the World Series ties the "rivals" together.

The upshot of this discussion is that it illustrates that cartel theory probably explains sports leagues better than the natural monopoly model. Further cartels can suggest that league arrangements can exist with potentially different objectives. The literature suggests that they can be understood in terms of the distinctions between US and European leagues. This comparison is now explored further by examining firm objectives and some characteristics of the forms of leagues.

7.5 US AND EUROPEAN LEAGUES

7.5.1 Club objectives

Drawing on the historical development of professional sports in Europe and the US, most US writers assume that profit maximization is the goal of team owners. In contrast, Sloane (1971) argued that European club owners might be viewed more accurately as utility maximizers, where a major determinant of utility is playing success, although profit is important for the club's long run financial stability. Forgoing profits, and even underwriting losses, therefore, suggests that club ownership is an act of consumption more than investment.

The impetus for this assumption was the relegation and promotion of hierarchical sports systems in Europe, coupled with the historic desire in European football for success in international competition. Sloane's (1971) proposed team utility function is given in Equation 7.15:

$$U = U\{P, A, X(\Pi - \Pi^{MIN})\} \qquad (7.15)$$

Where "U" is the utility level attained, which depends on performance on the field "P," home attendance "A," UO "X," and on the excess of post tax profit "Π" over a minimum acceptable level of post tax profit "Π^{MIN}." The notion of an acceptable minimum profit reflects factors such as the club's need to secure its long-run future. Any club that has outstanding debt has to display the ability to service that debt. Over and above servicing debt, the club may need to generate an acceptable level of profit; if it is a publicly quoted limited liability company the directors need to produce enough dividends to keep the shareholders happy. If they cannot, the share price will fall and the company may become the subject of a hostile takeover. In contrast, if a club has access to a sympathetic and wealthy owner (Chelsea with Roman Abramovich, Juventus with the Agnelli (FIAT) family, AC Milan with Silvio Berlusconi, Shaktar Donetsk with Rinat Akhmetv) or to favourable treatment from local or national government (Real Madrid, Barcelona) the minimum acceptable level could actually be negative. Sometimes, a large public company has a supportive relationship with a sports team, for example Philips Electrical with PSV, Bayer Chemicals with both Leverkusen and Munich, and Yukos Oil with Moscow Dynamo.

Theoretically, one can expect that, other things being equal, an increase in any one of the four factors identified by Sloane will make the supporters, the owners and the management happier. As Sloane (1971) notes, the more closely the four explanatory variables are correlated with each other the more probable it is that the predictions of the profit maximizing and utility maximizing models will resemble one another. Unless the predictions differ in some readily identifiable manner, attempts to distinguish the objectives of teams will fail. This is not to say that the differences are trivial. Chapter 9 explores the consequences of these differences for league management policies in detail.

7.5.2 League characteristics

Table 7.4 indicates some summary characteristics of US and European leagues, drawing on and extending Andreff and Staudohar (2000, 2002). Based on these characteristics, Andreff and Staudohar (2000, 2002) indicate that the amateur model of European sports shared some characteristics of early professional sports, particularly through the rise of gate revenue receipts, as

TABLE 7.4 Evolution of sports leagues

Basis of comparison	European amateur sport (traditionally and current)	Traditional European (1900–1980s)	Contemporary European (1980s–current)	US (traditionally and current)
Ownership	Members	Small number of shareholders	Public companies, media companies Entrepreneurial investment	Private owners (previously some collectives) Media companies
Finances	Membership fees, subsidies and donations, hospitality Gate revenue, some advertising and sponsorship (more for highest performers)	Gate revenues (e.g., 68–96%) Industrial patronage and subsidy (e.g., Fiat, Bayer, Peugeot 4%–21%) Sponsorship (e.g., 5%–35%) Merchandising (e.g., 1.4%–11%) Television rights (e.g., 0%–33%)	Gate revenues (e.g., 50%–20%) Sponsorship (e.g., 20%–25%) Television rights (e.g., 15%–39%) Merchandising (e.g., 10%–34%)	Gate revenues Sponsorship Merchandising Subsidy – stadia National and local television rights
Redistribution	None	Gate sharing Television rights sharing Maximum wages/salary caps Transfer systems	Some television revenues Some salary caps Modified transfer system	Gate sharing National television rights sharing drafts Reserve option (modified over time) Salary caps
Forms of competition	Traditional fixtures Knock-out cups Leagues at highest level All domestic, though informal tours	Domestic leagues National and international Knock-out cups	Domestic leagues International multi-stage tournaments	Domestic leagues and play-offs
League structure	Vertical with promotion and relegation	Vertical with promotion and relegation	Vertical with promotion and relegation	Closed Players developed in minor leagues, college sports
Team location	Traditional/multi-team cities	Traditional/multi-team cities	Traditional/multi-team cities Some "franchises"	Franchise/local monopoly
Labour market	Voluntary local	Local developed into national/ international	National/international	Traditionally national e.g., football Some international development

discussed earlier, and league competition. Indeed, the vertical promotion and relegation of the leagues ensured that the professionalism of the teams increased with performance within the hierarchical structure.

The traditional European professional system of organization emerged as discussed earlier and is labelled by Andreff and Staudohar (2000, 2002) as the Spectators–Subsidies–Sponsor–Local or SSSL model. Ownership of the club was either by an individual entrepreneur or a set of local investors receiving limited financial return, sometimes by regulation of the role of directors. The main source of trading revenue was typically gate revenues, with some minor sources of sponsorship and merchandising, but little television rights income. Its labour market was essentially closed to competition by restrictions on the number of overseas players that could be fielded, although some international trade occurred. Product markets, i.e., the leagues, were also closed and based nationally. By the 1980s it is argued that the contemporary model, labelled Media–Corporations–Merchandising–Markets–Global or MCMMG by Andreff and Staudohar, began to appear, of which the developments in Box 7.1 are a part. In contrast to the traditional SSSL model, the MCMMG model indicates that clubs were increasingly driven by media income, supported by large-scale merchandising and sponsorship activities. Gate revenues fell to minority sources of income for the larger clubs, i.e., 33% for the Premier League, 13% for Serie A and 25% for the Bundesliga in 2005–2006 (Deloitte, 2007). The clubs have evolved from local ownership into publicly quoted corporations or into being owned by business consortia or single wealthy entrepreneurs, many of whom are from overseas. According to Deloitte (2007) Serie A derived 62% of its revenue from broadcasting rights in 2005–2006, the Bundesliga 27% and the Premier League 42%. The Big Five, according to Deloitte (2005a) account for about 68% of all the broadcast revenue in European football. The giants of the Big Five, e.g., Real Madrid, Barcelona and AC Milan, each earn as much, if not more, from broadcasting than the entire Dutch league. In 2005 even Holland's giants, PSV and Ajax each earned about 8 million from television – approximately a tenth of what Chelsea earned from that source and about one sixth of what the average European top league club earned (Vrooman, 2007). While leagues (the product market) are still domestic, the labour market is international in scope; increasing emphasis is placed on a primary product market funded by media income and then international (European) club competition at the highest levels, also funded by media income. This illustrates some convergence of European leagues towards the model provided by US leagues which, as noted earlier, tend to be closed leagues with admission by geographical franchise, which provides local monopolies to the teams, although new franchises can be offered and they can move between cities.

There are also other broad economic similarities between the contemporary European and US sports leagues. In the US, geographic survival of teams has tended to be linked to their market potential for franchises. In Europe over the long-run, teams from areas of sustained weak economic and population growth tend to go out of business or drop into lower leagues. Evidence that the geographical location of professional football clubs in England has responded to long-run economic forces is offered by Waylen and Snook (1990). As Fort (2000) also argues, the play-off form of US sports, plus the feeding of talent into the major leagues from the minor leagues, are economically equivalent to the emergent European multi-stage tournaments and vertical structure, in that both are mechanisms which drive talent to the highest level of competition in the light of spectator demand.

In summary, it is clear that structural differences are evident between the leagues, but common economic processes appear to operate. It also remains that the economic objectives identified for teams may be different between the US and Europe, which for some authors, like Primault and Rouger (1999), derives specifically from the relegation and promotion structure in Europe. While Sloane (1971) acknowledged that it may be difficult to distinguish between the objectives this issue does matter. If, as contest theory predicts, economic value is likely to reside in smaller numbers of higher quality teams, then the ability of a larger cohort of vertically integrated teams to effectively coexist seems to be doubtful and suggestive of the need for changes in the current design of tournaments. This could explain the origins of the elite leagues at national level competition and the subsequent emergence of the Champions League or Heineken cup as a stepping stone in the direction of further elite level competition, where more money is available than in the Premier League, Premiership or Magner's League. In this respect some authors, for example Hoehn and Szymanski (1999) and Vrooman (2007), propose a European super league for soccer based on a closed franchise, leaving national leagues acting as minor leagues. Kesenne (2007b) argues that the perceived need of many national teams to compete with teams that dominate access to European competition is currently a stumbling block to cross-subsidization within national leagues. A closed European league would go some way to removing this obstacle, although it may be unpalatable to fans whose support is based on a tradition of promotion and relegation.

7.6 CONCLUSION

In this chapter the process of the transition of sports from amateur to professional status has been discussed, noting the shift in both the economic organization and motivational dimensions of sports clubs. Contest theory has been used to develop a more general set of principles that underpin the nature of sports competition as an economic contest and provide the basis for examining where the economic incentives lie in tournament design. Particular attention has been paid to the exercise of joint effort that is required to produce a contest, deriving from a key production externality and the subsequent tension that emerges based on the link between the exercise of effort by a competitor to produce success and the uncertainty required to produce a contest. The chapter argues that sports leagues are probably best viewed as cartels – groups of teams that have to cooperate to generate and distribute revenues, but that frequently have divergent interests and can have different institutional features. Chapters 8 to 11 explore elements of sports leagues in more detail.

Appendix 7.1 Some Properties of Tournament Discrimination

Given tournament probabilities:

$$P_1 = \frac{\Pi_1{}^\gamma}{\Pi_1{}^\gamma + \Pi_2{}^\gamma} \tag{A7.1.1}$$

Then, if γ is 0, it follows that:

$$P_1 = \frac{\Pi_1{}^0}{\Pi_1{}^0 + \Pi_2{}^0} \tag{A7.1.2}$$

As any value raised to the power 0 is 1, then Equation 7.1.2 becomes:

$$P_1 = \frac{1}{1+1} = \frac{1}{2} \tag{A7.1.3}$$

which suggests a 50% chance of success in a two-contestant competition. If the denominator of Equation A7.1.1 was $\sum \Pi_i$ for $i = 1, 2 \ldots n$ contestants, then it naturally follows that for any contestant the probability of success would be $1/n$. Table A7.1.1 reveals a little more of how variations in γ affects the teams' success probabilities in a two-team league. The effects are, in all probability, more extreme than those that would occur in a league of, say, 20 teams, but they are of qualitative interest. Because this is a two-team league, when Team 1 supplies a proportion x of total effort, Team 2 inputs the proportion $(1 - x)$. The "standard" model of competitive balance, discussed further in Chapter 9, is the special case in which $\gamma = 1$, when each team's success probability equals its share of league effort. The bottom row reveals that if the teams make identical efforts, their success probabilities are independent of the design parameter γ, although it seems unlikely that they would not adjust to change in γ. The penultimate row shows that, where teams' efforts are very closely matched, changing the value of γ does not greatly affect their probabilities of success, at least up to the value 4. But, as the differences between their efforts increase, so does the effect on their success probabilities when γ changes. Although γ might in theory assume any finite

TABLE A7.1.1   Success probabilities as γ varies, for given levels of team effort

Relative team efforts 1,2	Probabilities when $\gamma = 0$	Probabilities when $\gamma = 0.5$	Probabilities when $\gamma = 1.0$ standard model	Probabilities when $\gamma = 2.0$	Probabilities when $\gamma = 4.0$
0.3	0.5	0.4	0.3	0.16	0.03
0.7	0.5	0.6	0.7	0.84	0.97
0.4	0.5	0.45	0.4	0.31	0.16
0.6	0.5	0.55	0.6	0.69	0.84
0.49	0.5	0.495	0.49	0.48	0.46
0.51	0.5	0.505	0.51	0.52	0.54
0.5	0.5	0.5	0.5	0.5	0.5
0.5	0.5	0.5	0.5	0.5	0.5

value, however large, it is clear that even at $\gamma = 4$, the success probability of the team that supplies 30% of league effort is down by a factor of ten compared to the standard model. Only the values in the last row and in the fourth column are precise; the others are rounded-off to the nearest two decimal places, except for the third row third column entry where we need a third place of decimals to show what is happening. As already predicted, $\gamma < 1$ increases the prospects of clubs that supply less effort, while $\gamma > 1$ increases the probability of success for the team supplying most of the effort.

Appendix 7.2 The Derivation of Optimal Tournament Effort

Given the payoff to one specific contestant, 1:

$$R_1 = P_1 V - c_1 \Pi_1 \tag{A7.2.1}$$

and substituting equation A7.1.1 for P_1, leaves:

$$R_1 = \frac{\Pi_1^\gamma}{\Pi_1^\gamma + \Pi_2^\gamma} V - c_1 \Pi_1 \tag{A7.2.2}$$

Using the quotient rule, this suggests that the first order conditions for a maximum return would be, for a contestant choosing effort:

$$\frac{\delta R_1}{\delta \Pi_1} = V \gamma \frac{\Pi_2^\gamma \Pi_1^{\gamma-1}}{(\Pi_1^\gamma + \Pi_2^\gamma)^2} - c_1 = 0 \tag{A7.2.3}$$

Because it is assumed that each contestant is homogenous and competition is symmetric, then it follows that $\Pi_1 = \Pi_2 = \Pi$ so:

$$V \gamma \frac{\Pi^\gamma \Pi^{\gamma-1}}{(2\Pi^\gamma)^2} = c \tag{A7.2.4}$$

or:

$$V\gamma \frac{\Pi^{2\gamma-1}}{(2\Pi^\gamma)^2} = c \qquad\qquad \text{(A7.2.5)}$$

or:

$$V\gamma \frac{\Pi^{2\gamma-1}}{2\Pi^\gamma \times 2\Pi^\gamma} = c \qquad\qquad \text{(A7.2.6)}$$

or:

$$V\gamma \frac{\Pi^{2\gamma-1}}{4\Pi^{2\gamma}} = c \qquad\qquad \text{(A7.2.7)}$$

or:

$$V\gamma \frac{1}{4\Pi^{-1}} = c \qquad\qquad \text{(A7.2.8)}$$

or:

$$V\gamma \frac{1}{4c} = \Pi \qquad\qquad \text{(A.7.2.9)}$$

As detailed in the text, noting that the number of contestants is 2 shows that "1" in the numerator is equivalent to "n − 1" and "4" in the denominator is "n^2," as detailed in the text for "n" contestants.

CHAPTER 8

Uncertainty of Outcome, Competitive Balance and Bias in Sports Leagues

- To understand what is meant by uncertainty of outcome and competitive balance
- To appreciate how uncertainty of outcome and competitive balance are measured, and the difficulties with this measurement
- To appreciate the balance of evidence for and against the uncertainty of outcome hypothesis
- To understand the role of home advantage and why it is not easy to account for it connected with uncertainty of outcome

8.1 INTRODUCTION

Chapter 7 identified that uncertainty of outcome (UO) is theorized to be potentially a key component of the economics of professional team sports. This chapter explores, in some detail, how UO is understood and measured by economists, because it plays a prominent role in the analysis of sports leagues as shown in Chapter 9. Research into the extent to which UO influences both spectator and media demand for professional sports is discussed in Chapter 10 and serves as a rationale for restrictive labour contracts which enable teams to share revenues at the players' expense, discussed in Chapter 11.

Consequently, Section 8.2 explores the time-dependent nature of UO and draws distinctions between the short-run and long-run. Subsequent sections explore each element of UO in more detail. The chapter concludes with a discussion of home advantage in sports. Chapter 7 indicated that sports leagues have tried to account for this in offering balanced schedules of home and away fixtures. Indeed, Cairns, Jennett and Sloane (1986) argued that the most attractive game for spectators is that in which the visiting team is just sufficiently ahead of the home side for home advantage to equalize prospects. Further, Forrest and Simmons (2000) suggest that home advantage may be important in permitting weak sides to survive in leagues historically dominated by stronger ones. The link between home advantage and UO thus requires discussion.

8.2 THE TIME-DEPENDENT NATURE OF UNCERTAINTY OF OUTCOME

Chapter 7 outlined the UO hypothesis advanced by Rottenberg (1956) and Neale (1964), and in particular, argued that the nature of sporting competition requires a balance between competition and cooperation between contestants. While the UO hypothesis has been deeply ingrained in the economics of professional team sports literature, this chapter will demonstrate that its quantitative impact is not at all well-established. It will become apparent that this is partly due to the difficulty of deciding what precisely is meant by "uncertainty of outcome" and how it can be measured.

Cairns et al. (1986) distinguished four temporal forms of UO. First, they identified short-run UO where the emphasis is on the outcome of a particular game; secondly, medium-term UO where the identity of the season's winners is unknown; thirdly, within-season UO where several teams are "in contention." Finally, they recognized long-term UO (competitive balance), which is concerned with persistent domination that may damage the whole league. Each of these concepts is now discussed in some detail. The literature reviewed employs the various measures of UO as an independent variable in a regression equation that estimates the effect of UO and other factors on attendances and (more limitedly) broadcast audiences for sports in a research agenda examining the demand for sports from fans. Chapter 10 examines the impact of other variables on attendance and broadcast demand in more detail. Focus here is on the concept of UO as this is referred to in the literature in various guises.[1]

---

[1] It is always tempting to assume that more recent studies are improvements on earlier studies. It is true that the econometric tools available to the researcher have improved over time (Borland and MacDonald, 2003). However, as will become apparent in Chapter 10, research often tends to focus on specific issues and refinements, and does not necessarily address others. Evaluation of the work thus requires a careful reading of the specific studies concerned.

8.3 SHORT-RUN (MATCH) UNCERTAINTY OF OUTCOME

Match UO is the idea that spectators prefer close contests and are more likely to attend the next game if the teams are of much the same level of ability. There have been three broad approaches adopted to measure this dimension of UO: relative league standings; implied prior probabilities (p) of a home win through the use of betting odds; and direct estimates of the probabilities of home wins. Other things being equal, two teams immediately juxtaposed to one another in the league are of similar quality, and ignoring both home advantage and the probability of a draw suggests that both have an equal chance of winning. Likewise, this might be measured by betting odds of "evens." This suggests that the closer p is to 0.5 the more attractive the match should be and the greater the attendance. In the presence of home advantage and ignoring draws the most attractive game would be where p is less than 0.5. This is to allow home advantage to offset the visitors' greater quality, and research can be designed to estimate the value of p that maximizes attractiveness in the presence of home advantage. These alternative approaches are now discussed.

8.3.1 Relative league standings

Hart, Hutton and Sharot (1975), in an early paper on attendance demand for English soccer, made use of the teams' immediate pre-match league positions as indicators of the likely result and found the home team's standing insignificant as a determinant of attendance. One flaw with the approach adopted was that they used the absolute differences in league positions of teams. This is because they wanted to use logarithmic measures of the variables in their analysis, which has some statistical advantages. However, this cannot account for the relative pre-match standings of the teams, as the sign of the difference between home and away teams is lost (see Downward and Dawson, 2005a,b).

  Subsequent studies examining the effect of relative league standings on attendance are given in Table 8.1. It is worth noting that some recent innovations in measurement have occurred. Forrest, Simmons and Buraimo (2005) studied the audience for live broadcast Premier League games from 1993 to 1994 and 2001 to 2002. They devised a new index of uncertainty (partly in order to refine any potential bias problems in betting markets, which are discussed below) that incorporates both a measure of home advantage and one of match UO. Home advantage is computed within their sample to be, on average, about 0.57 points and is defined as the difference between points per game won by all home sides and points per game won by all away sides, evaluated over the previous season. They also identify a league performance component as the difference between the home and away sides' mean points

TABLE 8.1 Some findings on the effects of match uncertainty

Author/date	Sport/period	Dependent variable	Indicator(s)	Comment
Hart, Hutton and Sharot 1975	English soccer; 4 teams; 3 seasons starting 1969–1970	Log of match attendance	Log home standing	Insignificant
Borland and Lye 1992	Australian Rules football 1981–1986	Log of match attendance	Log away standing	Significant
			Log of absolute difference	Insignificant
Peel and Thomas 1988	Football League all teams 1981–1982	Log of match attendance	Difference of league standings	Insignificant
			Home standing	Significant
			Away standing	Significant
			Prob of home win	Significant (not a test of home advantage)
Dobson and Goddard 1992	Football League; 24 teams; 2 seasons starting 1989–1989	Log of match attendance	Log home standing	Significant
Wilson and Sim 1995	Malaysian semi-pro soccer 1989–1991	Log of match attendance	Log away standing	Significant
			Absolute difference of league points	Insignificant
			Square of above	Insignificant (not a test of home advantage)
Baimbridge, Cameron and Dawson 1996	Premier League football 1993–1994	Log of match attendance	Absolute difference of standings	Insignificant
			Square of above	Insignificant (not a test of home advantage)
Peel and Thomas 1997	English rugby league 1994–1995	Match attendance	Absolute value of the handicap betting spread	Significant
Dawson, Dobson, Goddard and Wilson 2005	English Premier League football 1996–2003	Log of disciplinary points y = 1, r = 2 issued per match	Home team uncertainty	Significant
Kuypers 1996	English Premier League football 1993–1994	Match attendance	Away team uncertainty	Significant
			Estimated odds on a home win	Insignificant

Study	Data	Dependent variable	Uncertainty measure	Result
Carmichael, Millington and Simmons 1999	English rugby league, season 1994–1995	Proportion of Sky subscribers watching live football	As above	Insignificant
		Log of match attendance	Pre-match odds	Significant
Falter and Perignon 2000	French soccer 1997–1998	Log of match attendance	Home standing	Significant
			Away standing	Insignificant
			Goal difference	Significant
			Absolute difference	Insignificant
Price and Sen 2003	NCAA Div 1-A Football	Match Attendance	Home wins in last 11 games	Significant
			Away ditto	Significant
			Squared difference of above	Insignificant
Forrest, Simmons and Buraimo 2005	BskyB live Premier League football 1993–194–2001–2002	Log of television audience (millions)	Composite index involving league form and home advantage*	Significant
		Probit of decision to broadcast	As above*	Significant
Garcia and Rodriguez 2002	Spanish League football 1992–1993 to5–1996	Log of match attendance	Pre-Boxing Day difference in relative wages**See F S &B	Significant
			Difference of league positions	Significant
			Square of above	Significant, wrongly signed
Forrest, Beaumont, Goddard and Simmons 2005	The Football League 1997–1998	Log of match attendance	PROBRAT (ratio of the probability of a home win relative to that of an away win) PROBRAT^2	Both probability ratios were correctly signed and significant
			HOMEPPG (home team prematch points per game)	Significant correctly signed

TABLE 8.1 (*Continued*)

Author/date	Sport/period	Dependent variable	Indicator(s)	Comment
			AWAYPPG (away team prematch points per game)	Insignificant FBG&S regard the PPG's as indexes of absolute team quality rather than of u/o *per se*
Meehan et al 2007	MLB 2000–2003	Match attendance	WINDIFF (Abs) (absolute difference in teams' win percents)	Significant
			WINDIFFP (+ home team difference in win percent)	Significant
			WINDIFFN (– home team difference in win percent)	Significant
			Games left	Significant** Interacted with WINDIFFP and WINDIFFN
Owen and Weatherston 2004	Super 12s rugby union, New Zealand 1999–2001	Log of match attendance	SUMPLACE (sum of the places each team lies behind fourth in the table)	Insignificant
			PROBH (probability of home win)	Insignificant
			$PROBH^4$	Insignificant
Alavy, Gaskell, Leach and Szymanski 2006	Premier League Football, 248 games broadcsat on Sky 2002–2005	The (minute by minute) rate of change of TV ratings	SQDIFF (squared difference of probability of home/away win)	Significant
			PSDRAW (probability of score draw)	Significant
			PNDRAW (probability of no-score draw)	Significant
			SUMSQ (sum of squared deviations of probabilities)	Significant

per game, evaluated using all available current season data. "Outcome uncertainty" for Forrest, Simmons and Buraimo (2005) is then defined as the absolute value of the sum of these components, which is at a maximum when the sum is close to zero. They find this index statistically significant in the explanation of television audiences, at least for games played after Boxing Day, when the broadcaster Sky's choice of matches is more likely to be influenced by current team performance.

8.3.2 Betting odds

Using information on league standings (and form) as an indicator of match UO is simple and appears intuitive. However, an implication is that the resulting indicator is based on partial (past) information. Viewing team performance as a production function, league standings reflect the past employment of playing talent as labour. However, it is conceivable that knowledge about injuries, suspensions and loss of form may be available, and would not be ignored by supporters as they make their decisions to attend matches. There may even be forward-looking information to hand, for example, that a particular player will have worked off a three-match suspension in time for the next game. Bookmakers will have utilized such information in deciding what odds to offer bets on a given result. The same will be true of bettors in deciding whether or not to stake a bet and how much they might stake. In this respect, betting odds can be associated with UO.

Peel and Thomas (1988) exploited published betting odds to obtain a forward-looking indicator of the probability of a home win. They estimate the probability of a home win (HP) directly from betting odds by making two simplifying assumptions, neither of which can be strictly true in soccer although the first is fine for baseball. First they assume that there is no probability of a draw. Secondly they assume that bookmakers have zero "spread" – i.e., margin for covering costs. This is discussed in Box 8.1. Under these circumstances, quoted odds of 4 to 1 against a home win convert into a probability of a home win equalling 0.2. While Peel and Thomas exploit this relationship, they fail to test the UO hypothesis by inquiring if, other things being equal, the value of the home win probability that maximizes attendance is significantly different from 0.5, as the theory suggests it should be. Furthermore, a problem with the use of betting odds is that it is not known if the "probabilities" identified by the betting public differ systematically from those perceived by potential spectators. In this regard Peel and Thomas' approach may suffer from sample selection bias. Nonetheless, a number of studies follow up their lead, as detailed in Table 8.1.

BOX 8.1 THE RELATIONSHIP BETWEEN BETTING ODDS AND UNCERTAINTY OF OUTCOME

The following examples hold when the bookmaker is assumed to provide their services free of charge. Peel and Thomas estimated the probability of a home win on this basis, but were under no illusions that real bookmakers behaved in this way. They accepted the inevitable loss of descriptive accuracy against the possibility of a gain in predictive power.

Suppose, for simplicity, that two teams due to play a game have prior win probabilities P1 and P2 respectively. Ruling out the possibility of a draw, it follows that P1 + P2 = 1. The implied odds on a win by Team 1, assuming that neither the bookmakers (nor taxation authorities) take any of the money staked, are equal to:

Odds of a win by team $1 \equiv P1/(1 - P1)$

Thus, if the bookmakers are offering 1/1 (even money) the researcher would deduce that the probability of a win by

Team 1 is 0.5 – the match is perfectly balanced. Those who backed Team 2 lose their stakes. Those that backed the winners get back their stake money plus an equal amount of winnings. On average, the bookmakers simply recycle money between gamblers.

If the bookmakers are offering 3/1 against Team 1, the implied probability is found by solving:

Three to one against $= 1/3 = P1/(1 - P1) \Rightarrow P1 = 0.25$

In which case, P2 equals 0.75 and the odds are three to one ON of Team 2 winning. If Team 1 wins, those who backed Team 2 lose their stake and the successful bettors get back their stake plus winnings equal to triple the sum staked. Had Team 2 won, the bettors would have got back their stakes plus winnings equal to a third of the stake. On average the bookmakers would be simply recycling money between those who made bets.

8.3.3 Direct estimates

An alternative approach to using betting odds to identify the probabilities of results is to predict, in advance of each match, the probabilities of a home win, an away win and a draw. Dawson, Dobson, Goddard and Wilson (2005) take this approach, addressing the incidence of disciplinary sanctions in Premier League football. They model the number of disciplinary points earned in a match (one for a yellow card, two for a red) as a function of team qualities, match uncertainty, match significance and attendance. UO indices seem to have significant positive effects on the number of disciplinary points collected by each team. The inference is that a closer, more uncertain, contest perhaps tempts players to stretch the rules of play.

Owen and Weatherston (2004) compute an estimate of the probability of a home win and employ it in an attendance study of Super 12 Rugby Union, but it is found to be insignificant. Alavy, Gaskell, Leach and Szymanski (2006) use data on minute-by-minute changes in television ratings to inquire whether uncertainty affects the size of the audience for a Premier League football match while it is being played. The probabilities of scoreless draws, score draws, home and away wins evolve through the game and their computation forms the basis of the work. They find some support for the UO hypothesis, but also that viewers prefer to see a game that has a winner and that people are attracted to games that take an unexpected turn.

In a further innovation, Forrest, Beaumont, Goddard and Simmons (2005) find that teams' current season pre-match points per game at home and away, and estimates of the ratio of the probability of a home win relative to that of an away win to help to explain attendance at football league matches in the 1997–1998 season. While points per game are viewed as indicators of team quality, Forrest, Simmons and Buraimo (2005) regard points per game as a match UO variable; clearly the precise role played by points per game is somewhat unclear.[2]

8.3.4 Summary

To summarize this section, Table 8.1 presents some of the studies in summary form, with the sport, the period analyzed, the dependent variable, indicator of UO and results summary. As can be seen, a mixed set of results are apparent although on balance league standings, rather than their differences, and betting odds appear to be significant determinants of attendance. There is also some indication that this is more likely to be discovered with more recent studies.

8.4 MEDIUM-TERM UNCERTAINTY OF OUTCOME

8.4.1 Within-season uncertainty of outcome

Within-season UO concerns which team will take the championship title, as opposed to the UO about the outcome of a particular game. There is also limited agreement on how to measure this facet of UO. An early classic piece, however, is Borland (1987) which used four measures of UO in an analysis of annual attendance at Australian Rules football.[3] In each of the four measures an average of observations was made at four points during the season. The intention was to obtain measures of UO as the season develops, rather than to compute a single measure for the whole season. The last two observations were also given double weight so that a given amount of UO is of more importance as the season draws to its close. The first of the four measures

---

[2] The authors also simulate how many spectators would be lost if perfect UO is established. It seems safe to infer from the paper that the pursuit of greater UO, ignoring home advantage, may reach a point at which further "improvements" in UO (as Cairns et al hypothesized) begin to reduce attendance and gate revenue. But the point estimate of 2 million fewer tickets sold appears rather more speculative than the authors admit.

[3] This paper is also noteworthy, being an early attempt to simultaneously model both long- and medium-term UO.

considers the spread between the top and bottom teams in the league. The second measure is the sum of the coefficients of variation of the numbers of games won by all teams, which incorporates information about the performances of all teams.

> *The coefficient of variation is a standardized measure of dispersion of data. It is calculated by dividing the standard deviation of the data by its mean value.*

The third measure is the average number of games a team is behind the leader. Other things being equal, the fewer the number of games in hand the lower the probability that the lead will change. The final measure is the number of teams that have been in, or at most two games out of, the leading four (at that time) teams that are eligible for the (play-off) finals, at each of the four measurement points. There was some evidence that the third measure affected attendance. As with earlier studies that used similar variables, for example, Demmert (1973) and Noll (1974), there is inevitably some arbitrariness in how one defines "close to" championship success. Table 8.2 presents some studies and also measures of UO.

8.4.2 Seasonal (team-specific) uncertainty of outcome

The seasonal (team-specific) UO literature exploits the externality property of UO inasmuch as while attention is on the seasonal outcome, as opposed to a specific game as with the measure of UO just discussed, the underlying concept is that spectators go to matches primarily to see their own teams win. UO is a by-product of having several teams "in contention" for the championship, preferably as late into the season as possible to maintain spectator interest. There are differences of opinion about how to model this and Appendix 8.1 shows how differences between two of the classic approaches may be reconciled. It has been observed that researchers have obtained slightly more robust estimates of the impact of this form of UO (Borland and MacDonald, 2003).

The pioneering work of Jennett (1984) based on an analysis of Scottish football attendances merits careful consideration, not least because his method has been adopted and/or modified by others, among them Borland and Lye (1992), Dobson and Goddard (1992, 2001) and Kuypers (1996). Jennett proposed a simply-measured variable to capture the development of UO through the season, match by match. His evolutionary approach stands in stark contrast to the computation of a single statistic to represent uncertainty in an entire season. He aimed to measure the uncertainty that attaches to every game. In any given match, one or both teams may start with a chance of championship "glory." Matches where one team (preferably both) may win

TABLE 8.2   Some findings on the effects of medium-term uncertainty

Author/date	Sport/period	Dependent variable	Indicator/s	Comment
Jennett 1984	Scottish Premier League football 1975–1976 to1980–1981	Match attendance	Home significance	Significant
			Away significance	Significant
			Relegation (H&A) significance	Insignificant
Borland 1987	Australian Rules football 1950–1986	Log of attendance per round* per capita *See Borland	Average number of games in hand over leader	Insignificant
Borland and Lye 1992	Australian Rules football 1981–1986	Log of match attendance	Three other indexes	All insignificant
			Sum of the number of games required for both teams to reach the finals	Significant
			Games where both are in the top 5	Significant
Dobson and Goddard 1992	Football League; 24 teams; 2 seasons starting 1989–1999	Log of match attendance	Log of home significance	Significant
Bairnbridge, Cameron and Dawson 1996	Premier League football 1993–1994	Log of match attendance	Log of away significance	Insignificant
			Both in top 4	Insignificant
Kuypers 1996	English Premier League football 1993–1994	Match attendance	Both in bottom 4	Insignificant
			Team has won title	Insignificant
			Home champ sig, games left times points behind	Significant
	Live Sky football matches 1993–1994	Proportion of Sky subscribers watching live football	Home relegation sig index	Significant
			Home champ sig	Significant
Falter and Perignon 2003	French soccer 1997–1998	Log of match attendance	Home rel sig	Significant
			Season dummies for each match	Significant

TABLE 8.2 *(Continued)*

Author/date	Sport/period	Dependent variable	Indicator/s	Comment
Dawson, Dobson, Goddard and Wilson 2005	English Premier League football 1996–2003	Log of disciplinary points y = 1, r = 2 issued per match	Home team champ sig*	Insignificant
			Away team champ sig* *See D & G above	Significant
Carmichael, Millington and Simmons 1999	English rugby league, season 1994–1995	Log of match attendance	Pre-season odds on the division title	Significant
Garcia and Rodriguez 2002	Spanish League football 1992–1993 to 1995–1996	Log of match attendance	Product of points behind and games left	Significant
Owen and Weatherston 2004	Super 12s RU	Log of Match Attendance	SEASON, numbers matches 1–11	Significant

the championship have more "championship significance." Ideally research-ers would be able to observe spectators' subjective expectations of their own teams' championship prospects prior to every match but, of course, this is impossible. Consequently, Jennett proposed a measure based on the mathe-matical possibility of winning the title in any given year, and found statistically significant results.[4] The estimated significance of any forthcoming match in this model is simply the reciprocal of the number of wins currently needed (WN) for the team to win the championship. This is indicated in Equation 8.1:

$$\text{Sig}_J = 1/\text{WN} \qquad (8.1)$$

In subsequent studies, Wilson and Sim (1995) found Jennett's measure significant in their study of attendance at Malaysian semi-professional soccer games. Dobson and Goddard (1992) provided a modified measure, converted into an index that always takes a positive value. They find the home side's match significance variable has a positively significant effect on English soccer attendance, but not the away side's match significance variable.

Cairns (1990) noted that Jennett's model is essentially backward-look-ing inasmuch as it requires one to know how many points the winners accumulated. In contrast, a forward-looking model would enable the po-tential spectator (and the investigator) to estimate the championship po-tential of every game for each side in advance. Some success with a semi-forward-looking index of match significance was obtained by Dobson and Goddard (2001, Chapter 3) who examined twenty-seven years' of football league match data between 1973 and 1999. They estimate a match-level forecasting model that includes both teams' league success over the previ-ous 24 months, plus more recent success and indicators of whether the match has championship and/or relegation significance for the home and away sides. Their model proved superior to random forecasts in predicting home and away wins and the coefficients of the match significance vari-ables were both correctly signed and statistically significant.

Dawson, Dobson, Goddard and Wilson (2005) used the same forward-looking index of seasonal match significance in their study of the occurrence of disciplinary sanctions, finding it to have a statistically significant effect on sanctions imposed on the visitors, but not on the home team. Whether this is primarily because visitors feel under more pressure playing away from home and try a little too hard or because (see below) match officials tend to give the benefit of the doubt to home sides is an interesting question.

---

[4] This model cannot be applied to the current season, since it requires the researcher to know exactly how many points will be required for championship success.

One of the less satisfactory aspects of Jennett's model, pointed out by Borland and Lye (1992), is that while it gives sensible results for teams that have to win every remaining game, it produces rather nonsensical results when a team has more games left than wins required, suggesting the same significance level for any number of matches left, say if only one more win is required. Borland and Lye suggest (but do not implement) a revision of the original model that takes into account the number of games left (GL) as well as WN. It incorporates both WN and GL, as detailed in Equation 8.2:

$$Sig_{BL} = (WN/GL) \qquad (8.2)$$

Another example is Kuypers (1996), who proposes a number of indices of forward-looking match significance involving GL and WN. The preferred index is given in Equation 8.3:

$$Sig_K = GL \times PB \qquad (8.3)$$

PB is points currently behind the leader, which plays a role equivalent to Jennett's WN. Kuypers (1996) finds Sig_K statistically significant in a study of English football from 1993 to 1994. Garcia and Rodriguez (2002) employ Sig_K in their study of Spanish league football and find it statistically significant.

One of the problems with these approaches is that they assume that winning, say, two from two games is the same as, say, ten from ten, and do not account for the difference in cumulative difficulty. Downward and Dawson (2005b) offer a suggestion for combining these approaches, as given in Equation 8.4:

$$Sig_{DD} = (1/GL)exp(WN/GL) \qquad (8.4)$$

Exp is the base of natural logarithms, while the exponent is clearly seen to be Sig_{BL} so that Borland and Lye's contribution is directly represented in the exponential model. Jennett's contribution is represented indirectly via GL, in other words Sig_{DD} encompasses the earlier models. Appendix 8.1 indicates how it resolves the anomalies of each approach.

8.4.3 Summary

As with match UO, within-season UO research produces some mixed results, although here there is less agreement that the UO hypothesis receives support. Studies summarized in Table 8.1 and 8.2 suggest that, in the shorter run at least, a team's success is at least as important as UO for determining match attendances.

8.5 LONG-RUN UNCERTAINTY OF OUTCOME

8.5.1 Competitive balance

The desire to promote long run UO or competitive balance in sporting leagues is due to the fear that domination by a few teams may result in a loss of spectator interest, revenue and profit, as implied in Chapter 7. As noted above Borland (1987) produced a seminal piece of work investigating medium-term UO. However, another contribution was to employ a variable to try to capture the effects of long-term UO on Australian Rules football match attendance by the number of teams that have reached the previous three years' play-offs, divided by the number of places available. A larger value of the variable is consistent with a lower level of long-run concentration. No significant results were identified, but it could be that three years does not constitute a sufficient indication of the long run. In turn Borland and Lye (1992) employed a related index that consisted of the sum of the number of times both contestants had made it to the final stages in the previous three years. The significance of this variable was uncertain.

In a long-run study of English soccer Dobson and Goddard (1992) used the logs of the teams' mean final league positions and the season prior to that in which the match took place as indexes of historical success, and found them to be significant and correctly signed determinants of attendance. Furthermore, while few attempts have been made to model the long-run significance of individual games, there is one index that consistently shows the expected (positive) effect on attendance and is almost consistently statistically significant; this measure is to identify derbies.

Most research focusing on competitive balance has examined the evolution of the dispersion of seasonal rankings of teams over time. Many researchers focusing on US professional team sports have used the standard deviation of win percent (a measure of dispersion of success) as an indicator of within-season UO. For example, Fort and Quirk (1995) inquire whether the sample standard deviation of win percent is significantly greater than the level that would characterize a perfectly balanced league. Appendix 8.2 indicates how this can be measured.

TABLE 8.3 Mean SDWPs in baseball and football by sub-periods, 1901–1990

League	1950–1959	1960–1969	1970–1979	1980–1990	1901–1990 average
AL	97(40)	83(39)	76(39)	65(39)	n.a.(40)
NL	80(40)	82(39)	68(39)	65(39)	n.a.(40)
NFL	210(144)	222(135)	208(132)	191(125)	n.a.(140)

Note: n.a. = not applicable.

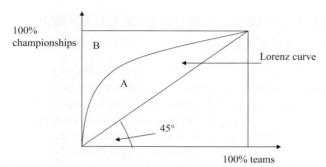

FIGURE 8.1 *The Lorenz curve and Gini coefficient.*

Some standard deviations of win percent (SDWP) covering five US sports leagues for the period 1901–1990, are presented in Table 8.3, taken from Quirk and Fort (1992). The numbers not in brackets in columns 2–5 are average SDWPs computed for the periods indicated. The numbers in brackets are the corresponding SDWPs for perfectly balanced leagues. Note that every number has been multiplied by 1000 to avoid decimal points.[5] In these leagues win percent was less evenly distributed than as would occur in perfectly balanced leagues.

Another way to report this phenomenon is to count the number of win percents in the tails of the distribution. Fort and Quirk (1995) report that, for the major league US professional team sports, there are too many win percents in the tails of the distribution, to be consistent with the sports being perfectly balanced, suggesting a wide variation in performance.

Schmidt and Berri (2001) examined how well-balanced major league baseball has been since 1901, using the Gini coefficient. This is related to the Lorenz curve, which is illustrated in Figure 8.1. Here, the percentage of teams and championship successes are plotted against one another. The 45° line indicates a situation of equal distribution of wins between teams, and would constitute a perfectly balanced league. The Lorenz curve, which is the curved line, plots the "actual" distribution of championship wins per club. Because the curve lies above the 45° line this shows that fewer clubs have won more championships than in the balanced case. The area,

---

[5] These figures are approximations, as is made clear elsewhere in this chapter. Ideally, the leagues should exclude draws, but the NFL does not satisfy this criterion and every team should play every other league member the same number of times per season, none of these leagues possesses this property.

A, divided by the sum of areas A and B can be used to derive the Gini coefficient, whose value must lie between 0 and 1, with the latter indicating complete inequality.

Schmidt and Berri's (2001) analysis suggests that concentration is not a serious problem and has, if anything, declined since 1901. However, their procedure was criticized by Utt and Fort (2002) on the basis that the Gini coefficient is useful in measuring horizontal industrial concentration as its values range from "1," where the industry is a pure monopoly, to around "0" where it comprises many very small firms. But, as Utt and Fort point out, no team can monopolize a season's wins in baseball. They adjust the Gini coefficient by comparing the actual distribution of win percents against the most unequal case, where the champions win all their games, the runners-up win all but those lost to the champions, and so on down to the bottom team which loses every game. Not surprisingly, their adjusted Gini coefficients exceed those of Schmidt and Berri, suggesting the leagues are in fact rather less competitively balanced than the latter authors had concluded. Utt and Fort's criticism applies equally to Michie and Oughton (2004) who estimate Lorenz curves of team shares of total points earned in English soccer for the seasons 1950–1951, 1993–1994 and 2004–2005.

Reflection Question 8.1

Why would the Gini coefficient of points share be calculated rather than win percents in English football?

Hint: Consider the form of game results in soccer compared to baseball.

The calculations are based on point shares to allow for the fact that, in football, games can be won, drawn or lost, and consequently win percents are misleading. Michie and Oughton (2004) find that competitive balance in English soccer has (apparently) declined sharply since 1993–1994 (see also Szymanski and Kuypers, 1999). Significantly, Utt and Fort suggest that, as nobody knows how to adjust for these departures from the ideal, researchers should stick to standard deviations of win percents as indexes of competitive balance.

The problem with this recommendation, however, is that standard deviations measured over several seasons do not permit a reliable distinction between cases where the overall spread of results is more or less identical year-on-year, but the distribution of success is more highly concentrated in one instance than another. This question is addressed by Eckard (2001) and Humphreys (2002). Using essentially the same approach, they partition the total league win percent variability into a component that captures the variation of teams' annual win percents about their own mean win percent or "time variance" and "cumulative variance" that captures the variation in teams' cumulative win percents across all teams.[6] Other things being equal, an increase in the first element implies an increase in competitive balance, whereas an increase in the latter element implies a decrease in competitive balance. The ratio of the first element to the total variation of win percents defines a competitive balance ratio (CBR). Eckard (2001) finds that competitive balance in the American League (AL) may have been markedly lower in 1995–1999 than in the other periods, while in the National League (NL) competitive balance may have been lower but not markedly so. Applying this approach to European sports may be more problematic, because promotion and relegation changes leagues' memberships annually, and draws are commonplace.

Eckard also examines the degree of concentration among the top four and (separately) the bottom four teams in both the NL and AL in all sub-periods; with five years in each there are 20 slots available in each sub-period. Herfindahl indexes (HI) of team shares in those leading positions are calculated. The Herfindahl index is the sum of squares of team shares (win percents in Eckard's study) in the 20 positions available in each five-year period. For example, if the same four teams feature every year (the highest concentration by this definition) each obtains 25% of all the places, so the HI takes the value $HI = 25^2 + 25^2 + 25^2 + 25^2 = 2500$.

Reflection Question 8.2

What value would the index take if shares of wins rather than percents were used?
Hint: Introduce the appropriate decimal points to the calculation.

If genuine shares of wins were used in the analysis, then the HI would emerge as 0.25. In this regard, the index reveals the "representative" number of teams that dominate the championship, in this respect 0.25 implies four teams. Eckard finds that the HI for the AL is highest in 1995–1999, which is also the five-year period in which the number of teams securing places in the top four is at its lowest, i.e., six. This is consistent with the findings based on his decomposition of win percents. In every sub-period more NL (than AL) teams made it into the top four, while the HI tended downwards consistent with his findings that competitive balance in the NL improved over the period.

---

[6] Humphreys uses standard deviations.

Humphreys (2002) computes decade-by-decade CBRs and HIs of first place finishes, again only for teams that played each year in the decade. Note that the HIs were computed from shares not percents (see Reflection Question 8.2). The CBRs trend slightly upward and the HIs downward over the period, suggesting improved balance in both the NL and the AL. Humphreys examines whether CBR, HI and the standard deviation of win percent affects attendances, and finds that only the CBR is statistically significant and positively signed suggesting that, other things being equal, more competitive balance drew more spectators to MLB. Elsewhere in the world Lee (2006) models the attendance at Korean professional baseball for the 21 seasons 1982–2002, making use of the win percents of the top and bottom 20% of teams and finds that the more evenly win percents are distributed the greater is attendance, as expected.

More informally, Szymanski and Kuypers report (1999) that between the start of the English football league in 1889–1890 and 1939, seventeen teams won the championship; Aston Villa and Sunderland won on no fewer than six occasions each, while Everton and Arsenal each won five. This constituted almost half of all the seasons then contested – the World Wars disrupted the Football League's programme. Since the resumption of professional football in 1946, Liverpool has taken their championship tally to 18, Manchester United to 15 and Arsenal to 13. In the Netherlands Ajax with 29, PSV with 19 and Feyenoord with 14 dominate the top division, while the Spanish domestic league championship has been won 29 times by Real Madrid, 18 times by Barcelona and 9 times by Atletico Madrid. Anderlecht on 28 occasions and Brugge on 13 have won the league championship of Belgium. At the top level, the European Cup/European Champions' League has been won nine times by Real Madrid, six times by AC Milan, five times by Liverpool and four times each by Bayern Munich and Ajax. The major domestic knockout cup competitions have been similarly dominated. In cricket the England and Wales County Championship – first contested in 1890 – has been won by Yorkshire on thirty occasions with four shared wins, while Surrey have compiled 18 wins and four shares. Of the 18 teams now participating Durham, Northamptonshire, Gloucestershire and Somerset have never won a championship.

Further, the Sheffield Shield interstate championship in Australia and the comparable series (the Currie Cup) in South Africa have been dominated by the most populous provinces; New South Wales and Traansvaal/Gauteng respectively, with the next most populous provinces Victoria and Natal/Kwa Zulu the closest rivals. Tasmania, the smallest and least populous Australian state, has never won the Sheffield Shield. In these latter cases, however, one should bear in mind that these data tell only a part of the story as (unlike win percents) they ignore the teams that finish the season in lower positions.

Different conclusions might be reached if all teams' annual points' totals were computed and analyzed. The more general point is that, as with UO in the short- and medium-term, there is no ready-made index that one could argue comes closest to capturing the multi-dimensional phenomenon that is competitive balance. Moreover, what one wants to know is not so much whether imbalance exists in sports leagues, but whether it is of a sufficient degree to warrant concern. Nonetheless, Table 8.4 summarizes the effects of some studies examining competitive balance on attendance. There is some evidence that attendances are affected by competitive balance.

8.5.2 Evolution of competitive balance

Finally, although there is limited research there seems to be no convincing body of evidence that sports leagues do evolve towards perfect balance. Dobson, Goddard and Ramlogan (2001) inquire whether English football between 1926 and 1997 obeys Gibrat's law of proportional effect (Gibrat, 1931).

> *Gibrat's law suggests that the size of a firm and its growth rate are independent. If Gibrat's law holds, one would expect the size distribution of the firms in an industry to remain constant.*

Clearly, if the bigger members of an industry systematically grow more rapidly than smaller ones, and if the process continues, the industry will become more concentrated. If the small firms grow faster and if the process continues, the industry will tend to become less concentrated. Given enough time, the sizes of all firms (as measured by, say, revenue or assets) would converge on an "equilibrium" value, although whether this occurs also depends on random factors. Dobson, Goddard and Ramlogan find that from the 1920s until the late 1950s there was a period of steady adjustment towards equilibrium. From the late 1950s until the late 1970s it is suggested that there was no tendency to revenue convergence, but this occurred from the late 1970s until about 1990 and convergence also seems to have broken down in the 1990s; the authors conclude there may have been two periods of relative equilibrium, followed by two of major change.

The causes are not identified from the model itself, but the earlier breakdown of stability came during a period of marked social change. Population drift towards southern England and also from the inner cities, and increased access to private transport may have been important, as well as the influence of the media in the creation of national support for some teams. It also begins around the time that the maximum wage was abolished, forcing clubs to increase admission charges that had been virtually unaltered since the 1920s. The 1990s breakdown of convergence took place against the simultaneous effects

TABLE 8.4 Some findings on the effects of competitive balance on attendance

Author/date	Sport/period	Dependent variable	Indicator/s	Comment
Borland 1987	Australian Rules football 1950–1986	Log of attendance per round* per capita *See Borland	Number of teams in the final stages previous three years divided by places available	Insignificant
Borland and Lye 1992	Australian Rules football 1981–1986	Log of match attendance	Sum of times both teams in finals previous three years	Borders on significance
Humphries, 2002	Baseball, AL and NL 1901–1999	Log of total league annual attendance	Comp balance ratio	Significant
			H Index of win percent	Borders on significance
			Std deviation of win percent	Insignificant
Schmidt and Berri 2001	Baseball AL and NL, annual data 1901–1998	Log of team annual attendance	Lagged Gini measures** See S&B	Significant
		Log of league annual attendance	As above	Significant
Lee 2006	KPBL 1982–2002	Log of aggregate season attendance	LTL, captures the dispersion of the win percents of the top and bottom 1/5 of teams	Significant

of the Bosman Ruling that enhanced players' bargaining power, the influx of money from broadcasters, and the (related) setting up of the Premier League. Add the transition to all-seater stadiums and the necessary rise in ticket prices, and there are plenty of factors that would be expected to shake up the industry structure.

8.5.3 Summary

In summary, as Downward and Dawson (2000) argued, the upshot of this discussion and that of previous sections is that the UO hypothesis seems to be rather overworked as a phenomenon that affects attendances inasmuch as it is not ubiquitously important, despite the ingenuity with which it has been measured.

8.6 HOME ADVANTAGE

As indicated in Chapter 7, and noted above, UO is to an extent inextricably bound up with the potential occurrence of home advantage. The phenomenon of home advantage is well-established in some sports, e.g., soccer, baseball and ice hockey, although not in major golf and tennis tournaments. Neville and Holder (1999) survey the field discussing measurement issues and potential causal factors. The simplest cases to analyze are balanced leagues, where it might be expected that, in the absence of home advantage, the home team should win 50% of games (exclusive of draws). Win percents that are significantly in excess of 50% are noted based on two (alternative) measures. HWP[a] includes drawn games; a team gains two points for a win, one for a draw and zero for losing. HWP[b] is the number of games won at home as a percentage of decided (won) games. Combining the results of nine studies of soccer (40 493 games) HWP[a] is equal to 63.9% and HWP[b] is equal to 68.3%. (Clearly the second measure must always be at least as great as the first.) In balanced leagues the home advantage passes around competitors, which tends to eliminate differences in team quality, so this factor does not need to be accounted for before computing HWP.[7]

---

[7] Golf, athletics and tennis championships and other unbalanced tournaments create new problems. For example, it is not safe to infer from the fact that US golfers often win the Open and (almost without exception) the USPGA that there is positive home advantage in the US and a negative home advantage in Britain. The observation is perfectly consistent with the alternative hypothesis that, by and large, American (male) golfers are better at stroke play than their British counterparts. This may be allowed for, using players' pre-match performance rankings as quality indexes, when the apparent ground advantage tends to diminish, Nevill and Holder (1999). Chapter 11 discusses sample selection issues.

Downward and Jones (2007) found four main causal factors that have been identified and their influence investigated in the literature: familiarity with the location; the effects of travel; location-related rules; and the crowd. It seems the crowd is likely to be the most important of these in European sports. Barnett and Hilditch (1993) found a significant home advantage in English soccer accruing to clubs, such as Luton Town, that had invested in artificial pitches. These have since been banned in English and Scottish football. On the other hand, there was no pressure in the US to standardize playing surfaces in baseball, suggesting that it is not seen there as a serious problem. Koning (2004) finds evidence of a small but significant level of home advantage in women's speed skating, probably related in part to familiarity with the locations. There is some suggestion that travel, especially across time zones, may contribute to home advantage in the US, but this can hardly be a factor in European national sports leagues (apart from Russia). Nevertheless, these sometimes show considerably higher degrees of home advantage (see Pollard, 2006a), although it might operate in UEFA competitions. There is no European equivalent of the rule in baseball that the home team bats last, which is often assumed to confer an advantage.

Some studies have suggested that home advantage increases with crowd size, e.g., Schwartz and Barsky (1977) in baseball, Dawson, Dobson, Goddard and Wilson (2005) in English soccer, while Downward and Jones (2007) and Pollard (2006b) find that the effect may be nonlinear. One possible explanation is that the most attended matches are ones that attract more away and neutral spectators, so the crowd is less supportive of the home side. Nobody is quite sure just how the crowd effect operates; it might be that players are more confident in front of their home crowds or that match officials' decisions are sensitive to the crowd. Neville, Balmer and Williams (1999a) report that crowds may well influence officials' decisions, as indicated by experimental tests of observees watching video replays of 52 soccer tackles, 26 by the home and 26 by the away sides, with half the participants hearing no sound. The participants who heard sound tended to judge statistically significantly but slightly to the benefit of the home side. Mascarenhas, Collins and Mortimer (2005) show considerable inconsistency in the rulings of even well-qualified match officials examining videos of rugby union tackles chosen from 60 hours of tapes shown to three groups of expert officials (referees, referee coaches and line judges) ranked by their experience. Dawson, Dobson, Goddard and Wilson (2005) also find that there is inconsistency in soccer referee's decisions. If (say) two or three decisions in a single match go in the wrong direction, the effect on one of the clubs might be quite serious, e.g., elimination from the

TABLE 8.5 Some findings on home advantage

Author/date	Sport/period	Dependent variable	Indicator/s	Comment
Morley and Thomas (2005)	One-day English Cricket 1996–1997	Win or loss (logistic regression)	Venue, attendance, home and away performance	57% home wins but inconclusive on why
Boyko et al (2007)	English Premier league 1992–2005	Goal differential	Attendance, referee identity	Evidence of bias
Johnston (2008)	English Premier League 2006–2007	Goal differential	Attendance, referee identity	No evidence
Morton (2006)	Super-14 and Tri-Nations rugby 2000–2004	Points difference	Venue	Home advantage
Clarke (2005)	Australian Rules football 1980–1998	% of games won; margin of victory	Venue	80% home advantage
Pollard and Pollard (2005)	NL 1876–2002			
	AL 1901–2002 NHL 1917–2003 NFL 1933–2002			
	English Football 1888–2003	% of home wins (baseball and basketball) % of total points for others	Time series description	Greater in early years
Jacklin (2005)	English football 1946–2002	Ratio of home to away wins	Time series description	Reduction in home advantage since 1945
Pollard (2006)	Association Football 1998–2003 72 countries	% of total points	Geographic area	Home advantage
Page and Page (2006)	Champions League/European cup 1955–2006 (knockout matches) UEFA Cup 1971–2006 Inter-Cities Fairs Cup 1955–1971 Cup Winners Cup 1960–1999	Probability of win when second-leg is at home (logistic regression)		Significant but decreasing (53–59% approx)

European Champions' League. More worrying (although the sample size is small), in view of the immense match-fixing scandal that has recently shaken up Italian soccer, is the potential that inaccuracy and disagreement between qualified officials may create for corruption. Table 8.5 summarizes some of the literature.

The above brief discussion suggests two important factors connected with uncertainty of outcome. The first is that, clearly, home advantage should be controlled for in seeking to examine the UO hypothesis. The second point is that, to the extent that bias affects results and thus UO, and inasmuch as attendance affects the bias, then it suggests a degree of simultaneity exists between attendance and UO which should be allowed for in studies of the demand for professional team sports. As Chapter 10 illustrates, this has not always been accounted for.

8.7 CONCLUSION

The above discussion suggests that there has been considerable innovation in the design of indices of UO, but disagreement between studies remains as to the effect of outcome uncertainty on match attendance (the traditional focus of attention). However, there is stronger evidence that home bias affects sports encounters. The main welfare concern is over long-term domination, its possible effect on interest and ultimately on league revenue and profitability, and it is these issues and their potential sources which now need further analysis, which is undertaken in subsequent chapters.

Appendix 8.1 Reconciliation of Jennett's and Borland and Lye's Models of Medium-term Uncertainty of Outcome

Downward and Dawson (2005b) suggest a simple equation determining match significance to encompass both Jennett's and Borland and Lye's indices of UO. This is presented in Equation A8.1.1:

$$\mathrm{Sig}_{DD} = (1/GL)\exp^{(WN/GL)} \tag{A8.1.1}$$

Exp is (as earlier) the base of natural logarithms, while the exponent is clearly seen to be Sig_{BL} so that Borland and Lye's contribution is directly represented in the exponential model. Jennett's model is represented indirectly via GL, in other words Sig_{DD} encompasses the earlier models. To show how Jennett's model is incorporated requires some explanation of, and justification for, the underlying model.

The rationale behind Sig_{DD} is relatively simple. It is assumed that the championship winner is the team that does most cumulative work during the season; in this context the one that accumulates most wins. Jennett's index may be seen primarily as an index of duration, WN wins cannot be acquired in fewer than WN games, the successful team is the one that stays the course. In contrast, Borland and Lye's index tracks the required work rate, crudely expressed as (WN/GL). Work rate and cumulative work are different concepts; Manchester City took four of a possible six Premier League points from Chelsea in 2004–2005, a unique work rate against Chelsea. However, they did not sustain that effort long enough to mount a title challenge. Neither the duration nor the work rate by itself measures work completed, although as total work is essentially a sum of products of work rates and durations some combination of the two is the minimal requirement for an index that aims to capture cumulative work. This is what Sig_{DD} is designed to accomplish. GL in the denominator acts as a clock, determining how long any required work rate (WN/GL) must be sustained. A team remains in contention only as long as (WN/GL) ≤ 1. The clock mechanism captures Jennett's model. High significance near the end of the season identifies a team that is close to championship success; early in the season it signifies a team that is heading for failure. This model differs in several respects from either of its progenitors. First the maximum significance level (one to win, one to play) is exp, not one. In this regard the incorporation of a "glory"dummy as with Jennett makes sense. That the model successfully avoids the pitfalls discussed in the chapter is simply demonstrated in Table A8.1.1.

Table A8.1.1 shows that the encompassing model gives sensible outcomes whether Team A has to win every game or not. The second column represents the case in which every game must be won and the team enters a winning streak; this is the case in which Borland and Lye's model fails, because it attaches the same score to each match. Given that the number of games left declines, Jennett's argument is that each successive game should be accorded more significance and the encompassing model satisfies this requirement. The third column shows that, as expected, match significance goes to zero when the team loses its first game. The fourth column shows that, needing to win one of three, if Team A succeeds in the first game it plays out the season as champions; again there is no problem here. In the fifth column, Team A is advancing towards the title very uncertainly, dropping two games. The significance of each remaining game increases just as Jennet requires, although his own model did not have this characteristic. The encompassing model (Sig_{DD}) clearly outperforms its antecedents, considered as a theoretical construct; how it might fare in empirical work remains to be seen.

TABLE A8.1.1 Significance of Team A's last three games under various assumptions about how many wins are needed (encompassing model)

Match	Team A, WN = 3, wins first two	Team A, WN = 3, loses the first	Team A, WN = 1, wins the first	Team A, WN = 1, loses the first two
16th	0.33exp	0.33exp	0.33exp0.33	0.33exp0.33
17th	0.50exp	0.0	exp Champions	0.50exp0.5
18th	exp Potential Champions	0.0	exp Champions	exp Potential Champions

Appendix 8.2 Calculating the Dispersion of Sporting Success in Sports Leagues Using Standard Deviations

Computing the sample SDWP for a given season

Let the league have N members. At the close of the season every team's win percent X_i (for the ith team) is known.

- STEP 1 Compute the deviation of each team's win percent from the mean; viz., for the ith team compute $(X_i - 0.5)$ – the ith team's mean deviation.
- STEP 2 Square each of the N mean deviations.
- STEP 3 Sum the squares.
- STEP 4 Divide the sum of squares by N*.
  *For small samples one often divides by $(N - 1)$.
- STEP 5 Take the square root of the number you calculated at STEP 4. The resulting figure is the SDWP of the league for that season.
- To arrive at the SDWP for a decade, compute the ten relevant SDWPs and take the average.

Computing the sample SDWP for a balanced league

The key to understanding the mean and standard deviations of win percents in a competitively balanced league lies in noting that sporting leagues in the US can be understood in terms of the binomial probability distribution. This distribution provides a means of answering binomial probability questions that are common in many aspects of business and economics. Typically, binomial problems have the following characteristics:

- there are "n" independent trials;
- there are two possible outcomes to each trial, success or failure;
- the probability "p" of a particular outcome occurring is the same in each trial.

Under these conditions, the binomial random variable is the number of successes that occur in "n" trials. This distribution describes some US sporting leagues that are balanced. For example, taking the league just described, there are:

1. "n" fixtures;
2. fixtures have to be won or lost;
3. crucially, the probability of a win for a team is the same in each fixture and must equal 0.5 in a balanced set of fixtures.

This means that one can define win percents as a binomial random variable. The mean of a binomial distribution is "np" which, in a sporting context, must be equal to 0.5n. The standard deviation of a binomial distribution is $\sqrt{np(1 - p)}$, which in a sporting context is $\sqrt{0.25n}$. As the win percent for any team is w/n, the mean win percent will be given by n(w/n) = w = 0.5. The variance of the win percent will be equal to Var (w/n) = Var (w)/n2. As Var (w) = np(1 - p) = 0.25n, Var (w/n) = $0.25n/n^2$ = 0.25/n. The standard deviation of a balanced league win percent will be equal to $0.5/\sqrt{n}$.

CHAPTER 9

Cross-Subsidization in Professional Sports Leagues

- ■ To understand the economic theory of sports leagues
- ■ To understand the rationale for, and forms of, cross-subsidization in professional sports leagues
- ■ To assess the impacts of cross-subsidization on competitive balance in sports leagues
- ■ To appreciate the empirical evidence relating to the effectiveness of cross-subsidization

9.1 INTRODUCTION

Chapter 7 introduced the "peculiar economics" of professional team sports, suggesting that there is a need to coordinate clubs' activities in leagues. In this chapter the main forms of cross-subsidization policy employed in leagues, purportedly to ensure that competitive balance is preserved, is discussed. The next section clarifies the economic rationale for cross-subsidization. Section 9.3 then outlines the variety of policies that have been employed in sports leagues. Section 9.4 outlines the "standard model" that has been employed to theoretically analyze sports leagues. It can be argued that the model has the character of US sports leagues, inasmuch as it is assumed that teams have a profit maximization objective, as discussed in Chapter 7, and that the labour market for players is closed. Section 9.4 considers the implication of changing the objectives from clubs to a version of utility maximization, in which teams seek to maximize their wins subject to a profit constraint. It is argued that this might be a more appropriate assumption for European leagues. Section 9.5 then further relaxes these assumptions to explore the impact of having spectators caring about absolute playing quality, that the scale of markets may produce diseconomies of scale from playing talent, and that the supply of talent

233

might be variable because of open, international markets. In short, the chapter argues that the potential for a corrective impact of cross-subsidization of teams appears to lie with revenue sharing in a win maximizing league, but remains an area requiring further theoretical and particularly empirical analysis. The chapter concludes with a discussion of the relevance of the UO hypothesis.

9.2 THE RATIONALE FOR CROSS-SUBSIDIZATION

An economic rationale for cross-subsidization lies in the market structure of sporting leagues which, as discussed in Chapter 7, can be viewed as oligopoly markets operating as producer cartels within which clubs need to compete in sporting terms, but also to cooperate to ensure that the sports are managed effectively. To attain these ends, leagues have traditionally set the terms of sporting competition and have directly influenced the economic aspects of competition, influencing admission price structures, negotiating television deals and sponsorship arrangements and last, but not least, controlling the terms on which players may move between clubs. It is important to note in this regard that sports leagues have practised these policies in spite of them being generally prohibited in other industries. Public policy agencies have traditionally taken the view, informed by economic theory, that an industry's attempt to regulate the terms under which its members operate will act contrary to the public interest. This is enshrined in legislation such as the Sherman Act (1890) and the Clayton Act (1914) in the US, the Monopolies and Restrictive Practices Act (1948) and the Restrictive Trade Practices Act (1956) in the UK. Nowadays, UK competition policy, as with other European countries, is subsidiary overall to EU competition policy, as discussed in Chapter 2.

Despite these legal frameworks there has been little historical government intervention in sporting markets. In 1922 the US Supreme Court ruled that baseball was exempt from the provisions of the Sherman Act, because it did not represent interstate commerce and although this ruling has often been criticized it has never been overturned. While other US team sports have never attained the same degree of immunity from the provisions of competition policy, they have been relatively leniently treated. Matters have tended to change, however, since the 1960s with a general reduction in the degree of regulation in both the product and labour markets in which cross-subsidization has typically operated. This has generally arisen concurrently with the reorganization of league financial arrangements, as well as a general political shift towards the advocacy of free market allocation of resources.

9.3 METHODS OF CROSS-SUBSIDIZATION

While differing in detail, leagues have traditionally intervened in sporting labour markets or regulated the distribution of club revenues. Targeting sports labour markets may seem to be an unusual way to affect competitive balance insofar as one is seeking directly to influence the price and availability of inputs (players) rather than output (sporting results), which is the ultimate object of the policy. However, players' salaries and wages comprise the bulk of professional sports teams' costs in both the US and Europe. Secondly, unlike other forms of production, it is labour in the production function of sport, the players, who ultimately determine performance on the field.

9.3.1 Sporting labour markets

Leagues have attempted to influence clubs' talent, finance and results by applying three major types of labour market policy instrument: drafting systems; salary caps; and reserve option arrangements. The best known example of a drafting system is the "Rookie Draft" in American football, introduced by the National Football League (NFL) 1936. The National Basketball Association (NBA) employed a similar system in the 1950s and Major League Baseball (MLB) introduced a draft in 1965. The National Hockey League (NHL) followed this pattern a few years later.

For example, the source of recruitment to the NFL is college football, which comprises amateur players. The reverse draft ensures that every year the professional teams obtain bargaining access to the new crop of graduates in reverse order of how they finish in the professional league. The intention is to give last year's least successful teams the first option to pick new recruits. Consequently, the weaker teams have the opportunity to enhance their stock of playing talent at a price that is probably discounted on the player's genuine market value. Over time the intention is that such a system reallocates talent between the teams to promote competitive balance. Of course, in hierarchical leagues, with promotion and relegation, the replacement of weaker teams with stronger teams reallocates talent in a similar way (Fort, 2000). There is, however, one potentially major flaw in the thinking behind drafts or, for that matter, how promotion and relegation affects talent distribution. For example, in the draft system, despite the opportunity for weak teams initially to sign new, higher quality talent, there remains an economic incentive for the stronger teams to buy talent from the weak ones, and the weak teams to sell talent to the stronger teams.

Reflection Question 9.1
Why would there be an incentive to trade rookie players?
Hint: Think about the relative cost of the players.

Leaving aside the personal ambitions of players to wish to play for stronger teams, the clubs would have incentives to trade because the player will probably be offered a contract with a wage below their market value by the team allocated first pick in the draft. Consequently, the gap between what the player can earn for the weaker team and the true market value of the player becomes an economic rent over which teams can bargain. The stronger team can offer the weaker team more than they have paid for the player, while not paying the player their market value. It follows that both clubs can make a relative financial gain through the trade. The player may or may not receive some of this gain; this will depend on the player's contract.

Salary caps, unlike drafting systems, directly target the financial cost of talent. Salary caps can either involve fixing the cost of individual and thereby aggregate player costs by establishing a maximum wage, such as existed in UK in soccer from 1901 until 1960, they can represent a maximum absolute amount that clubs can spend on players in total, or they can be expressed as a percentage of team (or league) turnover. In the US, the NBA, hoping to strengthen weaker teams' finances, adopted a salary cap in 1980, after the alternative of gate revenue sharing was blocked by the combined efforts of the strongest drawing teams.

Given that small-town clubs are forced by the salary cap to buy more success than their revenues can profitably support, the league as a cartel has a perpetual enforcement problem. In European rugby union, the financial difficulties that some clubs and unions from smaller countries have experienced following rugby union becoming professional have led to the introduction of a salary cap. The relative financial fragility of rugby league, despite its early professionalism as discussed in Chapter 2, has meant that a salary cap has been in place in the Super League. Of course, the frequently offered justification for the control of wages and/or wage bills is that, in principle, it makes the best talent affordable to all teams and/or it prevents teams from hoarding talent, which will help to produce competitive balance. As with the draft, however, potential problems apply to salary caps. On the one hand, illicit "side payments" may be offered to players to ensure that they play for the clubs that have the economic resources to attract them.[1] On the other hand, the "farm" system developed in baseball, discussed in Chapter 11, to provide opportunities to hoard players, while not having them appear on the payroll. It follows that economic incentives do exist to avoid the policy intent of the salary cap.

The other major labour market policy instrument employed by sporting leagues has been the reserve option clause, the most famous example of which has persisted in baseball since 1880. Chapter 11 discusses the impact of these clauses in more detail, however, the main point is that baseball's clause essentially tied players to clubs for their working lifetimes; when a club signed a player the relevant clause gave the club the option to renew the contract when it expired. In the early days, the player had little choice but to accept the new contract, as unless the club released him he could not seek employment with another club, and thus had no option but to retire from the sport. The "retain and transfer" system in European soccer is another example; for a player to move between clubs required the transfer of the registration document of the player with the governing body. However, it remains, as discussed above, with the other forms of cross-subsidization that incentives exist for teams to trade players. Indeed, one can view the fees that are paid between teams to transfer registration as a literal representation of the rents that exist.

9.3.2 Revenue redistribution

The other main form of cross-subsidization adopted by sports leagues is the redistribution of revenue. Traditionally, of course, this has concerned the gate revenue – monies paid by spectators at the turnstiles. At the outset, professional baseball operated a 50:50 split of gate revenue, one half going to the away team.

Reflection Question 9.2
How does gate sharing produce a more equitable allocation of resources?
Hint: Think about the relative scale of demand for different clubs.

Because imbalance is created by teams with different revenue base, as revenues are then spent on playing talent, to redistribute some home team revenue implies that a greater absolute amount of income is transferred from a

---

[1] Such payments might be "in kind," such as the provision of housing, use of a car or other perquisites. Amateurism might be thought of as an extreme form of salary cap. Much anecdotal evidence exists of the use of "boot" money, the offer of employment in owner-firms, etc., to attract players to specific clubs.

larger club to a smaller club than the other way around. This means that the larger club experiences a net reduction in revenue, while the smaller team obtains a net gain in revenue.

As in many other team sports, away team shares of gate revenue have fallen steadily over the years, and currently a variety of arrangements exist in the US ensuring that the home team receives the largest share of revenue. The NFL operates an unusually generous 60:40 split in favour of the home club, while the NBA and NHL have no gate sharing. In Europe, similar arrangements have applied. In association football, for example, in England between the 1920s and the 1980s an 80:20 split on gate revenue existed in favour of the home club. An alternative form of gate revenue sharing is a "pool" system, whereby a predetermined share of league-wide gate monies goes into a central fund to be distributed from the centre, one example being the EFLs 4% levy on all receipts, the proceeds of which were distributed equally. Similar arrangements existed in rugby league in the UK, but currently no gate sharing arrangements exist. Gate revenue is still shared in cup competitions.[2]

As far as television revenue is concerned, in the US local television coverage provided no revenue for visiting teams (Fort and Quirk, 1995), although national television revenue was shared. Fort and Quirk hypothesized that in a one-team-one-vote world, egalitarian distribution of national television revenue is more or less certain, as signing the national television contract requires virtual unanimity among league members. As discussed in Chapter 7 and further in Chapter 10, this system broke down in the EFL, whose First Division, with FA support, departed to form the Premier League, taking most of the television revenue with it. Sharing local television revenue is virtually a non-starter given the supermajorities required to change the rules of US sports leagues. Notwithstanding these details, it should now be clear that the effectiveness of revenue distribution actually depends on the labour market. The aim is to endow weaker teams with income streams that can help them to buy better playing talent. For the reasons noted earlier, there is no reason why players would move to the weaker teams.

Having discussed the forms of cross-subsidization, attention now turns toward the theoretical approaches by which economists have sought to

---

[2] Pool and direct gate sharing can have very different effects on club's finances, except in the pedagogic two-team league where each team participates in all the league's games. In an N team balanced league where each team plays the others twice a season there are $N(N-1)$ matches, which amount to 90 in a ten-team league, of which any one team plays in 18. Under direct (one to one) gate sharing how much a team gains (loses) is determined independently of the revenue from the other 72 matches. Under a pool scheme, what each team gets depends on the gate receipts at all 90 games.

evaluate their effects. This requires outlining the construction and controlled manipulation of a variety of theoretical models of sports leagues. It should be noted at the outset that this literature is relatively technical and much debate exists about the specification of the models and their implications. What follows, therefore, is an inevitably circumscribed account.

9.4 AN ECONOMIC FRAMEWORK FOR UNDERSTANDING CROSS-SUBSIDIZATION

A starting point for the analysis is that leagues are constructed in which there is imbalance, deriving from different scales of demand for their output, defined as wins, by fans, as teams look to hire playing talent according to its costs. Following the economic methodology outlined in Chapter 1, the various policies are then introduced to the analysis and predictions made about the effects on the league; for example, what happens to competitive balance, profits, player remuneration, etc.

There are two important zero–sum relationships in these models, one of which can be relaxed in the process of exploring alternative scenarios. The first, inescapable, zero–sum restriction arises from the fact that win percents in a sports league sum to 0.5N in an N team league in which no draws are possible. In a two-team league, therefore, win percents sum to unity. If N = 4 then the sum of win percents is 2, etc. This is because if Team A wins, its opponent must lose; if Team As win percent goes up by 1%, the sum of the win percents of all the other teams must fall by 1% (in the two team case the other team's win percent falls by 1%). The second zero–sum restriction is that the sum of changes in teams' stocks of talent is zero, which arises from the assumption that the amount of talent is fixed and that teams hire it all at the going market equilibrium price. If one assumes either that the supply of talent is variable or that teams do not necessarily hire the entire stock, this second zero–sum restriction no longer applies. This possibility is discussed in Section 9.5.

To begin the analysis, a highly influential two-dimensional model evolved by Fort and Quirk (1995) is presented that draws on earlier work by El Hodiri and Quirk (1971), Quirk and El Hodiri (1974) and Rottenberg (1956). The two-team league is pedagogically convenient as the questions may be posed and solutions found graphically rather than algebraically. The original model assumes that team owners pursue maximum profit and that they buy talent in a perfectly competitive market,

9.4.1 Profit-maximizing competitive equilibrium

Fort and Quirk's (1995) two-dimensional model assumes that a club's total revenue (R) is driven by two factors; their win percent (w) and their home market size (m), which is usually assumed to be proportional to local population. The relevance of these assumptions is presented in Chapter 10. The "ith" club's total revenue R_i (i = 1, 2) is given by Equation 9.1:

$$R_i = R_i(m_i, w_i) \qquad (9.1)$$

It is further assumed that $\partial R_i/\partial m_i > 0$, which means that big market (big city) teams, other things being equal, have higher revenues than small market teams. This is consistent with the demand for the output of large market teams being greater than in the case of small market teams, for any given level of performance. In general, it is also assumed that the MR of winning is positive, i.e., $\partial R_i/\partial w_i > 0$, but that it also declines $\partial^2 R_i/\partial w_i{}^2 < 0$ as the win rate increases. This is consistent with a declining growth of interest by spectators in a winning team (see for example Vrooman, 1995). Fort and Quirk (1995, 2004) and Kesenne (2004, 2006) also argue that eventually declining short-run UO causes the team's total revenue to fall. By implication this means that its MR eventually becomes negative. This is consistent with the externality effects of UO reducing demand.

Fort and Quirk (2004) further impose the restrictions that total revenue is zero whenever the team has either no talent or has monopolized the league's talent. In either event production is impossible. Another property of the model (see also Appendix 9.1) is that a 1% change in the amount of talent "t" hired by a team produces a 1% increase in win percent, independent of the existing level of win percent. Szymanski (2004) argues this is the result of a combination of assumption: (a) that the entire fixed supply of talent is hired; and of assumption (b) that talent can be measured on a scale such that the sum of talent adds to unity. In combination, they ensure that it is immaterial whether a club is viewed as choosing its talent or its win percent.

This can be illustrated by considering that a team's win percent "w" can be related to the amount of talent it hires relative to total talent, in the two-team case, where t_i is the actual number of talents hired by the ith team, i.e.:

$$w_1 = t_1/(t_1 + t_2) \qquad (9.2)$$

This is a contest success function, as discussed in Chapter 7, in which the likelihood of winning a contest is directly connected with the relative share of talent held by a team. Differentiating the above expression with respect to t_1 leaves:

$$(\partial w_1/\partial t_1) = \{t_1 + t_2 - t_1(1 + dt_2/dt_1)\}/(t_1 + t_2)^2 \qquad (9.3)$$

or:

$$(\partial w_1/\partial t_1) = 1 \qquad (9.4)$$

if $dt_2/dt_1 = -1$, which is made possible by the assumption that a fixed amount of talent is available and is wholly hired by teams, and that the "t_i" sum to unity, i.e., talent, is measured on a scale such that it can be summed to unity. In other words, whatever the amount by which Team 2 alters its stock of talent, it is exactly equal and opposite in sign to that of Team 1's change. Consequently, when the total amount of talent can be normalized on unity, a 1% increase in t_1 produces a 1% increase in w_1. Clearly, under these conditions, it is immaterial whether the team chooses a level of talent or a level of win percent.

The model can be illustrated in Figure 9.1, which depicts the MR curves (in the positive zone) of big city Team 1, MR1, and small city Team 2, MR2. The horizontal axis measures the teams' win percents and consequent share of talent, because of the discussion above, and the vertical axis measures revenue and costs. As drawn, Team 1's MR exceeds that of Team 2 at all win percents, reflecting the former's greater drawing power. The intercepts of the marginal revenue curves with the horizontal axis show that at zero MC the teams' win percents sum to a value in excess of unity. This is consistent with the idea that teams potentially seek to buy more talent than is available, ensuring that talent will have a positive price, it is a scarce good, and any price below the market equilibrium price will not be sustainable and will be adjusted back towards equilibrium.

The assumption that all talent is hired in equilibrium enables Figure 9.1 to be redrawn in a more convenient form as a two-team league. Figure 9.2 measures Team 1's share of talent reading from left to right and Team 2's share reading from right to left. This now illustrates nicely that any increase in Team 1's win percent must be met by a reduction in Team 2's win percent. It is important to note that the teams' MR's are equal at E, where Team 1 has a win percent of 0.6 and Team 2 a win percent of 0.4. This is the equilibrium level of production in the league, in which the larger team produces more wins than the smaller team, and consequently provides a visual example of an unbalanced league.

Reflection Question 9.3

Why is position E an equilibrium position in the market?
Hint: think about the conditions required for a profit maximizing firm to set its output level.

Point E is the equilibrium level of "output" (for each team) in the league, because here any point to the left implies that for any given win percent Team 1 has a higher MR than Team 2, and *vice versa* with any point to the

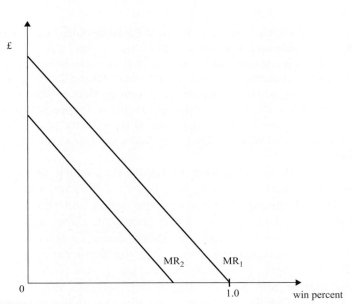

FIGURE 9.1 *Two-team league with Team 1 as the large market team.*

right. Under such circumstances the team with the greater marginal revenue would be able to hire more talent relative to the other team, who would likewise seek to sell talent. Because talent produces wins, this means that the win percent moves towards the position associated with E, which here is Team 1 at 0.6 and Team 2 and 0.4. As MR falls with increases in win percents, it is only at point E that talent will cease to be hired and hence become an equilibrium, because here both teams are prepared to pay the same price for talent. In this sense the market determines the MC of talent, as illustrated.

More specifically, one can argue that the team's total cost "C" is a function of the talent it hires "t" as indicated in Equation 9.5. Here, C also includes a fixed cost component "k." Fixed cost is irrelevant to short-run profit maximization, which depends solely on marginal (ultimately variable) cost, thus fixed cost is often left out of the equation or subsumed under variable cost on the grounds that clubs' fixed costs tend to be proportional to their variable (mainly labour) costs:

$$C_i = ct_i + k \qquad (9.5)$$

In this chapter it is assumed that $k = 0$, following convention. The parameter "c" is then the price (to be determined) of a unit of talent.[3] Implied in Equation 9.5 is that all clubs pay the same price per unit of talent, which is equivalent to assuming that in the labour market clubs behave like perfect competitors. As the league hires all the available talent, c is the market clearing price of talent, as described earlier.[4] An important point to note in this regard is that win percents could be driven to equality (0.5), but then the marginal revenue of Team 1 would exceed that of Team 2 by the amount FG. Clearly the market is not going to produce this outcome.[5] In short, at any other distribution of wins than point E, both teams could increase their profits by, and thereby have an incentive to engage in, trading talent.

Figure 9.1 (and by implication Figure 9.2) represent the MR curves as parallel lines (having the same slope). This implies that each team's supporters have identical dislike of short-run predictability of outcome. Should Team 2's supporters have a weaker distaste for predictability than Team 1's, its MR curve will be flatter, in which case for some range of win percents Team 2's MR may exceed that of Team 1. If Team 2's MR exceeds Team 1's at win percent 0.5 (see Kesenne 2004), the small city team will dominate the league. Furthermore, it is unlikely but not impossible that a small town club may, by superior management on and off the field, dominate the big city team at all win percents; in terms of Figure 9.1 this would mean that Team 1 is the small town side. Having set up the standard model it is now possible to examine how the introduction of cross-subsidization affects the distribution of talent, win percent and competitive balance.

---

[3] A player is viewed as a bundle of talent, the more gifted player simply has more talent than the average player and as each is paid according to the talent she/he possesses individuals (and teams) earn differing amounts (see Appendix 9.1).

[4] The stock of talent $\sum t$ is given at any moment, which is probably not too unrealistic an assumption for US team sports, which are relatively unique to that country, although Latin America is increasingly producing talented baseball players, some of them employed by the major US leagues. Should soccer finally take off in America, the fixed stock of talent assumption would be less realistic for US team sports. European sports teams, especially in soccer and rugby union and league, find talent worldwide, i.e., in elastic supply, therefore the standard model is not so obviously applicable to Europe. Vrooman (1995) allows for the possibility that the big city team may have to pay more per unit for its talent, which might act as a restraint on the amount it wants to hire. There may be something in this as the earnings of superstars in sports and entertainment often seem to be much higher than their talent would suggest is appropriate. Rosen (1981) provides a plausible explanation of the phenomenon.

[5] Most models build on the implicit assumption that causation flows in one direction only, from performance (win percent) to revenue. There is some statistical evidence, see for example Davies et al (1995), that causation could also flow in the opposite direction; teams that enjoy higher revenues can invest more in talent and therefore obtain more success.

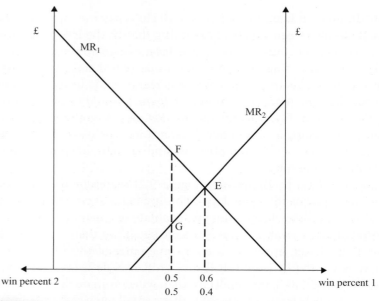

FIGURE 9.2   *Equilibrium win percent and no incentive to trade players.*

9.4.2 Cross-subsidization in a profit-maximizing league
9.4.2.1 Reserve option clause

Consider what ensues if a reserve clause is introduced into the sport, implying that players' contracts are owned by their employers. This has the effect of depressing the price of talent below its equilibrium value, c, therefore the teams will both want to hire more talent than is available, but the reserve clause prevents the price being bid up to c. Suppose once more that Team 1 has bought enough talent to attain a win percent of 0.7. Irrespective of whether its MR of winning is above or below the constrained price of talent, its MR is below that of Team 2. Provided teams are permitted to buy and sell players' contracts, Team 1 can sell talent to Team 2 and both will become more profitable, and this process can continue until their marginal revenues are equal and league revenue is maximized. It can be concluded, therefore, that the effect of a reserve clause on a league where teams are profit maximizers is not to redistribute talent in favour of weak drawing sides, but to restrain players' wages. Weak drawing teams will benefit financially from the introduction of a reserve clause, at the expense of players and of strong drawing teams to whom they can sell talent. Consistent with their prior expectations, Fort and Quirk found no evidence from standard deviations of win percent that competitive balance in MLB improved following the introduction of (partial) free agency in 1975.

9.4.2.2 Player draft

Consider the effect of a successfully operating reverse order draft as a result of which weak drawing teams will have acquired more talent at a lower price than the market would suggest, and will obtain a higher win rate than they can profitably employ using talent that could be profitably employed by the strong drawing teams. As implied earlier, profit maximizing teams have strong incentives to trade talent (since the 1960s the NFL has restricted cash sales). If trading should continue until both teams MRs are equalized, the distribution of players will be what it would have been in the absence of the draft. Once again, the real effect of the draft is to lower salaries in favour of profits; weak teams are made more profitable than they would otherwise be, through paying lower wages and selling talented players to stronger teams. Fort and Quirk again found no evidence (comparing standard deviations of win percent) that the draft introduced by the NFL had any significant effect on competitive balance; they found mixed evidence for MLB where there did seem to be a slight reduction in the AL. They also found contrary evidence, in that the concentration of championships increased in both leagues.

9.4.2.3 Salary cap

Consider the effects of introducing a salary cap to the sports league and suppose that it succeeds in pushing win shares closer to equality than they would otherwise be in a profit maximizing league. This would be the case if the weaker team bought more talent than otherwise might have been the case relative to the stronger team. Once again, the problem now arises that teams collectively and individually could make more profit by redistributing talent from the weak drawing sides (where it adds less to revenue). There are perpetual incentives for weak drawing teams to spend less than the agreed minimum on talent and for strong drawing ones to spend more, by the expedient of trading players. It is clear under such circumstances that if the salary cap can be enforced – and historically leagues have permitted exceptions – as Fort and Quirk argue, competitive balance in profit maximizing leagues can be affected by the adoption of a salary cap. However, their data on the NBA suggested that the introduction of the salary cap had no significant effect on standard deviations of win percents in basketball. They hypothesize that part of the reason might have been relatively poor adherence to the salary cap.

9.4.2.4 Revenue sharing

The final case to consider is revenue sharing. A formerly widespread practice is for the league to fix a proportion (α) of gate monies that the home side retains, the balance $(1 - \alpha)$ going to the visitors. The logic of what follows applies to any direct revenue sharing, however, such as television revenue sharing or total revenue sharing. The team's post-redistribution total revenues $(R^\star)$, for Teams 1 and 2 are given by Equations 9.6 and 9.7:

$$R_1^\cdot = \alpha R_1 + (1 - \alpha)R_2 \qquad (9.6)$$

$$R_2^\cdot = \alpha R_2 + (1 - \alpha)R_2 \qquad (9.7)$$

In competitive equilibrium the teams select win percents that maximize profit, by setting MR equal to MC as set out in Equations 9.8 and 9.9. MR is the change in total revenue that follows from a change in win percent, i.e., $\partial R_1/\partial w_1 > 0$. As changes in win percent for a given team affect those of the other team, in a two-team league, but in the opposite direction, because of the zero–sum property discussed earlier, then $\partial R_2/\partial w_1 < 0$. This means that the MR for Team 2 falls as the MR for team 1 rises, so:

$$MR_1^\cdot = \alpha MR_2 - (1 - \alpha)MR_2 = c \qquad (9.8)$$

$$MR_2^\cdot = \alpha MR_2 - (1 - \alpha)MR_2 = c \qquad (9.9)$$

Because of the negative sign on the second term in each equation, revenue sharing reduces both teams' marginal revenues below what they would have been otherwise, that is in the absence of the reallocation of playing talent. Equilibrium with gate sharing occurs where the post-sharing MRs are equated and league revenue is maximized, i.e., $MR^\star_1 = MR^\star_2$. Expanding the terms and cancelling common items reveals that this is equivalent to $MR_1 = MR_2$. The solution is shown in Figure 9.3, which shows, that each club's MR curve falls by the same amount. Equilibrium in the presence of revenue sharing is at $E^\star$ where win percent is identical to that at E and the price of talent has fallen to $c^\star$ below c.

An alternative form of revenue sharing is "pool" sharing, where teams contribute to a central pool which the league makes a redistribution from. This system is identical in its effects to gate sharing with N = 2, but not for N > 2. For example, a 20 team no-draw league provides $N(N - 1) = 380$ fixtures per season. Therefore, what Team 1 gets under a pool arrangement depends on gate receipts from 380 matches. If the league adopts gate sharing, the amount that Team 1 gets depends on receipts from the 38 games in which it is directly involved. Unless all teams MR's fall by the same amount, which is highly improbable, redistribution will affect the competitive balance. The main conclusion that Fort and Quirk draw from their analysis is that, of the policy instruments considered, only a salary cap can generally be expected to assist the finances of weak drawing teams and simultaneously

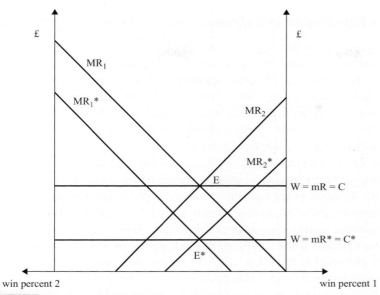

FIGURE 9.3 *Effect of revenue-sharing.*

improve competitive balance. Reserve option clauses and reverse order drafts affect players' wages and therefore act primarily to redistribute incomes between clubs and players – they might be expected to improve weak teams' finances, but not to improve competitive balance, suggesting that competitive balance is invariant to changes in league policies. This is known as the "invariance proposition," which is an example of the Coase theorem. It is shown that, because property rights can be established, market forces seek an efficient (profit maximizing) solution to talent allocation regardless of the ownership of the property rights.[6] This idea was noted in the seminal work of Rottenberg (1956).

---

[6] It should be noted that the evidence on the effect of such policies is potentially problematic. For example, Larsen et al (2006) report a significant impact on competitive balance of the NFL's simultaneous introduction of free agency and a salary cap in 1993. The salary cap was brought in to help teams survive the likely inflationary effect of free agency on players' wages. As Larsen et al (2006) state, the simultaneous introduction of two measures made it impossible for them to determine whether the effect was due to the salary cap alone (consistent with prior expectations) or to free agency (inconsistent). Economists frequently find themselves in similar situations – due essentially to the inability to conduct controlled experiments (ones in which causal factors are varied one at a time). Similar comments apply to the "before and after" studies reported by Fort and Quirk (1995), and others. One cannot be sure that the only "significant" differences between the period before and after the introduction of (say) free agency in baseball is the introduction of free agency; conceivably some unobserved factor or factors may have changed, leading to erroneous interpretation.

9.4.3 Equilibrium in a win-maximizing league

As discussed in Chapter 7, Sloane (1971) argued from the perspective of European football that clubs pursue utility maximization, i.e., mainly success on the field, subject to a minimum satisfactory level of profit. In a large body of work Stefan Kesenne (1996, 2004, 2007) has championed a particularly tractable form of the utility maximizing model – win maximization subject to a zero profit constraint – to determine how different owner's objectives affect the results of cross-subsidization measures.

Market equilibrium in the win-maximizing league (subject to zero profit) occurs where the clubs' ARs equal the marginal cost of talent c, shown as E_w in Figure 9.4, compared to equilibrium in the profit maximizing league E_p. Since AR always exceeds MR, as discussed in Chapter 1, it follows that talent is more highly priced in the win-maximizing league. Assuming that big city Team 1 dominates Team 2, the distribution of talent is less equal under win maximization. However, if Team 1 is a highly successful small city team and Team 2 is a comparatively less-well-run big city team, the small team will be more dominant under win maximization than under profit maximization. In this sense, win-maximization leagues can have closer competitive balance. This consideration led Kesenne (2004) to distinguish between "good" and "bad" over-domination; while one might be happy to redistribute revenue to correct an imbalance that currently favours the large city team, one might be reluctant to take an action that effectively punishes a dominant small city team for its success.

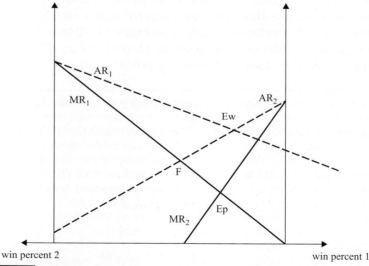

FIGURE 9.4 *Equilibrium in profit-maximizing (Ep) and win-maximizing (Ew) leagues.*

Another implication of win-maximizing behaviour is that total league revenue is not maximized. Figure 9.4 shows that at win-maximizing equilibrium E_w the teams' MRs are unequal, implying that if players transfer from Team 1 the revenue it loses is less than the revenue gained by Team 2.

9.4.4 Cross-subsidization in a win-maximizing league

It has been established that reverse order drafts and reserve option clauses have no effect on the balance of competition under profit maximization. It is now shown that the same applies under win maximization. In Figure 9.4 a win-maximizing league has win percent share E_w; if, say, a combination of draft and option clauses force the cost of talent below its (win percent) equilibrium value, teams can trade talent until E_w is attained, at which point the incentive for further trade is gone. The effectiveness of these instruments is zero in win-maximizing leagues, thus they are not considered further. There is little point in further considering the effect of a salary cap for the opposite reason; it is generally expected (although Vrooman, 1995, disagrees) to be effective if it can be enforced. In the interests of brevity, therefore, the remaining discussion focuses on the effectiveness of revenue redistribution.

It can be shown that, provided the redistribution benefits Team 2, its AR function will rise and that of Team 1 will fall, but relatively less than Team 2's rises, since Team 1 began with more revenue. Therefore, the distribution of talent and success will shift in favour of Team 2 and the cost of talent will increase. Other things being equal, revenue redistribution is expected to influence the balance of competition in win-maximizing leagues. This is an important result, as it indicates that the invariance proposition need not apply if owner objectives change. This means that cross-subsidization can, in principle, affect competitive balance. This issue is now further addressed by relaxing some of the other assumptions of the model.

9.5 RELAXATION OF ASSUMPTIONS

9.5.1 Introducing the effect of spectator preference for absolute quality

To begin the analysis take a quadratic revenue equation model from Kesenne (2000a, 2004, 2006a) to produce the simplest equivalent model to the Fort and Quirk case above. This is presented in Equation 9.10:

$$R_i = m_i w_i - b_i w_i^2 \tag{9.10}$$

The function implies that, as win percents increase, revenues increase linearly according to the first term on the right-hand side, and decrease non-linearly according to the second term on the right-hand side, assuming b >0, at an increasing rate. In fact the combination of these terms produces an inverted curve, in which revenue achieves a maximum and then declines. This is an indication of spectators' aversion to the increasing certainty of outcome. In this model the corresponding cost function is Equation 9.5.

The value of Team 1's (and by implication Team 2's) win percent can be derived, assuming that both owners pursue win maximization. The derivation under the alternative assumption of profit maximizing follows in Appendix 9.2. Both solutions are presented in Kesenne (2006). The teams' AR functions are given as Equations 9.11 and 9.12. Total revenue is divided by w to arrive at AR and at equilibrium, AR equals MC, c (which is consequently higher than under profit maximization).

Reflection Question 9.4

Why would marginal cost be greater under win maximization compared to profit maximization? Hint: Consider how the win-maximizing club decides on its win percent

A win-maximizing team will hire as much talent as it can to generate wins, provided it does not produce an economic loss. This will be indicated where the ARs and not MRs are equal to MC, which are equivalent to AC if MCs are constant. As ARs are always above MRs, this implies that a talent cost greater than under profit maximization will occur, as well as a greater degree of competitive imbalance. AR is then given as:

$$AR_1 = m_1 - b_1 w_1 = c \tag{9.11}$$

$$AR_2 = m_2 - b_2 w_2 = c \tag{9.12}$$

Equating and rearranging leaves the solution for Team 1's equilibrium share of talent (equivalently its win share) as Equation 9.13 where, to simplify notation, Σb is used to denote the sum of the b parameters:

$$w_1 = \{(m_1 - m_2)/\sum b\} + b_2/\sum b \tag{9.13}$$

If Team 1 has the larger market and if both teams' spectators have the same degree of taste for UO, then Team 1 has the larger share of the talent, because the first term on the right is positive and the second equals 0.5 whenever the b parameters are equal. If Team 1's spectators are exceedingly more averse to sporting certainty than Team 2, the small city team may dominate the league, consistent with the message of Fort and Quirk (2004). Kesenne gives the condition for this "good" imbalance where, even though $m_1 > m_2$, it is also true that $w_2 > w_1$, i.e., it is required for the smaller team (Team 2) to have greater win percents as:

$$b_1 - b_2 > 2(m_1 - m_2) \qquad (9.14)$$

which means that for "good" imbalance to appear in this league the large drawing team supporters' extra aversion to certainty of outcome must double its team's advantage in market size. The comparable condition for a "good" imbalance in a profit-maximizing league is as derived in Appendix 9.2:

$$(b_1 - b_2) > (m_1 - m_2) \qquad (9.15)$$

This suggests that the small market team is more likely (but still relatively unlikely) to dominate the league if team owners are profit maximizers. Playing quality can be added to the analysis, following Kesenne (2000b, 2006a), Vrooman (1995) and others in adding the assumption that teams' revenues depend also on the visitors' playing strength. Revenue now becomes:

$$R_i = m_i w_i - b_i w_i^2 + e_i w_j \qquad (9.16)$$

Here "e" is a parameter that converts the visiting teams' success, w_j (indirectly via its travelling support), into gate revenue for the home club. It would be expected that "e" is positive, although not identical across teams, i.e., the greater the drawing power of the home side the greater is e_i (in this context $e_1 > e_2$).

Kesenne (2001) found that adding a taste for absolute quality to the basic model, revenue redistribution can affect competitive balance even under profit maximization. If neither club's supporters value absolute quality both values of "e" are zero; if both sets have the same taste for quality then the values of "e" are equal and non-zero. In either case, Team 1's win percent depends on market size and the taste for UO, as in the basic model. When the values of "e" are equal, Team 1 has the same win percent as in the basic model under profit maximizing, but a smaller share than under win maximization.

9.5.2 Market size diseconomies

Vrooman (1995) suggests that the advantages in sports leagues conferred by market size might be offset by either the declining marginal productivity of talent and/or by size diseconomies. These assumptions imply that, for example, a given player may be more valuable to the weaker team since its win rate is lower than the stronger team. Recall that diminishing marginal productivity suggests that more employment of a variable factor of production leads to an increase in output, but at a declining rate. Consequently, teams with more talent can employ that talent at the margin in a less productive manner than a team with less overall talent. This might apply across all resources, suggesting that larger teams are relatively less productive in producing wins than smaller teams. This may result in less competitive imbalance than the basic model suggests and it also suggests that revenue redistribution can affect competitive balance. Figure 9.5 illustrates the equilibrium.

Team 1 maximizes profit at "A" paying a premium price "c_p" for every unit of talent hired. Team 2 maximizes its profit at "B" paying a discount price "c_d." Industry revenue would be maximized at "E," where both teams pay the competitive equilibrium price "c" for their talent, but E is not attainable given the imperfect market for talent that results in a dual price. Profit-maximizing equilibrium under market diseconomies is more balanced than at E. Talent hired by Team 1 is paid more than in equilibrium and that of Team 2 is paid less. It should be emphasized that this is a very naïve model of a market in which different prices are paid for units of identically productive talent.

Revenue sharing causes both teams' MR curves to fall, but unlike the standard model the actual win percents do change in Team 1's favour – why? An equal fall in both teams' MR curves lowers both the competitive equilibrium price of talent c and MCs, the latter equiproportionally. But, as Team 1 has a higher level of MC at w_1, the absolute fall in its MC exceeds that of Team 2's. Thus, the same w_1, w_2 cannot be a post-sharing win percent combination for profit-maximizing teams. At the new profit-maximizing

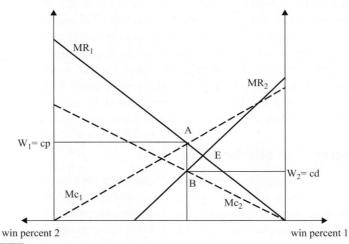

FIGURE 9.5 *Market size diseconomies (Team 1 maximizes profit at A, wages Cp, Team 2 maximizes profit at B, wages Cd).*

win combination both teams' MCs must have fallen by the same absolute amount, equal to the reduction in their MRs. To reach this new win percent combination, Team 1 must start buying extra talent to raise its MC slightly while Team 2 sells talent to lower its MC. At the end of this process both teams' MCs will have fallen (relative to pre-sharing) by the same amount, equal to the common reduction in their MRs. Each team will have restored equality between its MC and its MR and will be once again maximizing its profit at the new win percent combination. In the course of moving to the new equilibrium win percent the differential between "c_p" and "c_d" is squeezed. Declining marginal productivity is a factor that might amplify the results of market size disadvantage, but to pursue that line of inquiry demands a "standard" model not based on constant returns.

9.5.3 A variable supply of talent

So far the analysis has maintained that teams compete to hire a fixed amount of talent at a constant MC, c, in a closed market. Clearly, if the supply of talent is variable and/or it is no longer assumed that the entire stock is traded, the restriction that $dt_2/dt_1 = -1$ no longer applies and the choice of win percent is now distinguishable from the choice of talent; in other words $\partial w_i/\partial t_i \neq 1$. A team chooses to buy a number of talents, but it is unable to select any particular percentage of the total; its actual share of talent is known only after the whole industry has made its purchases. In this case the concept of MC relevant to the profit-maximizing team is not $\partial C/\partial w$, the MC of a win, but it is $\partial C/\partial t$, the MC of a unit of talent. European sports teams operate in open markets for talent, they are free to buy from clubs inside and outside of their own national leagues, and from other continents. To a lesser extent, there is an international market for players in US professional team sports.

To relax these restrictions Szymanski (2004) and Kesenne (2006b, 2007a) model leagues using game theory to take decision makers' interdependence into account, and argues that this is more appropriate than a Walrasian (competitive equilibrium) theory as a descriptor of behaviour when there are few participants, in other words an oligopoly market as discussed in Chapters 5 and 7. Szymanksi and Kesenne (2004) proved that in a Cournot–Nash profit-maximizing league revenue sharing worsens competitive balance – in effect the sharing of revenue goes some way to internalizing the negative externalities of teams' decisions, so the league moves closer to joint profit maximization. As the number of teams increase the outcomes of Cournot–Nash models get closer to competitive models; the misallocation of talent in a 20-team Cournot–Nash league is likely to be much less marked than in the two-team league.

9.6 WHEN DOES THE "INVARIANCE PROPOSITION" HOLD?

The above discussion has attempted to offer an overview of some of the main issues from a complex literature in which, with considerable ingenuity, economists have attempted to explore sports leagues. However, an important question remains, which is under what conditions may we assume that competitive balance is invariant to the application of (or changes in) cross-subsidization policies?

A summary might be as follows. First it appears that reserve clauses (transfer systems) and rookie drafts affect the distribution of value added between players and owners, but do not affect competitive balance, whatever the goals of owners, i.e., profit or win maximization or whatever the preferences of fans. Secondly, it appears that, with some exceptions (for example, see Vrooman 1995), salary caps are the one cross-subsidization policy that most writers believe can affect competitive balance, if it can be enforced. This leaves revenue sharing as the one method of cross-subsidization worthy of further discussion, as its ability to affect competitive balance does appear to depend on factors such as owner objectives and spectator preferences, the number of teams in the league, whether teams behave like oligopolists, and the particular form of cross-subsidization. In most of the models reviewed it appears that revenue sharing in win-maximizing leagues benefits the smaller teams relatively more than it harms the dominant ones and thus promotes more competitive balance while simultaneously raising the price of talent. Table 9.1, therefore, summarizes some findings on the effectiveness of revenue sharing as a means of influencing competitive balance in profit-maximizing leagues about which debate remains.

Table 9.1 is organized to illustrate the outcomes under four model specifications. A is Kesenne's quadratic version of the (Fort and Quirk) standard model. B differs from A by introducing fans' preferences for absolute quality. C departs from A by bringing in market size diseconomies. D differs from A by abandoning the notion of a fixed supply of talent, all of which is hired, and by treating clubs as oligopolists who compete via quality variations. The fourth column shows exceptions to the general rule, and gives references.

9.7 HOW FAR DOES COMPETITIVE BALANCE MATTER? THE EUROPEAN CHAMPIONS' AND OTHER LEAGUES

An implication of the above research is that only salary caps and revenue sharing may possibly affect competitive balance. Kesenne (2007b) is pessimistic about the prospects for a return to revenue sharing, which has been allowed to wither in, for example, European soccer leagues. Given the international

TABLE 9.1   Revenue sharing in leagues with profit-maximizing teams

Model specification	Effect on talent price	Effect on win percent	Qualifying remarks with respect to effects on win percent
A. Standard model equations and $\partial w_i/\partial t_i = 1$	Lowers	None	Requires all revenues shared and by same method (Fort and Quirk, 1995) Gate and pool sharing may give different outcomes. If MRs do not shift identically may have an effect (Kesenne, 2000a) Requires N>2 for an effect on win percentage
B. Standard model plus taste for absolute quality and $\partial w_i/\partial t_i = 1$	Lowers	Improves	If all e's zero or all identical – very unlikely indeed – no effect. (Kesenne, 2000) No effect under pool sharing (Kesenne, 2001) Requires N>2 for there to be any effect, irrespective of the e's (Kesenne, 2000)
C. Standard model plus market size diseconomies and $\partial w_i/\partial t_i = 1$	Lowers the revenue maximizing equilibrium price c	No effect on the revenue maximizing win percent	Operates irrespective of whether MR's fall by the same amount so works even when N = 2 (Vrooman, 1995)
	Reduces the spread between the unit prices of star and ordinary talent	Worsens balance, shifting it towards the revenue maximizing value where all MR's are equalized	
D. Cournot–Nash and $\partial w_i/\partial t_i \neq 1$	Lowers	Worsens balance, shifting it towards the revenue maximizing point where all MR's are equalized	Differs from A above in that $\partial w_i/\partial t_i \neq 1$, permitting the stock of talent to vary or some to be unemployed (Szymanski, 2004)

nature of the single European and broader market in soccer talent, and the extent and economic importance of supra-national competition, it is hard to see how any league acting on its own could resume more revenue sharing. Revenue sharing works for clubs in part through reducing the prices teams pay for talent; any single European league seeking financial salvation through revenue sharing would quickly find its leading members unable to attract enough talent to compete at supra-national level. Kesenne (2007b) notes that football clubs in European leagues are unlikely to give serious consideration to national revenue sharing schemes in view of a perceived need to compete with clubs from Spain, Italy, Germany, England and France, the leagues that have historically produced most of the supra-national title wins. The same implication would follow from the imposition of a salary cap in a single league. Likewise, it seems difficult to conceive of the effectiveness of salary caps in a sport with a truly international labour market. In other professional sports, such as rugby, this is possible as evidenced by their implementation.

The only realistic chance for revenue sharing or salary caps to be introduced into European soccer is for all leagues to act in concert – most probably under pressure from UEFA. In this context the important difference between European and North American professional sports leagues may not be so much that the latter have no equivalent to the formers' supra-national competition, but rather that the latter have fewer leagues, making agreement on cross-subsidization schemes easier to reach, even in the presence of what is a *de facto* supra-league as noted by Fort (2000) through the existence of the World Series and the Super Bowl, which may exert similar effects on competitive balance in American leagues and conferences.

It can also be hypothesized that outcomes in the Champions' League and the UEFA Cup have recently become more predictable, thanks to the partial replacement of the two-game knockout format of tournament by multi-stage semi-league formats and by the admission of larger numbers of competitors, which implies that a team must play more games than formerly to reach any particular stage or round. As discussed in Chapter 7, increasing the minimum number of games required to attain any given stage tends to enhance the prospects of the most successful teams. Other things being equal, the joint probability of multiple wins is lower than the probability of a single outcome against any one of the opponents and this will make it much less likely that teams with lower probabilities of wins are successful. In general, the more matches there are per round and the more rounds there are to any competition the greater the probability that favourites will reach the final stages. This makes intuitive sense, in that teams with a larger playing staff, through growing attrition, enhance the probability of their success.

Simultaneously, of course, such competitions produce a greater number of hours of live sport that can be sold. This perspective may help to explain why league titles in team sports tend to be more concentrated and more valued than knockout cup wins and why in an era when television exercises a strong influence on sports organizations fewer competitions continue to use the pure knockout format. It remains, however, to note that while sports economists are agreed that competitive balance is theoretically important to the survival and development of leagues, they are by no means agreed on how important it is. As Sanderson (2002) argues, while leagues impose measures on their members that recognize mutual interdependence they simultaneously pursue others that tend to exacerbate competitive imbalance. The evolution of the European Champions' League from the two-game knockout format involving only national league champions into a fully blown league format (and more entrants) is a case in point. As discussed in Chapter 8 one form of UO, deriving from Jennett (1984), argues that sports leagues are populated by supporters whose main object is to see their own teams win. Sports leagues have survived and expanded while displaying plenty of imbalances. This suggests that competitive balance is only one of many factors that determine their long-run health and may, in fact, be an outgrowth of their evolution rather than necessarily what causes them to change.

9.8 CONCLUSION

Chapters 7 and 8 have argued that there is a need to coordinate clubs' activities to ensure that UO or, as indicated in Chapter 8, competitive balance is preserved. Because it is argued that spectators prefer closer contests, the public's welfare may, therefore, be enhanced and the potential failure of leagues averted if stronger teams cross-subsidize weaker teams. In this chapter the main forms of cross-subsidization have been outlined, together with an exploration of their impact in leagues characterized by clubs maximizing profits and maximizing win percents. These respective objectives, it is argued, apply to US and European leagues respectively. It is shown that under conditions of profit maximization when the supply of talent is fixed, in general a version of the Coase theorem applies, making competitive balance invariant to any policy. It is argued that salary caps may affect competitive balance, but may fail because of enforcement problems. The chapter then argues that changes in the assumptions connected with modelling sport leagues produce challenges to the invariance proposition. These assumptions include shifting owner objectives to win maximization, having spectators caring about absolute playing quality, that the scale of markets may produce diseconomies of scale from playing talent, and that the supply of talent might be variable because of open, international markets. The chapter concludes that, under such circumstances, any potential for a corrective impact of cross-subsidization of teams appears to lie with revenue sharing in a win maximizing league, but the ability of domestic leagues to implement this remains dubious given the need to coordinate across countries. Attention now turns towards an empirical analysis of the demand for professional team sports.

Appendix 9.1 Why Win Percent and Talent Distribution are not Formally Equivalent

The logic of cross-subsidization policies is to try to produce competitive balance by ensuring a more equitable distribution of talent. This presupposes that production functions for wins "W" are as described in Equation A9.1.1, a function of labour "L" for team "i":

$$W_i = W_i(L_i) \qquad \text{(A9.1.1)}$$

If playing talent "t" is a function of labour, i.e.:

$$t_i = t_i(L_i) \qquad \text{(A9.1.2)}$$

this implies that:

$$W_i = W_i(t_i) \qquad \text{(A9.1.3)}$$

or, if wins are proportional to talent:

$$W_i = t_i \qquad \text{(A9.1.4)}$$

Win percents "w" will then become:

$$w_i = W_i/W_i + W_j = t_i/t_i + t_j \qquad \text{(A9.1.5)}$$

which is a "contest success function," as described in Chapter 7. Competitive balance will then be given by:

$$w_i/w_j = t_i/t_t \qquad \text{(A9.1.6)}$$

In which the relative supply of talent determines competitive balance. The use of talent rather than labour enables the consideration of homogenous talent units, as opposed to players that might differ in skills. However, the results in Equations A9.1.5 and A9.1.6 are potentially false. Consider a team that hires X% of the talent; obviously the number X is drawn from the large set of rational numbers.

Rational numbers may be expressed as ratios of integers e.g., 4/5 and 193/26079, integers being "whole" numbers. Numbers, such as π and the square root of 2, belong to the set of irrational numbers; i.e., numbers that cannot be expressed as ratios of integers (whole numbers).

Games, points and wins are measured in integers, based on the number of teams in the league N – usually less than 30. In an N team balanced league where teams play each other twice a season the number of games each club plays is equal to $2(N-1)$. Therefore, win percents are restricted to a very small subset of the rational numbers between zero and one, implying that it is impossible to hire X% of the talent and enjoy exactly X% of the wins for every possible value of X.

Appendix 9.2 The Quadratic Model Under Profit Maximization

The basic quadratic model under profit maximization is:

$$R_i = m_i w_i - b_i w_i^2 \tag{A9.2.1}$$

$$C_i = ct_i + k \tag{A9.2.2}$$

or:

$$C_i = ct_i \tag{A9.2.3}$$

if $k = 0$.

Profit maximization requires the teams to equate MR and MC leaving:

$$m_1 - 2b_1 w_1 = c \tag{A9.2.4}$$

$$m_2 - 2b_2 w_2 = c \tag{A9.2.5}$$

Using the fact that win per cents sum to unity, one can substitute $(1 - w_1)$ for w_2, set the equations equal and obtain:

$$m_2 - 2b_2 w_2 = c \tag{A9.2.5}$$

$$m_1 - 2b_1 w_1 = m_2 - 2b_2(1 - w_1) \tag{A9.2.6}$$

and, on rearranging, arrive at:

$$w_1 = \{(m_1 - m_2)/(2\sum b)\} + b_2/\sum b \tag{A9.2.7}$$

As one would anticipate, the only difference between Equation A9.2.7 and the equivalent with spectator preferences for absolute quality, is that the former has no terms "e" to represent consumer preference for better quality of play. Comparing A9.2.7 with the expression for the value of w_1 in a win maximizing league, as presented in the text, it is clear that the denominator is larger under profit maximization, suggesting that other things being equal, competitive imbalance is worse under win maximization.

CHAPTER 10

The Demand for Professional Team Sports: Attendance and Broadcasting

- To understand how the economic theory of demand is applied to attendance at professional sports matches
- To appreciate the evidence on the determinants of attendance demand
- To understand how broadcasting affects attendance demand and the determinants of broadcast demand
- To appreciate the role that broadcasting has had on the supply structure of professional sport

10.1 INTRODUCTION

In this chapter the demand for professional team sports is investigated in some detail, beginning in the next section with a brief resume of the theoretical framework presented in Chapter 3. Some theoretical and empirical extensions are then discussed in Section 10.3, to indicate how the theory requires refinement to apply to professional sports. Section 10.4 reviews evidence of the demand for professional sports, providing a selective summary of recent studies. The impact of television broadcasting of sport on attendance demand is discussed as part of this review and Section 10.5 then explores the sources and growth of broadcast sport in more detail. Initial research exploring the broadcast demand for sport is reviewed, as well as the implications of funding from the growth of this sector. It is argued that this growth has been primarily driven by supply-side changes in the media market and that the funding arrangements involved have helped to reshape the supply structure of professional sports leagues, enabling the league evolution discussed in Chapter 7.

261

10.2 THE DEMAND FOR PROFESSIONAL TEAM SPORTS

Chapter 3 presented the "derived" demand for sports goods and equipment as a result of a primary or parent demand for sports participation. The same theoretical framework used to examine the demand for goods and equipment can be applied to the decision of utility-maximizing sports fans, as consumers, to demand professional team sports. The basic conceptual relationship and qualitative set of predictions are illustrated in Figure 10.1, where a demand curve for match tickets is drawn. Changes in ticket price, other things being equal, will cause demand to increase or decrease by movements along the curve, whereas changes in income or preferences or the price of other goods will, for each change other things being equal, cause the demand curve to shift to the left or right, respectively, as less or more tickets are demanded at any given price.

10.3 THEORETICAL AND EMPIRICAL ISSUES

While the above analysis suggests that application of the standard economic theory of demand to professional team sports appears to be relatively straightforward, it should be noted that extensions to the theory and empirical complications of measurement and analysis need to be considered.

10.3.1 Measuring quantity

The above analysis, and indeed that of Chapter 1, suggests that the demand for sports is the match or event whose price is the ticket price. Yet, as Chapter 7 indicates, the core product of sport is really a contest, a meeting of competitors in a sports arena allied to many multifaceted characteristics concerning the timing and significance of the contest, such as the arena in which it takes place and its location, as well as the opponents and the historical and organizational elements of the contest (see also Borland and MacDonald, 2003). In this respect the researcher has to make some assumptions about the nature of demand.

One of the first and established assumptions is that gate paying attendance is the proxy for the demand for the contest as a live event. While this seems to be reasonable, it carries with it certain presumptions. For example, counting the aggregate number of seats at a match as a measure of

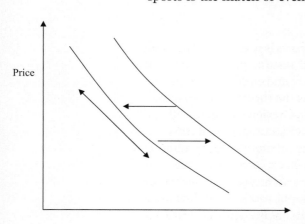

FIGURE 10.1 *A theoretical demand curve for match tickets.*

Price

Sports match tickets

demand presupposes that the experiences of the season ticket holder and the corporate client entertained in the firm's own "box," and the casual spectator buying a "one-off" ticket are all the same.

A further complication is that now, in many sports, events such as the Champions' League Final, the Superbowl and the World Series or games between local or international rivals (for example Celtic and Rangers, Manchester United and Manchester City or AC Milan and Inter Milan), can generate so much demand that stadiums are sold out. Indeed regular fixtures in the English PL are now mostly played in front of full capacities. Under such circumstances attendance for such matches measures supply (as constrained demand) and not demand as the free choices of fans. This is illustrated in Figure 10.2 where, for the lower ticket price, "demand" is indicated by supply capacity.

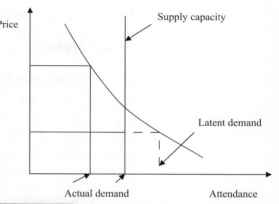

FIGURE 10.2 *Actual and latent spectator demand.*

A related question is how to treat the demand for sport on television. It is possible to add live gate paying spectators to television viewers to get a total match audience. One justification for this approach might be that the demands are "complementary" inasmuch as given the opportunity, the spectator would rather attend the live match. This suggests the prediction that screening live sport will at worst leave attendances unaffected, but at best may increase them by galvanizing interest in the sport. An alternative perspective would be to view television broadcasts as a substitute good that offers spectators the opportunity to watch live sport in settings that are more amenable. From this point of view one would expect live broadcasting to reduce attendances.

10.3.2 Measuring price and income

It might be reasonably assumed that the price of a stadium ticket is readily apparent. However, the price of attendance, i.e., the full opportunity cost of the match, is not. There will also be other costs, such as travel costs. Furthermore, the effects on demand of changes in substitute goods should be accounted for in price effects. Intuitively, however, it seems likely that "cross price" effects on demand are likely to be non-existent for fans of a particular team, or even sport. If their own team's ticket prices rise fans are much more likely to substitute other activities for watching their particular sport rather than switch to another team in the same sport.

Finally, it is clear that the real personal disposable income of fans should be the measure of income used in analysis. In the absence of primary research determining this information, it follows that any assumed proxy, such as industrial earnings in the region will tend to normalize earnings, rather than reveal their genuine variance and hence their potential impact on attendance.

10.3.3 Consumer preferences

The basic theory of consumer demand suggests that preferences could be treated as constant or fixed, in order to derive standard predictions. However, in the context of professional sports demand it seems clear that spectators' preferences may be affected by a number of factors. These include the quality of the experience associated with the sports contest, as noted above, and the fact that fans preferences, almost by definition, may be shaped by others in the community or by past experiences of watching their team. These last two factors are directly analogous to and further examples of, the social and consumption capital that has been argued to play a role in participation demand. In this respect, fans may exhibit interdependent preferences and habit persistence. Finally, there may be a spatial context to preferences. This suggests that attendance demand will be influenced by the geographical area for two reasons. On the one hand, it is likely that loyalty and habit persistence are likely to emerge from a local environment and historical connections with a club, as discussed in Chapter 7. On the other hand, the local geographic area approximates the scale of potential demand.

10.3.4 Estimation issues

As discussed in Chapter 1, the typical strategy employed in economic research is to estimate a regression equation to identify the impact of the various determinants of behaviour on the choices of individuals or firms. Stylized examples of the forms of regression models used in professional team sport literature to explain attendance demand are given in Equations 10.1 to 10.3. These represent a cross-sectional regression equation, a time series regression equation and a pooled/panel data regression equation, respectively.

$$A_i = \beta_1 + \beta_2 P_i + \beta_3 Y_i + \beta_4 UO_i + \beta_5 D_i + \beta_6 MS_i + \epsilon_i \qquad (10.1)$$

$$A_t = \beta_1 + \beta_2 P_t + \beta_3 Y_t + \beta_4 UO_t + \beta_5 D_t + \beta_6 MS_t + \beta_7 A_{t-1} + \upsilon_t \qquad (10.2)$$

$$A_{it} = \beta_1 + \beta_2 P_{it} + \beta_3 Y_{it} + \beta_4 UO_{it} + \beta_5 D_{it} + \beta_6 MS_{it} + \beta_7 A_{it-1} + \omega_{it} \qquad (10.3)$$

In these equations, "A" represents the dependent variable, which could be measured as the numbers of spectators, for example in thousands, at games for a club. In accordance with economic theory this variable is assumed to depend on the following causal or independent variables. "P" represents admission price, measured in a particular currency, for example pounds sterling, US dollars or Euros. "Y" represents the income of supporters, measured in the same currency, UO represents uncertainty of outcome that could be measured in a variety of ways, as discussed in Chapter 8, and "D" refers to a dummy variable that could measure any quality characteristic that could affect the game, such as whether the match was a derby match, whether it was raining or not, whether the match involved the league champions or not and so on. In practice, a large number of such variables are employed. MS refers to the market size or local population in some spatial dimension around the location of the match; ε, v and ω represent other factors that randomly cause attendance to vary; and i and t represent indices of observation, with the former referring to cases, such as clubs at a point in time, and the latter a particular case, for example, a club or set of clubs, over time. Where both appear, this indicates that observations are on a set of cases, such as clubs, over time.

In Equations 10.2 and 10.3 the lagged value of attendance is included as an independent variable. This is often used by researchers to measure "habit persistence" or the loyalty of support, which is a proportion of last period's attendance directly affecting this period's attendance. The degree of habit persistence would be given by the estimate of β_7 from the data. More generally, the estimate of β_2 would indicate the movement along the demand curve, that is change in attendance, following a unit change in the ticket price, with estimates of the other coefficients $\beta_3 \dots \beta_5$ indicating how much the demand curve shifts, i.e., attendance changes, following a unit change in income, UO or if the qualitative characteristic is applied or not.

10.3.4.1 Simultaneity

There are some potential problems associated with the econometric strategy noted above. To begin with, Equations 10.1 to 10.3 are examples of reduced form equations, measuring attendance as the joint outcome of a set of structural equations describing different aspects of behaviour. Box 10.1 provides an example of this in a simple examination of attendances, and Appendix 10.1 provides an example illustrating why it is problematic to assume that a lagged attendance variable, as in Equations 10.2 and 10.3, measures habit persistence. In a strict sense it can be shown that the presence of the lagged attendance variable can simply be viewed as providing a distinction between the short run or impact effect of a change in one of the (other genuine) independent variables on attendance, as given by $\beta_3 \dots \beta_6$, from the long run effect which is given by $\beta_3 \dots \beta_6$ divided by $1 - \beta_7$.

BOX 10.1 THE IDENTIFICATION PROBLEM

Consider a sports league in which the planned demand for seats "Ad" depends inversely on ticket prices, "P" as $AD = a - bP$, and the planned supply of seats, "As" depends directly on ticket prices as $AS = c + dP$, i.e., ignoring capacity constraints. When demand equals supply in equilibrium, i.e., $AD = AS$, this means that $a - bP = c + dP$, or that the equilibrium ticket price of a seat is $P = (a - c)/(d + b)$. Substituting this price into either AD or AD to identify equilibrium attendance would yield $A = (da+bc)/(d+b)$.

This shows that any set of observations on ticket prices and attendances, which must represent market equilibrium (where demand and supply cross) or the actual purchases and sales of seats, is a set of values representing the combination of the demand and supply coefficients and thus *not* what a fan alone might be prepared to pay for a ticket, as theorized in the demand curve. In this simple model, therefore, price and attendance are simultaneously determined and for any observed change in price and attendance one could not identify whether this was due to demand or supply separately. A regression of these equilibrium attendances on these equilibrium prices *cannot* be presumed to represent an estimate of attendance demand!

To identify the separate demand and supply (attendance) functions would require specifying additional variables that only appear in the opposing equation. Additional data on supply would therefore help to identify demand and *vice versa*. The intuition is that shifts in one of the functions help to trace out the other, as illustrated below in identifying the demand curve. A more detailed example of this issue is presented in Coates and Humphreys (2005).

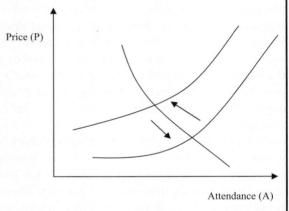

Estimating a single equation that is actually part of a set of equations also raises statistical problems. An estimated coefficient that is derived from an equation in which the independent variable is actually determined from another equation will suffer from simultaneous equation bias. As a consequence, a number of general strategies are open to the researcher to avoid simultaneous equation bias. They are beyond the scope of this book, but involve replacing the offending variable (often using its predicted value that will not contain a random element, unlike the original variable) with an appropriate alternative. This is referred to as instrumental variable estimation or two-stage least squares (2SLS) estimation. Finally, the researcher can use (multivariate) estimation techniques that allow for more than one dependent variable in a set of equations. Examples would be cointegration analysis, used in time series analyses to explore the possibility of a long-run equilibrium relationship between variables. An important feature of this analysis is that it directly addresses the problem of spurious regression occurring, such that apparent relationships between variables arise because of common random trends in the data. Another form of system modelling is to use seemingly unrelated regression (SUR), that attempts to allow for common random influences across a set of equations.

10.3.4.2 Multicollinearity

As well as simultaneous equation bias, the possibility of interaction between the regressors may raise problems of multicollinearity. This would, potentially, make it difficult to identify the impact of specific variables on attendance, as multicollinearity suggests that there is not really a problem of simultaneity of the variables but rather that the regressors are measuring different dimensions of the same influence on demand. In this context, it might well be that market size is closely correlated with the purchase of quality players and also with playing success and UO, as it provides a key resource base for clubs. It might be the case that price and travel costs are closely related or income and unemployment. A number of strategies are open to researchers to deal with these issues, such as combining the variables using factor analysis to identify latent variables representing combinations of the set of original variables. Tests of the joint significance of sets of variables could also be employed.[1]

10.3.4.3 Heteroscedasticity and serial/autocorrelation

Finally, heteroscedasticity could arise because of the potential for variability in the behaviour of fans from different population segments. A general form of adjusting the standard errors of estimates to produce more robust, i.e., consistent, t-ratios on which to base statistical inferences, such as White's adjusted standard errors, have now become a standard feature in econometric work. Similarly, generalized least squares procedures and other approaches have become common for estimating equations rather than adjusting the standard errors. The same applies to treating serial correlation which occurs when the random errors affecting attendance are linked over time.

10.4 EVIDENCE

Historically, the scope and scale of research has been relatively limited, reflecting the novelty of the economic analysis of sports. For example, Borland and MacDonald (2003) reviewed 57 studies since 1974 covering the following sports (and number): soccer (20); cricket (2); rugby league (7); Major League Baseball (13); Australian Rules football (4); National Football League (6); hockey (2); National Basketball Association (2); and all four US major league sports (excluding Major League Soccer) (1). It is noted that 23 of the studies are

---

[1] This would use the F-distribution in OLS or equivalent with other estimators, as discussed in Chapter 1.

single season analyses, 15 cover between 2 and 6 seasons, 5 cover between 7 and 10 seasons, 3 cover between 11 and 25 seasons, and 11 studies cover between 26 and 98 seasons. To update this work, an additional 22 studies have been reviewed for this chapter. These cover Spanish soccer (2), German soccer (2), English soccer (4), Belgian soccer (2), French soccer (1), Korean baseball (1), Super 12 rugby union (1), Major League Baseball (5), Minor and Junior League Hockey (1), Major League Baseball, National Basketball Association and National Football League combined (2) and National Basketball Association (1). Of these studies, 6 cover 1 season only, 6 cover between 2 and 6 seasons, 2 between 7 and 10 seasons, 1 between 11 and 25 seasons and 7 between 26 and 53 seasons. Table 10.1 provides some details.

There is some evidence, therefore, of a broadening scope of study, but soccer and baseball still dominate the literature. Furthermore, the typical study is a pooled cross-section–time series analysis of less than 10 seasons, with a substantial number being only one season. However, there is evidence now of a growing body of longitudinal analysis, with 18 studies covering periods in excess of 26 seasons.

10.4.1 Measuring quantity

As discussed earlier, the main variable used to measure the quantity of demand for professional team sports is gate attendance. However, the quality and detail of data varies. Most studies examine sets of individual clubs' match attendances within and across a number of seasons. Recent examples are Owen and Weatherston (2004), Forrest, Simmons and Szymanski (2004), Buraimo, Forrest and Simmons (2006) and Meehan et al. (2007). As the study period increases, aggregate league attendance tends to be examined, for example, in the more recent studies by Winfree et al. (2004), Coates and Harrison (2005), Lee (2006), or seasonal club attendances are used across longer time periods, such as in Feddersen et al. (2006) and Feddersen and Maennig (2007). Earlier studies that pioneered this approach are Simmons (1996) and Dobson and Goddard (2001).

Simmons (1996) is also significant in that it was one of the first studies to disaggregate attendance demand by considering the difference in behaviour of season ticket and casual spectators, thereby recognizing that attendance is not necessarily homogenous. Garcia and Rodriguez (2002) concentrate on non-season ticket holders and Falter et al (2008) distinguish between season and non-season ticket holders. A number of other studies attempt to control for different types of ticket holders implicitly by, as noted further below, making use of weighted ticket prices being paid by different sets of spectators; such an example is the study by Lee (2006). The issue of capacity constraints is now

TABLE 10.1 A selection of recent econometric findings on team sport demand

Author	Context, sample size	Model, method and estimator	Significant variables and comments
Butler (2002)	MLB 1999, 2428 games	Aims to determine effect of interleague play on attendance	Weekday dummies (+) (Monday is default)
	MLB seasons occur within a single calendar year	OLS	Away teams starting pitcher's wins minus losses (+)
			Hot (−); bad weather (−)
		(inferred)	Closing stadium (+)
		Dependent variable	Home team games behind leader (−)
		Log attendance	Log away team payroll (+)
			Inter-league game (+)
			Inter-league games few in number but very attractive
			Weekday dummies (+) (Monday is default)
Forrest, Simmons and Feehan (2002)	Premier League soccer 1995–1996.	Aims to measure sensitivity of attendance (by club) to travel cost	General travel cost (including time) (−)
	Fan survey by Norman Chester Centre	Weighted OLS	Proportion zone population within socio-economic classes 1–2 (+)
	20 479 questionnaires returned out of 58 000	Dependent variable	Proportion of zone population who attend 3 or more away games (+)
		Log of per capita local ticket sales	Fixed effects - 4 clubs (+)

TABLE 10.1 (*Continued*)

Author	Context, sample size	Model, method and estimator	Significant variables and comments
Garcia and Rodriguez (2002)	Spanish First Division soccer 1992–1993 to 1995–1996 1580 games	Aims to explain match attendance	OLS
		OLS (Column 1) Dependent variable log match attendance	Log real ticket price (−) Log real income (+) (inelastic) Weekday dummy (−) No rain (+)
		IV log real ticket price is instrumented (Column 6) Dependent variable log match attendance IV preferred as it does not ignore the endogeneity of the ticket price	Distance (−) UO (various) (+) Team budget (+) home, away
			On public television (−) IV As above but income no longer significant
Allan (2004)	Aston Villa, home league games 1995–1996 to 2000–2001 114 games	Aims to explain home attendance	Distance (−) and squared (+)
		OLS Dependent variable log home attendance	Cumulative away trophies (+) Away Euro run (+) England qualifier win (+) England qualifier draw (−) Bank Holiday (+) Weekday evening (−) Sky dummy (−)

Forrest, Simmons and Szymanski (2004)	English soccer, PL and First Division 1992–1993 to 1997–1998 PL 3214 games, FD 3312 The large number of PL sell-outs suggests TOBIT as an estimator For both divisions, the facility fee likely makes up for the home team's lost ticket revenue	Aims to estimate effects of broadcasting on match attendance and revenue TOBIT (PL) Dependent variable Log attendance 688 right censored observations, 2526 other OLS fixed effects (FD) Dependent variable Log attendance	TOBIT Dist (−) and squared (+) Weekday dummy (−) April–May dummy (+) Lpos (−) and squared (+) home, away Log last season mean attendance (+) home, away Promoted dummy (+) Log last season mean attendance if just promoted H (−) Season effects (+) Weekday dummy (−) OLS FE Similar to the above
Owen and Weatherston (2004)	Super 12 RU, NZ fixtures involving the five NZ teams, each played at one of 17 (rotating) grounds. 83 games of which 13 were capacity constrained. Seasons 1999, 2000 and 2001.	Aims to investigate UO effects on attendance	Significant variables from the final log-linear estimate N = 70; liberal strategy

TABLE 10.1 (Continued)

Author	Context, sample size	Model, method and estimator	Significant variables and comments
General-to-specific modeling (GETS) in contrast to informal selection and estimation of equations	NB Lagged attendance relates to the GROUND. Not to the home team. Thus it is NOT an index of team loyalty	PCGETS	Log of lagged attendance (+)
A liberal strategy permits more explanatory variables to "survive". See the corresponding final "conservative" strategy model		At each stage the model is simplified IFF it passes a battery of tests for functional form, normality of the errors, homoscedasticity, simultaneity, etc. Dependent variable Log attendance	Match-day nearest recorded rainfall (−) Cake Tin stadium (+) Home tries in last game (+) Traditional NZ rival (+) Away from overseas (+) Away's proportion of possible points earned so far (+)
Winfree, McCluskey, Mittelhammer and Fort (2004)	MLB 1963–1998, 884 team-seasons in all, regular play only.	Aims to measure the effect on a club's annual attendance of the distance from its nearest rival, and the impact effect of a new team.	Distance to nearest rival (−)
	New Team dummy is unity if a franchise opens within 500 miles of the team in any year.	NL-GLS allows for the nonlinear form and for heteroscedastic errors Dependent variable Annual attendnce (100 000)	New Team dummy (−) Real ticket price (−) (inelastic) Real per cap inc (+) (inelastic) Local pop (+) Win% (+), change win% (+) New stadium dummy (+) Lagged attendance (+) Current season runs (+) Div champs (+) Strike (−) Attendance growth (+) Team fixed effects (+)

Clapp and Hakes (2005)	MLB 1950–2002, 1232 potential franchise years,	Aims to measure the effect of new stadiums on mean annual (normal play) attendance.	Results for whole-period regression.
		N = 1179	
		GLS	Team win% (+)
	53 lost due to lack of data on stadium construction costs	Allows for serial correlation and for heteroscedastic errors	Lagged win% (+)
	New team dummy captures the arrival in a given year of a new franchise within the city	Dependent variable	Ln real ticket price (−) (inelastic)
		Log of mean annual game attendance.	Ln real stadium cost (+)
		Allows for the effect of league expansion on the number of games in normal play	Other teams in city (−)
			Ln stadium capacity (+)
			No of all stars (+)
			Classic stadium dummies (−)
			Last year of stadium (−)
			Stadium aged<6 (+)
			New team impact (+)
			Ln local pop (+)

TABLE 10.1 (*Continued*)

Author	Context, sample size	Model, method and estimator	Significant variables and comments
Coates and Harrison (2005)	MLB 1969–1996 all US based franchises, 725 franchise years	Aims to measure effect of industrial disputes on franchises' mean season attendance (normal play)	Results for whole period regression.
		IV	Ln lagged attendance (+)
	Strikes and lockouts are themselves endogenous. A model that takes this into account might produce different conclusions. Compare Putsis and Sen, who endogenized NFL TV black outs.	Recognizes the endogeneity of ticket price and that it is observed with error Dependent variable Ln of mean season attendance	Ln population (+) Ln stadium age (−) Win% (+) Lagged win% (−) Post-season last year (+) Strike-lockout impact dummies (−) Disputes have no effects beyond the year in which they occur
Coates and Humphreys (2005)	MLB, NFL and NBA, 1969–2001 780, 891 and 729 franchise years respectively	Aims to measure effect of new facility provision on mean season attendance, from reduced form equations	Per capita income (+) not NBA
	NHL excluded due to the number of Canadian teams	OLS	Win% (+) ALL

Notes	Study details	Method / description	Variables
Looks like NBA may be an inferior good	Rather confusingly they call it "team trend" "Other franchises" means the number of teams in ANY of the three sports within the city	One reduced from per sport	Stadium age (−) ALL
		Dependent variable	Stadium age squared (+) MLB
		Season mean attendance	Team duration (+) MLB and NFL, (−) NBA; Team duration squared (−) MLB; Other franchises (−) MLB and NBA; Last year post-season (+) ALL; Stadium age < 10 (+) ALL
Forrest, Simmons and Buraimo (2005)	English soccer, 1993–1994, 2001–2002 Sky audiences	Aims to explain how broadcasters select matches to televise	The paper also presents an OLS study (qv) of the audiences for the 522 televised games
*The author's Table 3 has confusing nomenclature	552 games were broadcast live out of 3346	Probit	All season variables
Do these dummies pick up games based on current PL standings, as Table 3 suggests or (as the names suggest) do they pick up games that involve PL teams that currently were, or had been, PL and Euro Champions?	Derbies and weekend scheduling work all season	On the 3346 games	Derby (+)
	Matches played before Boxing Day matches had been selected pre-season	Dependent variable	Weekend (+)
	After BD selection is sensitive to current form	Dichotomous dummy = 1 if match is broadcast, otherwise = 0	Pre-BD variables
		UO as defined is expected to have a negative effect on audience	Combined wages (+)
		Broadcasters' Audience Research Board (BARB) data are used in the complementary OLS study of live audiences	Wage differential (||)
The first seems more probable			Post-BD variables; Combined wages (+); UO proxy (−); Dummy 1 (+)*; Dummy 2 (+)*; Dummy 3 (+)*

TABLE 10.1 *(Continued)*

Author	Context, sample size	Model, method and estimator	Significant variables and comments
Alavy, Gaskell, Leach and Szymanski (2006) An extremely interesting extension to the concept of SRUO	English PL soccer, Jan 2002 to May 2005 248 games for which BARB possessed audience figures taken at one minute intervals NB Vars other than within game time dummies appear in rate of change (Δ) form in the regression	Aims to detect UO effects on changes (per minute) in the television audience during the game AB GMM estimator for the dynamic model of the TV audience (Step 2) Dependent variable The per minute change in the BARB rating Δr	Dummy 4 (+)* Dummy 5 (+)* *See first column. Results at Step Two Δr at lags of 1 to 3 minutes (+) Δtotal goals (+) home, away Δgoal in last minute (+) Δprob no score draw (−) Δprob score draw (−) Δ(prob home win − prob away win)^2 (−) Δsum of squares of changes in probabilities since kick-off (+) Some minute dummies are significant
Multinomial logit model is used to estimate the probabilities of home wins away wins score draws and no-score draws. From these UO measures are derived for modelling the television audience at Step Two Buraimo, Forrest and Simmonds (2006)	FL Championship soccer 1997–1998 to 2003–2004, 2884 games	Aims to model match attendance to assist clubs in decision-making.	Years in Champ (+) home, away

Innovative approach (qv) to measuring market size	The authors' Table 2 probably stacks only the more significant variables from a regression that may have involved many more, e.g., lagged values That they refer to "results from our estimation" is suggestive	Hausman-Taylor RE Model Allows for unobserved variable effects Dependent variable Ln of match attendance	LnPop < 5 mls (+) home, away Close rivals (–)home, away Relative wage (+) home, away Derby (+) Dist (–), dist squared (+) Midweek not television (–) Bank holiday (+) Month dummies Terrestrial television English team in Euro comp (–) Points per game thus far (+) Home, away Game on ITV (–) Game on ITV Digital (–) Game on Sky (–)
Forrest and Simmons (2006) Suspect Table 2 contains the most significant regressors only		Aims to measure the extent to which FL attendances suffer from match congestion and live broadcasting of higher league matches Prais-Winsten with panel corrected errors – same equation includes all divisions Dependent variable Log of match attendance	Lagged home attendance (+) all divisions Lagged Away attendance (+) Divisions 2, 3 Promoted dummy interacted with lagged attendance (+) all divisions Derby dummy (+) all divisions Distance (+), distance squared (-) All divisions Home points (+), away points (+) all divisions Recent home form (+) Divisions 2, 3 Game on ITV (–) Division 1 ITV CL dummy (–) Divisions 2, 3 England on television (–) Division 3

Football league normal play 1999–2002, 4320 games

TABLE 10.1 (Continued)

Author	Context, sample size	Model, method and estimator	Significant variables and comments
Lee (2006)	Korean professional baseball, 1982–2002, total annual attendance, 21 observations. Korean born C H Park pitched in MLB. Until the end of 2002 only these games were televised in Korea. ParkI is a proxy for MLB competition with KPBL	Aims to identify the main causes of the decline in total attendance. OLS. Dependent variable. ln of annual mean attendance per game. Takes into account changes in the number of normal play games	Midweek dummy (−); Divisions 1, 2; Interactive fixture congestion dummies; Ln real per capita income (+); (inelastic); Park I (−); 2002 W Cup dummy (−)
Coates and Humphreys (2007)	MLB, NBA and NFL attendance 1991–2001; 264, 298 and 308 franchise years respectively. Table 2 reports only some of the authors' results	Aims to investigate the elasticity of attendance demand w r to the prices of complementary items as captured by the Fan Cost Index. GMM. To allow for simultaneity and unobserved effects. One equation per game. Dependent variable. Ln of mean annual home gate per franchise	From Table 2; Ln FCI (−) NBA; Ln real ticket price (∥) MLB, NBA; Win% (+) ALL; Stadium age years (∥) NBA; Ln real per capita income (+) (inelastic) NBA; Ln lagged attendance (+) ALL; Population (+) MLB, NBA
Feddersen and Maennig (2007)	Bundesliga soccer, 1963–1964 to 2005–2006, 13 100 games, 772 club seasons	Aims to identify the effect on attendance of a dedicated arena relative to an all-purpose stadium	Real monthly earnings (+)

Panel unit root tests applied before estimation	The fixed (club) effects are very significant (qv)	End season league position (−)
The absence of any price variable might suggest that the authors regard their equation as a reduced form	Borussia Dortmund, Bayern Munich and Schalke 04 have much larger than average base support	%games midweek (−)
	Tobit fixed effects and OLS fixed effects	
	Dependent variable	
Or that they are imposing the restriction that spectator demand is completely price-inelastic	Bribery scandal 1970–1971, dummy set 1971–1972 to pick up possible effect in following season	Δcapacity (+)
	The club's mean season attendance	No of rivals within 100km (−)
	The paper shows no marked differences in the two sets of estimates	Financial scandal dummy (−)
	As only 7 observations were right censored, this is not surprising.	Novelty effect (+)
		Dedicated arena (+)
Meehan, Nelson and Richardson (2007)	MLB 2000–2002, 7189 normal season games, after 45 had been deleted due to lack of attendance data	The results below are taken from their Model 3
	Aims to test for significance of UO effects on attendance and whether symmetrical	
This paper (and others herein) could have made advantageous use of Jennett's and Kuppers' work to arrive at a more systematic treatment of medium term UO	Every team's first 10 games deleted each season. UO not very significant early on, see Chapter 8	Weekday dummies (−) Sat is default daytime (+)
	Cf issue of home advantage (Chapter 8) Also to test for time-varying significance of UO	
See Chapter 8 and appendices		Temp(+) rain (−)
	Censored regression – 344 sell-outs, out of 6828 games under study	
****Must be a statistical artifact; an incorrect sign produced by a particular combination of errors		Covered stadium (−)
	Dependent variable match attendance	New stadium (+)
It is not credible that MLB is a Giffen good	Support for asymmetry of UO effects	Income (+)
		Fan cost index (+)****
		Inter-league (+)

TABLE 10.1 *(Continued)*

Author	Context, sample size	Model, method and estimator	Significant variables and comments
			Playoffs last year (+) home, away
			Allstars (+) home, away
			Games behind leader (−) home, away
			Home win% (+)
			Abswin%diff (−)
			Poswin%diff (−)
			Negwin%diff (+)
Rascher and Solmes (2007)	NBA 2001–2002 all 1189 matches	Aims to model UO effects on attendance.	Probability home win (+)
		Censored regression	Square probability home win (−)
Three models (qv) set up and estimated. For brevity only the second is considered.	****Another statistical artifact Estimated from January onward FCI has no significant effect	There were 446 sell-outs	M Jordan (+)
			All stars (+)
		Dependent variable	Weekend (+)
		Game attendance	Fan cost index (+)****
			Median local household income (−)
			%non-white local pop (−)
			Local population (+)
			Local unemployment rate (+)
Coates and Humphreys (2007)	MLB, NBA and NFL attendance 1991–2001; 264, 298 and 308 franchise years respectively	From Table 2	
	Aims to investigate the elasticity of attendance demand w r to the prices of complementary items as captured by the Fan Cost Index Table 2 reports only some of the authors' results	GMM	Ln FCI (−) NBA
		To allow for simultaneity and unobserved effects	Ln real ticket price (−) MLB, NBA
		One equation per game	Win% (+) ALL
		Dependent variable	Stad age yrs (−) NBA

Brown and Link (2008)	MLB 1995–2001, 204 franchise seasons only. Arizona and Tampa Bay joined MLB in 1998	Ln of mean annual home gate per franchise	Ln real per cap inc (+) inel NBA
In economics a "bandwagon effect" is observed when the number of people who buy a product depends positively on the number who currently buy it	Brown and Link take 84 wins as the threshold at which bandwagon effects may begin	Aim to detect possible bandwagon effects on local revenues (gate, local television, etc. and concessions)	Ln lagged att (+) ALL Pop (+) MLB, NBA Comments relate to their Model 5 of Table 3
Brown and Link use it in a different sense	It will normally get the team into post-season play	OLS	Time trend (+)
Successful teams attract people who are not traditional fans	Several models and estimators used	Dependent variable	Pop×wins (+)
		Local annual REVENUE* in 1999 $	Pop×postseason games (+), lagged (+)
			Retro state of art stadium (+) Post-season games are intended to capture the bandwagon effect Not so easy to distinguish the two bandwagon effects Model 5 Table 3
			Total attendance
Falter, Perignon and Vercruysse (2008)	French first division soccer 1996–1997 to 1999–2000, 1298 games	Aims to measure the effect on attendance of France winning the World Cup in 1998	WC dummy (+)
The authors leave ticket price out on the grounds of simultaneity. Better to incorporate and use IV to deal with the problem	No evidence of a WC effect on the total number of transient spectators although if the model (qv) is estimated with a percentage capacity audience figure this conclusion is reversed	OLS	
But if demand is totally price inelastic their specification is correct		Dependent variable	
		Ln attendance OLS	Host city (+) Lpos (−) home, away

TABLE 10.1 *(Continued)*

Author	Context, sample size	Model, method and estimator	Significant variables and comments
		Dependent variable ln non season ticket holders	Team budget (+) home Last score (+) home Sunshine (+) Transport cost (−) Derby (+) Fixed effects home N-S attendance Similar except WC, host city and team budgets insignificant
Winfree and Fort (2008)	US Minor and Junior Hockey leagues 1998–1999 to 2005–2006. 707 ML games and 531 JL games in the sample	Aims to measure the extent to which NHL fans substituted ML and JL hockey during the lockout of 2004–2005 GLS	Time trend (+) ML, JL
A lockout during 2004–2005 caused the loss of the entire NHL season Time trend to capture effects of unobserved change in prices, population, incomes, etc.	25% ML teams with local NHL team are in Canada		Ln points per game (+) ML, JL
	80% JL teams with local NHL team are in Canada	Some evidence of serially correlated errors	NonNHL teams (|) ML
		Dependent variable Ln per game attendance	Strike dummy (+) ML NHL team (+) JL Seems as if whatever substitute there is goes into ML ML teams (not JL) are affiliates of NHL

increasingly addressed in demand studies. One of the first studies to account for this problem was Kuypers (1996), who recognized that 10% of English football matches were sell-out fixtures. Explicit treatment of capacity constraints is now, however, much more common. This is the case in Price and Sen's (2003) Tobit analysis of match attendance at US college football, Forrest et al's (2004) analysis of Premier League attendances, Meehan et al's (2007) "Censored Normal Regression," i.e., Tobit, analysis of Major League Baseball, Feddersen and Maennig's (2007) analysis of the Bundesliga, and Falter et al's (2008) analysis of French soccer.

Finally, the earlier research that exists offers mixed results on the effects of television broadcasting on attendance demand. The ambiguity persists with more recent research; in Falter and Perignon (2000) and Falter et al (2008) the broadcasting of French football matches is not significantly associated with attendances, which is echoed by Verhaegen (2006) in Belgian football, while Price and Sen (2003) show that the scheduled broadcast of college football on television is positively correlated with attendances. In contrast, Garcia and Rodriguez (2002) find that televised Spanish soccer matches have lower attendances. The same is true for English soccer for Aston Villa according to Allan (2004) and for matches outside of the Premier League according to Forrest et al (2004), Buraimo et al (2006) and Forrest and Simmons (2006). A significant contribution of these latter studies is that they do control for the scheduling of matches and the possibility of substitution effects, because it is Premier League clubs competing in the Champions' League. Overall, the results show that televised matches are more likely to generate substitute effects when higher quality and lower quality matches are compared and that it may be difficult to disentangle the effects from scheduling changes.

10.4.2 Measuring price and income

As noted above, measuring the price of sports matches typically depends on relatively imprecise data. Indeed, as a result of this, many studies end up having to ignore prices because of lack of data. Of the more recent studies this applies to Jones et al's (2000) study of British rugby league, Owen and Weatherston's (2004) study of Super 12 rugby union, Forrest et al's (2004) study of Premier League and First Division soccer, Barajas and Crolley's (2005) study of Spanish soccer, Coates and Humphrey's (2005) study of Major League Baseball, Buraimo et al. (2006) and Forrest and Simmons' (2006) studies of the English Football League, Feddersen and Maennig's (2007) study of the Bundesliga, and Brown and Link's (2008) and Winfree and Fort's (2008) studies of Major League Baseball.

BOX 10.2 PRICE ELASTICITY OF DEMAND

A price elasticity of demand of exactly −1.0 means that a 1% price rise or fall in ticket prices (other things being equal) reduces or increases attendance by 1%. As revenue is equivalent to price × attendance, i.e., quantity, the increase or decrease in revenue that would follow from a price rise or fall is exactly offset by the reduction or increase in revenue from the reduction or increase in attendance. Total sales revenue remains constant.

Price elasticities less than −1, for example −1.5, suggest that a rise or fall in ticket prices of 1% would decrease or increase attendance by 1.5%, hence sales revenue falls or rises. This means that it pays to cut prices and demand is referred to as price elastic. A price elasticity of between 0 and −1, for example −0.5, suggests that a rise or fall in ticket prices of 1% would decrease or increase attendance by 0.5%, hence sales revenue rises or falls. This means that it pays to raise prices and demand is referred to as price inelastic.

When price has been measured, in earlier studies minimum adult admission prices have been used or an average price based on revenues and attendance. It follows that, if sports engage in price discrimination, such an average price will be a biased estimator of the actual prices paid by any given supporter. More recent research studies, such as Falter and Perignon (2000), identify that ticket price changes do not affect attendance at French soccer and Coates and Harrison (2005) found the same in Major League Baseball. However, the conventional wisdom is that most studies (see also Fort 2004) identify that attendance and ticket prices are negatively related and, moreover, that demand is price inelastic. Elasticity is a unit-free measurement indicating the percentage change in the dependent variable that will follow from any given percentage change in the independent variable. Price inelasticity suggests that sports fans are not sensitive to changes in ticket prices, as illustrated in Box 10.2.

The finding that sports fans have price inelastic demand raises two important issues. The first is that it provides a rationale behind teams raising prices to increase their revenues from price increases. In this regard, Dobson and Goddard (2001) chart the extremely close relationship between ticket price increases and revenue increases in English soccer.[2] The second implication, however, calls into doubt the assumption of profit maximization for teams. The reason for this is illustrated in the figure in Box 10.3, where it is shown that profit-maximizing teams should price in the elastic portion of their demand curve. The finding that teams face price inelastic demands has, thus, generated debate. For example, Fort (2004) suggests that in the US profit maximization still follows if the analysis allows for the impact of larger-than-average local television revenues being earned by a team. This suggests that MR from gate attendance can be negative if offset by a positive MR from

---

[2] See also Dejonghe (2007).

BOX 10.3 INELASTIC PRICING

Profit maximization occurs where marginal cost (MC) and marginal revenue (MR) are equal. With ticket prices (p) on the vertical axis and attendance (A) on the horizontal axis, attendance demand, i.e., average revenue (AR) and MR can be illustrated as shown in the figure. As shown in Appendix 10.1, MR will have twice the slope of a linear AR curve. If MC is positive this means that MR has to be positive. Given that the formula for the ticket price elasticity of attendance demand is $-(\partial A/\partial p \times p/A)$, with a straight line demand curve of constant slope, price elasticity of demand can be inferred from the ratio p/A. Intuitively, elastic demands will lie at higher prices/lower attendances and inelastic demands at lower prices/higher attendances.

More specifically, because MR measures the change in revenue following a change in price, as discussed in Box 10.2, a falling price can only reduce revenue with an inelastic demand. Reducing revenue means that MR must be negative, so it follows that a negative MR following a price fall must imply that demand is inelastic. As can be seen from the diagram below, for teams to set their ticket prices in the inelastic portion of their demands must mean that MR and MC are not equal, as is implied in profit maximization. Some profit must be forsaken.

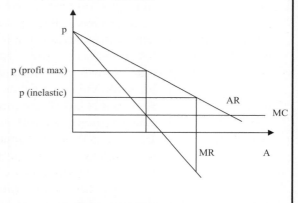

television. However, this argument has been formally challenged, suggesting that "the paradox of inelastic sport ticket pricing persists." (Porter, 2007, p. 158.)[3]

Qualifications can be made to the general claim; Simmons (1996) shows that it is season ticket holders that have inelastic demands relative to casual spectators. Researchers have also attempted to identify the full economic price of attendance that might suggest that inelasticity masks the true effects of price on attendance. One strand of research developed in the US has been to make use of the "Fan Cost Index" instead of just the ticket price. This covers the cost of two adults and two child tickets, four small soft drinks and hot dogs, two small beers, programmes, two adult sized baseball caps and parking. This index clearly captures a broader set of costs. *A priori*, however, it is not apparent which sign this variable would take according to the theory of demand. On the one hand, as a broader set of opportunity costs are associated with game attendance one might expect to see a negative sign. On the other hand, it is an example of product bundling, providing a discount on individual tickets. If

---

[3] Formally it is argued that Fort's (2004) analysis confuses the MR attributed from price changes with the MR associated with the acquisition of playing talent. See also Chapter 9.

this is the case, then one might expect to see a positive stimulus to demand. The literature reflects this ambiguity, with Meehan et al. (2007) identifying a positive impact on attendances in Major League Baseball, while Coates and Humphreys (2007) and Rascher and Solmes (2007) found a negative and insignificant impact in the National Basketball Association, respectively.

The second and more traditional approach has been to integrate some indication of the travel costs associated with match attendance. In the earlier studies, such as Baimbridge et al (1995, 1996), the distance between venues acts as an indication of travel cost in studies of English soccer and British rugby league, with a negative sign being consistent with a "price" effect. More recent studies, such as Garcia and Rodriguez (2002) for Spanish soccer, Allan (2004) for Aston Villa soccer club, Winfree et al (2004) for Major League Baseball, and Forrest et al (2004) Buraimo et al (2006) and Forrest and Simmons (2006) for English soccer, identify similar effects. Other studies, such as Falter and Perignon (2000) and Falter et al (2008), use return second-class rail fare as a direct proxy for travel cost in studies of French football. In both cases a significant negative sign is detected.

A particularly innovative study by Forrest et al (2002) combines both distance and direct cost of travel measures to produce a "generalized cost of attendance" of Premier League soccer, based on a large-scale fan survey in 1998 and 1999. This comprised a weighted average ticket price for season and non-season tickets, plus a measure of the direct- and time-costs of attending. Based on this generalized cost it was revealed that 8 clubs had price elastic demands and 12 had inelastic demands.

There has been less detailed research into the availability of substitute products on attendance demand. However, where it exists, the evidence suggests a broadly negative influence on attendance which could also help to account for price inelastic demands. Consequently, Dobson and Goddard (2001) note that the presence of professional rugby league in the north of England could account for the lower attendances, other things being equal, of northern English football clubs compared to their southern counterparts. Price and Sen (2003) also note that the number of college teams per state population can reduce attendances at college football games, Clapp and Hakes (2005) that the number of teams in the city can reduce Major League Baseball attendances, a view supported by Coates and Humphreys (2005). Likewise, Buraimo et al (2006) show that other English soccer teams in the same city can reduce attendances for clubs, and Feddersen and Maennig (2007) demonstrate that the number of rival teams within 100 kilometers of Bundesliga teams reduce attendance. Further pertinent results are provided by Winfree et al (2004) and Winfree and Fort (2008), who note respectively that attendances at Major

League Baseball teams can fall following the relocation of a franchise to within a 500 mile radius of a team, or that an increasing number of non-national hockey teams in the same standard metropolitan statistical area (SMSA) can reduce attendances in Minor League Hockey. In contrast, Owen and Weatherston (2004) do not identify a significant effect of other Super 12 rugby union franchises being on the same land mass on their attendances, and Winfree and Fort (2008) that the presence of a National Hockey League team in the same SMSA can increase attendance in Junior League Hockey. The latter results suggest complementarity in consumption.

Similar problems of data availability apply to attempts to measure the income of fans and the impact that this has on attendance. As the theory of demand refers to the individual's disposable income, it follows that lack of data or the fact that it varies inconsequentially over the study period has meant that many studies exclude its influence. Of the more recent literature this applies to Forrest et al (2004), Buraimo et al (2006) and Forrest and Simmons (2006) for English soccer; Clapp and Hakes (2005) and Brown and Link (2008) for Major League Baseball; Winfree and Fort (2008) for Minor and Junior League Hockey and Falter et al (2008) for French soccer. Where attempts have been made to include income, researchers have tended to rely on averages of earnings, employment status or some classification of fans according to socio-economic status.

Most of the more recent studies identify a significant positive but income inelastic affect on attendances, but make use of a measure of earnings. These include Garcia and Rodriguez (2002) who use regional per capita income in Spanish soccer; Winfree et al (2004) who use real per capita income in the state for Major League Baseball; Lee (2006) and Meehan et al (2007) who use per capita income for Korean baseball and Major League Baseball respectively; Coates and Harrison (2005) who use real income for Major League Baseball; and Feddersen and Maennig (2007) who use real gross earnings in trade and industry for German soccer. An exception is Falter et al (2000) who find a negative effect using average earnings in the department, suggesting that French soccer is an inferior good, a finding that is confirmed when using the unemployment rate as an alternative proxy for income. A positive sign on unemployment is identified.

Reflection Question 10.1

Why does a positive relationship between unemployment rates and attendance suggest an inferior good?

Hint: Think about the relationship between income and employment.

Because one would expect to have an inverse relationship between unemployment and income, the fact that the latter is associated with a rise in attendance suggests that attendance rises with falls in income and *vice versa*. This is the definition of an inferior good.

10.4.3 Consumer preferences

As well as the typical economic determinants of demand suggested by theory, sports researchers have adapted the theory to the sports context, which might be understood as reflecting elements of fans preferences which include quality characteristics, as well as interdependent preferences.

10.4.3.1 Quality characteristics

As far as the qualitative attributes connected with the viewing of a contest are concerned, to begin with, aspects of the stadium have been investigated. For example, Owen and Weatherston (2004) note increased attendance in Super 12 rugby union for games played in the "Cake Tin," a distinctive stadium in New Zealand. Winfree et al (2004) and Meehan et al (2007) suggest that new stadiums generate a positive stimulus for Major League Baseball attendances, but the latter also find that this is not the case for domed or roofed stadiums. This finding is supported by Brown and Link (2008), who identify increases in Major League Baseball attendances for "retro state-of-the-art" stadia. Moreover, Coates and Harrison (2005) identify that older stadiums reduced attendances in Major League Baseball. This is a result confirmed by Coates and Humphreys (2005, 2007) in Major League Baseball, the National Basketball Association and the National Football League. These results are contrasted by Clapp and Hakes (2005), who identify that older stadiums increased attendances in Major League Baseball, but classic stadiums reduced them, as did the final year of old stadiums. Finally, Feddersen and Maennig (2007) identify that dedicated soccer stadiums receive greater attendances than other German stadiums in which soccer is played, and that construction and novelty can decrease and increase attendances respectively. In general, the results suggest that fans appreciate dedicated stadiums, and that they are loyal to their stadiums but also receptive to new construction.

In general, the scheduling of fixtures appears to matter, with most studies identifying that moving games from traditional weekend slots reduces attendances. For example, Garcia and Rodriguez (2002) identify reductions in attendance at Spanish soccer for games during the week, Forrest et al (2004) find likewise for the Premier League and English Football League First Division, Allan (2004) for midweek games for Aston Villa football club, Forrest and Simmons (2006) for midweek games for Divisions 1 and 2 for English soccer,

Meehan et al (2007) for Major League Baseball for weekday games compared to Saturday, and Feddersen and Maennig (2007) for midweek German soccer games. Natural exceptions to this are public holidays where there is a ubiquitous finding that attendances increase, as illustrated by Allan (2004), Buraimo et al (2006) and Forrest and Simmons (1996) for English soccer.

Predictable results are identified for the impact of the weather on attendances, with them increasing with higher temperatures and reducing with rain. Garcia and Rodriguez (2002), for example, show that attendances at Spanish soccer increase in the absence of rain, and Owen and Weatherston (2004) found that attendances at Super 12 rugby union matches decrease when it rains. The same result is identified for Major League Baseball by Meehan et al (2007). Likewise, Falter et al (2008) show that French soccer attendance rises with the percentage of sunshine. Many studies also include significant seasonal dummy variables which, in part, may also identify the effects of weather on attendance, as well as factors such as championship contention.

As far as the quality of the contest is concerned, naturally UO is of great importance to researchers. The effect of UO on attendance was reviewed in Chapter 8, where it was argued that the evidence was mixed, although it was noted that support for the hypothesis is increasingly evident in more recent studies. The only point worth adding to this discussion is that many studies identify that "derby" matches involving local rivalries can increase attendances. For example, this is the case for Garcia and Rodriguez (2002) in Spanish soccer, Owen and Weatherston (2004) in Super 12 rugby union, Forrest et al (2004), Buraimo et al (2006) and Forrest and Simmons (2006) in English soccer and Falter et al (2008) in French soccer. However, the literature balances this hypothesis with the finding that attendances for clubs increase with the success of the specific club.

This suggests that the quality of the team is important for attendance. As well as the success of the team, a number of other methods have been used to identify team and specific player qualities, such as budgets for players (Garcia and Rodriguez, 2002), wage bills (Buraimo et al. 2006) and the visit of some historically dominant teams (Buraimo and Simmons, 2007; Verhaegen, 2006). The importance of star players being present in a team has also been investigated (Rascher and Solmes, 2007; Meehan et al. 2007) and shown to increase attendance.

10.4.3.2 Interdependent preferences and habit persistence

There is a large body of evidence which asserts interdependent preferences in professional team sports. On the one hand, it is argued that bandwagon effects are identified by Brown and Link (2008), because of the impact of post-season play increasing local revenues in Major League Baseball. Strictly speaking, however, this is not a bandwagon effect, through consumption being determined by other's consumption, but is more properly connected with some fans attending because of the team's success, as discussed above.

Likewise, there are numerous studies indicating that loyalty and habit persistence are demonstrated by the significance of lagged attendance on current attendance. Borland (1987) and Simmons (1996) are earlier examples in Australian Rules football and English soccer respectively. Owen and Weatherston (2004) in Super 12 rugby union, Winfree et al (2004), Coates and Harrison (2005) and Coates and Humphreys (2007) in Major League Baseball, Forrest et al (2004) and Forrest and Simmons (2006) in English soccer are more recent examples. As noted earlier, it is by no means clear that such a measure correctly identifies habit persistence, and hence interdependent preferences, i.e., fans consuming more games because of past experience or because others do. However, Dobson and Goddard (2001) do note that the age of the club is connected with increased attendances in English soccer, and Buraimo et al (2006) that the duration of a fan's club membership increases attendances. Intuitively, therefore, the results are suggestive of habit persistence and tradition, although Appendix 10.1 cautions against this interpretation.

10.4.3.3 Spatial context

The spatial nature of the demand for professional sports is, of course, clearly recognized in theories of sports leagues, as discussed in Chapter 9 in which it is argued that teams with larger potential market sizes draw higher gates. The evidence supports this argument with most of the literature identifying the market size of the home team having a positive impact on attendances. More recently, Dobson and Goddard (2001) make use of population census data for the city in which the club is located to examine English soccer, Garcia and Rodriguez (2002) use population in the province of the club in Spanish soccer, Owen and Weatherston (2004) make use of the regional population in Super 12 rugby union and Buraimo and Simmons (2006) use population within five miles of the home and away club in English soccer. The population of the away team is often included in studies, but is typically deflated by the distance between the clubs. This suggests that market potential dissipates with an increase in travel costs.

In the US it is common to use the population of the Standard Metropolitan Statistical Area to proxy market size. This is the case in Meehan et al's (2007) analysis of Major League Baseball and Coates and Humphreys' (2007) analysis of Major League Baseball, National Basketball Association and National Football League attendances. Rascher and Solmes' (2007) analysis of the National

Basketball Association makes use of the population in the Consolidated Metropolitan Statistical Area (CSMA), which is an updated definition of population. Some studies, such as Winfree et al (2004) make use of the city population in their analysis of Major League Baseball.

If more than one club is located in the area, researchers use some mechanism to allocate the population. For example Kesenne and Janssens (1987) divided the population of the arrondissement by the number of teams; Garcia and Rodriguez (2002) used the proportion of season ticket holders. This measuring criterion may not be the most appropriate, however. Professional team sport allegiance may vary spatially and Dejonghe et al (2006), for example, note that for the Netherlands the market areas of most of the clubs may be more strongly related with "marketing zones," for example as reflected in coverage by local newspapers. It remains, however, that "local" population seems to be ubiquitously associated with attendances and larger population bases raise attendance.

10.4.4 Estimation issues

While it is noted above that much of the earlier literature makes use of rather elementary applications of OLS estimation, there is evidence of an increasingly sophisticated econometric approach to both estimation and diagnostic checking. Developments are not consistent, however. In terms of simultaneity, studies such as Davies et al (1995), Dobson and Goddard (1998) and Jones et al (2000) identify the possibility of "reverse causality" between attendance and success in studies of English rugby league and soccer, suggesting simultaneity. A number of studies also note that prices and attendances may be simultaneously related. On this basis, recent work by Falter and Perignon (2000) drops the price variable from their analysis of French soccer, while Garcia and Rodriguez (2002) account for it in their instrumental variable estimation. It is explicitly accounted for in the application of multivariate systems by Owen and Weatherston (2004) for Super 12 rugby union, and in Schmidt and Berri's (2001) time series analysis of Major League Baseball.

Negligible attention is paid in the literature to multicollinearity, although it is tacitly accepted by researchers inasmuch as many researchers routinely categorize sets of variables together, such as "economic," "sporting success," "UO" or "controls." One of the few studies to address such issues empirically is Garcia and Rodriguez (2002) who perform F-tests on these blocks of variables to test for their joint significance, consistent with their conceptual groupings in an analysis of Spanish soccer.

Finally, the more recent research now routinely addresses serial correlation and heteroscedasticity. For example, Winfree et al (2004) used generalized least squares to estimate attendance in Major League Baseball because of heteroscedasticity; Lee (2006) undertakes generalized least squares to correct for serial correlation in estimating attendances in Korean baseball; Forrest and Simmon's (2006) use a Prais–Winsten estimator to control for autocorrelation and adjusted standard errors to control for heteroscedasticity in an analysis of English soccer; Winfree and Fort (2008) tested for heteroscedasticity in their study of Minor League and Junior League Hockey, finding none; and Falter et al (2008) corrected their standard errors for heteroscedasticity in an analysis of French soccer.

10.5 BROADCAST DEMAND

The discussions above indicated that the broadcasting of sports events may affect gate paying attendance, suggesting that the demands are substitutes. This issue is worth further investigation because, as discussed in Chapter 7, the development of sports leagues has become increasingly dependent on media income, as evidenced by the conceptualization of the contemporary European sports league as a Media–Corporations–Merchandising–Markets–Global or MCMMG model, in which for the largest clubs the single biggest source of income derives from the media. Understanding how and why this change in the "product" market occurred is an important issue that is addressed in the remainder of this chapter.

10.5.1 A brief outline of sports and broadcasting history

The evolution of modern sports leagues is directly linked with the growth of media income for sport and its distribution has fed directly back into the structure of sport. For example, the Premier League (PL) was directly connected with the offer of £43 million for the rights to broadcast live games of the larger, more powerful, clubs by the emerging satellite broadcaster, Sky. Until then the BBC and Independent Television Network (ITV), which began as a commercial provider in 1955, shared the televising of sport, which was relatively limited, as a "public" good. Indeed, the BBC had its rights to broadcast major sporting events enshrined in the 1981 and 1984 Broadcasting Acts. This benign cartel was broken with the arrival of Sky, with developments then following a model that had been experienced in the US with CBS funding the AFL, a rival league to the NFL, which ultimately led to the merger of the leagues. The PL consequently was established as an independent league, although promotion to and relegation from the EFL remained. Other sports have followed this model of development. The EFL attempted to emulate the funding model of the PL by securing a contract with ITV Digital for £315 million.

However, the market for championship football failed to attract subscribers, leading to the bankcruptcy of the broadcaster and considerable financial dislocation for the league.

In addition to the Premiership, Broadcasting Rights provide the financial backing for the Champions League in European football which evolved, as discussed in Chapter 7, from the European Cup. Outside of soccer in the UK, both rugby league and rugby union have followed the Premier League broadcasting model for football, as have the Super League and Premership respectively, while rugby union also has a European club championship, the Heineken Cup, in which teams from France, Italy and regional teams from Scotland, Ireland and Wales compete. In these smaller rugby unions traditional teams compete in national leagues, while the franchises compete in the Celtic (now Magner's) League.

Elsewhere in Europe, as noted by Szymanski (2006b), the evolution of broadcasting has been similar, with the removal of monopolies by public broadcasters and a general migration to pay television through satellite broadcasting, although in August 2006 the monopoly position of Sky in the UK was broken following a European Commission ruling, with Setanta sports emerging as a rival. Interestingly, however, as Andreff and Bourg (2006) point out, different models of rights allocation exist. In the UK and Germany cartels of clubs negotiate rights' deals. In France, the league owns and negotiates rights, whereas in Spain and Italy individual clubs undertake this function. Regardless of these differences, soccer has been the main driver, accounting for over 50% of sports broadcasting rights. Furthermore, a common implication of these developments is a redirection of funds towards the bigger clubs in leagues (this is programmed into Sky's funding formula for the PL) and towards the bigger leagues. While all clubs in the PL receive an equal fixed fee from 50% of the television revenues, for example approximately £743 000 in 1993–1994, rising to £8 885 000 in 2006–2007, the remaining 50% of revenues are allocated unequally. One half of this (25% of the total) is allocated according to the teams' positions in the league. This is known as a Merit Award. In 1993–1994 the Premier League champions, Manchester United, received approximately £856 000. They received £9 357 000 as champions in 2006–2007. Likewise, Swindon Town, the team relegated in 1993–1994, received approximately, £38 000 and Watford, relegated in 2006–2007, received approximately £487 000. The remaining 25% of television revenues are allocated according to the number of live matches that a team features in. Each team must appear in at least three live fixtures. This is known as the facility fee. Not surprisingly, above the minimum number of televised matches, fixtures involving more successful teams are broadcast more often (as discussed further below). Consequently, for the seasons noted above, Manchester United received a facility fee of approximately £1 011 000 and £9 357 000, respectively. Likewise, Swindon Town and Watford received approximately £243 150 and £3 271 000, respectively (Baimbridge et al, 1996; Findlay et al, 1999; Deloitte, 2007).

Across Europe, however, while the growth in funding has been similar, the distribution has varied. Vrooman (2007) estimates that total earnings of the Premier League grew at an annual average (compound) rate of 16% during the nine years from 1995–1996 (when the Bosman Ruling came into play), reaching 1987 million in 2004–2005. Of this total, broadcasting revenue comprised 862 million, about double the broadcasting revenues in Germany, France and Spain, and substantially above that in Italy. In turn, broadcasting revenue in the PL increased at an average annual rate of 33%, increasing as a proportion of total PL revenue from about 12% in 1995–1996 to 43%. Average revenue growth rates have been slower in the rest of the "Big Five" leagues in Spain, Germany, France and Italy. The price paid annually for television broadcasting rights to the Bundesliga increased from DM255 million in 1997–2000 to DM750 million in 2000–2004. The annual price of television broadcasting rights to the French Ligue rose from 125 million in 2001–2004 to 600 million in 2004–2007.[4] In this regard, the PL is the biggest sports league in Europe.

Elsewhere in the world similar situations apply with, for example, Fox Sports broadcasting Australian Rules football, the National Rugby League and the emergent A-league for soccer, as well as the Super 14 and Tri-nations rugby union competitions in Australia. The increased funding in rugby league, which provided the largest Australian market, and which threatened to absorb the best rugby talent, led to the formation of the latter rugby union competitions. A significant part of these deals was to repackage games such as rugby union into a franchised competition that aggregated talent into regions and was not broadcast on free-to-air television.

Similar developments are beginning to occur in cricket. The duration of cricket games has always led to problems attracting spectators, leading to the development of one-day cricket in the 1960s, in contrast to multiple-day County and test matches. "Twenty-20" cricket was developed in 2003 by the England and Wales Cricket Board with the direct intent of courting new fans and being attractive to the media as a complement to existing forms of the game. In June 2008, however, an Indian Premier League (IPL) emerged, developed by the Board of Control for Cricket in India, and underwritten with a television rights deal of $1.026 billion over ten years from a consortium of businesses from India's Sony Entertainment Television network. The IPL

---

[4] According to "The Political Economy of Football" web address (http://www.footballeconomy.com/stats/stats_tv_03.htm).

franchises have been signing the star players from around the world, which has caused consternation in countries such as the UK, as the Indian season overlaps their traditional season. This could limit the availability of players for their traditional teams and competitions, but nonetheless they stand to earn far more money from playing in the IPL. Matters are complicated further because of a rival unofficial league, the Indian cricket league, underwritten by a rival broadcaster in India. To meet this challenge, the English and Wales Cricket Board is, at the time of writing, looking for financial backing from Sir Allen Stanford, a billionaire who has underwritten Twenty-20 cricket in the West Indies. The English Premier League would look to involve teams from its counties plus others from India, Australia and South Africa. The England and Wales board faces the dilemma of seeking to protect and to promote all elements of the game, but faces the potential leakage of its best players.

The upshot of these discussions is that media income has grown substantially for sport and its distribution feeds back directly into the structure of sport. While this situation persists, it is difficult to see how sports leagues and competitive structures can evolve independently of the demands of the media, as the media provides financial incentives to change. It also suggests that uncertainty of outcome may not play the role traditionally thought in sports' league evolution, although it may be an outcome of restructuring with the intent of drawing together the best talent available in a specific competition. The economics underlying these issues are now discussed.

10.5.2 The economics of broadcasting and sport

The successful inroads made by broadcasting companies into the sports industry can be understood in terms of Neale (1964), who identified that professional team sports confer an externality on the public by the league standing effect, i.e., widespread interest in a successful sports team exceeds those that pay gate fees. A distinct element of this, the "fourth estate" benefit carries over directly to the media, who can earn income at no direct cost to themselves. It can be argued that public television broadcasting was a means of accommodating this externality. However, as discussed in detail in earlier chapters, the Coase theorem states that if property rights can be established for a resource and if a market can be organized to price the resources correctly, optimal allocation or something akin to it should follow. As the property rights to broadcast sporting fixtures can be easily established, because of restricted access to sporting stadiums, it follows that there was always the option to supply sports through such media. What ultimately mattered for the more recent changes to broadcasting was the technical ability to supply broadcast coverage with restricted access and an economic incentive to do so. The general growth of broadcasting technology into cable and satellite (digital) forms has made restricting access to broadcasts possible, which was not the case with traditional broadcasting.[5] Likewise, the economic regulatory climate of the 1980s and 1990s was conducive to the deregulation of industries. In turn, the scale of demand for sports has provided the economic conditions to promote these forms of supply. Historically, then, it is not surprising that sports leagues have acted collectively to sell the rights to broadcast live matches and highlights. This "internalizes" the external benefits. Moreover, the rise of the new media required explicit subscriptions to the appropriate technology to generate effective demand. As an expression of the derived demand for sport, broadcasters had to channel these funds towards sporting leagues to provide the incentives for leagues to supply them with access to fixtures in opposition to rival broadcasters.

As noted above, one of the ways in which this might have been prevented is through explicit economic policy. However, regulators have been relatively muted on the need to rule against collective selling of television rights. The collective selling of media rights is sometimes defended, on the grounds that it is likely to produce more revenue in total and to produce a more equal distribution of broadcasting revenue than if clubs sell rights individually. On the other hand, it creates the potential for monopolistic restriction of output and over pricing, and the EU has expressed concern. The logical justification for the league, rather than clubs selling television rights, is that no club can create a saleable product in the absence of the league which therefore has a property right in every league match. This is clear in Neale (1964) who went so far as to regard the league as a monopoly supplier and the clubs as its "plants." What is interesting is that the US and Europe have developed different models, in spite of the sustained increases in value of the markets noted earlier.

In the US, collective bargaining exists with revenue distribution, while in Europe sports rights have become associated with premium pay television channels. Szymanski (2006b) argues that this has been due to four main reasons. The first is that, unlike the US, one major sport dominates Europe, which means that the willingness to pay of European consumers will be greater than in the US, where all four main sports share the market. The second is that the US has economies of scale, in that markets for sports are national. This means that national carriers cannot pay as much as pay television networks,

---

[5] There are, of course, still potential leakages to property rights. Signs are emerging that the owners of rights face problems similar to those experienced by the owners of recording rights in the music industry. Websites exist that offer (for a small charge or none at all) software to connect your PC via telephone to the People's Republic of China where, by agreement with the rights holders (Sky), Serie A matches are broadcast free-to-air.

who can operate in separate segments, i.e., national markets, in Europe. These points imply that sports are not substitutes in Europe, and that national leagues are also not substitutes. The third point is that US leagues have been receptive to designing their competitions around media needs. The final point offered, and the one favoured as an explanation, is that US regulations have remained tighter on opening up the media market to competition than those in Europe. As discussed earlier, in Europe there has been an attempt to deregulate the market, but this has taken place in an environment in which some leagues have collective selling of rights and others have decentralized selling.

This naturally raises the question of which model is most appropriate. It is clear that some form of decentralized selling is preferred by the European Union, yet the impacts on consumer welfare are not that straightforward (Jeanrenaud and Kesenne, 2006). On the one hand, as discussed earlier, decentralized selling has led to UK rights values actually increasing. This could be the results of multiple downstream monopolies being created, although overall more games are being televised. On the other hand, non-exclusivity in some form for broadcasters would undermine the pay television market, because of the presence of perfect substitutes. Moreover, one could argue that having individual clubs make their own deals could benefit the larger clubs most, thereby affecting competitive balance. However, this is already happening in the UK with pooled rights. What seems to matter then, for competitive balance, is revenue sharing or not, rather than if rights are pooled or not, as discussed in Chapter 9. As noted there, moreover, the impacts on competitive balance will also depend on the objective of clubs, with revenue sharing potentially contributing to competitive balance in a league of win maximizing clubs.

What does seem to be clear is that there is a form of tripartite trade-off of rents involved, in which rights deals extract some rents from consumers and transfer these in part to the sport. Any wholesale reintroduction of public broadcasting, then, may increase consumers' surplus at the expense of funds in the industry. At the same time, as Szymanski (2006b) argues fans want to watch the highest level of competition that sports have to offer and broadcasting money may well have helped to provide this.[6] Significantly, this may well have helped to promote uncertainty of outcome as a market solution.

There is evidence to support these claims. In the studies of attendance demand noted above, it is shown that, while televised games reduce attendances, overall televised games correspond with increased revenues for the

---

[6] However, as noted in the next chapter, it is also the case that much of this rent has found its way to the players.

clubs in the Premier League and First Division (see Baimbridge et al, 1996; Forrest et al, 2004). The current deals thus benefit the clubs as a transfer from consumers. This naturally provides incentives for the clubs to have the deals, because it is able to cross-subsidize its gate paying demand from broadcast demand. Secondly, in two innovative studies, Forrest et al (2004) and Alavy et al (2006) examine the choice of broadcasters to televise a game and broadcast viewing figures on a minute-by-minute basis respectively. In the former case it can be shown that in the second half of the season when broadcasters have more discretion over which games to show, uncertainty of outcome increases the likelihood of a game being shown live. In the latter case it is shown that viewers prefer eventful contests with a result rather than UO *per se* and certainly are not interested in "tame draws." Under such circumstances, it can be suggested that broadcasters and their audiences appear to be much more interested in exciting close games, probably between high-level competitors. Both of these studies point to the strong influence of UO on broadcast demand for sport, in contrast to the relatively mixed results for attendance demand. It is perhaps not surprising that in a closed league system such as the US broadcasters will be happier with a more centralized system, but in Europe broadcasters have also been happier to encourage development of the games to promote higher-level and more equal competition. In the absence of closed leagues this has meant producing supra-national competition. In this regard, UO has become an outcome, rather than an initial driver, of league developments, as suggested earlier.

10.6 CONCLUSION

In this chapter the demand for professional team sports has been investigated and shown to involve a modified version of the theoretical framework presented in Chapter 3. In general, it is argued that the literature has increasingly come to terms with some conceptual and econometric issues associated with modelling demand, such as the need to account for capacity constraints and the endogeneity of key independent variables, such as price, and that a number of general findings emerge. These include that demand is generally found to be price and to a lesser extent income, inelastic consistent with a normal good. Market size is ubiquitously significant along with team quality, the success of teams, favourable weather, local rivalries, significant matches, and rescheduling games away from traditional times and days. As detailed in Chapter 8, there is some growing evidence that uncertainty of outcome matters, but the results are mixed, and the same can be said for habit persistence, but this time because of problems of interpretation. Finally, much of the evidence suggests that broadcast and attendance demands are substitutes if the effects of scheduling are accounted for. The evidence that is available suggests that teams still benefit, however, because of the revenue differentials. The chapter concludes by noting that the broadcast industry has had increasing effects on the development of sports leagues, made possible because of technical and regulatory developments in the media market and the incentives that media deals offer to clubs. It appears that UO matters more with broadcast demand.

Appendix 10.1 Problems of Measuring Habit Persistence

This appendix, although not necessarily representing precisely how particular authors arrived at their models of demand, illustrates some problems that arise in the interpretation of habit persistence. Consistent with the discussion in the chapter, in a simple case we might specify a linear demand for attendance as Equation A10.1.1:

$$A_t = a_1 + a_2 P_t + a_3 A_{t-1} \qquad \text{(A10.1.1)}$$

Here, A is the level of home game attendance – perhaps by club by season – P is a measure (possibly ticket revenue divided by attendance) of price, and the subscripts are date observations. The parameters a_1, a_2 ($a_2 < 0$) and a_3 ($0 < a_3 < 1$) are to be estimated by some regression procedure. It follows that, by analogy, a set of equations associated with previous time periods can be written as indicated in Equations A10.1.2–10.1.4.

$$A_{t-1} = a_1 + a_2 P_{t-1} + a_3 A_{t-2} \qquad \text{(A10.1.2)}$$

$$A_{t-2} = a_1 + a_2 P_{t-2} + a_3 A_{t-3} \qquad \text{(A10.1.3)}$$

$$A_{t-N} = a_1 + a_2 P_{t-N} + a_3 A_{t-N-1} \qquad \text{(A10.1.4)}$$

Based on these equations, successive backward substitution can be used to remove past attendance levels from the right-hand side (hereinafter RHS) of Equation A10.1.1 in order to discover what actually drives attendance other than the current price. This leaves:

$$A_t = a_1 + a_2 P_t + a_3 A_{t-1} = a_1 + a_2 P_t + a_3(a_1 + a_2 P_{t-1} + a_3 A_{t-2})$$
$$= a_1(1 + a_3) + a_2(P_t + a_3 P_{t-1}) + a_3^2 A_{t-2} \qquad \text{(A10.1.5)}$$

which, after further substitutions, resolves into:

$$A_t + a_1(1 + a_3 + a_3^2 \ldots + a_3^{N-1}) + a_2(P_t + a_3 P_{t-1} + a_3^2 P_{t-2} \ldots + a_3^{N-1} P_{t-N+1})$$
$$+ a_3^N A_{t-N} \qquad \text{(A10.1.6)}$$

Equation A10.1.6 states that today's attendance is a geometrically weighted distributed lag function of price. Unfortunately, Equation A10.1.6 is not consistent with habit persistence, and the very last RHS term shows why. Since, as N goes to infinity, a_3^N goes to zero, past attendance (A_{t-N}) plays no role whatsoever in determining current attendance, A_t. In a supposed habit persistence model past attendance insignificant! This is actually a partial adjustment model with a_3 determining the speed with which attendance responds to price change. Downward and Dawson (2000) indicate how habit persistence can be introduced into the model.

CHAPTER 11

The Labour Market in Professional Team Sports

- To understand the institutional structure of the players labour market in professional sports
- To appreciate profit and win maximizing models of wage and employment determination
- To become aware of the main results of research into the labour market

11.1 INTRODUCTION

The discussions in Chapters 7 and 9 have suggested that labour plays a paramount role in the supply of sports. Ultimately, the exercise of labour creates the sports contest. This chapter explores the labour market in more detail. In the next section, the labour market in a perfectly competitive market is briefly re-presented. This will help to indicate conceptually the novelty of the sports labour market, and to indicate what, in economic terms, an efficient or theoretically justifiable wage rate would be. Section 11.3 reviews the historic institutional forms of labour market in the US and Europe, arguing that sports leagues' monopoly power has endowed teams with monopsonistic power in sports labour markets, but that this situation has now changed. Some descriptive evidence to support predictions associated with the labour market changes are presented. Section 11.5 then examines the formal econometric evidence associated with the labour market in the US and Europe. Section 11.6 briefly reviews the market for coaches and managers in professional sports, before conclusions follow in the final section.

11.2 PERFECT COMPETITION AS A BENCHMARK LABOUR MARKET

The model of perfect competition is a useful benchmark for the economic analysis of sports labour markets for two reasons. The first is that it provides a conceptual basis for deriving a "just wage," i.e., one that players deserve based on their productivity. The second is because it highlights some peculiarities about the labour market in sport. The first claim was presented in Chapter 1, where it was argued that teams would hire labour up to where the wage was equal to the marginal revenue product of labour (MRPL), which is the revenue earned for the firm from the last unit produced by the worker being sold at the market price.[1]

Now, in general terms, these conditions for maximizing profits apply to all factors of production. Appendix 11.1 illustrates this for the case in which two factors of production are concerned, labour, "L" and capital, "K," the latter could represent the stadium and related land, etc. Each factor of production will be employed up to the point at which its marginal revenue product (MRP) equals its marginal factor cost or price, i.e., the wage rate "w" for labour and the profit rate "r" for capital. An interesting possibility arises from this discussion. By direct analogy with the theory of consumer demand, if the price of labour rises, i.e., "w" increases, it follows that profit-maximizing firms will reduce their demand for labour and increase it for capital, that if they have an incentive to substitute capital for labour, and *vice versa* if the cost of capital, "r" rises.[2] It is here that an interesting difference between sports and other industries arises. Because labour ultimately produces the sports contest, it is not possible for teams to substitute capital for labour if the wage rates increase.[3] This is simply a "technological" restriction of the production of sport. In this respect in sports, both the long-run and short-run decisions of firms are effectively the same. Under such circumstances there would appear to be strong incentives to constrain wages in sports leagues, which suggests a less benign reason than the motive of

---

[1] It is worth noting that, in general, the price at which output is sold is not equal to MR. Thus, in general, the marginal product of labour multiplied by the price of the firm's product, known as the value of labour's marginal product (VMP), is not equal to the MRP. For example, the VMP of a monopoly would be greater than the MRP of a monopoly.

[2] In general, investment also tends to bring technological advance with it. These predictions are thus made assuming technology remains constant.

[3] This is not to say that capital does not matter. In sports such as motor racing, yachting, cycling and other capital-intensive sports, investment in capital does matter to a degree, although labour is still the key resource.

UO to explain polices aimed at the labour market. The historic institutional nature of the labour market is now discussed.

11.3 HISTORIC EVOLUTION OF THE LABOUR MARKET IN SPORT

11.3.1 The United States

As Szymanski and Zimbalist (2005) note, after the foundation of the National League (NL) in baseball in 1876, it soon became customary to compensate the owners of other teams for their "reserve" rights over their players, because of the upward pressure that trading players had on salaries. Indeed, as the NL became more dominant, the reserve clause was established in 1879. This clause gave the club power to rollover the player's contract, by having them re-sign within a one year period. This "anti-competitive" practice was upheld in 1922 by the US Supreme Court in the light of challenges to the policy. The court ruled that baseball was exempt from anti-trust legislation because it did not comprise interstate commerce. As they developed, other US professional team sports adopted similar reserve option policies, although they did not obtain legal exemption. It is probably fair to say that, initially, team owner profits were a key consideration in this policy, but as Fort and Quirk (1995) note:

"Over time as the reserve clause faced court challenges, owners of sports teams developed the argument that, whatever the consequences of the reserve clause on players' salaries, it was needed to preserve competitive balance. Owners argued that free agency would allow the richest teams to acquire a disproportionate share of the playing talent in the league. Competitive balance would be destroyed, driving weaker franchises out of business." (Fort and Quirk, 1995 p. 1174)

Since the 1970s there has been a much freer labour market. Impetus for these changes began with the 1970 *Flood versus Kuhn* case in the US Supreme Court, in which Curtis Flood, a star player with the St Louis Cardinals, was traded to the Philadelphia Phillies in 1969, but he refused to play, wanting instead to be considered by other teams. The US Supreme Court ruled that the case was subject to the 1922 ruling.[4] Nonetheless, in 1970, a forceful baseball players' union negotiated a collective bargaining agreement that brought into existence an impartial arbitrator to help sort out contractual grievances. Some crucial developments followed. By 1973 final offer arbitration (FOA) for salary

---

[4] Earlier failed challenges to the ruling exist in the 1950s, but the courts were not entirely unsympathetic and prevented the anti-trust exemption carrying over to football.

TABLE 11.1 US sport salaries ($)

Sport	2000	2007
National Football League		
▪ Highest	▪ 619 050	▪ 1 102 880
▪ Lowest	▪ 361 200	▪ 440 520
% spread	▪ 71.4%	▪ 150.4%
Major League Baseball		
▪ Highest	▪ 2 225 000	▪ 3 591 667
▪ Lowest	▪ 268 500	▪ 380 000
% spread	▪ 729%	▪ 845%
National Hockey League		
▪ Highest	▪ 1 600 000	▪ 2200 000
▪ Lowest	▪ 500 000	▪ 800 000
▪ % spread	▪ 220%	175%
National Basketball Association	2001	2006
▪ Highest	▪ 4 475 688	▪ 5 215 000
▪ Lowest	▪ 590 850	▪ 1 347 000
▪ % spread	▪ 657%	▪ 287%

Source: http://content.usatoday.com/sports/

grievances was instituted.[5] Furthermore, in 1975 two star pitchers, Andy Messersmith of the Los Angeles Dodgers and Dave McNally of the Montreal Expos, refused to sign contracts, played for a year without contracts for their clubs and at the conclusion argued they had worked off their clubs' reserve option periods, and asked to be regarded and treated as free agents. Crucially, the arbitrator, Peter Seitz, favoured the players and was consequently sacked by the team owners. However, the courts refused to reverse the decision. The outcome of the Messersmith–McNally judgement was to give the club an exclusive six-year option on the player's services, after which time they automatically become a free agent.

As Sanderson and Siegfried (1997) note, the move back towards free agency in US sports has culminated in a situation in which "rookie" players of one or two years' experience are subject to a reserve clause. Intermediate players of between three and six years experience are eligible for FOA and veterans of seven or more years' service are free agents or eligible for FOA.

With regard to other policies, Staudohar (1998) notes that the NBA was the first league to reinstigate a salary cap in 1984 and the National Football League

---

[5] In final offer arbitration, the two sides to a dispute, the players and the team, make salary offers and then the arbitrator picks one of the two offers as the settlement. This is distinct from conventional arbitration settlements in which the arbitrator is free to impose any settlement they deem fit.

initiated a cap in 1994. The impetus came from the asserted financial difficulties experienced by clubs following the rise in player's salaries after the move to free agency. Indeed, the increases in salary have been quite extraordinary. Sanderson and Siegfried (1997) note that average baseball salaries rose by approximately 730% between 1975 and 1985; between 1967 and 1977 basketball salaries rose by approximately 615% and football salaries grew by 110%; and between 1977 and 1987 ice hockey salaries grew by approximately 180%. More recent data is presented in Table 11.1, for the median annual salary. It should be noted that the dispersion in salaries has increased in both football and baseball.

11.3.2 The UK and Europe

As noted in Chapter 10, in much the same way as baseball has tended to dominate both academic and general sporting discussion in US sports, this has been the case with soccer in European sport. However, this is not to say that other professional team sports such as rugby league and rugby union do not have active labour markets. Soccer provides the most detailed exemplar, however, and has driven European sports labour markets. There are strong parallels with the development of US sporting labour markets in which labour market restrictions have applied to both player remuneration and player mobility. As Szymanski and Kuypers (1999) argue:

"At its foundation in 1888 the Football League expressly set out the twin aims
   of imposing a maximum wage and preventing the movement of a player
   from one club to another without permission of the former."
   (Szymanski and Kuypers, 1999 p. 99)

However, the post-war boom in interest for soccer, with attendance figures at their all-time high (Dobson and Goddard, 2001), coincided with increased player and union militancy. In 1960, Jimmy Hill coordinated a campaign that led to the abolition of the maximum wage. Player mobility was controlled by the "retain and transfer" system. Only a player registered with the Football Association (FA) can play professional football. Because the registration is held by a club, historically, it could control the player's movements much in the same way as the reserve option clause in US sports. At the end of a season, for example, a club could retain players if it wished or let them leave. In principle it could retain the registration of a player, even if it did not renew the contract. Moreover, clubs could charge a fee – a transfer fee – for allowing the player to move to another club. Note that this could apply even in the absence of the maximum wage so, effectively, the terms and conditions of the players' contracts lay with the club under this system. The first effective challenge to the transfer system came in 1963 when George Eastham took his club, Newcastle

United, to court for refusing to let him leave the club on a transfer. The courts upheld his claim.

"From then on, the club holding the registration had to offer a new contract at least as remunerative and of the same duration as the expired contract . . . in order to retain the player's registration; if such a contract was not forthcoming, the player became a free agent." (Dobson and Goddard, 1998 p. 776)

Moreover, in 1977 players were awarded the right to decide on a move at the end of their contracts. However, if the club wanted to retain the player or demand a fee, the player could go to arbitration to the Football League Appeals Committee. As this increasing "freedom to contract" occurred, not surprisingly, salaries and transfer fees escalated rapidly as larger clubs competed to sign talent. Nonetheless, in the latter case there was a desire to keep transfer fees in the game because of their purported revenue-generating ability for smaller clubs (Dobson and Goddard, 1998, p. 777). It is also worth noting that while the case of the UK has been discussed, the general thrust of institutional developments has been similar in other countries.

"In other countries similar though not identical arrangements apply. Thus, under the rules of the Union of European Football Associations (UEFA) a board of experts makes a binding judgement in the case of a disputed fee . . . but differences remained. Thus, within France a transfer fee is payable only in the case of a player's first change of club and within Spain players aged 25 or more can transfer freely without a fee being required." (Sloane and Campbell, 1997 p. 2–3)

It is perhaps for this reason that the Bosman ruling has received much attention although it was, in many respects, a relatively minor legislative change to the changes in the system that had already occurred. The ruling arose because Jean Marc Bosman took two clubs (RC Liege, his current club, and US Dunkerque, the club which sought to buy him) to the European Court of Justice under Article 177 of the Treaty of Rome, which enshrines the free mobility of land, labour and capital in the European Union, for damaging his employment opportunities by fixing a transfer fee (over which they could not agree). The court declared that, in the absence of pressing reasons of public interest, the transfer rules did constitute an obstacle to the free movement of workers. The substantive outcome of the Bosman ruling was that no fee could be expected by clubs on the transfer of an out-of-contract player.

A new transfer system was agreed in 2001 which specifies two "transfer windows" for the purchase and sale of players in which players are allowed to move, but only once per season unless they are on loan. Unilateral breaches of contract can take place at the end of the season, but require the payment of a fee so as to protect the interests of the training clubs (Dimitrakopoulos, 2006). In addition, for players less than 24 years' of age compensation needs to be paid for transfers, with players under the age of 18 requiring agreed conditions and distribution of the fees between clubs. Players over 24 years of age become free agents at the end of their contract. A player can move in the final year of a four- or five-year contract if they hand in a request to the club no more than 15 days after the end of the previous season (FIFA, 2005). Under these circumstances the club would be entitled to compensation. In this way the labour market has become structured according to experience, as with the US. The Bosman ruling has been consolidated by the Kolpack ruling in 2003, which has essentially made the Bosman ruling international for European clubs trading with countries with which the EU has association agreements, and it has also had impacts in cricket and both rugby codes. A European Union association agreement involves a treaty with a non-EU country to promote cooperation, trade and other links.

Further liberation of the players' labour market is expected with the Webster ruling. The Webster ruling is a test case in soccer law involving Andy Webster, a former player with Heart of Midlothian football club in Edinburgh, Scotland. In September 2006 he became the first player to exploit the updated transfer regulations of FIFA (Article 17) that players who sign a contract when aged 28 or under are able to terminate those contracts after three years, and can do so in two years if aged 28 or over. Compensation should be paid, but clearly the player can now decide where they wish to play even within the contract period. The ruling was initiated in response to fears that the EU would abolish the transfer system altogether. The upshot of this increasing liberalization has meant that player wages and also transfer fees have increased, as in the US. It is argued that by 1978, more freedom of contract:

"... led to a wage explosion in the late 1970s and early 1980s. Between 1977 and 1983, wage expenditure by clubs trebled in the first, third and fourth divisions, while it more than doubled in the second." (Szymanski and Kuypers, 1999 p. 95)

This led to much concern over the financing of soccer in the UK with the 1983 Chester report examining the growing indebtedness of clubs. More recently many other sports such as rugby union and rugby league in the UK, and rugby league in Australia have introduced salary caps. Soccer is an exception, which is probably connected with the difficulties of enforcement that a genuinely international labour market brings, as discussed in Chapter 9. Notably, for Premier League clubs, the range of wage bill increases for clubs between 1996 and 2001 was 54% to 476%, and between 2001 and 2005 ranged from a cut of 33% and an increase of 319%. Over the same periods, for Division

TABLE 11.2 Premiership transfer spending

Season	English £ million	Overseas £ million	Total £ million	Overseas/ English %
1992–1993	51	n.a.	51	n.a.
1993–1994	67	n.a.	67	n.a.
1994–1995	84	29	113	35
1995–1996	94	69	163	73
1996–1997	95	84	179	88
1997–1998	95	118	213	114
1998–1999	136	142	279	104
1999–1990	105	150	255	143
2000–2001	135	229	364	170
2001–2002	118	195	323	152
2002–2003	86	101	187	117
2003–2004	132	254	386	192
2004–2005	108	232	340	215
2005–2006	134	301	435	225

Source: Deloitte (2007).
n.a. = not available.

1 of the EFL, the range was 21% to 1164% and a cut of 71% to an increase of 175% (see Deloitte, various years). The data reveal not only sustained and large growth, but also increasing dispersion of growth, with teams facing relegation having to curtail expenditure absolutely, and teams continuing to maintain their positions or looking to get promoted having to increase expenditures.

A direct consequence of the Bosman and subsequent rulings has been the growth in the market in overseas players, particularly in the Premier League which, as noted in Chapter 7, is the richest European league. As a result of such trade, FIFA have recommended a "six-plus-five" rule for leagues, with home country teams needing to field at least six domestic players, but such a restriction would be contrary to European law.[6] Table 11.2 provides some comparative data in which transfer spending on English and overseas players is charted.

11.3.3 Player agents

A potentially important element of the players' labour market that has arisen with market liberalization in both the US and Europe has been the growth in

---

[6] http://www.dailymail.co.uk/te95xtbased/sport/football/article-1023043/FA-support-FIFA-rules-stop-foreign-players-dominating-Premi95er-League-bid-strengthen-English-game.html.

the role of player agents. Semens (2008) argues that in the US agents have been in operation since the 1920s (see also Shropshire and Davis, 2003), but became more prevalent in the 1960s (Joyce, 1997; Mason and Slack, 2001, 2003; Mason and Duquette, 2005; Shropshire and Davis, 2003; Karcher, 2006). In the US, as part of the process of labour market changes, agents have become complementary to player unions in becoming the main vehicle for salary negotiations (Shropshire and Davis, 2003, p. 11) and tend to act solely for the player (Holt et al., 2006, p. 5).

In the UK and Europe, Semens (2008) argues that agents have also been in evidence since soccer became professional, but traditionally clubs internalized the activity through scouting networks (Roderick, 2001). Moreover, in 1936 FIFA banned the use of agents in transfers, over concerns that they promoted illegal moves (Berlin Congress, August 1936, displayed in FIFA collection, NFM). As with the US, it is argued that agents became more prevalent in the 1960s, particularly in Italy in the 1970s and 1980s when clubs wished to recruit talent from eastern Europe and employed a middleman to "facilitate" the deals, overcoming political and legal barriers (Holt et al., 2006, p. 4). Asser (2005) also notes that the growth of revenues from sport, for example the broadcasting income noted in Chapter 10, and the Bosman ruling promoted the widespread use of agents and the widening of their roles to exploit the playing and commercial opportunities arising from the expanded international market.

The existence of player agents may also help to explain why transfer fees have persisted. Under a more liberal labour market one might expect that players benefit at the expense of clubs, through their wage increases, but a fee being paid means that some revenue is still directed to the selling club, as noted earlier. As agents receive a fee based on a percentage of the transfer, and as Semens (2008) notes, it could be argued that buying clubs are only interested in the total cost of the player, including wages and fees, this suggests that the payment of fees remain in the interests of selling clubs and agents, who potentially benefit at the expense of players. For example, agents might have an incentive to move a player while they are within contract to obtain a proportion of the fee. In essence there is a three-way principal–agent relationship.

11.3.4 Contract duration

The above discussion suggests that contract durations have become a significant feature of players' labour markets. Under the reserve clause or traditional soccer contract, clubs faced no potential financial loss from losing a player to a rival bid for the player's services from another team.

HIGH	Monopoly: "Star model"	Bilateral monopoly: "Bargaining over rents"
LOW	Perfect competition: "Just wage"	Monopsony: "Exploitation of players"
Player power/ Club power	**LOW**	**HIGH**

FIGURE 11.1 *Labour market structures*

In essence, there was a long-term contract between the club and the player – although a particular contract might be nominally specified for a set number of years. However, in moving towards a more competitive environment, nominal contract lengths assume a real economic significance.

Commensurate with the risks of injury and loss of earnings faced by players, clubs face the real economic risk of losing their better players with no recourse to compensation in a free market. In the aftermath of the Bosman ruling, in a context of relative aversion to risk, it would be expected that player contract lengths would generally increase as a form of insurance, and also to attract fees, should a player wish to leave a club. Once again, there is descriptive evidence to support this claim according to Szymanski and Kuypers (1999) and Simmons (1997). However, the more recent changes in the labour market will have limited this incentive.

11.4 THEORIZING THE PLAYERS' LABOUR MARKET

The above discussion has argued that a growth in the freedom of contract for players in sports leagues has led to greater player salaries, a greater dispersion of salaries and also a growth in the total cost of players if transfer fees are included, as well as an influx in overseas players to leagues with an open labour market, such as Europe. Explaining such developments can be made with reference to a variety of different theories of the labour market.

Figure 11.1 presents a taxonomy of labour market structures, which essentially maintains that firms, in this case teams, are profit maximizing. A win maximizing approach is discussed later. Each axis measures power and, as drawn, suggests that low power of clubs and players results in perfect competition, as discussed in Section 11.2. Moving horizontally the diagram indicates increasing club power with player power remaining constant. This could imply that the number of clubs is smaller than in the competitive case or that particular clubs are perceived to be so good that players want to play for the club. At a rudimentary level, there will always be more players than clubs. It is clear that these assumptions are closer to sporting leagues than the perfectly competitive assumptions. The limiting theoretical case of this scenario is a monopsony, which has been used to describe the historical position of sports labour markets in

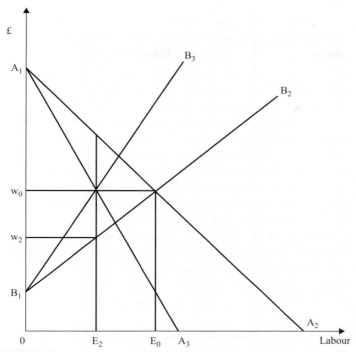

FIGURE 11.2 *Wages and employment under monopsony (W2, E2) and competition (W0, E0).*

their historic context as described above. This labour market leads to the monopsonistic exploitation of players.[7] This exploitation arises because players will receive salaries below their MRP, as is now illustrated.

11.4.1 Monopsony

The monopsony model differs from the perfectly competitive model inasmuch as the MC of hiring another employee comprises the wage received by that person plus the extra wages paid to those who were already on the payroll. This drives a wedge between the MRPL and the wage. The intuition is that the higher wages needed to attract additional workers are also paid to other employees. Appendix 11.2 presents the result more formally.

Figure 11.2 illustrates the comparison between monopsony and competition, and illustrates the associated equilibrium levels of the wage rate and

[7] This is a general case of exploitation. Other forms, such as due to race, would then be additional extensions of this general case.

employment, defined as hours of labour purchased per week. A_1A_2 is the perfectly competitive firm's demand for labour, MRPL, defined over hours of work, while A_1A_3 is the corresponding MRPL of the monopsonist. B_1B_2 is the weekly supply of hours to price-taking firms in the labour market. B_1B_3 is the monopsonist's marginal cost of labour (MCL). The perfect competitor maximizes profit where B_1B_2 intersects A_1A_2, giving W_0, E_0 as the perfectly competitive equilibrium wage–hours combination. The monopsony firm maximizes its profit where B_1B_3 (MCL) intersects A_1A_3, but the monopsony equilibrium wage–hours combination is W_2, E_2. Note that under monopsony the MRPL (given by A_1A_3) exceeds W_2, signifying exploitation of labour. The general inference is that wages and hours, and (implicitly) numbers in employment, will be lower (other things being equal) where the firms exercise increasing power to determine prices. It naturally follows that as club power, monopsony, diminishes, wages will increase, with corresponding increases in employment. Moreover, it is to be expected that with payment commensurate with productivity wages would increase faster for segments of the labour market associated with higher skills. This, of course, is what the evidence discussed above suggests.

The adjustment to wages can be viewed as players recapturing economic rents. Consider Figure 11.2 once more. A perfectly competitive firm operating at equilibrium pays a wage W_0 equal to the competitive MRP and hires E_0 hours of labour at that wage. But the competitive firm's labour supply curve B_1B_2 indicates that most of these hours could have been purchased at lower wage rates. It is important to distinguish between the actual wage paid (in equilibrium W_0) and the "reservation wage" – the wage that is just enough to persuade somebody to supply that particular hour, read in Figure 11.2 as the height of the labour supply curve B_1B_2 at the hour in question. If the equilibrium wage rate W_0 is slightly reduced the marginal hour will not be supplied, but intra-marginal hours will continue to be supplied because a small reduction will leave the actual wage in excess of most intra-marginal workers' reservation wages. An earnings equivalent corresponds to the reservation wage; wage rates are usually measured by the hour, the ensuing earnings are usually measured on a weekly, monthly or annual basis. A person's "transfer earnings" is the level of earnings below which they quit the payroll. Earnings over and above transfer earnings (actual wages in excess of reservation wages) provide their recipients with "economic rent," which like consumer surplus is a pure welfare gain.

With the growth of player power one might expect increasing wages to lie somewhere between W_2 and MRPL, depending on relative bargaining power. This possibility is now discussed.

11.4.2 Monopoly

The predictions connected with wage increases *etcetera* from an initial monopsony position could also be explained with reference to other labour market structures than a simple adjustment towards the competitive case. Moving diagonally up from the monopsonistic case in Figure 11.1 indicates increasing player power with club power remaining low. Here it is assumed that particular players have unique talents and are monopolies as there is no effective substitute for them. In this case competitive pressure applies to clubs wishing to hire the player. One can think of many examples of sporting monopolies such as: Mark McGuire; Deion Sanders; Jerry Rice; Michael Jordan; Shak O'Neal; David Beckham; Christiano Ronaldo; Daniel Carter. In the case of sporting monopolies, as Neale (1964) points out, the supply curve of the athlete is vertical and, as a consequence, wages are demand driven. This is consistent with the superstar model proposed by Rosen (1981), where the ability for players to attain monopoly power is related to the notion of scarcity.

11.4.3 Bargaining

The final quadrant of Figure 11.1 refers to the case of bilateral monopoly. Here, both clubs and players have market power and under such conditions it is clear that decisions would be made paying explicit attention to the likely responses of other parties. As discussed in Chapter 5, this suggests a game theoretic model. As "games" can involve conflict or non-conflict this requires some deliberation. In a sporting context one can see that signing a new player to strengthen a team may not produce conflict between clubs and players. However, if the new player is seen as a replacement player, then the context is different – conflicts of interest arise. Likewise, games can be characterized as cooperative or non-cooperative. Cooperative games imply that agents can make binding commitments on one another. Non-cooperative games do not. It is clear that in the former case players' labour markets, which are governed by the law of contract, have this characteristic. Game theoretical models can also account for differences in the information possessed by the parties to a deal. Thus, it can be assumed that information is symmetrically distributed. In contrast, it is possible that games might be characterized by asymmetric information, in which one party to a deal has more information than the other. In the former case it is likely that, other things being equal, an experienced player will know their true ability relative to the competition. Moreover, because of the scrutiny of sports players it is also likely that teams will have an accurate perception of established players' abilities. Under such circumstances it seems plausible to think of the player's contractual conditions as being characterized by symmetric information. However, in the case of a relatively new talent, the situation is clearly different. Finally, an appropriate solution concept needs to be identified.

As indicated in Chapter 5, a common approach adopted in cooperative games is to invoke the Nash bargaining solution. The assumption underpinning this solution is that the bargained outcome will maximize the product of the incremental utilities of all parties. Basically, this solution makes the value judgement that parties to a bargain will settle on a solution that maximizes overall utility rather than that of a particular individual. Thus, in the case of monopsony we can note that the difference between the salary paid to a player and the revenue received by the club, in the form of the MRP of the player, represents an increment of income that could be reallocated to the player. Clearly there is a disagreement point based on the current level of player's pay from which bargains can be made. As shown in Appendix 11.3, in general the split of incremental income will depend on the form of the utility function. Nonetheless, the model predicts that the new agreed wage will lie somewhere between the player's MRP and their monopsony wage.

11.4.4 Non-profit-maximizing behaviour

The above approaches maintain the (implicit) assumption that teams maximize profit which, as discussed in Chapter 7, is disputed for European sports. As discussed in Chapter 9, Kesenne in various publications addressed the behaviour of a club that seeks to maximize its wins subject to recovering a predetermined level of cost (k) that conceivably might incorporate an element of profit. The conclusion he reached is that the club will pay a wage equal to its average net revenue (ANR), and that since ANR will exceed MRP in the neighbourhood of win-maximizing equilibrium, the club will pay wages in excess of MRP. By implication, win-maximizing clubs systematically overpay their players, with potentially inimical implications for the game's survival. The origin of this conclusion is presented in Appendix 11.4. However, it suggests that win maximizers are expected to pay higher wages and to hire more talent than their profit-maximizing equivalents, which Kesenne argues might explain some of the financial problems in European soccer. From this perspective it can be argued that soccer in Europe has evolved from a set of profit-maximizing national monopsony leagues into a set of win-maximizing leagues that operate in a (largely) unified talent market.

11.5 THE PLAYERS' LABOUR MARKET: SOME ECONOMETRIC FINDINGS

This section examines a selection of econometric studies that have aimed to test for the historic degree of monopsonistic exploitation in more detail, whether this has reduced following changes to the labour market and whether a particular labour market structure fits the evidence best. The potential stock of econometric studies is large so the aim of this section is to cover seminal work, and that which illustrates some of the more recent main findings and methods of investigation. Because the availability of data is different in the US and elsewhere, the discussion is divided into consideration of the US (typically baseball) and Europe (typically soccer). It should be noted throughout the discussion that player characteristics and performance are often central to the research. One can think of the characteristics as indicative of the human capital of the player (as discussed in Chapter 3) that governs their productivity. In the European literature, team characteristics are also measured which, it will be shown, refer to the relative powers of the teams in terms of controlling player contracts and availability. In the US literature, the tendency is to focus on measuring the labour market structure more directly.

11.5.1 The United States

11.5.1.1 The reserve option

The seminal contribution to the econometric analysis of the sports labour market is provided by Scully (1974), who analyzed the 1968 and 1969 baseball seasons, predating both arbitration and the movement towards free agency. Because data on individual player performances and salaries is freely available in the US, Scully's objective was to estimate the MRPs of players, compare these to the players' annual salaries, and determine from that comparison the extent of monopsonistic exploitation suggested by the reserve option clause. Scully specified a causal chain (recursive) model of two structural equations in the first of which player inputs influence win percent, i.e., through their productivity (measured by the team "slugging average" and team's "strike-to-walk ratio" for hitters and pitchers). In the second equation, win percent influences revenue by attracting fans.

> A recursive model suggests that the values of the dependent variables in a set of equations are not simltaneously determined, but that the values of one variable subsequently feed into determining the other variable.

Coefficients were estimated by OLS. By multiplying the coefficient measuring the impact of player performance on win percents with that measuring the impact of win percents on revenues, MRPs were obtained to be compared to salaries. It was suggested that players tended to be paid about 10% to 15% of their gross MRPs. Medoff (1976) argued that Scully's specification of a recursive model was problematic, because it did not address the possibility of simultaneity between win percents and revenues in the two equations. Using 2SLS to address this possibility it was suggested that players received around 30% to 50% of their MRPs.

MacDonald and Reynolds (1994) researched the period during which FOA and free agency were both operating, using data for 1986–1987. The authors' findings suggested that MRPs have no significant influence on the salaries of those ineligible for FOA, but that they significantly affect the salaries of FOA eligibles and are most important in determining the salaries of players eligible for free agency. MacDonald and Reynolds also tested for superstar effects in baseball salaries, i.e., the presence of the monopoly power of players is such that as a performer's ability increases so does their salary, but at an increasing rate. For both batters and pitchers superstar effects were identified.

Marburger (1994) modelled baseball salaries via a one-step process that takes account of the bargaining structure and dispenses with the estimation of MRPs, and reached very similar conclusions. Marburger estimated expected 1992 salary levels for eight years of a player's career and identified that attaining FOA status added about 50% to a batter's expected salary and 30% to a pitcher's. Secondly, between attaining FOA and becoming eligible for free agency, the player's expected salary increased to the free agent level.

11.5.1.2 Contract length and salaries

Kahn (1993) examined the impacts of free agency and FOA eligibility on MLB salaries, contract duration and total compensation (defined as duration times salary) in a reduced-form study derived from a structural model. Data on 1144 non-pitchers and 831 pitchers active between 1987 and 1990 were used. Perhaps the most important finding was that free agency has a very powerful positive effect on players' contract durations, but less on salary, which agrees with earlier findings. Krautmann and Oppenheimer (2002) postulate a structural model connecting salary and contract duration. The sample consisted of 272 MLB free agent batters covering the seasons 1990 to 1994. They find that while better performers tend to enjoy longer contracts and higher salaries, there is a performance-related trade-off between wages and contract length.

Consequently, the literature for the US suggests that removal of labour market restrictions has tended to produce higher wages, indicative of a reduction in monopsonistic exploitation, and an increase in contract duration, consistent with teams insuring themselves against the loss of quality players. However, the evidence on which form of labour market structure dominates is unclear, and is probably linked to differences in player attributes and the

TABLE 11.3 A selection of econometric evidence on US labour markets in sport

Author	Context	Model, method and estimator	Results
Scully (1974)	Major league baseball Testing for player exploitation Two regressions were used to compute MRPs for comparison with batters' and pitchers' salaries	**Period 1968–1969** 148 salaries observed **OLS regression** **Dependent variables** ■ win percentage ■ team revenue **Independent variables** ■ slugging average ■ strike-to-walk ■ NL dummy ■ in contention ■ SMSA pop ■ age of stadium ■ percentage non-white players	Estimated that players earned on average about 10–15% of their gross MRPs
MacDonald and Reynolds (1994)	Major league baseball Testing for player exploitation Two regressions were used to compute MRPs Two subsidiary regressions (for batters and pitchers) testing for superstar effects in salaries	**Period 1986–1987** 1300 salaries: all players rostered Aug 31 in both years **2SLS** **Dependent variables** ■ win percentage ■ team revenue **Independent variables** ■ team runs ■ earned run average ■ contention dummies ■ local pop ■ personal local income ■ local MLB rival ■ arbitration dummies ■ free agent dummy ■ years played as a proxy for experience **Period 1986–1987** 792 batters 572 pitchers **OLS** **Dependent variables**	Young players are paid below their estimated MRPs Experienced players are paid in accord with their estimated MRPs Positive significant coefficients on the squares of MRP terms support the superstar hypothesis Suggests that as the level of talent increases the salaries of the most talented players increase faster than their talent

TABLE 11.3 (Continued)

Author	Context	Model, method and estimator	Results
		■ batters' salaries ■ pitchers' salaries **Independent variables** ■ MRP ■ MRP squared ■ FOA eligible ■ Free agent eligible	Expected salaries of young players increase significantly once they attain FOA eligibility Thereafter salaries increase gradually, attaining parity with free agency after six years
Marburger (1994)	Major league baseball Tests whether pay adjusts from rookie to FA level smoothly or in steps MRPs not directly estimated Salaries directly regressed on independent variables Data separated prior to estimation into: ■ ineligibles ■ FOA eligibles ■ FA eligibles as an alternative to using dummies as independent variables	**Period** 1991–1992 1360 salaries observed OLS* **Dependent variables** ■ hitters' salaries (logs) ■ pitchers' salaries (logs) **Independent variables** ■ own runs ■ own home runs ■ career runs ■ career home runs ■ years played ■ own ERA ■ innings pitched last season ■ career innings ■ career ERA *We infer from the fact that Marburger does not specify the estimator that it was OLS (the default estimator)	
Maxcy and Mondello (2006)	National basketball association, national football league, national hockey association Tests if competitive balance has improved following free agency	**Period** 1951–2004 54 end season measures of competitive balance in each sport	In the NHL and NFL at least one measure of competitive balance has improved with free agency. But in NFL it may be the salary cap that is responsible Not so clear-cut in NBA, which had a soft salary cap

Kahn (1993)

Equations estimated for each sport, and for every definition of competitive balance the authors include

*Unit root tests suggested the errors are stationary, thus OLS is a suitable estimation method

Major league baseball

Author aims to test for effects on both salary and contract duration of eligibility for FOA and of free agency

Two markets – one for each type of player

Kahn estimates reduced form equations for salary and contract duration

The H–T estimation method allows for omitted variable bias

Independent variables differ between the equations for pitchers and for non-pitchers

Using the same set would assume pitchers and non-pitchers are almost perfect substitutes

Separate equations for black and white non-pitchers as opposed to a single dummy variable

OLS after unit root tests*

Dependent variables
- ratio of SDWP to its ideal value
- SRCC of end-season standings

Independent variables
- lagged SDWP variable
- free agency dummies
- salary cap dummies
- strike dummies
- rival league dummies
- expansion dummies

Period 1987–1990

Panel data on 1144 non-pitchers and 831 pitchers

Hausman-Taylor fixed effects estimator

Salaries model

Dependent variables
- logs of pitchers' salaries
- logs of non-pitchers' salaries

Independent variables
- 3 FOA dummies
- experience
- performance data
- team chars
- year contract signed

Duration model

Dependent variables
- pitcher contract durations
- non-pitcher contract durations

Independent variables
As above

Obviously not identical for both types of player

The pitcher's salary and his duration are determined by one set of independent variables

The empirical results are broadly consistent with the invariance principle; labour market restrictions principally affect the distribution of economic rent

H–T test rejects the null hypothesis of no unobserved fixed effects

Chow test rejects the hypothesis that all coefficients are the same for white and other non-pitchers

No clear pattern of differences

Overall arbitration eligibility and free agency had similar effects on salaries

Free agency increased contract duration

TABLE 11.3 (Continued)

Author	Context	Model, method and estimator	Results
		Another set determines those of non-pitchers Some independent variables, e.g., FOA, feature in both reduced forms	
Krautmann and Oppenheimer (2002)	Major league baseball: free agent batters only Structural equation estimation Main purpose is to detect whether contract duration is traded against salary OLS and 2SLS are inconsistent in the presence of unobserved quality variations By sampling free agents only Krautmann and Oppenheimer reduce the scale of this problem Hard to say what the "expected" sign is for the race dummy	**Period** 1990–1994 272 free agents **2SLS (and OLS)** **LHS dependent variables** ■ log of real salary (1990 = 100) **RHS dependent variables** ■ DUR ■ DUR*PERF **Independent variables** ■ minority dummy ■ team revenue (1990 = 100) ■ experience ■ ABYEAR	2SLS results reported below Positive significant coefficient on DUR, negative on the interaction term favours the insurance hypothesis Experience not significant – may be the result of restricting the study to free agents, which reduces within-sample variation in experience MINORITY dummy "wrongly" signed and insignificant in 2SLS results

structured nature of the labour market. This suggests something of a transition from monopsony, through bargaining and arbitration towards competitive outcomes with free agency or superstar "overshoots" in wages. Table 11.3 presents a summary of the literature reviewed.

11.5.2 Europe

Research into the labour market in European soccer has not followed the same lines as that in the US, partly because of relative lack of data on salaries and also because of the existence in Europe of a well-organized transfer market where players trade for cash, other players and on free terms, unlike the US where teams trade players either for other players or for prior rights in future drafts. Consequently, researchers have investigated the transfer market for evidence of rent-sharing between buying and selling clubs in terms of the fees paid and received.[8]

11.5.2.1 Monopsony rent-sharing

Carmichael and Thomas (1993) seek to explain the determination of transfer fees in English soccer as an outcome of two-sided Nash bargaining between selling and buying clubs. The authors examine transfers that occurred between the end of the 1989–1990 and 1990–1991 seasons, during which 255 transfers were reported, although only 214 cases were analyzed because of the need to exclude free transfers, transfers involving payment by means of player exchange, and transfers involving clubs from other leagues, including overseas ones. The former two cases preclude bargaining, while the latter lacked data on overseas clubs.[9] The coefficients on player characteristics were correctly signed and statistically significant at or above the 5% level. In general, buying club characteristics had significant coefficients, but not selling clubs, which suggested to Carmichael and Thomas that the upward trend in fees had been buyer-led, consistent with the occurrence of rent sharing.

---

[8] Frick (2007) presents a very useful summary of labour market research in football, noting that as well as the issues discussed in this chapter, contract duration can affect the performance of players, as is consistent with tournament theory, and institutional changes such as the Bosman ruling have lengthened player career durations suggesting that it has enhanced the need for players to raise their productivity (see also Frick et al., 2006).

[9] Free transfers actually suggest some form of truncation in the data, which would make OLS problematic. This issue has also affected other studies of the transfer market, as discussed in the chapter.

Dobson and Gerrard (1999) examine six seasons' of data from the EFL from 1990–1991 through to 1995–1996, plus the closed season of 1996–1997. During these years 2215 permanent transfers took place involving football league teams only. Of these, in 198 cases the fee was not disclosed, another 98 were exchanges, and there were 432 free or nominal fee transfers and others that were problematic. Part-exchange transfers were included, where a cash valuation was published. After exclusions 1350 transfers – about 60% of the total – could be used in the study. The Bosman ruling led to an increase in the proportion of free transfers, and thus the proportion of current transfers that could be used fell as time passed. Most player characteristics appeared to be individually significant. Selling club characteristics appeared to be statistically significant. The most important finding was that both sets of characteristics were significant, supporting the rent-sharing hypothesis.[10]

11.5.2.2 Fees in a competitive labour market

A paper by Carmichael, Forrest and Simmons (1999) notes that about 10% of players were transferred every year and suggested the possibility that those who do transfer are not a random sample of soccer professionals. To correct for selection bias the authors use Heckman's (1979) two-stage estimator. In the first stage they model the probability that a given player will transfer, using the information on all players in the sample. In the second stage they use the data on those who have transferred to model fees, adding a correction term derived from the residuals from the probability model.

The sample studied was all active professionals (i.e., those who played in at least one league game) in the football league between May 1993 and May 1994, and who were still contracted to a club at the end of the season. Of 2100 players, 59 were deleted for lack of information on player attributes and 11 because their transfers involved exchange of players, leaving 2029, of which 240 transferred within the season.[11] The selection model meant that information on the 42 free transfers in their sample could be used rather than excluding them, although this represents a censored distribution of fees from below which would make OLS estimates of the

---

[10] Did the authors go too far in assuming that the amount of rent sharing is constant? Drop this assumption and the simple test cannot be applied. In an earlier (1997) discussion paper Dobson and Gerrard had split the sample into three groups (N = 450) graded by price. For each group they found buying club characteristics to be significant, but the Chow test rejected the hypothesis that the parameters were the same for each subsample. This runs counter to a constant rate of rent sharing, but not to rent-sharing as such.

[11] It is perhaps ironic that this sample selection issue is not addressed!

fee equation inconsistent. Therefore, in the second stage the authors used the Tobit estimator.

It is shown that support exists for the authors' hypothesis that unobserved player characteristics make their possessors more likely to be transferred and to command higher fees when transferred. Traditional player characteristics are also significant. In the Tobit equation that corrects for sample selection bias, variables that capture age, experience, scoring ability and international status attain at least the 5% level of significance. Inasmuch as the emphasis is on these characteristics, a competitive market explanation has some support. A decisive test with a bargaining approach in which buying and selling clubs characteristics are included is not possible because one cannot include the former for players that have not transferred. Nonetheless, the proliferation of players' agents, as discussed earlier, suggests that some form of market imperfection remains.

11.5.2.3 Salary determination in football

With the emerging availability of salary data a number of studies assessing salary determination have been published. Lucifora and Simmons (2003) model individual salaries in Italian football, Serie A and Serie B. Salary data existed for 730 players; the authors were able to obtain sufficiently informative career histories for 533. Some evidence of superstar effects for forwards is identified. Frick (2006) reports estimates of player salaries in the first division of the Bundesliga. The sample contained 1025 players and 2381 player years, on average about 2.3 years of a player's first division career during the seasons 2001–2002 through 2005–2006. No superstar effects were identified, but overseas players (controlling for position, age and experience) were generally paid more than equivalent native Germans, although the only groups paid significantly more were other Europeans and South Americans. Table 11.4 summarizes the literature reviewed.

11.6 MANAGERIAL EFFICIENCY[12]

The above discussion has focused primarily on the contribution of playing talent to the production of team sports, and then analyzed the impact of regulations on issues such as their remuneration and contract duration. In

---

[12] In the UK and Europe the term "manager" is used, particularly with soccer, to describe what the US and other sports would typically refer to as the coach. There is clearly increasing specialization of managerial and coaching roles in professional sport, but the effects of their organization have not been researched.

TABLE 11.4 A selection of econometric evidence on transfers and wages in European sport

Author	Context	Model, method and estimator	Results
Carmichael and Thomas (1993)	English soccer Using transfer fees (£) to investigate monopsony rent sharing	**Period** 1990–1991 214 intra-league transfers, exclusive of free transfers **OLS** **Dependent variables** transfer fee (log) **Independent variables** ■ player characteristics (PC) ■ age squared ■ goals ■ tribunal ■ position ■ buyer characteristics (BC) ■ profit ■ gate ■ goal difference ■ league position squared ■ division ■ seller characteristics (SC) ■ as above	Equation accounts for about 80% of sample variation in the log of the fee BCs generally more significant than SCs Most significant BCs are gate, goal difference, league position and division Most significant SCs are goal difference, league position and division League appearances and age the most significant of the PCs Hints at asymmetrical bargaining power
Dobson and Gerrard (1999)	English soccer Modelling real (1990 = 100) transfer fees to investigate rent sharing Model specifically designed to test for rent sharing	**Period** June 1990–Aug 1996 1350 intra-league transfers exclusive of free transfers **OLS** **Dependent variables** ■ real transfer fee (log)	BCs statistically significant as a group, favourable to rent sharing Equation accounts for about 79% of the in-sample variation in the log of the real transfer fee over six years NB: not directly comparable with Carmichael and Thomas above, which is for current price fees in a single year BCs more significant as a group than SCs (agrees with Carmichael and Thomas) Most significant PCs are age, league appearances, number of previous clubs, international goals, interaction terms with goal variables, premium prices for forwards and defenders

Carmichael, Forrest and Simmons (1999)

English soccer

Modelling transfer fees and the probability of being transferred simultaneously

A competitive market determines both the probability of a transfer and the fee

Heckman estimator to deal with possible selection bias in the fee equation

Independent variables

- PC
- age, agesquared
- previous club
- league total, league total squared
- goals (various)
- internat
- pos
- BC
- pos, possq
- lastpos, lastpossq
- goal diff
- gate
- division
- SC as above
- TIME
- month dummies
- football season dummies

Period May 1993–May 1994

2029 footballers

240 intra-league transfers including

42 free transfers

Heckman; second stage is Tobit

Very low value transfers gave trouble.
Better treated as free transfers

Overall some commonality with Carmichael and Thomas's findings

Heckman estimator rejects the absence of unobserved quality variations

Most significant of the PCs are age, league appearances, some goal terms, goals conceded by defenders, midfielders, under-21s

Most significant club variables are loans, previous clubs and change of manager

λ tests significant, favouring the selection bias hypothesis

TABLE 11.4 (*Continued*)

Author	Context	Model, method and estimator	Results
	Probit equation estimates transfer probabilities, using data on all players. The residuals are used to construct a term (λ) to remove sample selection bias in the fee equation The equation to estimate the transfer fees, estimated by Tobit to permit CFS to include free transfers *Loans and previous clubs may indicate human capital	**Probit** 2029 obs **Dependent variables** ■ dummy, 0 or 1 as transfer does/not occur **Independent variables** ■ PC ■ age, agesquared ■ league appearances ■ goals ■ position ■ international ■ club characteristics ■ division ■ goal ratio ■ loans* ■ previous clubs* ■ change of manager* ■ promotion risk* ■ relegation risk* **Tobit** 240 transfers **Dependent variables** ■ fee (£) **Independent variables** ■ all those from the Probit, plus λ, minus the asterisked club characteristics	Age, appearances, goals, international status, division are significant Of club characteristics, only the division is significant
Lucifora and Simmons (2003)	Soccer, Serie A and B Modelling the logs of player salaries using a reduced form Testing for superstar earnings Is it possible to identify this as something different from tournament outcomes? *lagged one year **lagged and related to position ***career rate lagged one year ****banded career scoring rates	**Period** 1995–1996 533 of 730 players **OLS with fixed team effects** **Dependent variables** ■ log of salary **Independent variables** ■ age, agesquared ■ *appearances	Positive sign coefficient on square of forward strike rate (Equation 11.1) and on superstar variables (Equation 11.3) broadly consistent with convexity Club fixed effects could not be rejected No test for unobserved player effects Age, appearances and forward scoring rates all very significant, also international status

- ** goal rate
- ** assist rates
- *** strike rate squared
- * under 21
- * it int
- * other int
- *** superstar1/2

Period 2001–2002 to 2005–2006
2381 player years (1025 players)
Fixed (club) effects
Dependent variables
- log of salary

Independent variables
- age (and its square)
- career games (and square)
- international caps (and square)
- 4 position dummies
- tenure with current team
- region of origin dummies
- year dummies

Hausman test rejects suitability of OLS as an estimator

No evidence of any convexity in the response of salaries to age, career games and international caps

Tenure a significant positive factor

Native born players, other things being equal, are often paid less than overseas colleagues

Players from Europe and South America earn significantly more than native-born players

Frick (2006)

Bundesliga

Modelling logs of salaries

Author also considers the wage bill performance nexus

Club characteristics are picked up by the club effects alone

No club specific indexes are included

Goals not included separately, as the positional dummies identify players that are more or less likely to score sports, however, the role of the coach/manager is also perceived to be important in affecting the productivity of talent, as evidenced by the popular media's attention to their being hired and fired.

Evaluating a coach/manager's contribution to the team's sporting success is as important and as difficult as evaluating a player's. In economic terms, the coach/manager can be assumed to affect the form of the production function described throughout this book, that is the technology by which labour and other inputs combine to produce output. One problem is to disentangle this effect from that of the players' efforts. Another problem is to relate the productivity of the coach/manager to either their reward or prospects of retaining their job.

One possibility is to use the regression residuals from a team production function as an indicator of technical efficiency. This is the approach undertaken by Carmichael and Thomas (1995) who estimate a production function for English rugby league during 1990 and 1991. Teams (and by implication their coaches/managers) that enjoy higher than expected win percents are regarded as being more efficient than those that produce lower than expected win percents on the basis of available resources. A problem with the analysis is that OLS always produces positive and negative residuals, as defined in Chapter 1. Negative residuals suggest that output is below the maximum possible, but positive residuals suggest that output can exceed the maximum that the production function is supposed to determine.

One solution to this technical problem is to model a stochastic frontier production function, as used by Dawson, Dobson and Gerrard (2000) and Dawson and Dobson (2002). In the former case this is used to analyze a sample of 147 coach/managerial observations, covering 72 appointments, to examine their ability to maximize team performance for a given quality of playing resources. In the second case this analysis is augmented to include the possible effects of human capital on 660 coach/managerial observations covering 318 managerial appointments. Both studies examine English soccer during the 1992–1993 to 1997–1998 seasons. The general conclusion is that efficiency has been falling due to increasing demands for success. Dawson and Dobson (2002) identify that variations in efficiency are linked to the human capital characteristics of coaches/managers and particularly to experience prior to an appointment.

This raises the important issue that the duration of a coaches/manager's tenure at a club is likely to be linked to their performance. To this end, Scully (1994) uses a stochastic production function analysis of coaching efficiency in basketball, baseball and American football and adds their efficiency to a hazard model exploring the duration of the coach's tenure. Scully identified that the expected duration was positively related to efficiency. Audas,

Dobson and Goddard (1999) used this approach to examine 918 coaching/managerial spells between 1972–1973 and 1996–1997 in English soccer and identify that job security is highly contingent on current team performance, a finding reinforced in an updated piece of work in Dawson and Dobson (2006) examining 1100 managerial terminations between 1972–1973 and 2002–2003.

The implication is that, as far as the output of sports teams is concerned, coaching and managerial inputs matter and in turn team performance is crucial to the duration of tenure of these inputs. To the extent that this simultaneous process can affect the trajectory of the impact of playing talent, it is clear that the previous analysis in this book assumes this complexity away.

11.7 CONCLUSION

Labour is the most important input into professional team sports. The interest of economists has ranged widely, over wages, monopsonistic exploitation, transfer fees, discrimination and contract durations. The broad thrust of the literature suggests that historically endowed monopsonistic exploitation has been reduced or removed as labour markets have evolved in the light of regulatory reform. Superstar effects, competitive markets where players are paid their MRPs and bargaining effects can be identified from the evidence, suggesting that no one theory describes all aspects of the labour market, but that a range of ideas can help us to understand the process of their transition, with bargaining being likely to persist in the presence of active European player agents, but with competitive outcomes with US athletes moving towards being free agents. It is also likely that less talented players and younger players are likely to experience degrees of exploitation, while superstars will be the exceptions in any sport.

A theoretical conundrum does remain. As with the conceptualization of sports leagues, either profit or win maximization can be assumed to drive labour markets. The above discussion broadly presupposes profit maximization. If win maximization is dominant then one might expect players to have always received greater payment than their MRP, as teams hoard talent. European analysis has not tested this proposition. It could apply if linked to longer-term profitability problems with European sport that has been exacerbated with labour market freedoms for some clubs. Approaching the labour market from this perspective, though, is also suggestive of a need to examine how the redistribution of impacts has occurred.

What is clear is that, regardless of profit or win maximization (subject to a profit constraint), rising player costs affect all teams, but will affect those least able to raise their revenues most. As discussed in Chapter 7, therefore, this could help to explain the financial difficulties in large-scale leagues such as soccer in England, for the lower quality teams and why, as discussed earlier, salary caps may be perceived to be acceptable for lower drawing sports generally. The labour market, both in terms of harnessing talent to generate saleable productivity, i.e., contests for fans, as well as in terms of dominating costs, thus remains of central importance to sports leagues.

Appendix 11.1 General Conditions for the Demand for Factors of Production

The general profit-maximizing conditions for perfect competition have a direct corollary in the general theory of consumer demand presented in Appendix 3.1 It is assumed that the firm maximizes profits, Π, which is the difference between total revenue, R, and total costs, C, subject to the constraint of the level of output that it can produce according to the production function. Note that output constrains the firm's decisions because both revenues and costs depend on output and the price of output and inputs respectively. The latter are given to the firm in competitive markets. This can be written as:

$$\text{Maximize } \Pi = R - C \text{ subject to } Q = Q(L, K) \tag{A11.1.1}$$

as:

$$R = P \times Q \text{ or } PQ \tag{A11.1.2}$$

and:

$$C = wL + rK \tag{A11.1.3}$$

then substitution for C and Q leaves:

$$\Pi = PQ(L, K) - C \text{ subject to } Q = Q(L, K) \tag{A11.1.4}$$

First order conditions for a maximum then become:

$$\partial\Pi/\partial L = P\partial Q/\partial L - w = 0 \tag{A11.1.5}$$

$$\partial\Pi/\partial K = P\partial Q/\partial K - r = 0$$

or:

$$\partial\Pi/\partial L = P\partial Q/\partial L = w \tag{A11.1.6}$$

$$\partial\Pi/\partial K = P\partial Q/\partial K = r$$

which are the conditions where marginal revenue productivities are equal to marginal factor costs. An important feature of these two FOCs is that they imply:

$$\partial Q/\partial L / \partial Q/\delta K = w/r \tag{A11.1.7}$$

That the ratio of marginal products – notice that the constant prices cancel – is equal to the ratio of the factor costs. This is the equilibrium condition implied in Figure A11.1.

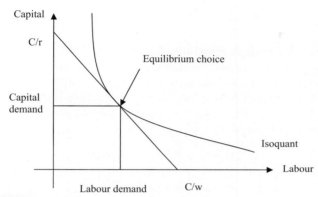

FIGURE A11.1 *Equilibrium demands for labour and capital.*

Appendix 11.2 Profit-Maximizing Monopsony

The Monopsonist has to maximize profits as:

$$\text{Maximize } \Pi = TR - TC = P(Q)F(L, K) - w(L)L - rK \qquad (A11.2.1)$$

Partially differentiating Equation A11.2.1, using the product rule for the revenue component with respect to labour and capital, setting the derivatives to zero and rearranging, we obtain for marginal revenue productivity of labour (MRPL) and marginal revenue productivity of capital (MRPK):

$$MRPL = P(\partial F/\partial L) + (\partial P/\partial Q)(\partial F/\partial L)Q + (\partial w/\partial L)L = w \qquad (A11.2.2)$$

$$MRPL = P(\partial F/\partial K) + (\partial P/\partial Q)(\partial F/\partial K)Q + (\partial w/\partial K)L = r \qquad (A11.2.3)$$

The MRPL under monopsony equals MRPL under perfect competition, the first term on the left-hand side plus two others. One of these, the last term, is the cost of having to pay a higher wage rate to the existing labour force when the firm hires extra labour. To the monopsonist, the marginal cost of labour (MCL) equals the wage rate plus the additional cost of intra-marginal labour. The other component is the revenue lost on intra-marginal sales when the price is cut to sell the extra product; $(\partial P/\partial Q)Q$ is the rate at which the price falls and Q is intra-marginal sales. Hence, the whole term corresponds to the change in revenue. Note that the rate of change is multiplied by $(\partial F/\partial L)$ in order to get a measure of the rate at which a change in L (labour input) affects the product price (P). Other things being equal, the profit-maximizing monopsonist pays a lower money wage than the profit-maximizing imperfect competitor.

Appendix 11.3 The Nash Bargaining Model

The Nash bargaining solution assumes that the product of the incremental gains to utility is maximized in striking a bargain. If we define M as the player's MRP, W0 as the player's monopsonistic wage and W the wage that players seek to achieve above W0, the players utility, G, will be a function of the wages received and the joint utility function for the team and the player can be written as:

$$U = (M - W)(G(W)) - G(W0)) \tag{A11.3.1}$$

Differentiating this function with respect to W yields:

$$\partial U / \partial W = M(\partial G / \partial W) - (\partial G / \partial W)) + G(W0) \tag{A11.3.2}$$

To identify the necessary conditions for a maximum this equation can be set equal to 0. Rearranging this condition implies that the newly-bargained wage will be equal to:

$$W = M - [G(W) - G(W0)/(\partial G / \partial W)] \tag{A11.3.2}$$

The top line of the term in square brackets will be positive, because W will lie above W0 – or there would be no bargain – and hence the player's total utility will be higher in the case of W than W0. The bottom line of the term in square brackets will also be positive, because it is the marginal utility of the player's wage and this is positive by assumption. This suggests that the overall term in square brackets is positive. Thus, the newly-bargained wage, W, will lie somewhere below the marginal revenue product of the player and above the monopsonistic wage W0.

Appendix 11.4 A Win-Maximizing Labour Market

The basis of Kesenne's (2002) argument can be illustrated by assuming that the ith club's total revenue (TR) is a function R(x) of the amount of talent (x) that it employs, with the property that MR is always positive but that it decreases with talent hired, as presented in Equation A11.4.1. To simplify the expression the subscript that identifies the ith team is dropped:

$$TR = R(x) \tag{A11.4.1}$$

To impose Kesenne's restrictions on MR requires $MR = \partial R/\partial x > 0$, and $\partial MR/\partial x = \partial^2 R/\partial x^2 < 0$; i.e., MR is positive but decreases as more talent is added to the team, which the author argues is consistent with the idea that spectators value UO. The team's total cost (C) is taken to be a linear function of talent hired plus a fixed cost element (k) that might incorporate a desired minimum profit component, embodied in Equation A11.4.2, where W is the wage rate:

$$TC = Wx + k \qquad (A11.4.2)$$

If the team's object is to maximize performance (x) subject to the constraint that it recovers fixed cost k, a constrained maximization (Lagrangean) equation L where x is the maximand and λ (positive) is the Lagrange multiplier can be presented as A11.4.3. Choosing x and λ to maximize function L ensures that the financial constraint (recovery of the club's fixed cost) is met at the equilibrium value of x:

$$\text{Minimize } L = x + \lambda[R(x) - W(x)x - k] \qquad (A11.4.3)$$

To find the highest level of talent the club can afford, subject to meeting its cost target, requires partial differentiation of L with respect to x and λ, and setting both derivatives equal to zero leaves:

$$\partial L/\partial x = 1 + \lambda(\partial R/\partial x) - x(\partial W/\partial x) - W(x)] = 0 \qquad (A11.4.4)$$

$$\partial L/\partial \lambda = [R(x) - W(x)x - k] = 0 \qquad (A11.4.5)$$

Equation 11.4.4 may be rearranged (compare Kesenne's 10) to give:

$$\partial R/\partial x = x(\partial W/\partial x) + W(x)x - \lambda^{-1} \qquad (A11.4.6)$$

Given that λ is positive, Equation 11.4.4 implies that the MR of talent ($\partial R/\partial x$) is less than the MC of talent [$x(\partial W/\partial x) - W(x)$] suggesting that cost-constrained win maximizers would hire more talent in equilibrium than profit maximizers, a result that fits Kesenne's prior expectations well. Equation 11.4.5 reveals that when $\partial L/\partial \lambda$ is zero, the cost constraint holds, which is precisely why the Lagrange multiplier λ is used in simple constrained optimization problems. The equation may be rearranged into the form below (compare Kesenne's 11) the interpretation of which is that the equilibrium wage paid per unit of talent equals club net average revenue ANR. Total net revenue is R(x) minus fixed cost k. Dividing by x gives average net revenue.

$$W(x) = [R(x) - k]/x = TNR/x = ANR \qquad (A11.4.7)$$

Under cost-constrained win maximization the wage exceeds that paid by clubs in a profit maximizing industry. The relevant zone of ANR for cost-recovering win maximizers is always where ANR>MR, implying that talent tends to be overpaid.

CHAPTER 12

The Economics of Sports Events and Infrastructure

- To understand the economic rationale for public sector investment in sports events and infrastructure
- To understand the difference between market and non-market impact of sports investment
- To understand the difference between economic impacts, the full economic value and cost–benefit evaluation of sports investment
- To appreciate the main findings of the empirical evidence evaluating public sector sports investment
- To appreciate the empirical evidence on the provision of sports
- To assess the rationale for public policy on the provision of sport

12.1 INTRODUCTION

In this chapter attention turns away from a specific focus on professional team sports and returns to consider elements of the economics of sports events more generally. This is for two main reasons: on the one hand, from the point of view of policy, as discussed in Chapter 2, a sports "event" has come to represent a sports contest that is taking place in a context different from a league-based competition of professional teams, which is less regular and can involve individuals or teams. This brings with it a need to examine some distinct elements of economics. On the other hand, as discussed in Chapter 5, one of the major policy issues connected with sports events is for the public sector to invest in hosting and/or the infrastructure required for hosting events. However, the distinction between types of sports contests and the arbitrariness between team and individual sports are not, of themselves, of major conceptual significance. It can be shown that both the economic rationale for, and the principles of evaluation of, any public sector investment in sports is common to *all* sports contests, although naturally the scale and types of investments differ.[1]

To explore these issues in more detail, Section 12.2 revisits the concept of a sports event discussing the variety of types identified in the literature. It is noted that, in the absence of professional teams, a central economic problem with event design is to balance the conflicting incentives required to encourage participation in an event, but also to promote high level performance which makes the event attractive, as predicted by contest theory. The role of adverse incentives, such as cheating (as a form of rent seeking), are discussed.

Section 12.3 then discusses the policy rationale for public sector investment in sport and, in particular, the role that externalities and other "spillover" effects are perceived to play in hosting events. The role of adverse incentives is also discussed. Section 12.4 then focuses in much more detail on the sports investment decision. Section 12.5 argues that the evidence suggests that dubious recommendations for investment decisions have often been made in sport. The chapter concludes by suggesting that, while a coherent theoretical case can be made for public sector investment in sports, the evidence in support of this case is weak, and suggests considerable caution and planning is required to harness the spillover effects from the investments.

12.2 SPORTS EVENTS

Depending on the literature or policy organization, the specific definition of a sports event can vary although, as noted earlier, they tend to be united in recognizing that events do not directly refer to professional sports leagues. Many criteria have been taken into account in describing an event but some of the more common are given in Table 12.1 (see Rahmann et al., 1998; Toohey and Veal, 2000; Gouguet, 2002; Barget and Gouget, 2007; Dejonghe, 2007b).

In addition in the tourism and management literature, the implicit scale, impact and prestige of certain events, such as the Olympic Games or world cups, means that they are referred to as "hallmark" or "mega" events (Getz, 1991; Torkildsen, 1994). In the UK, the Sports Industry Research Centre (SIRC), based on empirical case studies, has also provided a specific taxonomy of events connected with their sporting significance, economic impacts, regularity and scale (see Gratton et al., 2000; Gratton and Taylor, 2000).

---

[1] Consequently this chapter does not focus on any specific event, but assimilates the evidence. For an authoritative account of the economics of the Olympic Games, the reader is referred to Preuss (2004).

TABLE 12.1   Types of sports events

Frequency	**Irregular** ■ Olympic Games ■ Commonwealth Games ■ World Championships **Regular** ■ Wimbledon ■ Six Nations' rugby
Level of competition	International ■ World Cup ■ Champions League **National** ■ FA Cup Final **Regional/Local** ■ Amateur club championships
Single or multi-sport	**Single** ■ Henley rowing regatta ■ Tour de France **Multi** ■ Olympic Games ■ Commonwealth Games ■ Asian Games ■ School/university championships
Economic scale and impact	**Large- or small-scale (with respect to)** ■ Attendances ■ Media coverage ■ Sponsorship ■ Investment requirements
Ownership of the event	**International sport federation** ■ IOC ■ FIFA ■ ICCB **Private** ■ Tour de France ■ Paris–Dakar Rally
Location and assignment	**Same** ■ National stadia ■ London, Paris, New York marathons **Rotating requiring bids** ■ Olympic and other games ■ Champions League Final ■ Final stage of Tour de France

SIRC identify:

- Type A: irregular, one-off, major international spectator events generating significant economic activity and media interest (e.g., Olympic Games, football world cup, European football championship).
- Type B: major spectator events, generating significant economic activity, media interest and part of an annual domestic cycle of sports events (e.g., the FA cup final, six nations' rugby union internationals, test match cricket, open golf, Wimbledon).
- Type C: irregular, one-off, major international spectator/competitor events generating limited economic activity (e.g., European junior boxing championships, European junior swimming championships, world badminton championships, IAAF grand prix).
- Type D: major competitor events generating limited economic activity and part of an annual cycle of sports events (e.g., national championships in most sports).

Despite these differences in emphasis and classification, from an economic perspective, two particular issues are of interest for this chapter. The first is participation in the event. This requires consideration of the decisions of spectators to watch the event and also of competitors to enter in the event, which the remainder of this section discusses. The second issue concerns the economic significance of the event, to which much of this chapter is devoted. Discussion of this issue commences in the next section.

In the former case there is little specific economic research on attendance at events, with most emphasis being connected with attendance at professional sports leagues, as discussed in Chapter 10. However, the empirical grounding of SIRCs taxonomy suggests that the highest level of sporting competition does not necessarily attract the highest spectatorship, in the sense that the economic significance of some of the events are low.[2] This suggests that, outside of the major multi-sport events, most economic activity appears to be associated with the popular team sports and some individual sports, such as golf and tennis. The reasons for this are, of course, difficult to identify. It might be suggested, following the discussion of Chapter 10, that elements of personal consumption and social capital, i.e., habit persistence, apply to the demand in this case although, clearly, detailed research is required for a proper understanding. In general, moreover, SIRC note that in lower-level competitions, spectatorship is broadly associated with the athletes, their families and broader social groups.

As far as attracting competitors is concerned, then naturally some form of selection mechanism must apply. On the one hand governing bodies will

---

[2] The term "significance" is used deliberately, as will become evident later in the chapter.

establish performance criteria, which are required to be met for further representation at regional, national and international competition. Selection here is primarily from "within" the sport and founded on linkages between mass participation and elite performance as discussed, for example, in Chapter 5. Naturally, this applies to team and individual sports. In many respects there is no choice to be made about participation. What is more interesting from an economic perspective, therefore, is when choice is exercised by a competitor to enter a specific event, given that they have options of alternatives at their disposal. As discussed in Chapter 7, such choice problems conform to those analyzed using tournament theory, where it was shown that a broadly positive feedback between levels of sporting performance and economic performance existed. This has obvious implications for the current context. Organizers need to offer a large enough prize and distribution to attract competitors and to elicit high levels of effort from them and also to attract spectators, broadcast and sponsorship revenues, while at the same time not incurring losses. It is important to note here that the prize need not be monetary. For many athletes or event holders the opportunity to participate in or offer an Olympic qualification trial may be considered a high enough prize, which consequently attracts spectator and related interest and expenditure.

The link between economic and sporting performance is, however, quite subtle in contest theory. In Chapter 7 it was argued that prizes had to be increasing with the rank of competitors, to continue to elicit effort. This suggests that the highest prizes should be associated with the highest level of performance in tournaments, and that greater prize differentials would be associated with higher performances. Logically, however, this suggests that having a single prize is the most appropriate for event organizers, inasmuch as the highest level of sporting performance can be elicited. In fact, this is not the case in most sports. A range of prizes are offered and the economic reason for this can be understood as reflecting the view that competitive balance and the overall quality of the competition is more important to organizers and fans than a single record-breaking performance or domination of a competition. This is, of course, a mirror image of the UO argument in professional team sports. However, there is another reason for multiple prizes that applies to events more than professional sports teams, and this is that entry to tournaments may be low if participants have clear or predictable chances of losing. This was discussed in Chapter 7. The implication is that, from an economic point of view, organizers are prepared to sacrifice some level of effort to promote greater participation in the event. In the absence of this other participants may not be found, or they may engage in very low levels of performance as they have virtually no chance of success, and hence spectator, broadcast and other incomes fall which could undermine the economic sustainability of the event.

There is relatively little empirical evidence of the application of contest theory to sports events, and most has focused on the effort–performance–reward relationship of competitors.[3] Frick (2003) summarizes some of the earlier research. One of the seminal pieces is an examination of the 1984 US and 1987 European Professional Golf Association tours, in which Ehren-berg and Bognanno (1990a, b) found that player performance was positively correlated with the value of prizes, controlling for a wide range of variables including the quality of other players, the weather and course difficulties. Bognanno (1990) found similar results in US professional bowling, but a contradictory conclusion also, that greater skewness in the prize money pro-duces less performance (measured as pins knocked down per round).

More consistent with the predictions of contest theory, Fernie and Metcalf (1996, 1999) identified that British jockeys who had signed a contract that guaranteed them a certain fixed income showed deteriorating performances in comparison to when they had a contract without a certain guaranteed sum. Likewise, Lynch and Zax (1998) examined US horse riding and found that more effort is elicited with greater prizes and prize differentials, but the highest prize events often attract low quality as well as high quality competitors. Rationally, one would expect that over time poorer quality horses would not be entered into races where they expected to do badly. This is, perhaps, an example of long-shot gambling. In cases in which the prize differentials wid-ened, however, it is shown that the quality differences in competitors reduced, as would be expected.

In other sports, broadly consistent results are obtained. More recently Lynch and Zax (2000) analyzed 135 professional running contests held be-tween 1993 and 1995 and found that higher prize money resulted in faster finishing times. This result is supported by Maloney and McCormick (2000) who analyzed 115 professional running races in the US held between 1987 and

---

[3] There is a large and growing literature that examines the macroeconomic relationships between medal success and economic activity. Econometric analysis of medal performance, i.e., medal counts or proportions of medals won or, as recently proposed by De Bosscher (forthcoming 2007), the market share of points earned in competition, with 3 points corresponding to a gold medal, 2 for a silver medal and 1 for a bronze, is regressed on independent variables such as Gross Domestic Product (GDP), population, and host country status in reduced form equations as discussed in Chapter 10. These determinants act as proxies for implied demand and supply factors contributing to sports success. For example, population can be viewed as an indicator of the pool of talent available to countries, a supply-side factor. In contrast, GDP can be thought of as the ability of countries to "buy" success. In this regard it acts as a proxy for allocation of resources to sport, a supply-side factor, but also to the purchase of athletic effort, a demand-side factor. A summary of some of the studies is presented in Appendix 12.4.

1991 and identified that the average prize paid and prize spread had a positive effect on performances. Lallemand et al. (2008) also found that in women's official WTA tennis tournaments between 2002 and 2004 a positive and significant relationship between prize spread and performance was evident. However, they also found that players' ability and the difference in ability between players, given by their individual ranking, has a bigger influence on performance than incentives. Becker and Huselid (1992) examined prize money differentials in National Association for Stock Car Auto Racing (NASCAR) and International Motor Sports Association (IMSA) racing, and confirmed that performances increased with prize money. They also noted that the effects were possibly non-linear, peaking at a certain level. This result was supported by Von Allmen (2001) who investigated the team incentives and reward structure of the 1999 professional NASCAR Winston Cup. It was concluded that, in comparison with golf, rather "flat" prize money is more efficient than a winner-takes-all system, because the costs that may be inflicted on other participants, due to an increasing crash rate, could be too high. Becker and Huselid (1992) had also identified that riskier driving occurred with higher prize money. However, Schwartz et al. (2007) argued that drivers will increase their efforts as they see their overall ranking drop, so that unskilled drivers only tend to drive more aggressively in the early stages of the season.

This latter point is interesting, because it raises the issue of selection biases in the research. That is, competitors are only likely to enter tournaments which they perceive they have an opportunity to win and, of course *vice versa*, as discussed above. This means that better competitors are more likely to enter the highly paid tournaments. In this way average performances are likely to be higher regardless of the direct effects of prizes on effort. To try to account for selection effects Frick (2003) examined three golf tours in the US, the senior PGA tour, the PGA tour and the Buy.it.com tour, that differ in prize money and prestige. Selection into the tours is likely to require demonstrable skill. It is found that in the lowest value tour, the Buy.it.com tour, the survival rate of entrants is much lower, suggesting that lower quality players opt out of golf if they fail to make a living. Further, an earnings premium is identified for players progressing on to the other tours, in which performance is higher. It is argued, therefore, that both selection and performance are influenced by prizes. The upshot of this empirical research is that the evidence that is available broadly supports the positive feedback that it is proposed exists between sporting and economic performance, and also supports organizers offering more balanced tournaments than those that might occur with only one prize.

There are three important corollaries to this discussion. The first relates to the prize spread. As noted in Chapter 7, Frick (2003) argues that a key tenet of tournament theory is that the incentives to elicit effort should increase with rank. The evidence broadly supports this argument with respect to financial prizes. However, it seems reasonable to argue that this can also explain why a range of non-pecuniary prizes exist, such as the gold, silver and bronze medals in the Olympics and other games.[4] In the ancient games only the winner received the prize of the olive branch! This suggests, on the one hand, that athletes and their supporting administration place a differential weighting on these medals. In this sense, a gold medal is not just two places above a bronze medal. It might also not be appropriate to score its value 3, versus 2 for silver and versus 1 for bronze, as some medal tables comparisons suggest.[5] On the other hand, having a range of prizes can be viewed as a mechanism to increase participation of nations across the events, to avoid traditional specialisms, etc.[6]

The second point concerns the "darker" forms of incentive offered in tournaments, which is the possibility of cheating, as discussed in Chapter 7. Unlike the sports policy and philosophy of sport literature, the economics of cheating in sport is an under-researched area. Maennig (2002), however, drawing on Becker (1968) and the theory of rational behaviour discussed in Chapter 3, argues that rising prize money and related incomes from participation in sport raises the incentive to cheat, and consequently more cheating is likely if the returns for legitimate endeavour remain constant and efforts to tackle illicit behaviour also remain constant.[7] In this way cheating, such as doping, can be understood as the extraction of economic rents in the face of information asymmetries between athlete and monitor.

The third point is that hosting major events has now become a large and growing business and the supply of such events requires cities to "bid" to host

---

[4] This is not to say that funding for athletes from sports organizations, and related sponsorship deals etc., are not relevant, but that historically amateur activity even operated with this prize structure.

[5] In an interesting paper Blavatskyy (2004) shows that, in the typical symmetric contest modified to allow for asymmetric equilibria, that is when some contestants drop out of a tournament as with multiple elimination tournaments such as the Olympics, aggregate effort can rise with multiple prizes, whereas it would normally fall as the effort levels of competitors drop. In the former case, this is argued to be because of the likely greater number of competitors. The general proposition that effort levels fall with prize sharing is identified in the evidence above, inasmuch as greater prize differentials increase performance. The value of medals is discussed in Appendix 12.4.

[6] There is currently anecdotal evidence that countries target specific events, however, to boost their overall medal tally.

[7] A forthcoming volume edited by Rodriguez and Kesenne, based on a workshop at Gijon in Spain in May 2008, addresses the economics of doping and other threats to sport.

them. This process can also be viewed as a tournament. Tournament theory predicts that success is most likely to be the case where greater effort is expended. In this case, this suggests that cities (and governments) that are most prepared for hosting events are more likely to be successful in meeting the objectives of the tendering sports organization.

The Olympic Games illustrates this process. According to Preuss (2004) the IOC derives its power from the monopoly supply of the "product" – the Olympic Games – which it franchises to a specific Organizing Committee of the Olympic Games (OCOG) to a city or country, to deliver. Why cities bid to host the Games is a complex issue, which is partially addressed in the next section, however, whatever the specific reasons, the strong demand to host the games coupled with the need to cover infrastructural costs:

"... means that bid candidates will become limited to those cities which already have an adequate infrastructure to stage the Games. It is said that today there are only 20 countries able to stage the Olympic Games." (Preuss, 2004 p. 284)

Clearly, therefore, the allocation of the Olympic Games to host cities faces the same trade-offs between participation in a tournament and the performance of participants in the tournament, measured here in terms of its economic scale. Expenditures of "effort," i.e., resource and capability, to produce the Games raise the likelihood of success in bidding to become the host. This militates against the opportunity for developing countries to host the Games, although arguably these countries would benefit more.[8] As with tournaments generally, moreover, incentives to cheat exist. Corruption scandals have been noted, as indicated in Box 12.1.

This discussion reveals that many of the economic principles used to analyze professional team sports contests carry over to the process of organizing sports events when they are understood in the context of contest theory. As implied above, the similarity of aspects of analysis also applies to the decision to invest in sports, which is a central component of hosting sports event. This issue is now discussed at length.

12.3 INVESTMENT DECISIONS

12.3.1 Theoretical issues

Chapter 3, and particularly Appendix 3.2, introduced investment decisions in terms of increasing the capacity of an individual to undertake an activity

---

[8] Although, as discussed below, it can be argued that the benefits are more alleged than real in economic terms.

BOX 12.1 BRIBERY AT THE IOC

1. One of the most serious charges of corruption at the Olympic Games concerns allegations, in December 1998, suggesting that members of Salt Lake City's bid committee spent millions of dollars to improperly influence the votes of 14 International Olympic Committee (IOC) members. It is alleged that payments included cash, medical expenses, travel expenses, gifts and entertainment, and college tuition payments for IOC members' children. Policy responses followed including not allowing members to visit bidding cities and reconstitution of the bidding process and membership of the IOC. In addition, six IOC members were expelled and three others resigned. IOC president Juan Antonio Samaranch ruled out resigning, but pledged to lead an effort to purge the corruption, promising the formation of an ethics commission to review how the IOC members operate.

See: http://www.infoplease.com/spot/olympicscandal1.html

2. Ivan Slavkov, the Bulgarian IOC member, was investigated by the IOC when in 2000 it was alleged he offered support to a businessman who went on to try and solicit bribes from Cape Town when they were bidding to stage the 2004 Games. He was also secretly filmed by the BBC arguing that he could arrange votes to back London's 2012 bid for money. He was expelled from the IOC in 2004.

See: http://news.bbc.co.uk/sport1/hi/other_sports/olympics_2012/3531456.stm
See also Brown, G., Olympic Five-Ring circus: Bribery Scandal Tarnishes Olympic Gold.

by enhancing their skills (by acquiring human capital or consumption capital) or involving the purchase of goods and equipment that can be used more than once (durable goods) to yield a flow of services or utility over time that is not used up with one consumption act. More traditionally, investment decisions are connected with suppliers increasing their capacity to supply goods or services to consumers. This implies that suppliers incur costs to increase the capital required to facilitate their operations in the current period, or at least over some phased set of future periods, while seeking to at least pay back these costs from revenue streams being earned from future purchases of their goods or services.

Investment decision making requires consideration of two related points:

1. Establishing the decision rule for making an investment; and
2. Assessing the mutually exclusivity or independence of the decision.

The first point implies that to make an investment requires specifying a clear objective. Following the discussion of Chapter 5, it is assumed in economic theory that private sector suppliers seek to maximize profits. However, this objective was primarily discussed in a situation in which the current capacity of suppliers was fixed. As investment decisions take time to earn a return, the nature of profit maximization over time needs to be discussed. The second point is concerned with whether or not the investment is unique or part of a portfolio of investment options. For example, the building of an Olympic stadium or a new professional sports team stadium is an example of a mutually exclusive investment. Only one of the investment options for alternative designs and locations can be undertaken. In contrast, the equipping of a leisure centre constitutes independent investment decisions in that more than one type of equipment can be invested in simultaneously, at least up to a budgetary or spatial limit. Once either of these limits is met of course, options which might include alternative bundles of investment goods, become mutually exclusive. Appendix 12.1 demonstrates that accepting any project which yields a positive "net present value" (NPV) contributes to maximizing profits over time in theory, by maximizing wealth.

In economic terms "wealth" is the sum or stock of net income flows of an individual.

12.3.2 Public sector rationale

The discussions in Chapter 5 indicated that profit maximization might not be relevant for the theoretical analysis of the public sector. In general, however, the specific economic rationale for public sector investment in sport tends not to be explicitly discussed, although various benefits are identified as its outcomes. This is the case in the twin-track approach advocated for the UK, in DCMS/Strategy Unit (2002), in which investments in both elite sport, that is in the production of international success and the production of facilities that could host events, and mass participation mutually reinforce one another. Specifically, according to this approach, investment in international success will generate benefits (costs) from:

1. The feel-good (bad) factor stemming from sporting success (failure);
2. The enhanced (diminished) image of the UK;
3. The enhanced (reduced) productivity and consumer confidence following sporting success (failure).

While hosting sporting events and investing in infrastructure may:

1. Generate ongoing benefits for the community in the form of legacies, including urban regeneration, enhanced sports participation, increased tourism;
2. Attract new visitors helping to sustain economic activity;
3. Contribute to future sporting success.

Clearly these features are interrelated. Investment in events and infrastructure may generate sporting success and its related benefits. The "feel-good" factor may affect economic productivity, enhance the image of a country's tourism and bring success in sports, which in turn further enhance the legacies. Arguments such as these are not unique to the UK (Sandy et al., 2004, p. 187; Gratton et al., 2005, p. 986). There is, therefore, a strong and general policy impetus to invest in international sporting success, events and

TABLE 12.2 Forms of investment

Aim of investment	Type of investment	Examples
Facilitating international sporting success	Support national teams in competitions	UK Sport, Sport Canada, German Sports Confederation (see Chapters 2 and 6)
Facilitating professional sports teams	Build new/refurbish stadium	US major league sports franchises
Hosting national teams	Build/refurbish a national stadium	Wembley Stadium, Millennium Stadium
Hosting local, national and international events	Build new/refurbish stadia, arenas and related facilities	Olympic venues, Sheffield, Indianapolis

infrastructure. Table 12.2 summarizes the four main arenas in which this has happened and gives some examples of the investments.

Chapters 2 and 6 indicated a need for public investment in elite sports that do not have the requisite income from commercial activity to be self-sustaining. The administration of such investment is undertaken by various non-governmental sports policy bodies. As far as investment in physical infrastructure is concerned, the US has had a long tradition of civic authorities providing new, or refurbishing existing, facilities in the major league sports. Siegfried and Zimbalist (2000) report that since the 1950s public investment in new facilities has never dropped below 55% on average, has typically been in the region of about 70% and has, at times, been 100%. In the case of refurbishing existing facilities the proportion of total investment has never dropped below 78% on average over the same period and has typically been in excess of 90%.

As noted by Gratton et al. (2005), elsewhere investment has typically been in national stadiums or stadiums that have been designed for a variety of uses. In theoretical terms a defence of public sector investment is that, first, the private sector does not identify profitable opportunities to make such an investment but secondly, this lack of identification results from an understatement of the benefits to the economy that could occur with the investment. There are two main reasons why the economic benefits may not be accounted for, both of which are connected with market failure. The first is that the benefits exist as externalities. In this respect, the argument for supporting public investment in sport parallels that made for supporting sports participation activities, as discussed in Chapter 5.

Reflection Question 12.1
Which of the above impacts of international sporting success and hosting mega events are examples of externalities?
Hint: From Chapter 5 externalities were defined as occurring when the activities of an agent directly affect another agent and whose effects are incidental to the activity.

The impact of sporting success on general productivity would be an externality effect. The same would be the case of sporting success attracting tourists, increasing attendance at events or hosting of sports events raising sports participation. This is because the effects are incidental to the initial sports activity and not related through market transactions but through direct effects on the utility, and hence behaviour, of individuals.[9]

The second is that even though a specific investment might not be profitable, i.e., add to a private sector company's wealth and hence would be overlooked, wider economic benefits can be generated by the investment through multiplier effects, as first discussed in Chapter 1. In this case taking a broader as opposed to an individual organizational perspective, the costs of the investment overall might be met or exceeded by the subsequent economic activity that is generated beyond the investing organization. This makes the multiplier effect distinct from an externality, as the effects are mediated through market linkages rather than directly by the utility functions of individuals. The detailed nature of the multiplier and its possibility is discussed further below.

Reflection Question 12.2
Which of the above impacts of international sporting success and hosting mega events could bring about or rely on multiplier effects?
Hint: Which activities are likely to be generated from related market transactions?

In the examples above urban regeneration or new visitors sustaining economic activity would be examples of multiplier effects. This is because, in the former case, the initial investment in sports infrastructure stimulates additional economic activity in the markets providing the inputs to the investment asset. Likewise, these markets further stimulate economic activity in their respective input markets and so on. In the latter case, the spending of visitors at an event will support the investment in the event directly and thus

---

[9] As will become clearer below, it is the additional tourism generated from sports investment that is central to legitimately identifying economic impact.

stimulate related input markets, as just described, but will also stimulate other related consumption, such as accommodation, hospitality and transport. This makes it apparent that the effects of the multiplier are complex. Because of its centrality to discussions concerning public investment in sports infrastructure, the concept of the multiplier is discussed in more detail in the next section.[10]

12.3.3 The multiplier

As discussed in Chapter 3, a basic feature of economic analysis is that it constitutes a flow of resources between economic agents as described in the "circular flow of income." An important feature of the circular flow of income is that expenditure will correspond to income at the aggregate levels and, by implication, the value of economic output. Equation 12.1 summarizes this result:

$$\text{Expenditure} = \text{Income} = \text{Value of output} \qquad (12.1)$$

It was also noted in Chapter 3 that there are leakages from the circular flow in the form of savings by households, taxation by public authorities, and imports of goods and services. Each of these, other things being equal, will reduce the circular flow of income. Correspondingly, injections of income can increase the circular flow of income. These might comprise investment by firms or expenditures from public authorities and exports. If the injections and leakages of income balance, then the circular flow of income will be constant and will be in equilibrium.

The multiplier effect is linked to the injection of resources to the circular flow of income, and consequently the latter's expansion. Box 12.2 identifies the components of multiplier effects that describe this expansion. Because in theory, expenditures, incomes and the value of outputs must be equal, then these effects could in principle be calibrated in terms of either of them. Box 12.2 indicates that the multiplier is the scaling factor that links the value of the total economic activity generated by an investment to the value of the initial injection of resources. From a planning or evaluation point of view, once a multiplier is calculated or estimated, it can be used to scale-up the value of the initial proposed economic activity that will be generated from a subsequent investment to identify the overall new level of economic activity.

---

[10] As will become apparent discussed further below, the effects of the investment can either be understood through the demand side, i.e., the related expenditures involved, or the supply side, i.e., the incomes received.

BOX 12.2 COMPONENTS OF THE MULTIPLIER

Direct effect: the initial increase in expenditure or income connected with the injection of resources by the sports event. For example, the expenditure on building or spectators visiting facilities, or income received by facility owners or event organizers.

Indirect effect: the increase in expenditure or income generated as a subsequent result of the sports facility construction or hosting the event. For example, the expenditure on, or income received by, suppliers to and employees of a construction company or the company running the sports event.

Induced effect: the increase in expenditures on, or incomes received by, suppliers and employees of the organizations that supply those building the facilities or running a sports event. In principle the multiplier can be calibrated as:

Direct effect + Indirect effect + Induced effect

A final issue to note is that while Equation 12.1 calibrates economic value in terms of expenditures, incomes or the value of output, it is possible to identify the employment that might be generated by an investment. Recall from Chapter 1 and Chapter 11 that in economic terms output "Y" can be understood as deriving from a production function that depends on the inputs of land, "Ld," Labour, "L" and capital "K." This is represented in Equation 12.2:

$$Y = Y(Ld, L, K) \qquad (12.2)$$

Logically, the value of output will be equivalent to the value of the inputs. Consequently, if "p" is the price of output (for example a ticket price), "rt" is the rental value of land (for example price of land per acre), "w" is the wage rate (for example of athletes and employees of a stadium) and "r" is the cost of capital (for example, profit rate) then Equation 12.3 holds, in which the value of output is equivalent to the total costs of the factors of production:[11]

$$pY = rtLd + wL + rK \qquad (12.3)$$

This means that for any given moment, with prices known and land and capital fixed, then employment can be given as a proportion of the value of output as:

$$L = (pY - rtLd - rK)/w \qquad (12.4)$$

---

[11] Note here that profit is viewed in economic terms as a "cost." The profit rate is the cost of keeping the capital in the productive activity.

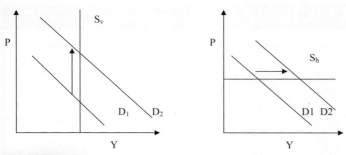

FIGURE 12.1 *The impact of injections on prices and resource employment.*

Calculations such as these are common in the literature and consultancy reports evaluating investment in sport, with L being forecast from the total value, pY, estimated to be generated by an investment and non-labour costs from current experience being extrapolated from current levels. There are problems with these calculations. On the one hand if technology changes as a result of the investment in K, then the form of the production function implied in Equation 12.2 will change, because of the changes to productivity. On the other hand, even with similar technology, greater employment of inputs will affect productivity as, for example, implied in the concept of diminishing marginal productivity. In both cases, therefore, in the long run as investments are undertaken, changing productivity will cause the prices of factors of production to change relatively in connection with the demands for them, and consequently alter the relative employment of the factors. Proportionate calculations of the likely employment of labour assume these complications away.[12]

The empirical calculation of the multiplier is discussed in more detail in Section 12.4. For now, attention focuses on the possibility of its existence. This is important because without the multiplier, a central argument for a public policy of investment in sports infrastructure is removed. Both the possibility and extent of multiplier effects are dependent on certain conditions existing in the structure of supply in the economy. To begin with, the basis for relying on multiplier effects to enhance regeneration and employment is connected to the possibility of subsequent increases in real economic activity, i.e., Y as defined above, following an injection of resources. In contrast, as discussed in Chapter 1, if all economic activity behaved according to the predictions of the model of perfect competition then the economy would always fully adjust to an equilibrium in which resources were fully employed and no increase in injections could produce a multiplier effect in the aggregate.

These alternatives are illustrated in Figure 12.1 in which two scenarios are presented. In both cases the vertical axis measures the price level in the economy and the horizontal axis the real value of output, Y. On the left hand side is an economy with fully employed resources, as indicated by a vertical

---

[12] The reader should note that this sort of argument resonates with the discussion of supply structures below and is central to differences in multiplier calculations according to input–output and computable general equilibrium models discussed later.

(aggregate) supply curve, S_v. If (aggregate) demand is increased, from D_1 to D_2, by an injection to the circular flow of income then prices have to rise, i.e., inflation occurs, and there is no increase in real economic output and no multiplier is possible.

In contrast, if there are unemployed resources in the economy, as indicated by a horizontal supply curve, then an injection to the circular flow of income can lead to an expansion of real economic activity, following the effects identified in Box 12.2, as prices do not have to rise to encourage the employment of the resources. This latter situation, however, reveals that markets must have failed to fully allocate resources in order for a multiplier to occur. In this respect, while externalities and multiplier effects are both indicative of spillovers from economic transactions due to market failures, the failures are of a different kind. The multiplier effect relies on an assumption about the failure of the market to allocate resources. In this respect the multiplier has its origins in the analysis of the sources and remedies of prolonged unemployment experienced in the Great Depression of the 1930s. The unemployment was characterized as structural, because the market system did not seem to have adjusted to re-employ the workers or other resources. It is this logic that is implied in arguments to regenerate an area. As traditional industries decline it is felt that the market, i.e., cheaper prices of land, and the possibility of employing workers more cheaply will not encourage new industries to invest in the area.[13] Consequently policy agencies should begin the process of reinvestment.

Reflection Question 12.3

What slope would the aggregate supply curve have to take for both prices and real resources to increase with an injection of demand?

Hint: Think of a position between the two extremes just discussed.

Of course, it is possible that both prices and the employment of real resources can increase following an injection to the circular flow of income, as implied above. This would require a supply curve that slopes upward from left to right. In such circumstances an injection of resources, i.e., demand,

---

[13] This can be viewed as a problematic claim. Whereas in the 1930s international trade collapsed, currently in a global economy many industries now make international investment decisions and typically manufacturing has been relocated to the newly-emerging markets in the Far East and Asia, to avail themselves of cheaper labour and also investment incentives. Consequently, the global market can be viewed as allocating resources but the process is slow and politically unpalatable.

must raise both prices and the level of real output. Clearly the steeper the curve the more that prices adjust relative to real resources and hence the lower the potential multiplier and *vice versa*.

The point that should be emphasized here is that the value of economic output, for example, as indicated in Equation 12.1, is the product of the price level and the level of real economic output as indicated in Equation 12.3. Any change in expenditure in the economy, i.e., an injection of income, can thus become manifest as a change in either prices or output (or both) because of differences in the supply conditions of an economy. The degree of price change that ensues from an injection of investment limits the potential size of multiplier effects.

The second supply-side issue to consider in reviewing the possibility and scale of multiplier effects is the spatial context within which investments take place. Implicit in the discussions above, and connected to the macroeconomic origins of multiplier analysis, is that an "aggregate" form of economy is considered. In this respect, the circular flow of income should be viewed as a conceptual device that refers to an economic system within certain boundaries. Historically, nations provided clear policy-related boundaries for this analysis. If a smaller region of the economy provides the focus for analysis, however, for example using sports investment to build a specific facility or to host an event to regenerate a specific urban area, then it is likely that any multiplier effects will depend on the spatial context of the venue or event. This implies that local spending is unlikely to contribute to economic impact, as it may simply be a diversion from other expenditure in the area. Likewise, an injection of investment in one area may "crowd out" expenditure in another area or increase the leakages from that area.

> Crowding out is a term used in economics, particularly macroeconomics, to indicate that if an economy is at full employment then public expenditure can only take place at the expense of private sector investment. These arguments have been used to counter the theoretical efficacy of public sector investment as a means of controlling the level of economic activity and also, empirically, for the growth in the proportion of public sector activity in the economy.

For example, if a new sports stadium helps to promote further investment into a region, elements of this may come from suppliers relocating their businesses. If the stadium helps to promote tourism, elements of this may include reduction in tourism and expenditure elsewhere.

The final supply-side issue concerns the timescale over which multiplier effects are likely to be experienced. Theoretically, the multiplier effect is calibrated by comparing two equilibrium positions: the level of real income before the investment; and that after it. The model of perfect competition, and indeed most economic theory, suggests that market prices will adjust rapidly to reallocate resources and consequently there can be no net increase in real economic activity. The question arises of what happens if this is not the case. It is conceivable that the supply side of the economy takes time to adjust to a demand side change following an injection of resources (and, of course, *vice versa*). A number of different scenarios now become possible.

One view might be that in Figure 12.1, the right-hand side diagram may represent the short-term, but the left-hand side diagram the long-term. The argument to support such a view is that an injection of investment or other expenditure initially appears to raise real output. However, this is because economic agents misconstrue the injection as leading to an increase in real income. In fact, the market system will generate full employment in the long-run and so only a nominal increase in income occurs. Consequently, as prices begin to rise, the economy is forced towards its long-term real output level, but higher prices will stabilize for the economy over time. This is connected with the adaptive expectations of economic agents. If economic agents have rational expectations this would imply a rapid change in prices consistent with perfect competition, such that the left hand-side of the diagram applies.

Another view is that the multiplier effects discussed in Box 12.1 implicitly presuppose that the level of supply capacity or potential is fixed. It is inherently a relatively short-run perspective. In other words, the multiplier works by the re-employment of previously unemployed resources. The analogy might be that a vacant stadium is once again used for activities following some refurbishment investment. Such an effect does not address any subsequent investment in the locality that may occur as a result of the initial injection of resources.[14] If investment decisions depend on increases in income (in the economic area) then the potential capacity to supply will also increase in that area. Investment depending on income can be represented as an accelerator model, a version of which was discussed in Appendix 3.2. The impact of this accelerator mechanism would be to reinforce the multiplier effect through an increase in the supply potential of the economy.

While the traditional multiplier–accelerator model relies on the idea that investment can also be induced from changes in income, suggesting a potentially greater long-run impact of the investment than just the multiplier, the more general point is that if investment raises productivity generally then there may be a shift in the supply curve to the right, even if the left-hand diagram of Figure 12.1 applies, as the capacity of the economy is enhanced. It seems unlikely, however, that such effects, relying on wholesale productivity

---

[14] As will be seen in the chapter below, this is not an issue typically addressed in the literature.

changes, could be triggered by sports investment directly in equipment and facilities and would need to rely on the productivity of employees being enhanced. Such claims are often made to support the public investment in science and technology.

Despite the detail of these different scenarios, a broad difference in perspective lies at the heart of the discussions. This concerns the ability of the market system to fully employ resources. If the market system can provide full employment, then there is no logical basis for arguing that sports investment can have wider economic benefits and it may have adverse redistribution effects. It follows that the case for sports investment having such spillover effects relies on the alternative position that markets cannot be presupposed to employ all economic resources fully.[15]

12.4 TYPES OF SPORTS EVENTS AND IMPACTS

12.4.1 Duration and scale of impacts

The above discussion has focused primarily on the rationale for public sector investment in sports events and infrastructure. In this section a clearer distinction is made between the duration and scale of impacts in different sports contexts, as well as noting important differences in the type of impact that can be monitored or assessed.

Table 12.3 includes the investment alternatives presented in Table 12.2 and, notwithstanding their likely interaction, identifies the primary externality and spillover effects that it can be argued are associated with each option in columns 3 and 4, respectively. Column 5 reports typically measured outcomes of the options, which are referred to later in the chapter. It can be seen from these columns that the infrastructural investments indicated in the last three rows appear to be theoretically equivalent, as was implied in the opening paragraphs of this chapter. However, there are two senses in which these alternatives can differ. First, in the final row it is indicated that existing infrastructure could be used to support economic events. In this respect subsidy of their use or the use of funds to attract the events, would constitute the investment.

Secondly, and of more importance, in column 2 it is noted that in addition to the initial investment subsequent economic stimuli can be identified from visiting spectators and regeneration activity. Different investment options will

---

[15] This concern over the efficacy of prices to allocate resources can be hinted at in noting that in the multiplier–accelerator model investment depended (primarily at least) on past income and not the rate of interest (or profit) as the cost of capital. In Chapter 3, it was argued that investment market needed to be linked to the price of investment funds, to govern economic behaviour consistently with the model of competition and fully employed resources.

TABLE 12.3 Summary of impacts of investment

Investment	Economic investment	Externalities	Multiplier/accelerator	Typically measured outcomes
Facilitating international sporting success	Support national teams in competitions	1. Increased consumer confidence 2. Increased productivity		1. Rise in consumer confidence surveys, increase in consumption 2. Rise in productivity indices 3. 1 & 2 Rise in share prices
Facilitating professional sports teams	Build new/refurbish stadium 1. Visiting spectators 2. Regeneration		Multiplier effect 1. Subsequent multiplier effect 2. Subsequent multiplier/ accelerator effect	Rise in employment, income or expenditure
Hosting national teams	Build new/refurbish a national stadium 1. Visiting spectators 2. Regeneration		Multiplier effect 1. Subsequent multiplier effect 2. Subsequent multiplier/ accelerator effect	Rise in employment, income or expenditure
Hosting local, national and international events	Build new/refurbish stadia and arenas, etc. 1. Visiting spectators 2. Regeneration Hosting events 3. Visiting spectators 4. Regeneration		Multiplier effect 1. Subsequent multiplier effect 2. Subsequent multiplier/ accelerator effect 3. Subsequent multiplier effect 4. Subsequent multiplier/ accelerator effect	Rise in employment, income or expenditure

have different temporal and scales of effect.[16] This raises a very important issue, as indicated by Preuss (2004) in a review of the impact of the Olympic Games, that notwithstanding the discussions of the supply-side of the economy discussed in the previous section:

> "... the effect of non-recurring expenditure weakens in the course of time and vanishes completely. This means that the increase declines with every new period and, in the long run, the falling demand leads back to the equilibrium income that existed before the Games..." (Preuss, 2004 p. 41)

This quotation reveals that to support the initial multiplier effects, i.e., on levels of economic activity, a continuous injection of resources is required. If these cease then the economy will shrink back to its previous level. In contrast, if the structure of supply changes, for example accelerator effects promote new investment and this becomes self-sustaining and supports new levels of activity, then when the injection of resources ceases the economy will shrink back to a higher equilibrium level of income.

It follows that a professional sports team is the case most likely to bring sustained additional expenditures than otherwise might have been the case (by either expanding the capacity of a stadium or providing attendance expenditures that were not previously available because the sport was not previously provided for). This is because the facility will be scheduled for regular use according to league and various other competitions. This will be more frequent than the provision of infrastructure to host the sports contests of national teams, and much more so than the investment in infrastructure to host an event like the Olympic Games or a world cup.

This may help to explain why in the former case, national stadia are often used by other sports and for events other than sports. It may also help to explain why the legacies of the Olympic Games are now viewed with such importance as an argument to justify public investment in the Games. Conversely, it may help to explain why in Germany the 2006 World Cup was primarily hosted at existing facilities, as has been the case with the rugby union World Cups. Although gains may be more temporary, they are likely to be larger. In the latter case, the world cup is seen as an opportunity for the IRB to raise most of its revenue for investing into the development of the sport (http://www.rugbyheaven.com.au/news/news/irb-retains-world-cup-format/

---

[16] The emphasis here is placed on spectators and regeneration as broad categories. In reality a whole host of additional activity might be stimulated. For example, as discussed in Chapter 10, broadcast income might be attracted. This, together with the facility, might bring with it additional sponsorship. Merchandising opportunities might also change as better facilities are built. These details are suppressed in the interests of conceptual clarity. Preuss (2004) gives a highly detailed account of the sources of impact from the Olympic Games.

accessed 15/1/08). Without such gains, as Szymanski (2002) argues, public expenditure on sports events could be thought of as a consumption rather than investment decision.

In addition to the potential fragility of longer-term sustainability of economic activity generated by sports investment, it has been argued that the scale of economic activity associated with various sports events is likely to vary significantly. One-off major sports events such as the Olympic Games and world cups are likely to have the greatest single value, followed by regular large-scale sports tournaments such as Wimbledon, the Six Nations competition in rugby and the Open in golf. Lower level tournaments and regular annual sports leagues are likely to generate the least value per event. In general, it is argued that the higher the level and the longer the duration of the event, the larger the economic value that will be connected with the sports contest (Gratton and Taylor, 2000; Gratton et al., 2000, 2005). This suggests that there may be a trade-off between the durability and the scale of activity supported by investment in sports.

12.4.2 Theorizing economic activity as an impact

Up until now, the specific nature of the impact of sports investment has been left broadly defined to refer to the impact on the level of real economic activity, i.e., real expenditure, income or output following an injection to the relevant circular flow of income. It is important to recognize, however, that there is a distinction between three main concepts that can be used to evaluate alternative scenarios of economic activity generated by investment. These are:

1. Economic significance;
2. Economic impact;
3. Economic welfare.

Economic significance is the broadest measure of economic activity and simply corresponds to the total values of all transaction involved. In contrast, "economic impact" has become identified specifically with identifying the net benefits to the economy as a whole as a result of the investment (Crompton, 2006). Finally, as discussed in Chapter 1, economic welfare is maximized where economic efficiency is maximized. As discussed in Chapter 1, in theory, perfect competition is consistent with maximum economic efficiency because market transactions will reflect the full economic costs and benefits of resources and, as such, guarantee productive and allocative efficiency. There are two implications of considering the welfare effects of sports investment in analysis. The first is that even if the main impact of the investment is to redistribute resources criteria can be employed to assess this redistribution in welfare terms, as discussed in Chapter 5, in which those who gain from a redistribution can compensate those who lose. The second is that a focus on economic welfare suggests that both the costs and benefits of alternatives should be taken into account in evaluating the investment, unlike an economic impact analysis. Cost benefit analysis (CBA) is viewed as appropriate in this case, a point made strongly by Kesenne (2005).

12.4.3 The practical measurement of economic activity as an impact

If one accepts the above arguments that changes in economic welfare following an investment are the most theoretically relevant indicator of economic impacts, then this raises the question of how might this take place. As far as both appraisal and evaluation are concerned, a focus on economic welfare suggests that the true opportunity costs and benefits of investments should be accounted for. There are a number of dimensions to this task.

12.4.3.1 Adjusting prices

The first is to ensure that prices are not distorted by taxation or subsidies, as these reflect policy interventions rather than the benefits and costs of the investment. Consequently, taxes should be added back to prices and subsidies removed. Prices should also be discounted at the appropriate discount rate and inflation taken into account.

12.4.3.2 Multiplier effects

Multiplier effects should be accounted for to ensure that genuine net benefits are identified. It follows that this must also apply to an economic impact analysis. Potential increases in economic activity that would have taken place without the investment should also be discounted from the analysis.[17]

There are a number of specific methods for calculating multipliers, but they essentially either focus on the demand side, i.e., expenditure, or supply-side structure of the economy (Hudson, 2001; Blake, 2005).[18]

---

[17] This is known as a "deadweight" effect. In the review of the evidence discussed later, the trend rate of output, employment or income can be viewed as an indicator of this. Also, the problems in the use of multiplier analysis in the past can be linked to including the deadweight value as an impact from the investment or failing to allow for crowding out, etc.

[18] These are the methods that tend to be employed in large-scale appraisals. In smaller-scale projects methods that evaluate the multiplier by investigating the supply chain of an organization or project exist. A good example is the LM3 model proposed by the New Economic Foundation in conjunction with the Countryside Commission in the UK (Sacks, 2002).

1. Export injection multipliers;
2. Input–output models;
3. Computable general equilibrium models.

Export injection multipliers draw on the Keynesian analysis of the expenditure multiplier discussed in Chapter 1 and presented in Appendix 1.2, to demonstrate that an initial injection of expenditure from outside the economic system – which constitutes visiting fans in the sporting context, hence the reference to exports – is magnified through interlinked spending in the (local) economy. Equation 12.5 presents the basic multiplier presented in Appendix 1.2, and Equation 12.6 presents the more developed "export" version, where the impact of imports and taxes reduces the value of the multiplier. The additional terms reduce the value of the multiplier because of leakages. The term $(1 - i)$ indicates the proportion of initial export-generated expenditure that remains an export. Multiplying by this term deflates the mpc to account for imports. The term $(1 - t)$ indicates the proportion of initial export generated expenditure that is not taxed.

$$\text{Multiplier} = \frac{1}{1 - b} = 3 \qquad (12.5)$$

$$\text{Export multiplier} = \frac{1}{1 - b(1 - i)(1 - t)} = 1.25 \qquad (12.6)$$

where:

b is the marginal propensity to consume (mpc) (<1), e.g., 0.667
i is the marginal propensity to import (<1), e.g., 0.5
t is the marginal tax rate (<1), e.g., 0.4

The input–output (IO) approach to multipliers is based on deriving the inter-sectoral, i.e., supply-side, transactions in a defined economic region. Based on an understanding of how various economic sectors trade with one another, a change in economic activity in one sector can be examined for its impact in another sector, and consequently multiplier effects established. There are a number of assumptions of IO analysis which can be summarized as in Dwyer et al. (2006):

1. There are no resource constraints;
2. The production function implies constant proportions between inputs and outputs;
3. Price effects are neutral;
4. Government budgets are neutral;
5. Components of demand (including government budgets) are exogenous (not given by the model).

These assumptions suggest that the supply-side of the economy is as given on the right-hand side of Figure 12.1, and that if there is an expansion of output in a given sector or industry, the derived demand for inputs for other industries or sectors and the employment of labour will increase in proportion, and prices will not rise to reduce the value of real output overall. The last assumption suggests that the impact of any expansion on government finances is ignored. How are the multiplier effects calculated? The basis of the approach is to present a set of input–output coefficients in a matrix "A" that summarize the trading flows of the economy for a unit of output.

A matrix is a table of elements or quantities. They can be added, subtracted, multiplied or, by multiplying by an "inverse" matrix, equivalent to divided. They are particularly useful for summarizing a set of linear equations. A vector is a matrix in which either the number of columns or rows are restricted to one. Likewise, it is equivalent to a linear subcomponent of a matrix.

It is then possible to show that:

$$X = [I - A]^{-1}D \tag{12.7}$$

X is a vector of the outputs of the industries, and D is the demand for the outputs. I is an identity matrix, in which each value on the (principal) diagonal running from top left to bottom right is 1 and all other values are 0. This matrix corresponds to the value of 1 in (scalar) arithmetic. The matrix I − A is calculated by subtracting the corresponding elements of the identity and input–output coefficient matrices. The superscript −1 indicates that the inverse of the resultant matrix is multiplied by D. Multiplying by the inverse of a matrix is used in mathematical operations to correspond to dividing in normal arithmetic. $[I - A]^{-1}$ is known as the Leontieff inverse matrix, after the originator of the analysis. It is this matrix which provides the multiplier effects. Consequently, Equation 12.7 indicates that for any change in consumption demands, D, the effect on industry output, X, is a multiple of D determined by $[I - A]^{-1}$ whose parameters are the input–output coefficients, A, that describe the structure of inter-industry trading (remember that I only contains 1s or 0s).

The assumptions of the IO approach have been challenged and, as a consequence, it is increasingly argued that computable general equilibrium (CGE) analysis is a more appropriate method for deriving economic impacts (Dwyer et al., 2006; Blake, 2005). In contrast to IO analysis, CGE:

1. Constrains the availability of labour and capital so that wages and prices can change only or as well as, output changes, following an injection to the economy;

2. Accounts for the feedback on the demand for labour, and capital and corresponding consumption of the changes in wages and prices;
3. Components of (real) final demand are endogenous as prices vary;
4. Changes in economic activity affect government expenditures and tax receipts.

The implication of these assumptions is to recognize that while input–output models can measure all of the positive impacts of an event, they are incapable of modelling most of the negative impacts, so they consistently overestimate the impact of events (Blake, 2005, p. 12). The possibility of price changes crowding out the effect of injections is taken into account in CGE, suggesting that the supply-side might be more akin to the left-hand side diagram in Figure 12.1, or at least the supply curve has a positive slope.

12.4.3.3 Non-market valued effects

A concern with economic welfare, in assessing the impact of sports investment, implies that attempts should also be made to estimate the externality effects of sports investment, i.e., to account for the wider social and environmental costs and benefits for which there is no market price. Conceptually speaking, this recognizes that the total economic value of a sports investment has more than one dimension. Gouguet (2002) and Barget and Gouguet (2007) argue that, drawing on the field of environmental economics, two broad domains of value can be identified with the investment, as illustrated in Figure 12.2. Total economic value breaks down into two main categories, use and non-use values. Non-use values are connected with the valuation

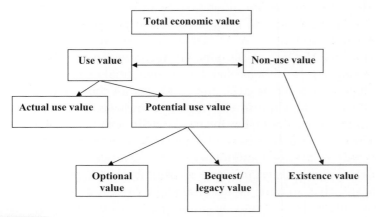

FIGURE 12.2   *The components of total economic value.*

placed by individuals, for example, on the existence of the investment. This might be because they identify with the investment, for example the sports franchise, facility or team, or because they feel that it is beneficial to them and the community even although they do not intend to make use of the investment. In contrast, use value is connected with the actual use or intended use of the investment. Actual use value would comprise, for example, the entrance or ticket price paid, but would also include any additional value or consumer surplus. As discussed in Chapter 1, this is the amount greater than the ticket price that a consumer would be prepared to pay. Potential use value, on the other hand, is the valuation placed on the intended future use of the investment. In the specific language of the Olympic Games, it is also possible that legacy values exist which correspond to the potential future values that would be generated from the investment for future generations. Of course, this also applies to any investment and in environmental economics is often termed bequest value.

A number of different methods exist to attempt to measure these elements of value and they were typically developed to value natural resources. The approaches broadly break down into two types. Revealed preferences, which makes use of the values of economic variables in related markets to identify use values, and stated preferences. Travel costs are an example of revealed preferences discussed in Chapter 10. Stated preferences require survey work to elicit the values attached to an economic activity or resource. For example, contingent valuation techniques capture statements of the highest "willingness to pay" to access an economic resource or lowest "willingness to accept" compensation for losing access to it (Downward, 2004; Tidsell, 2006).

A final point to note is that explicit concern for equity can be built into the analysis by allowing for differences in income distribution. For example, the marginal utility of consumption can be estimated for particular income bands and then some average level of income. Identifying the proportion that the former comprises of the latter provides a weight. With lower income levels it is expected that the marginal utility of consumption will be higher than the average, and *vice versa* for those with higher-than-average income. This means that for those on lower income, weights will be >1 and for those on higher income, weights will be <1. These weights could then be used to adjust estimated utilities so that lower-income utilities will be increased and higher-income utilities decreased. Naturally, when aggregating utilities to assess a redistribution of resources in policy, this means that welfare is reallocated in favour of those with lower incomes. Appendix 12.3 provides an example of how one might calculate such weights.

12.4.3.4 Increased productivity and consumer confidence

The above discussion has focused directly on the measurement of economic welfare, impact or significance as a result of (potential) changes in real economic resources. However, it was also noted earlier that international sporting success can yield changes in consumer confidence and productivity through its impact on feel-good factors, coupled with the expectation of a positive economic impact. The measurement of productivity and consumer confidence as outcomes of such impacts could be undertaken directly by examining data on each of these items, however, most of the literature focuses on the impact of sporting success, or its likelihood, and subsequent economic benefits on share price returns, because it is argued that the stock market will capture all available information that affects the profitability of companies. This might be as a result of enhanced consumer confidence or increased productivity. The typical approach used to examine the effects of sporting success or the announcement of the hosting of a major sporting event on stock price returns is an event study.[19] This approach uses a regression equation to examine the pattern of share prices and then makes use of a dummy variable to indicate a period of time over which, say, an international success occurs or the announcement of the decision to host an event takes place compared to before the success or announcement.

12.4.3.5 Other impacts

To close this section it is worth noting that research from an economic perspective into the other external benefits or costs, i.e., legacies, of sporting investment or hosting sports events, is relatively undeveloped. This might include examining the impacts on community cohesion, community image and sports development, including enhanced participation which, as noted earlier, is considered to be a symbiotic goal for sports policy in the UK. Indeed, as Crompton (2004) argues, an alternative rationale for assessing the impact of sports events than purely focusing on the impact on real economic output and employment is possible. This lies in focusing on the intangible benefit of "psychic" income. Primary research could also investigate the effects of sports investment on community and sporting behaviour.

---

[19] This terminology does **not** derive from the analysis of sports events but rather the event of changes in the regulations of market trading. The event study approach, as indicated below, has become common in the economic analysis of the impacts of sports events more generally than stock prices.

12.5 EMPIRICAL EVIDENCE

The empirical evidence on the impact of investment in sports infrastructure and events is the basis of much debate and, indeed, is clouded by some controversy. Despite the undoubted complexity of trying to tease out the complex effects of large-scale investment activity, the point is made by Crompton (2006) that while:

"There is a sound conceptual rationale for economic impact studies, and they have a legitimate political role in informing both elected officials and tax payers of the economic contributions . . . to community residents' prosperity . . . this legitimacy is predicated on the studies being undertaken with integrity. Because the motivation under-girding them usually is to prove the legitimacy of the sponsor's economic case, the temptation to engage in mischievous practices is substantial. In some cases the practices are the result of ignorance and are inadvertent, but too often they are deliberate and enacted with intent to mislead and distort."
(Crompton, 2006 p. 67)

This suggests that the evidence is also, at times, deliberately misleading. The earlier discussion of adverse incentives from contests suggests a rationale for this behaviour. There is a distinction in the literature, therefore, between the *ex ante* research that tends to derive from proponents of investment in sports infrastructure and events, which Crompton suggests at times is misleading, and *ex post* research which tends to come from independent academic sources (Coates and Humphreys, 2002; Downward, 2003; Kasimati, 2003).[20]

12.5.1 *Ex ante* evidence

The claim that the *ex ante* evidence is often deliberately misleading is a strong one, but Crompton presents evidence from US professional team sports. For example, in consideration of the use of public funds to invest in a new stadium for the Dallas Cowboys NFL team in Arlington Texas, four economic impact studies were produced each with widely varying results. Three were supportive of the investment, citing estimated impacts of between $51 million and $416 million in various cities and counties, whereas one study opposing the investment estimated a loss of $325.3 million.

---

[20] The point here is not that academics may not have been part of the *ex ante* research projects, which are typically funded by governments or organizers and carried out by state agencies of private consultancy firms or consortia, but that there is an implicit advocacy position as opposed to a more objective assessment of the impacts of the investment.

Variation in results seems endemic to the literature concerned with either forecasting or evaluating the hosting of major events worldwide.[21] Table 12.4 presents some studies. Comparison of the value of the impacts is problematic not only because of some currency differences, but because the year associated with the prices in which the overall impacts were measured varies. However, it is clear that there is considerable variance in the results, even for the same event and method of assessing impact.

12.5.2 Explaining the variance

The source of variance in economic impact studies could be due to technical difficulties. However, it has also been systematically researched. Crompton (1995) has argued that 11 potential flaws can be identified with economic impact studies, and which are potentially exploited by advocates of investment in sports facilities and events. These are reported in Table 12.5. Elements of these flaws apply to some of the studies of major events, such as focusing on gross impacts, not being clear about the type of employment generated and not always accounting for the costs in calculating net benefits (if not using a full cost-benefit analysis because economic impact is identified as a policy target). Significantly, from an economic perspective, perhaps of most importance is flaw number 10. No study attempts to evaluate what investment in an alternative facility or scheme would provide, although some include sensitivity analyses of their forecasts, such as Blake (2005) and the New South Wales (Australia) Treasury (1997).

In an interesting piece of work, Hudson (2001) conducted a meta-analysis of 19 economic impact studies connected with Major League Baseball, the National Football League or the National Hockey League between 1989 and 1997 to try to identify which factors accounted for most of the variation of economic impact valuations. The value of the economic impact was treated as the dependent variable and a range of independent variables were used to identify their contribution to the value estimate. These included the type of sport, the location of the franchise, the age of the stadium and the assumptions made about the location and nature of expenditures generated by the franchise investment. The results indicated the lack of statistical significance of a

---

[21] In addition to these studies that identify impacts in terms of the levels of employment and income generated by events, others, such as Bohlmann and van Heerden (2008), identify the percentage change in such variables. Using a computable general equilibrium model, they identify that the 2010 world cup in South Africa is likely to change GDP by 0.08–0.69% and employment by 0.72–(−)0.35%. The range of forecasts is based on low tax and high tax scenarios, respectively, as a result of the event.

TABLE 12.4 The economic impact of major events

Author	Event	Method	US $ billion (unless indicated. Date of prices if available)	Jobs	Impact period
Economic Research Associates (1984)	Los Angeles Olympics, 1984	Input output	2.3 (1984)	73 375	Not given
Kim et al. (1989)	Seoul Olympics 1988	Not given	1.6	336 000	Not given
Brunet (1995)	Barcelona Olympics 1992	Not given	30	296 640	Not given
KPMG (1993)	Sydney Olympics 2000	Input output	5.1 (1992)	156 198	Not given
Humphreys and Plummer (1995)	Atlanta Olympics 1996	Input output	5.1 (1994)	77 026	Not given
NSW Treasury (1997)	Sydney Olympics 2000	Computable general equilibrium	4.5 (1996)	98 700	1995–2006
Andersen (1999)	Sydney Olympics 2000	Input output	4.5 (1996)	63 000–90 000	Not given
Papanikos (1999)	Athens Olympics 2000	Macroeconomic expenditure	15.9 (1999)	445 000	2000–2010
Balfousia-Savva et al. (2001)	Athens Olympics 2000	Macroeconomic expenditure	10.2 (2000)	300 400	2000–2010
Cambridge Policy Consultants (2002)	Manchester Commonwealth Games 2002	Cost benefit analysis	Not given	6300	to 2007
Madden (2002)	Sydney Olympics 2000	Computable general equilibrium	(AUS)$6.5 (1996)	Not given	1995–2005
Yu (2004)	Asian Games 2002	Not given	(HK)$72.8	310 000	Not given
Blake (2005), Price Waterhouse Coopers (2005), EEDA (2006)	London Olympics 2012	Computable general equilibrium	(£)1.94bn (2005)	8164	2005–2016
Brunet (2005)	Barcelona Olympics 1992	Not given	Not given	20 000	1986–2004
Insight Economics (2006)	Melbourne Commonwealth Games 2006	Computable general equilibrium	(AUS)$1.6 (2002)	13 600	2002–2022
Maening and Du Plessis (2007)	World Cup Germany 2006	Cost benefit analysis	$0.997	Not given	Not given
Maening (2007)	World Cup Germany 2006	Not given	Not given	25 000–50 000	Not given
Grant Thornton (2003)	World Cup South Africa 2010	Cost benefit analysis	(R)21	150 000	Not given

TABLE 12.5 Flaws with economic impact studies

Flaw	Implication
1. Using sales instead of income multipliers	1. This models gross business turnover and not the income created in the locality which may be of more use to local planning and forecasts of government tax revenue
2. Misrepresentation of multipliers	2. Employment multipliers not allowing for changes in working hours, growth in casual part-time work only
3. Incremental multipliers used instead of proportional multipliers	3. The denominator used is direct income rather than visitor expenditure. This inflates the multiplier, as the latter is clearly larger
4. Failure to define the region of impact	4. Can overstate the impact in a region, part of a city, etc.
5. Inclusion of local spectators	5. Overstates expenditure
6. Failure to exclude casual spectators	6. Overstates expenditure
7. Fudging multipliers	7. Borrowing a multiplier, say, from an official regional source is misleading. National multipliers will be > state multipliers which will be > city multipliers because of leakages
8. Claiming total instead of marginal benefits	8. The return on the potentially incremental contribution of public funds should be considered otherwise benefits are overstated.
9. Confusing turnover with the multiplier	9. Aggregating spends incorrectly by double counting sales, etc., overstates the benefits as opposed to "value-added"
10. Omit opportunity costs	10. Would a shopping centre not attract more visitors and expenditure?
11. Measure only benefits	11. Omits costs of congestion, etc.

variable measuring the assumed multiplier, and that including local spending in the studies boosts the forecast economic impact by \$38 million, while not identifying that the sport was the sole reason for visiting spectators coming to the area, i.e., attributing visitors to the area as deriving from the attraction of the franchise investment *per se*) can boost the impact by \$41 million. This suggests that, independently of the multiplier calculations, it is important to get the direct impact of additional spending right in any study, as this can seriously over-inflate the value of the impact. More recently, Crompton (2006) has reaffirmed that including local residents in economic impact evaluations is the "most frequent mischievous procedure" (p. 70).

This is not to say that including local residents in the analysis is always wrong. If a major event keeps a resident at home, rather than going on a trip that would normally have taken place, for example, to go on holiday, then clearly this is additional expenditure that otherwise would not have taken place. It follows that any visitors that are deterred from the area as a result of the event should also be accounted for, as a reduction in direct impact. Likewise, it may be the case that if the event or infrastructure was part of the reason for attracting visitors to an area then logically a proportion of this visit can be considered attributable to the investment. Preuss (2004) provides a detailed discussion of these issues.[22]

Overall, however, this discussion suggests that the evidence being provided to justify public investment in sports infrastructure and events is unreliable in the specific sense in which research is classified, as different researchers, methods and contexts seem able to produce different results for the same or similar events. It would seem reasonable to account for this in policy related advice.[23]

In research, reliability is broadly concerned with the consistency of results deriving from various measurements or data collection tools. This contrasts with validity in which a measurement or measurement tool actually measures what it is intended to measure.

12.5.3 *Ex post* evidence

Standing in contrast is a body of research that evaluates the impact of investment in sports infrastructure and events *ex post*. Here, much more consistent and reliable results appear to be derived. The approach adopted in the analysis is also not based on any multiplier analysis or structural economic modelling, as implied in IO and CGE, but is based on the event study regression approach noted above. Here, measures of income and employment in a local economy across cities and/or time are regressed on variables measuring changes in the sports environment, such as the construction of new facilities or the relocation of franchises, to see if the latter affect the former. In one of the studies the authors conclude that:

---

[22] Primary research in which a set of attractor variables to an area could be used to weight the significance of the facility or event relative to others could be used to disaggregate a unit of expenditure in much the same way that marketers might attribute value to components of a product or service.

[23] It should be noted that UK Sport's advice on assessing the impact of sports events recognizes that there are problems with using multiplier analysis and consequently focuses on evaluating the direct impacts. However, this is not explicitly linked to the potential problems of multiplier analysis, but more that multipliers will be location-specific and consequently, not identify equivalent comparison across events (see UK Sport, undated).

"... Far from being engines of growth, these results indicate that at best SMSAs
    get nothing from their sports fanchises; at worst they pay dearly for
    professional athletic franchises." (Coates and Humphreys, 1999 pp. 362–363)

These are a gloomy set of results for proponents of sports-led economic
development, because Table 12.6 reveals that they are common. The first
column reports the authors of the work, and the second column the subject
of the analysis. The next column describes the model and estimator used and
the final column reports the conclusions.

The literature suggests that, at best, hosting unique events or hosting post-
season events adds nothing statistically to employment or the value of the
economy, and at worst can cost the locality.[24] What is interesting about this
research is the greater reliability, i.e., consistency of finding, that is lacking in
the *ex ante* literature. This naturally begs the question why this occurs.

A clear inference in the *ex post* research, as indicated by Crompton, is that
there is an incentive for policy makers to overstate the benefits from hosting
major events or investing in sports infrastructure. A number of economic
factors might promote this state of affairs. An obvious answer is corruption
or deliberate misleading behaviour connected with incentives to win bids in
the light of weak monitoring, as suggested by contest theory. Other answers
can be offered. Fort (1997) provides a discussion of public choice theory applied
to US sports and argues that in "direct democratic" systems of voting such as
referenda, organized lobby groups with economic interests can dominate by
trading votes to achieve a result of mutual interest. A number of specific
economic conditions could explain what make this political outcome possible.
To begin with, public investment in sports events infrastructure might be an
example of adverse selection, as discussed in Chapter 1, in which more risky
economic investment options are presented to the public than otherwise
would have been the case, because of the inability to effectively scrutinize
the options through a political process. Consequently, there is a government
failure in efficiency terms that is masked by political rhetoric. As discussed in
Chapter 5, the lack of frequency of the transactions of public investment in
sports franchises or major investments may add to the information costs of
transactions, i.e., the ability to exercise effective monitoring by the public.
This would stand in contrast to' the relative efficiency of the stock market.

---

[24] The ethos of this is captured in the following passage which is a book review by Tollison
(2001, p. 207), "... the discussion of so-called multipliers in this book is illuminating.
Somehow, local spending on sports creates extra local income. I thought Keynes was dead, but I
guess he lives on in these 'local effects' calculations of economists who study tourism and the
like. But, surely, the subsidization of sports is a poor example. At best these transfers from
taxpayers to teams are zero-sum transfers. At worst, they are negative-sum transfers..."

TABLE 12.6 Econometric evidence on economic impacts

Author	Context	Model, method and estimator	Results
Matheson and Baade (2008)	Baseball world series	**Period** 1972–2000 25 metropolitan areas hosting the play offs **OLS regression Dependent variable:** ■ change in real income **Independent variables** ■ lagged change in real income ■ time trend ■ taxes as a percentage of all cities (73) ■ nominal wages as a percentage of all cities (73) ■ oil price booms and related city specific impacts (e.g. Hurricane Andrew) ■ for 25 cities, compared model estimates with actual income growth to assess impact of play-offs	"Our detailed regression analysis reveals that over the period 1997–2000 cities appearing in the major league baseball post-season had higher than expected income growth by 0.003%. This figure is not statistically significantly different than zero, although a best guess of the economic contribution of a single post-season game is $6.8million, or at most $75 million, roughly half that of the typical *ex ante* projection" (p. 333)

Baade and Matheson (2004)	1994 World Cup	**Period** 1970–2000 13 of 73 largest US cities **OLS regression Dependent variable:** ■ percentage change in real income **Independent variables** ■ lagged percentage change in real income ■ time trend ■ taxes as a percentage of all cities (73) ■ nominal wages as a percentage of all cities (73) ■ oil price booms and busts ■ for 13 cities compared model estimates with actual income growth to assess impact of world cup	" . . . an overall negative impact on the average host city and the US economy overall" (p. 351)
Coates and Humphreys (2002)	Post-season play (e.g., World series, Superbowl, play-offs)	**Period** 1969–1998 Cities with professional sports teams **Fixed effects estimator (panel estimator)** **Dependent variable:** ■ real per capita income **Independent variables** ■ economic/demographic factors ■ sport environment ■ appearance in post-season play	"The mean overall impact of the vector of sports variables . . . is negative . . . the parameters on the post-season appearance variables are not statistically significant from zero" (p. 296)

TABLE 12.6 *(Continued)*

Author	Context	Model, method and estimator	Results
Baade and Matheson (2002)	1984 Los Angeles and 1996 Atlanta Olympic Games	**Period 1969–1997** 57 cities among largest 50 metropolitan areas hosting the play-offs **Pooled regression** **Dependent variable:** ■ percentage change in employment in an area **Independent variables** ■ population (log value) ■ real per capita personal income ■ nominal wages as a percentage of all cities (57) ■ taxes as a percentage of all cities (57) ■ oil boom and bust ■ regional location ■ metropolitan statistical area ■ Olympic host	"The estimated coefficients for the summer Olympic Games variable did not emerge as statistically significant in either Los Angeles or Atlanta" (p. 139)

| Lertwachara and Cochrane (2007) | Expansions, relocations of MLB, NBA, NFL and NHL | **Period** 1969–2000

33 franchises
Pooled regression (2 steps)
Estimate residual, unexpected per capita income and its growthregress residual on number of franchises
Dependent variable:
■ level and growth of MSA per capita income
■ unexpected values of i
Independent variables
■ US GDP
■ number of franchises | "… we find that a professional sport team does not have a positive economic impact on the local community … estimated local income in the presence of a professional sports franchise is lower than what would be estimated in the absence of a professional sports franchise." (p. 253) |

Further, as discussed in Chapters 7 and 9, sports leagues can be understood as cartels that can exercise monopoly power. Siegfried and Zimbalist (2000) argue that in the US the monopoly power of leagues is such that they permit enough franchises to make the entry of new leagues uneconomic and yet, at the same time, leave enough outside options to give teams the option to relocate. A similar argument could be made with respect to event organizers. Because the IOC and FIFA are the only bodies that can award the Olympic Games and the soccer World Cup, a state of affairs ascribed to other events and organizers as well, it is clear that monopoly status is present. Indeed, because mega events are completely unique, Leeds and von Almen (2002) have described the IOC as the "ultimate franchise monopolist." Under such circumstances, it can be argued that bidding cities face an all-or-nothing demand curve in which over-bidding, or the "winners curse," can occur.

> The winners curse can arise in auctions in which competitive bids are made to buy an item. Logically, the market price of an item must be the average revenue that is received by a supplier. In an auction this must be equal to the average value of bids. However, the winning bid must, logically, be greater than the average bid, which suggests that it overvalues the item.

Figure 12.3 illustrates the proposition. This reproduces the basic monopoly diagram introduced in Chapter 1 as Figure 1.3. In contrast to just a profit-maximizing monopolist, the all-or-nothing monopolist can fix the scale of output and extract additional expenditure beyond the market demand level. Clearly this can relate to public subsidy beyond what the paying public will contribute towards going to a major event.

Beside the potential political motives for overstating the impacts of sports investment and the potentially dubious assumptions that are made in the analyses, the reasons why little impact appears to be identified in the *ex post* studies requires some further deliberation. One argument might be that the *ex ante* research is invalid, as well as unreliable. In this regard, it might be argued that it is just not possible to capture the complex interactions that underpin possible crowding out. However, in this respect the validity, if not the reliability, of the *ex post* research can also be challenged. Baade and Matheson (2004) argue that in their analysis:

"... the standard error of the estimate for the typical city is above 1% meaning that one would expect the models to predict actual economic growth for the cities ... within 1% point about

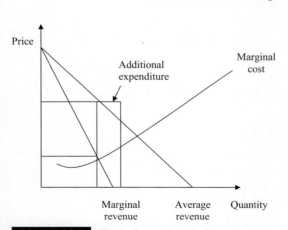

FIGURE 12.3   The "all-or-nothing" demand curve.

two-thirds of the time. For the cities in question, a 1% error translates into a $300 million difference for the smallest cities ... and over a $2 billion difference for the largest metropolitan areas ... While it is unlikely that the models for any individual city will capture the effects of even a large event, one would expect that across a large number of cities, any event that produces a large impact would emerge, on average as statistically significant." (Baade and Matheson, 2004 p. 350)

It is not entirely clear that this conclusion follows. Table 12.5 reports impacts that can lie within these statistical bounds and, as discussed earlier, it might be expected with sports franchises as opposed to major events that the impacts will be smaller. It follows that there is some doubt as to the validity of this line of research. The approach may just not produce sensitive enough measurements to be definitive. There could also be an issue of causality associated with the negative findings, that cities with lower incomes require investment in sports. Causality is not particularly investigated in the analyses. This is not to suggest that there may not be good reasons for accepting the results. Baade and Matheson (2002) note that structurally, an event like the Olympic Games imports "alien investment" to an industrial location, and probably lacks the linkages that effective clusters of industry have in promoting economic growth, as it requires entirely different physical and human capital. This is of course precisely the reason why legacies are sought. Further, in the case of US sports, franchise infrastructure has been described as resembling "walled cities" by Seigfried and Zimbalist (2000). This is because the possibilities of spillover effects for expenditure are essentially minimized by tie-in clauses to suppliers of refreshment and hospitality, etc. The effects are compounded if professional athletes do not live locally and they simply do not attract new visitors to the area which, given the geographic dimensions of the US, seems plausible. In this case spending is merely substituted from one leisure activity to another. This could account for the reduction in income in an area if the other spending would have been linked, say, to activities that were more closely articulated to the locality. Suffice it to say that it is not simply enough to say that the *ex post* research is necessarily adequate in rejecting calls for public investment in events.

12.5.3.1 Increased productivity and consumer confidence

As discussed earlier in the chapter, the event study approach has also been used to assess if investment in international sporting success can yield changes in consumer confidence and productivity through its impact on feel-good and that this might be reflected in share price returns. There is an emergent literature addressing this issue. Ashton et al. (2003) examined daily data drawn from the Financial Times Stock Index (FTSE) 100 index for the period 6 January 1984 until 3 July 2002 and regressed the stock returns on a dummy variable scored 1 if the English national soccer team won a match, 0 if it drew a match and −1 if it lost a match. The results suggested that wins were statistically associated with an increase in share returns and losses with decreases. The implication is that feel-good enhanced expectations of profitability.

More qualified impacts have been identified in two studies of the announcement of the Olympic Games being hosted on host nation stock prices. Berman et al. (2000) examined daily stock price data in Australia from 4 January 1988 to 29 November 1996 for the All Ordinaries Accumulation Index and the 23 Australian Stock Exchange Industry Accumulation Indices. The results indicated no effect on overall stock prices, but significant positive effects in sectors connected with building, developers, engineering and services, i.e., industries connected with the development and hosting of the Games. Significantly, too, it was revealed that these effects were confined to industries based in New South Wales.

In a study of the Athens and Milan Stock exchanges, Veraros et al. (2004) examined the impact of the announcement of the Games being awarded to a winner (Athens) and not the other main rival city (Milan). Weekly data, because of limits on daily price fluctuations, were examined between 1 September 1995 and 10 October 2003 in both cases. It was identified that the Athens stock market returns increased by 7.7%, which was primarily driven by significant expected returns in construction and industrials. In the case of Milan, no general (negative) impact on returns was identified, although an effect was identified for the construction and electrical industry, contrary to expectations, which is identified as being spurious.

12.5.4 Non-market valued effects

The literature measuring the non-market value of sports infrastructure and investment is now growing, with a number of contingent valuation analyses being undertaken. Table 12.7 presents analyses where willingness to pay has been elicited for individuals in a sample and then aggregated for the relevant population. Significantly, Barros (2006) also argues that the analysis reveals that the full costs of Euro 2004 of €282 million are not covered by the aggregate willingness to pay, which suggests that it would be inefficient to use public funds to support the project.

12.5.4.1 Other impacts

As far as the effects of investment in sport on community cohesion, social capital, sports development and other externalities is concerned, the literature is very sparse. One contribution, Downward and Ralston (2006), however,

TABLE 12.7 Contingent valuation analyses

Author	Context	Model and data	WTP	Total WTP
Johnson et al. (2000)	New university basketball and minor league baseball stadia for Kentucky	Tobit n = 230	Basketball $6.36 Minor league baseball $6.17	$610 293–$311 249 $59 061–$301 951 (over 95 958 residents)
Barros (2006)	Stadium construction for Euro 2004	Tobit n = 1600 Portuguese residents	€0.106 (2000)	€11.874 m (2000) (over 3.73 m households)
Johnson et al. (2006)	To ensure the NFL Jaguars remained in Jacksonville and to attract an NBA team	Probit and truncated regression[a] n = 367 and n = 139 or 167		NBA Range from $37.02–$67.23 (per capita) NFL Range from $94.24–147.70 (per capita)
Heyne, Maennig and Süssmuth (2007) Cited in Maennig and Du Plessis (2007)	*Ex-ante* and *ex-poste* valuations of the 2006 World Cup	Not stated	*Ex ante* $5.66 *Ex post* $13.38	*Ex ante* $467m *Ex post* $1.1 bn (Over 82 m inhabitants)
EFTEC (2005) cited in	London 2012 Olympics	Not stated	London £22 Manchester and Glasgow £12	£0.67 bn London £3.2 bn outside London
Blake (2005), Price Waterhouse Coopers (2005)				

TABLE 12.7 *(Continued)*

Author	Context	Model and data	WTP	Total WTP
EEDA (2006) Walton et al. (2007)	London 2012 Olympics	Weibull estimation[b] n = 167 or 147	£42.20	£5 833 095 (138 225 residents in Bath) £173 271 934 (4 105 970 residents in the southwest)

[a] *The two equation approach, described as a Heckman model in Chapter 4 allows the determinants of preparedness to pay to differ from the determinants of the amount that respondents are willing to pay, unlike Tobit. A Probit relationship was used to identify the probability that a respondent will be willing to pay, and then a log-linear truncated regression model is estimated on the sub-sample of those who presented a wtp value, as well as the inverse mills ratio which controls for the sample selection. The log-linear form was used because of the non-normality of the distribution of the total wtp.*

[b] *Weibull models are part of a class of models used to model "hazard" in economics. Typically this occurs in labour economics to model the duration of unemployment. The dependent variable is thus identified as such an interval in this analysis. Willingness to pay is thus identified as a discrete interval. Willingness to pay is identified as an interval in this analysis.*

examines a sample of 403 volunteers from the 2002 Manchester Commonwealth Games to identify whether their experiences of the games raised their interest in, and their potential for, greater sports participation and volunteering in sport. The results suggested that while volunteering at a major event can raise interest, participation and volunteering in sport generally, particularly for younger volunteers, there appeared to be a much stronger potential opportunity to generate wider social capital, i.e., volunteering in non-sports contexts, than necessarily producing changes associated with sport. It is clear that further research of a longitudinal and wider population is required.

12.6 CONCLUSION

This chapter has explored elements of the economics of events, suggesting that the design and allocation of non-professional team sports events can also be understood with reference to contest theory. It has also been argued that professional sports and events share other economic features, particularly connected with the impact of sport provision that is, at least partially, funded by public authorities. It has shown that both the economic rationale for, and principles of evaluation of, any public sector investment in sports is common to all sports contests, although naturally the scale and types of investments differ. The definition of investment decisions has been discussed, as well as the policy rationale for public sector investment in sport. It has been noted that externalities and other spillover effects are perceived to play a central role in evaluating sports investment decisions from a public sector perspective. The chapter identifies that the most appropriate form of impact to consider is that on economic welfare and this requires assessing both the tangible impacts of investments, as well as its intangible aspects.

In the former case it has been argued that *ex post* evaluation of investment decisions suggests that multiplier effects are weak. This may be due to the supply-side of the economy producing crowding out effects or be indicative of measurement errors. In either case, the evidence appears to be more reliable than many *ex ante* studies in which large-scale impacts are often forecast. The discussion also indicates that more reliability is associated with the measured impacts of sports investment on intangible impacts, for example value to communities, and expectations of future consumer confidence and productivity gains, although it is not clear that such gains would outweigh the costs of the investments. The chapter concludes, therefore, by suggesting that while a coherent theoretical case can be made for public sector investment in sports, the evidence in support of this case is relatively weak, and suggests considerable caution and planning being required to harness the spillover effects from the investments.

Appendix 12.1 NPV, Wealth and Profit Maximization

Recall from Appendix 3.3 that the present value of any amount "A" at interest rate "r" over "t" periods:

$$\text{Present value} = A/(1+r)t \qquad\qquad (A12.1.1)$$

Consider Figure A12.1.1 below, it represents a production possibilities frontier for all of the investment opportunities open to a supplier. The current period, "t" is represented by the horizontal axis, and the future, "t + 1" is on the vertical axis. Note that the concave shape indicates that the projects are ranked in order of their return. In other words, from a position of current investment funds, S_0, on the horizontal axis, investment of some of these funds, say S_0 to S_1 can yield future funds of 0 to S_2, etc. Wealth would comprise current resources $0 - S_1$ plus future resources 0 to S_2, from the investment. It follows that each point on the curve indicates an investment portfolio in which some resources are held over and some invested for the future. The marginal rate of transformation of this curve measures the yield or internal rate of return of the investments, "d." Note that this must decline as more and more funds are invested in projects. At which point on this curve will any investment decision maximize profits or wealth? To answer this question recall that Equation A12.1.1 indicates the present value of any amount "A." Central to this calculation is the market rate of interest "r." This represents the opportunity cost of funds to the supplier, inasmuch as it represents what can be earned from placing resources in savings, rather than investing in expanding their business, or the cost of borrowing money to invest in the business. It follows that a profit maximizing supplier would only invest in the business if the internal rate of return or yield from the business activity exceeded the market rate of interest. At the margin this implies that investment would stop where the internal rate of return, "d," is equal to "r." Drawing a line at slope "r" at the furthest point to the right of the origin in Figure A12.1.1 would consequently identify the maximum wealth from any investment indicated at point M, derived from the point of tangency where the slope of "r" would be equal to "d." This shows that the intercept of this line with the current time period axis must indicate the NPV of any investment combination (and by analogy, the intercept of this line with the vertical axis must indicate the future value of any investment). Note that the vertical distance

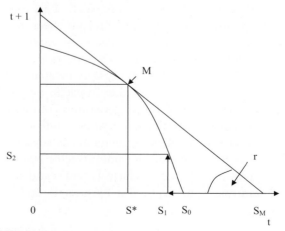

FIGURE A12.1.1 *NPV and wealth maximization.*

(M–S*) represents the future returns from the investment S_0 to S^*. In time "t," this would be equivalent to the horizontal distance $(S^*–S_M)$. In other words, because for investments up to S^*, $d > r$, this investment must add more to wealth than simply placing resources in financial markets. As wealth is the sum of flows of resources, maximizing wealth is simply the long-run equivalent of maximizing the flow of profits.

Appendix 12.2 A Simple Input–Output Analysis of Multiplier Effects Given a Simple Economic System

TABLE A12.2.1   A simple input–output account € million

		Consuming Industry M	Industry S	Household consumption	Output total
Producing	M	100	10	200	310
Industry	S	60	10	60	130
Input total		160	20	260	440

The rows of the table indicate the value of transactions corresponding to the output of the industry "X," where "M" is manufacturing and "S" is sport, and the columns show how much of this output is consumed by the sector itself, and by other sectors and consumers. Consequently, the two columns of the "consuming industry" part of the table represent how much output is bought and sold between industrial sectors, i.e., firms in the circular flow of income, whereas the column "consumption" represents how much is purchased by households, in the circular flow of income "D." For simplicity, the government sector and imports and exports are ignored, as are any other payments by industries to those not subsequently involved in inter-industry trade. This might involve wages to employees. Note that the row and column totals must sum to the same overall amount, as any input to an industry must be balanced by an output.[25]

A set of input output coefficients can be calculated by dividing the purchases of each industry, as obtained from the values in the columns of the input–output table of transactions, by the total value of output of the industry making the purchase.

---

[25] Strictly, each column total should be equivalent to the row total. For example manufacturing produces €310 million output and provides €160 million to other industries. This leaves €150 million for disbursement to other industries outside of the trading system or to wages and profits that might fund the household consumption, which is treated as exogenously given here. This means that in calculating the input–output coefficients, technically, one should divide each column entry by its total to indicate what proportion of the total inputs provided by the industry go to each producing industry, including itself. Numerically speaking one gets the same answer. In this example, to keep the numerical calculations simpler the row totals have been used, with the same logic that one is illustrating with the input–output coefficients the proportion of the industries output that is used as an input to itself and other industries.

TABLE A12.2.2   Input–output coefficients

	M	S
M	0.32	0.08
S	0.19	0.08

In equations this is:

$$0.32\,M + 0.08\,S + DM = M \tag{A12.4.1}$$

$$0.19\,M + 0.08\,S + DS = S$$

In matrix terms the input–output coefficient matrix is:

$$\begin{pmatrix} 0.32 & 0.08 \\ 0.19 & 0.08 \end{pmatrix} \tag{A12.4.2}$$

Consequently, given:

$$X = [I - A]^{-1}D \tag{A12.4.3}$$

If the component of sports expenditure rises, say, by €10 million, but manufacturing demand is constant, i.e., 0, then:

$$\begin{pmatrix} 1.5 & 0.13 \\ 0.31 & 1.1 \end{pmatrix}\begin{pmatrix} 0 \\ 10 \end{pmatrix} = \begin{pmatrix} 0 + 1.3 \\ 0 + 11 \end{pmatrix} = \begin{pmatrix} 1.3 \\ 11 \end{pmatrix} \tag{A12.4.4}$$

There is an increase in manufacturing output of €1.3 million and an increase in sports output of €11 million. The manufacturing demand rises, of course, because of the inter-industry transactions.

Appendix 12.3 Calculating Welfare Weights

Adopting a Cobb–Douglas utility function means that utility "U" can be derived as a function of the value of consumption "C" of an individual:

$$U = C^{\beta} \tag{A12.3.1}$$

or in natural logarithms (ln), as discussed in Chapter 4:

$$U = \beta \ln C \tag{A12.3.2}$$

where β is the elasticity of utility with respect to consumption. The marginal utility of consumption will be:

$$\partial U/\partial C = \beta/C \tag{A12.3.3}$$

or if $\beta = 1$:

$$\partial U/\partial C = 1/C \tag{A12.3.4}$$

or:

$$\partial U/\partial C^* = 1/C^* \tag{A12.3.5}$$

if C* refers to some average level of consumption. This means that utility declines in direct proportion to consumption from income in the case of Equation A12.5.4. A utility weight relative to average income can then be defined as C*/C by dividing Equation A12.3.4 by Equation A12.3.5.

Appendix 12.4 The Determinants of Medal Success

TABLE A12.4.1 Econometric evidence on performance (medals) in Olympic Games

Author	Context	Model, method and estimator	Results
De Bosscher, Heyndels, De Knop, Van Bottenburg and Shibli (2008)	Olympic Summer Games and Winter Games	**Period** Athens 2004 **Stepwise OLS regression Dependent variable** ■ Ln [Med] weighted points country ■ (gold = 3, silver = 2, bronze = 1) **Independent variables** ■ Ln Population, Ln GDP cap, Ln population density, dummies Muslim, protestants, and (former) communist countries **Period** Salt Lake City 2002 **OLS regression** **Dependent variable** ■ Ln [Med] weighted points country ■ (gold = 3, silver = 2, bronze = 1) **Independent variables** ■ Ln Population, Ln GDP cap, Ln population density, dummies muslim, protestants, (former) communist countries and mountains	"population size is responsible for 19.3% of the international success, wealth add another 19.5% and together with the political system for (former) communist countries, we end up with a model where 52.4% of the international success is explained" "the results revealed that only wealth and communism are significant . . . with a determination coefficient of 54.6%"
Rathke and Woitek (2007)	Olympic Summer Games	**Period** 1952–2004 **Translog product function** **Dependent variable** ■ (medal share) ■ Olympic diploma **Independent variables** ■ Ln of GDP, GDP^2, population, $population^2$, GDP:population Dummies for host country, Soviet, plan (China, Norrth Korea, Albania and Yugoslavia)	"GDP is a good predictor of success . . . The effect of population, however, is positive only for relative rich countries . . . Host and Soviet countries outperform . . ." (p.12)

TABLE A12.4.1 (*Continued*)

Author	Context	Model, method and estimator	Results
Mitchell and Stewart (2007)	Olympic Summer Games	**Period** Athens 2004 **OLS and Poisson** **Dependent variable** ■ total medals won by country ■ weighted medals won by country **Independent variables** ■ people: population, birth rate, fertility, infant mortality, life expectancy, literacy, migration ■ government: dummy (former) communist ■ economy: GDP, GDP², GDP/capita, GDP in agriculture, industry and services, openness, government budget, donor (development aid), Gini index income lowest and highest 10%, poverty, ■ technology: cell phone **Other variables** ■ dummy Africa	
Roberts (2006)	Olympic Summer Games	Period: Athens 2004 **Poisson and negative binomial count data regression** **Dependent variable:** ■ total medals won by country **Independent variables:** ■ GDP/capita, population, health expenditure per capita, age dependency ratio(people <15 + >64 divided by people 15–64), frost prevalence (proportion land with more than 5 frost-days a year), dummies for host or neighbour country, test playing cricket nations and top 10 rugby union nations	"GDP per capita, a relatively cold winter climate and the age dependency ratio all have statistically significant impact... population, health expenditure per capita, host/ neighbour effect and rugby and cricket effects all appear to hold no explanatory power." (p. 8)

Hoffman, Chew Ging and Ramasamy (2004)	Olympic Summer Games	**Period** Sydney 2000 OLS **Dependent variable** ■ total number medals won by country (ASEAN countries) **Independent variables** ■ share of world population, share of world GNP, dummies for (former) communist country, cooler humid climate, host country, having hosted since 1948, having hosted twice since 1948	"all variables chosen were significant at a 90% confidence interval"(p. 268)
Bernard and Busse (2004)	Olympic Summer Games	**Period** Rome 1960–Atlanta 1996 **Tobit regression** **Dependent variable** ■ medal share of country **Independent variable** log population, log GDP/capita, dummies host, Soviet, planned (not Soviet), lagged medal share (indicator for current success)	"the results for population and GDP per capita . . . remain positive and significant . . . The Soviet countries . . . and other planned economies have shares that are higher. . . The host effect . . . is also positive and significant . . . lagged medal share . . . is strongly significant" (p. 415)
Johnson and Ayfer (2004)	Olympic Summer and Winter Games	**Period** Summer 1952–1998 Winter 1952–1996 **OLS with nation fixed effects** **Dependent variable** ■ all participants by nation ■ female participants by nation ■ all medals by nation ■ gold medals by nation **Independent variables** ■ GDP/Cap, squared GDP/cap, population, dummy host, neighbour, politics(monarchy, single-party, military or other), light and heavy frost (share of land with less than 5 days and more	"per capita income has a positive impact . . . more populous nations win more medals . . . the home nation has a strong advantage . . . neighboring nations sharing marginally in the bounty in Summer Games . . . single party and communist systems outperform . . . Cold nations outperform in both Summer and Winter Games" [p. 984–987]

TABLE A12.4.1 (*Continued*)

Author	Context	Model, method and estimator	Results
Tcha and Pershin (2003)	Olympic Summer Games	than 20 days of winter), time trend, total medals that can be won **Period 1988–1996** **Tobit regression and patterns of specializing in sports by using the revealed comparative advantage (in line with neoclassical trade models)** **Dependent variable** ■ cumulative number of medals for each country and sport (swimming, athletics, weights, ball games, gymnastics, others) **Independent variables** ■ land mass, coast length, altitude, temperature GDP per capita, GDP and population ■ dummies for African, Asian and former socialist countries	"countries with higher GDP per capita ... collect medals from a diversified range of sports ... Asian countries did not perform well in swimming ... countries with RCA in athletics are relatively well endowed with land mass, high altitude and hogh GDP per capita ... AFD(Africa) also turns to be significant and positive in athletics" (pp. 229–234)
Hoffman, Chew Ging and Ramasamy (2002)	Olympic Summer Games	**Period Sydney 2000** **OLS** **Dependent variable** ■ number of medals won by country **Independent variables** ■ policy factors GNP/capita, population, dummies for current/previous communism, Sydney host, countries having hosted once, countries having hosted twice, ■ deterministic factors average temperature in capital, squared average temp, dummies for cooler humid zone, warmer humid zone, dry zone and tropical humid zone	"significant quadratic relationship between Sydney medal success and mean temperature,... optimal average temp of around 15 °C... countries in warmer and colder humid climates are expected to win an extra 14 and 20 medals respectively ... All factors(policy) are significant" (pp. 247–548)

Stamm and Lamprecht (2001)	Olympic Summer Games	**Period** 1964–1980, 1984–2000, 1992, 1996, 2000 **OLS** **Dependent variable** ■ total medals won by country ■ final participation **Independent variables** ■ GDP per capita, secondary education enrolment, extent of political and civil liberties, population size, sporting tradition, measured as degree of institutionalisation of elite sports: year, duration of IOC membership ■ political system: dummy for socialist countries; effect of authoritarian model of sport promotion	"of particular importance are population size . . . and level of economic development" (p. 5)
Den Butter and Van der Tak (1995)	Olympic Summer Games	**Period** Seoul 1988 and Barcelona 1992 **Bayesian method of Poission regression** **Dependent variable** ■ number of medals country Independent variables ■ equation 1,2,3: population, dummy (former) communist country; GDP/Pop (several forms is several equations such as national income/pop (eq1), NIpurchasing power/pop(eq2), "real" national income/pop (eq3) ■ equation 4,5: log pop, Human development index (eq4), log quality of life index (eq5), dummy communist	"All regressions prove that the level of welfare is a major determinant of the relative performance of nations at the OG multidimensional welfare indicators do not outperform NI . . . per capita income elasticity can be set equal to unity, but the elasticity with respect to population size appears to be smaller than one" (pp. 34–35)

References

Abbott, M., and Ashenfelter, O. (1976) Labour supply, commodity demand and the allocation of time. *Review of Economic Studies* **43:** 389–411.

Adams, F., Davidson, P. and Seneca, J. (1968) An Analysis of Recreational Use of the TVA Lakes, reprinted in Davidson, L. (ed.) (1991) The Collected Writings of Paul Davidson, Vol. 2, Inflation,Open Economies and Resources. London: Macmillan.

Alavy, K., Gaskell, A., Leach, S. and Szymanski, S. (2006) On the Edge of your Seat: Demand for Football on Television and the Uncertainty of Outcome Hypothesis. International Association of Sports Economists Working Paper, 06-31.

Allan, P. (2004) Satellite television and football attendance: The not so super effect. *Applied Economics Letters* **11:** 123–125.

Altergot, K., and McCreedy, C. (1993) Gender and family status across the lifecourse: Constraints on five types of leisure. *Society and Leisure* **16, 1:** 151–180.

Andreff, W., and Staudohar, P. (2002) European and US sports business models. In: Barros, C., Ibrahimo, M. and Szymanski, S. (eds). *Transatlantic sport: The comparative economics of North American and European sports*. Edward Elgar, Cheltenham.

Arrow, K. (1950) A difficulty in the concept of social welfare. *Journal of Political Economy* **58:** 328–346.

Arnout, J., (2006) Independent European Sports Review, European Union.

Arrow, K. (1963) *Social Choice and Individual Values*. John Wiley and Sons, New York.

Arthur, Andersen (1999) *Economic Impact Study of the Sydney 2000 Olympic Games. Centre for Regional Economic Analysis*. University of Tasmania, Australia.

Asser (2005) Professional Sport in the Internal market, Working paper, DG Internal Policies of the Union – Directorate A – Economic and Scientific Policy, European parliament, Brussels.

Ashton, J. K., Gerrard, B., and Hudson, R. (2003) Economic impact of national sporting success: Evidence from the London stock exchange. *Applied Economics Letters* **10:** 783–785.

Audas, R., Dobson, S., and Goddard, J. (1999) Organisational performance and managerial turnover. *Managerial and Decision Economics* **20:** 305–318.

Australian Sports Commission (2005) Participation in Exercise and Sport. Annual Report 2005.

Australian Bureau of Statistics. (2005) *Sport Volunteers and Other Volunteers: Some Data from the 2002 General Social Survey*. National Centre for Culture and Recreation Statistics.

Australian Sports Commission (2004) Participation in Exercise, Recreation and Sport: Annual Report. Belconnen, ACT.

Baade, R., and Matheson, V. A. (2002) Bidding for the Olympics: Fools' Gold? In: Barros, C. et al. (eds). *Transatlantic Sport: The Comparative Economics of North American and European Sports*. Edward Elgar, Cheltenham.

Baade, R., and Matheson, V. A. (2004) The quest for the cup: Assessing the economic impact of the world cup. *Regional Studies* **38, 4:** 343–354.

Baimbridge, M., Cameron, S., and Dawson, P. (1995) Satellite broadcasting and match attendance: The case of rugby league. *Applied Economics Letters* **2, 10:** 343–346.

Baimbridge, M., Cameron, S., and Dawson, P. (1996) Satellite broadcasting and the demand for football: A whole new ball game? *Scottish Journal of Political Economy* **43, 3:** 317–333.

Balfousia-Savva, S., Athanassiou, L., Zaragas, L., and Milonas, A. (2001) *The Economic Effects of the Athens Olympic Games*. Centre of Planning and Economic Research, Athens, Greece.

Barajas, A. and Crolley, L. (2005) A model to explain support in Spanish football, University of Vigo September, Online at http://mpra.ub.uni-muenchen.de/3235/ MPRA Paper No. 3235.

Barget, E., and Gouguet, J. (2007) The total economic value of sporting events; theory and practice. *Journal of Sports Economics* **8, 2:** 165–182.

Barnett, V. and Hilditch, S. (1993) The effect of an artificial pitch surface on home team performance in football (soccer). *Journal of the Royal Statistical Society*, A, part 156, 39–50.

Barros, C. (2006) Evaluating sports events at European level: The Euro 2004. *International Journal of Sport Management and Marketing* **1, 4:** 400–410.

Becker, B., and Huselid, M. (1992) The incentive effects of tournament compensation systems. *Administrative Science Quarterly* **37:** 336–350.

Becker, G. (1965) A theory of the allocation of time. *Economic Journal* **75, 299:** 493–517.

Becker, G. (1968) Crime and punishment: An economic approach. *Journal of Political Economy* **76:** 169–217.

Becker, G. (1974) A theory of social interactions. *Journal of Political Economy* **82:** 1063–1091.

Becker, G. (1976) *The Economic Approach to Human Behaviour*. The University of Chicago Press, Chicago, IL.

Becker, G. (1992) The economic way of looking at life. *The Journal of Political Economy* **101:** 385–409.

Bergson, A. (1938) A reformulation of certain aspects of welfare economics. *Quarterly Journal of Economics* **52, 2:** 310–334.

Berman, G., Brooks, R., and Davidson, S. (2000) The Sydney Olympic Games announcement and Australian stock market reaction. *Applied Economics Letters* **7:** 781–784.

Bernard, A., and Busse, M. (2004) Who wins the Olympic Games: Economic resources and medals totals. *The Review of Economics and Statistics* **86, 1:** 413–417.

Bittman, M., and Wajcman, J. (2000) The rush hour: The character of leisure time and gender equity. *Social Forces* **79, 1:** 165–189.

Blake, A. (2005) The Economic Impact of the London 2012. Olympics Working paper, No 5 Christel DeHaan Tourism and Travel Research Institute, Nottingham University Business School, Nottingham, UK.

Blavatskyy, P. (2004) Why the Olympics have three prizes and not just one. Institute for Empirical Research in Economics, December, University of Zurich, Switzerland.

Bognanno, M.L. (1990), 'An Empirical Test of Tournament Theory', Ph.D. Thesis, Department of Economics, Cornell University.

Bohlmann, H., and van Heerden, J. (2008) Predicting the economic impact of the 2010 FIFA world cup on South Africa. *International Journal of Sport Management and Marketing* **3, 4:** 383–396.

Borland, J. (1987) The demand for Australian Rules football. *The Economic Record* **63, 182:** 220–230.

Borland, J., and Lye, J. (1992) Attendance at Australian Rules football: A panel study. *Applied Economics* **24, 9:** 1053–1058.

Borland, J., and MacDonald, R. (2003) Demand for sport. *Oxford Review of Economic Policy* **19, 4:** 478–502.

Bourdieu, P. (1986) The forms of capital. In: Richardson, JG. (ed). *Handbook of Theory and Research for the Sociology of Education.* Greenwood Press, New York.

Boyko, R. H., Boyko, A. R., and Boyko, M. G. (2007) Referee bias contributes to home advantage in English premiership football. *Journal of Sports Sciences* **25:** 1185–1194.

Breuer, C. (2006) Sport Participation in Germany – a demo-economical model. German Sport University Cologne, Discussion paper 01/06.

Breuer, C. (2007) *Sport-entwicklungsbericht 2005/2006: Analyse zur Situation der Sportvereine in Deutschland.* Bundesinstitut für Sportwissenschaft, Bonn.

Brown, D., and Link, C. (2008) Population and bandwagon effects on local team revenues in MLB. *Journal of Sports Economics* **10:** 1–18.

Brown, E. (1999) Assessing the value of volunteer activity. *Non-Profit and Voluntary Sector Quarterly* **28, 1:** 3–17.

Brunet, F. (1995) An economic impact analysis of the Barcelona '92 Olympic Games: Resources, financing and impact. http://olympicstudies.uab.es/pdf/OD006_eng.pdf.

Brunet, F. (2005) The economic impact of the Barcelona Olympic Games, 1986–2004. www.olympicstudies.uab.es.

Buraimo, B., Forrest, D. and Simmons, R. (2006) Insights for clubs from modelling match attendance in football. Working paper, Lancashire University.

Buraimo, B. and Simmons, R. (2007) A tale of two audiences: spectators, television viewers and outcome uncertainty in Spanish football. Lancaster University Management School Working Paper 2007/043.

Burgham, M., and Downward, P. (2005) Why volunteer, time to volunteer? A case study from swimming. *Managing Leisure* **10:** 79–93.

Butler, M. (2002) Interleague play and baseball attendance. *Journal of Sports Economics* **3:** 320–334.

Cairns, J. (1990) The demand for professional team sports. *British Review of Economic Issues* **12, 28:** 1–20.

Cairns, J., Jennett, N., and Sloane, P. (1986) The economics of professional team sports: A survey of theory and evidence. *Journal of Economic Studies* **13, 1:** 3–80.

Cambridge Policy Consultants (2002) The Commonwealth Games 2002: A Cost and Benefit Analysis, Revised Executive Summary. http://www.gameslegacy.com/files/CG2002%20-%20SUMMARY%20REPORT%20-%20OCTOBER%202002.doc.

Carmichael, F., Forrest, D., and Simmons, R. (1999) The labour market in association football: who gets transferred and for how much? *Bulletin of Economic Research* **51, 2:** 125–150.

Carmichael, F., Millington, J., and Simmons, R. (1999) Elasticity of demand for rugby league attendance and the impact of BskyB. *Applied Economics Letters* **6:** 707–800.

Carmichael, F., and Thomas, D. (1993) Bargaining in the transfer market: Theory and evidence. *Applied Economics* **25:** 1467–1476.

Carter, P. (2005) *Review of National Sport Effort and Resources.* DCMS, London.

Cicchetti, C., Davidson, P., and Seneca, J. (1969) *The Demand and Supply of Outdoor Recreation: An Econometric Analysis*. Bureau of Outdoor Recreation, Washington, DC.

Clapp, C., and Hakes, J. (2005) How long a honeymoon? The effect of new stadiums on attendance in major league baseball. *Journal of Sports Economics* **6**: 237–263.

Clarke, S. (2005) Home advantage in the Australian football league. *Journal of Sports Sciences* **23, 4**: 375–385.

Cnaan, R., Handy, F., and Wadsworth, M. (1996) Defining who is a volunteer: Conceptual and empirical considerations. *Nonprofit and Voluntary Sector Quarterly* **25, 3**: 364–383.

Coalter, F. (1999) Sport and recreation in the United Kingdom: Flow with the flow or buck the trends? *Managing Leisure* **4**: 24–39.

Coase, R. (1960) The problem of social cost. *Journal of Law and Economics* **3**: 1–44.

Coates, D., and Harrison, T. (2005) Baseball strikes and the demand for attendance. *Journal of Sports Economics* **6**: 282–302.

Coates, D., and Humphreys, B. (1999) The growth effects of sports franchises, stadia and arenas. *Journal of Policy Analysis and Management* **18, 4**: 601–624.

Coates, D., and Humphreys, B. (2002) The economic impact of post-season play in professional sports. *Journal of Sports Economics* **3, 3**: 291–299.

Coates, D., and Humphreys, B. (2005) Novelty effects of new facilities on attendance at professional sporting events. *Contemporary Economic Policy* **23, 3**: 436–455.

Coates, D., and Humphreys, B. (2007) Ticket prices, concessions and attendance at professional sporting events. *International Journal of Sport Finance* **3, 2**: 161–170.

Collins, M. (2003) *Sport and Social Exclusion*. Routledge, London.

Collins, M. (2004) Driving up participation. Social Inclusion, in Sport England. (2004).

Cornes, R., and Sandler, T. (1986) *The Theory of Externalities, Public Goods and Club Goods*. Cambridge University Press, Cambridge, UK.

Council of Europe (1980) European Sport for All Charter. Strasbourg.

Council of Europe, (1992) European Sports Charter, http://www.coe.int/t/dg4/sport/SportinEurope/charter_en.asp.

Crompton, J. (1995) Economic impact analysis of sports facilities and events: Eleven sources of misapplication. *Journal of Sports Management* **9**: 14–35.

Crompton, J. (2004) Beyond economic impact: An alternative rationale for the subsidy of major league sports facilities. *Journal of Sports Management* **18**: 40–58.

Crompton, J. (2006) Economic impact studies: Instruments for political shenanigans? *Journal of Travel Research* **45**: 67–82.

Cuskelly, G., Hoye, R., and Auld, C. (2006) *Working with Volunteers in Sport: Theory and Practice*. Routledge, London.

Dardis, R., Soberon-Ferrer, H., and Patro, D. (1994) Analysis of leisure expenditures in the United States. *Journal of Leisure Research* **26, 4**: 309–321.

Davies, B., Downward, P., and Jackson, I. (1995) The demand for rugby league: Evidence from causality tests. *Applied Economics* **27, 10**: 1003–1007.

Davies, L. (2004) Valuing the voluntary sector in sport: Rethinking economic analysis. *Leisure Studies* **23, 4**: 347–364.

Dawson, P., and Dobson, S. (2002) Managerial efficiency and human capital: An application to English association football. *Managerial and Decision Economics* **23**: 471–486.

Dawson, P. and Dobson, S., (2006) Managerial Employment and Re-Employment Patterns: A Case Study of English Professional Football. In: Jeanrenaud, C. and Kesenne, S. (eds) conomics Applied to Sports: Five Case Studies, CIES Editions.

Dawson, P., Dobson, S., and Gerrard, B. (2000) Estimating coaching efficiency in professional team sports: Evidence from English association football. *Scottish Journal of Political Economy* **47:** 399–421.

Dawson, P., Dobson, S., Goddard, J. and Wilson, J. (2005). Modelling the incidence of disciplinary sanction in English premier league football. Paper delivered at the University of Groningen, March 2005.

DCMS/Strategy Unit (2002) Game Plan: A strategy for delivering government's sport and physical activity objectives.

DCMS/Strategy Unit (2008) Playing to win.

De Bosscher, V., Bingham, J., Shibli, S., Van Bottenburg, M. and De Knop, P. (forthcoming 2007) *Sports Policy Factors Leading to International Sporting Success: An International Comparative Study*. Oxford, UK: Meyer and Meyer Sport.

Dejonghe, T., Van Hoof, S. and Kemmeren, T. (2006) Voetballen in de kleine ruimte: een onderzoek naar de geografische marktgebieden en ruimtelijke uitbreidingsmogelijkheden voor de clubs in het Nederlandse Betaalde Voetbal, Nieuwegein, Mulier Instituut, Arko Sports Media.

Dejonghe, T. (2007a) *Sport en economie: een aftrap*. Arko Sports Media, Nieuwegein.

Dejonghe, T. (2007b) *Sport in de wereld: ontstaan, verspreiding en evolutie*. Academia Press, Gent.

Deloitte, Touche (2005a) *Annual review of football and finance*. Deloitte and Touche, Manchester.

Deloitte (2005b) The Football Money League: the Climbers and the Sliders. Manchester.

Deloitte (2007) Annual Review of Football Finance, Manchester.

Demmert, H. (1973) *The Economics of Professional Team Sports*. Heath, D.C.

Den Butter, F., and Van Der Tak, C. (1995) Olympic medals as an indicator of social welfare. *Social Indicators Research* **35:** 27–37.

Dimitrakopoulos, D.G., (2006) More than a Market? The Regulation of Sport in the European Union, Government and Opposition **41**: 561–580.

Dobson, S., and Gerrard, B. (1999) The determination of player transfer fees in English professional soccer. *Journal of Sport Management* **13:** 259–279.

Dobson, S., and Goddard, J. (1992) The demand for standing and seated viewing in English non-league football. *Applied Economics* **24, 10:** 1155–1164.

Dobson, S., and Goddard, J. (1998) Performance, revenue and cross subsidis-ation in the football league 1927–1994. *Economic History Review* **L1, 4:** 763–765.

Dobson, S., and Goddard, J. (2001) *The Economics of Football*. CUP, Cambridge.

Dobson, S., Goddard, J., and Ramlogan, C. (2001) Revenue convergence in the English soccer league. *Journal of Sports Economics* **2, part 3:** 257–274.

Downward, P.M. (2003), Sport and Sport Constructions in the Regional Competition of Cities: Some Observations from the USA and UK. In Buch, M.P., Maennig, W. and Schulke, H.J. Nachhaltigkeit von Sportstatten, Bundesinstitut fur Sportwissenschaft, Bonn.

Downward, P. (2004) Assessing neoclassical microeconomic theory via leisure demand: A post keynesian perspective. *Journal of Post Keynesian Economics* **26, 3:** 371–395.

Downward, P. (2005) Understanding Participation in Sport, Leisure and Tourism. In: Downward, P. and Lumsdon, L. (eds). *Essential Data Skills: Leisure and Tourism. A Guide to using Official Data Sources.* The Stationery Office, London.

Downward, P. (2007) Exploring the economic choice to participate in sport: Results from the 2002 General Household Survey. *The International Review of Applied Economics* **21, 5:** 633–653.

Downward, P., and Dawson, A. (2000) *The Economics of Professional Team Sports.* Routledge, London.

Downward, P., and Dawson, A. (2005a) Measuring short-run uncertainty of outcome in sporting leagues: A comment. *Journal of Sports Economics* **6, 3:** 303–313.

Downward, P. and Dawson, A. (2005b) Anomalies in the economics of professional team sports: examples from short and medium term models of outcome uncertainty. Paper delivered at the University of Groningen, March 2005.

Downward, P., and Jackson, I. (2003) Common origins, Common Future? A Comparative Analysis of Association and Rugby league Football in the UK. In: Fort, R. and Fizel, J. (eds). *International Comparisons in the Economics of Sports.* Praeger.

Downward, P., and Jones, M. (2007) Exploring crowd-size effects upon referee decisions: Analysis of the FA cup. *Journal of Sports Sciences* **25, 14:** 1541–1545.

Downward, P., and Ralston, R. (2006) The sports development potential of sports event volunteering: Insights from the XV11 Manchester Commonwealth Games. *European Sport Management Quarterly* **6, 4:** 333–352.

Downward, P., and Riordan, J. (2007) Social interactions and the demand for sport: An economic analysis. *Contemporary Economic Policy* **25, 4:** 518–537.

Dwyer, L., Forsyth, P., and Spurr, R. (2006) Economic Evaluation of Special Events. In: Dwyer, L. and Forsyth, P. (eds). *International Handbook on the Economics of Tourism.* Edward Elgar, Cheltenham.

Dwyer, L., and Forsyth, P. (2006) *International Handbook on the Economics of Tourism.* Edward Elgar, Cheltenham.

East of England Development Agency (EEDA) (2006) Economic Impact Study of the London 2012 Olympic Games and Paralympic Games.

Eckard, W. (2001) Baseball's blue ribbon report: Solutions in search of a problem. *Journal of Sports Economics* **2, 3:** 213–227.

Economic Research Associates. (1984) *Community Economic Impact of the 1984 Olympic Games in Los Angeles and Southern California.* Los Angeles Olympic Organizing Committee, Los Angeles.

Economics for the Environment Consultancy (2005) Olympic Games Impact Study – Stated Preference Analysis: Final Report, December 2005, Department of Culture Media and Sport. London.

Ehrenburg, R., and Bognanno, L. (1990a) Do tournaments have incentive effects? *Journal of Political Economy* **98:** 1307–1324.

Ehrenburg, R., and Bognanno, L. (1990b) The incentive effects of tournaments revisited: Evidence from the European PGA tour. *Industrial Relations Review* **43:** 74–88.

El-Hodiri, M., and Quirk, J. (1971) An economic model of a professional sports league. *The Journal of Political Economy* **79, 6:** 1302–1319.

European Commission (1999) The European Model of Sport. Brussels.

Falter, J.-M., and Perignon, C. (2000) Demand for football and intra-match winning probability: An essay on the glorious uncertainty of sports. *Applied Economics* **32:** 1757–1765.

Falter, J.-M., Perignon, C., and Vercruysse, O. (2008) Impact of overwhelming joy on consumer demand: The case of a world cup victory. *Journal of Sports Economics* **9:** 20–42.

Farrell, L., and Shields, M. (2002) Investigating the economic and demographic determinants of sporting participation in England. *Journal of the Royal Statistical Society (A)* **165, 2:** 335–348.

Feddersen, A., Maennig, W., and Borcherding, M. (2006) The novelty effect of new soccer stadia: The case of Germany. *International Journal of Sport Finance* **1:** 174–188.

Feddersen, A. and Maennig, W. (2007) Arenas versus multi-functional stadia – which do spectators prefer? Working paper, University of Hamburg.

Fernie, S., and Metcalf, D. (1996) It's not what you pay it's the way that you pay it –jockeys' pay and performance. *Centre Piece* **2:** 2–6.

Fernie, S., and Metcalf, D. (1999) It's not what you pay it's the way that you pay it. That's what gets results – jockeys' pay and performance. *Labour* **13:** 385–411.

Forrest, D., Beaumont, J., Goddard, J., and Simmons, R. (2005) Home advantage and the debate about competitive balance in professional sports leagues. *Journal of Sports Sciences* **23, 4:** 439–445.

Forrest, D. and Simmons, R. (2000) Outcome uncertainty and attendance demand in sport: the case of English soccer. Discussion Paper, Centre for Sports Economics, University of Salford.

Forrest, D., and Simmons, R. (2006) New issues in attendances demand: The case of the English football league. *Journal of Sports Economics* **7:** 247–266.

Forrest, D., Simmons, R., and Buraimo, B. (2005) Outcome uncertainty and the couch potato audience. *Scottish Journal of Political Economy* **52, 4:** 641–661.

Forrest, D., Simmons, R., and Feehan, P. (2002) A spatial cross-sectional analysis of the elasticity of demand for soccer. *Scottish Journal of Political Economy* **49, 3:** 336–355.

Forrest, D., Simmons, R., and Szymanski, S. (2004) Broadcasting, attendance and the inefficiency of cartels. *Review of Industrial Organization* **24:** 243–265.

Fort, R. (1997) Direct Democracy and the Stadium Mess. In: Noll and Zimbalist, (eds). *Sports, Jobs, and Taxes: The Economic Impact of Sports Teams and Stadiums.* Brookings Institution, Washington D.C.

Fort, R. (2000) European and North American sports differences(?). *Scottish Journal of Political Economy* **47, 4:** 431–455.

Fort, R. (2004) Inelastic sports pricing. *Managerial and Decision Economics* **25:** 87–94.

Fort, R., and Quirk, J. (1995) Cross-subsidization, incentives, and outcomes in professional team sports leagues. *Journal of Economic Literature* **33, 3:** 1265–1299.

Fort, R., and Quirk, J. (2004) Owner objectives and competitive balance. *Journal of Sports Economics* **5, 1:** 20–32.

Fox, K. and Rickards, L. (2004) Results from the sport and leisure module of the 2002 General Household Survey, TSO. London.

Freeman, R. B. (1997) Working for nothing: The supply of volunteer labour. *Journal of Labor Economics* **15, 1:** S140–S166.

Frick, B. (2000) Contest theory and sport. *Oxford Review of Economic Policy* **19, 4:** 512–529.

Frick, B. (2003) Contest Theory and Sport, Oxford eview of Economic Policy **19:** 512–529.

Frick, B. (2006) Salary Determination and the Pay-Performance Relationship in Professional Soccer: Evidence from Germany. In: Rodriguez, P., Kesenne, S. and Garcia, J. (eds). *Sports Economics after Fifty Years: Essays in Honour of Simon Rottenberg.* University of Oviedo, Oviedo.

Frick, B. (2007) The football players' labour market: Empirical evidence from the major European leagues. *Scottish Journal of Political Economy* **54, 3:** 422–446.

Frick, B., Pietzner, G., and Prinz, J. (2006) The Labour market for Soccer Players in Germany – Career Duration in a Competitive Environment. In: Jeanrenaud, C. and Kesenne, S. (eds). *Economics Applied to Sports: Five Case Studies.* Cies, Neuchâtel, Suisse.

Friedman, M. (1953) *The Methodology of Positive Economics in Essays in Positive Economics.* University of Chicago Press, Chicago.

Garcia, J., and Rodriguez, P. (2002) The determinants of football match attendance revisited. *Journal of Sports Economics* **3, 1:** 18–38.

Getz, D. (1991) *Festivals, Special Events and Tourism.* Van Nostrand Reinhold.

Gibrat, R. (1931) *Las Inegalites Economiques.* Libraire du Recueil Sirey, Paris.

Gouguet, J. (2002) Economic impact of sporting events: What has to be measured? In: Barros, C., Ibrahimon, M. and Szymanski, S. (2002). Transatlantic Sport: The Comparative Economics of North American and European Sports. Cheltenham: Edward Elgar.

Grant Thornton (2003), SA 2010 Soccer World Cup Bid Executive Summary. www.polity.org.za.

Gratton, C., and Taylor, P. (1985) *Sport and Recreation: An Economic Analysis.* E. and F. N. Spon, London.

Gratton, C., and Taylor, P. (2000) *Economics of Sport and Recreation.* E. and F.N. Spon, London.

Gratton, C. and Tice, A. (1991) Sports Participation in Britain: An Investigation into the Changing Demand for Sport. Manchester Polytechnic Working Paper.

Gratton, C., Dobson, N., and Shibli, S. (2000) The economic importance of major sports events: A case study of six events. *Managing Leisure* **5:** 17–28.

Gratton, C., Nichols, G., Shibli, S., and Taylor, P. (1997) *Valuing Volunteers in UK Sport.* Sports Council, England.

Gratton, C., Shibli, S., and Coleman, R. (2005) Sport and economic regeneration in cities. *Urban Studies* **42, 5–6:** 985–999.

Gravelle, H., and Rees, R. (2004) *Microeconomics.* Prentice Hall, London.

Green, M. (2004) Changing policy priorities for sport in England: The emergence of elite sport development as a key policy concern. *Leisure Studies* **23, 4:** 365–385.

Green, M., and Houlihan, B. (2005) *Elite Sport Development: Policy Learning and Political Priorities.* Routledge, London.

Gronau, R. (1973) The intrafamily allocation of time: The value of the housewives' time. *American Economic Review* **63, 4:** 634–651.

Grossman, M. (1972a) *The Demand for Health: A Theoretical and Empirical Investigation.* National Bureau of Economic Research, New York.

Grossman, M. (1972b) On the concept of health capital and the demand for health. *Journal of Political Economy* **80:** 223–255.

Hart, R., Hutton, J. and Sharot, T. (1975) A statistical analysis of association football attendance. *Journal of the Royal Statistical Society;* Series C (Applied Statistics), vol. **24, 1**: 17–27.

Heckman, J. (1979) Sample selection bias as a specification error. *Econometrica* **47:** 153–161.

Heinemann, K. (1999) Sports Clubs in Europe. In: Heinemann, K. (ed). *Sports Clubs in Various European Countries*. Hofmann, Schorndorf.

Heinemann, K., and Schubert, M. (1999) Sports Clubs in Germany. In: Heinemann, K. (ed). *Sports Clubs in Various European Countries*. Hofmann, Schorndorf.

Henry, I. (2001) *The Politics of Leisure Policy*. Palgrave, London.

Heyne, M., Maennig, W. and Süssmuth, B. (2007) Mega-sporting Events as Experience Goods? Working Paper, Bremen University, University of Technologie and Hamburg University.

Hicks, J. (1939) *Value and Capital*. Clarendon Press, Oxford.

Hoehn, T., and Szymanski, S. (1999) The Americanisation of European football. *Economic Policy* **14, 18:** 205–240.

Hoffmann, R., Chew Ging, L., and Ramasamy, B. (2002) Public policy and Olympic success. *Applied Economic Letters* **9:** 545–548.

Hoffman, R., Chew Ging, L., and Ramasamy, B. (2004) Olympic success and ASEAN countries: economic analysis and policy implications. *Journal of Sports Economics* **5:** 262–276.

Holt, M., Mitchie, J., and Oughton, C. (2006) The Role and Regulation of Agents in Football. The Sport Nexus.

Horch, H. (1994) Resource composition and oligarchization: Evidence from German sport clubs. *European Journal for Sport Management* **2, 1:** 52–67.

Houlihan, B. (1997) *Sport, Policy and Politics: A Comparative Analysis*. Routledge, London.

Houlihan, B. (2005) In: Slack, T. (ed). *The Commercialisation of Sport*. Frank Cass, London.

Hudson, I. (2001) The use and misuse of economic impact analysis: The case of professional sports. *Journal of Sport and Social Issues* **25, 1:** 20–39.

Humphreys, B. (2002) Alternative measures of competitive balance in sports leagues. *Journal of Sports Economics* **3, 2:** 133–148.

Humphreys, B. and Ruseski, J. (2006) Economic Determinants of Participation in Physical Activity and Sport. IASE Conference, Bochum.

Humphreys, J. and Plummer, M. (1995) The Economic Impact on the State of Georgia of hosting the 1996 Olympic Games: 1995 update. Selig Center for Economic Growth, Terry College of Business, University of Georgia.

Ibsen, B. (1999) Structure and Development of Sports Organisations in Denmark. In: Heinemann, K. (ed). *Sports Clubs in Various European Countries*. Hofmann, Schorndorf.

Insight Economics. (2006) *Triple Bottom Line Assessment of the XVIII Commonwealth Games: Executive Summary*. Insight Economics, Melbourne/Perth.

Jacklin, P. (2005) Temporal changes in home advantage in English football since the Second World War: What explains improved away performance? *Journal of Sports Sciences* **23, 7:** 669–679.

Jackson, N. (1899) *Association Football*. George Newnes, London.

Jennett, N. (1984) Attendances, uncertainty of outcome and policy in Scottish league football. *Scottish Journal of Political Economy* **31, 2:** 175–197.

Jeanreneaud, C., and Kesenne, S. (2006) Sport and the Media an Overview. In: Jeanrenaud, C. and Kesenne, S. (eds). *The Economics of Sport and the Media.* Edward Elgar, Cheltenham, UK.

Johnson, B., and Whitehead, J. (2000) The value of public goods from sports stadiums: The CVM approach. *Contemporary Economic Policy* **18, 1:** 48–58.

Johnson, B., Mondello, M., and Whitehead, J. (2006) Contingent valuation of sports: temporal embedding and ordering effects. *Journal of Sports Economics* **7, 3:** 267–288.

Johnson, D., and Ayfer, A. (2004) A tale of two seasons: participation and medal counts at the Summer and Winter Olympic Games. *Social Science Quarterly* **85, 4:** 974–993.

Johnston, R. (2008) On referee bias, crowd size, and home advantage in the English soccer premiership. *Journal of Sports Sciences* **26, 6:** 563–568.

Jones, J., Schofield, J., and Giles, D. (2000) Our fans in the North: the demand for British rugby league. *Applied Economics* **32, 14:** 1879–1890.

Joyce, K. (1997) The Ethics and Dynamics of Negotiating a Professional Sports Contract. *Texas Entetainment and Sports Law Journal* **6:** 7–11.

Kahn, L. (1993) Free agency, long-term contracts and compensation in MLB: Estimates from panel data. *Review of Economics and Statistics* **75:** 157–164.

Kaldor, N. (1939) Welfare propositions of economics and interpersonal comparisons of utility. *Economic Journal* **49:** 549–552.

Karcher, R., (2005) The NCAA's Regulations Related to the Use of Agents in the Sport of baseball: Are the Rules Detrimental to the Best Interests of the Amateur Athlete? *Vanderbilt Journal of Entertainment and Law.* (http://ssrn.com/ abstract=936898).

Kasimati, E. (2003) Economic aspects and the Summer Olympics: A review of related research. *International Journal of Tourism Research* **5:** 433–444.

Kesenne, S. (1996) League management in professional team sports with win maximising clubs. *European Journal for Sports Management* **2:** 14–22.

Kesenne, S. (2000b) The impact of salary caps in professional team sports. *Scottish Journal of Political Economy* **47, 4:** 422–429.

Kesenne, S. (2000a) Revenue sharing and competitive balance in competitive team sports. *Journal of Sports Economics* **1, 1:** 56–65.

Kesenne, S. (2001) The different impact of different sharing systems on the competitive balance in professional team sports. *European Sports Management Quarterly* **1:** 210–218.

Kesenne, S. (2004) Competitive balance and revenue sharing when rich clubs have poor teams. *Journal of Sports Economics* **5:** 206–212.

Kesenne, S. (2005) Do we need and economic impact study or a cost-benefit analysis of a sports event. *European Sport Management Quarterly* **5:** 133–142.

Kesenne, S. (2006b) The win maximisation model reconsidered. *Journal of Sports Economics* **5:** 981–1006.

Kesenne, S. (2006a) Competitive balance in team sports and the impact of revenue sharing. *Journal of Sport Management* **20:** 39–51.

Kesenne, S. (2007a) *The Economic Theory of Professional Team Sports.* Edward Elgar, Cheltenham, UK.

Kesenne, S. (2007b) The peculiar international economics of professional football in Europe. *Scottish Journal of Political Economy* **54, 3:** 388–399.

Kesenne, S., and Janssens, P. (1987) Belgian soccer attendances. *Tijdschrift voor Economie en Management* **3:** 379–400.

Kim, J., Rhee, S., and Ju, J. (1989) *Impact of the Seoul Olympic Games on National Development*. Korea Development Institute, Seoul.

Koning, R. (2004) Home Advantage in Speed Skating: Evidence from Individual Data. Paper given at the University of Groningen, March 2005.

Kooreman, P., and Kapteyn, A. (1987) A disaggregated analysis of the allocation of time within the household. *The Journal of Political Economy* **95, 2:** 223– 249.

Koski, P. (1999) Characteristics and contemporary trends of sports clubs in the Finnish context. In: Heinemann, K. (ed). *Sport Clubs in Various European Countries.* Hofmann, Schorndorf.

KPMG. (1993) *Sydney Olympics 2000: Economic Impact Study*. Sydney Olympics 2000 Bid Ltd., Sydney, NSW.

Krautmann, A., and Oppenheimer, M. (2002) Contract length and the returns to performance in major league baseball. *Journal of Sports Economics* **3:** 5–17.

Kuypers, T. (1996) The beautiful game? An econometric study of why people watch English football. *University College London Discussion Papers in Economics* , pp. 96–101.

Lallemand, T., Plasman, R., and Rycx, F. (2008) Women and competition in elimination tournaments: evidence from professional tennis data. *Journal of Sports Economics* **9, 1:** 3–19.

Lamb, L., Asturias, L., Roberts, K., and Brodie, D. (1992) Sports participation – How much does it cost? *Leisure Studies* **11, 1:** 19–29.

Larsen, A., Fenn, A., and Spenner, E. (2006) The impact of free agency and the salary cap on competitive balance in the NFL. *Journal of Sports Economics* **7, 4:** 374–390.

Lawson, T. (2003) *Reorienting Economics*. Routledge, London.

Lechner, M. (2008) Long-run labour market effects of individual sports activities. IZA DP Number 3359.

Lee, Y., and Bhargava, V. (2004) Leisure time: Do married and single individuals spend it differently. *Family and Consumer Sciences Research Journal* **32, 3:** 254–274.

Lee, Y. (2006) The decline of attendance in the Korean professional baseball league. *Journal of Sports Economics* **7:** 187–200.

Leeds, M., and von Allmen, P. (2002) *The Economics of Sports*. Pearson, London.

Leibenstein, H. (1966) Allocative efficiency versus x-inefficiency. *American Economic Review* **56:** 397–409.

Lera-Lopez, F., and Rapun-Garate, M. (2005) Sports participation versus consumer expenditure on sport: Different determinants and strategies in sports management. *European Sports Management Quarterly* **5, 2:** 167–186.

Le Roux, N., and Camy, J. (1999) An Essay on the French Sports System. In: Heinemann, K. (ed). *Sports Clubs in Various European Countries*. Hofmann, Schorndorf.

Lertwachara, K., and Cochran, J. J. (2007) An event study of the economic impact of professional sport franchises on local US economies. *Journal of Sports Economics* **8, 3:** 244–254.

Lipsey, R.G. and Lancaster, K. (1956–1957) The general theory of second best. *The Review of Economic Studies*, **24, 1**: 11–32.

LIRC. (2003) *Sports Volunteering in England 2002*. Sport England.

Lucifora, C., and Simmons, R. (2003) Superstar effects in sport. *Journal of Sports Economics* **4, 1:** 35–55.

Lukka, P., and Ellis, A. (2002) *An exclusive construct? Exploring different cultural concepts of volunteering*. Institute for Volunteering Research.

Lynch, J. and Zax, J.S. (1998) Prizes, selection and performance in Arabian Horse Racing. Discussion Paper, University of Colorado.

Lynch, J. and Zax, J.S. (2000) The reward to running: Prize structures and performance.

MacDonald, D., and Reynolds, M. (1994) Are baseball players paid their marginal products? *Managerial and Decision Economics* **15:** 443–457.

Madden, J. R. (2002) The economic consequences of the Sydney Olympics: The CREA/Arthur Anderson Study. *Current Issues in Tourism* **5, 1:** 7–20.

Maennig, W. (2002) On the economics of doping and corruption in international sports. *Journal of Sports Economics* **3, 1:** 61–89.

Maennig, W. (2007) One Year Later: A re-appraisal of the economics of the 2006 soccer World Cup. Hamburg Working paper Series in Economic Policy, No 10.

Maennig, W., and Du Plessis, S. (2007) World-cup 2010: South African economic perspectives and policy challenges informed by the experience of Germany 2006. *Contemporary Economic Policy* **25, 4:** 578–590.

Maguire, J. (1999) *Global Sport: Identities, Societies, Civilisations*. Polity Press, Cambridge.

Maloney, M., and McCormick, R. (2000) The response of workers to wages in tournaments: evidence from foot races. *Journal of Sport Economics* **1, 2:** 99–123.

Marburger, D. (1994) Bargaining power and the structure of salaries in major league baseball. *Managerial and Decision Economics* **15, 5:** 433–441.

Marshall, A. (1952) *Principles of Economics*, 8th edition. Macmillan, London.

Mascarenhas, D., Collins, D., and Mortimer, P. (2005) The accuracy, agreement and coherence of decision-making in rugby union officials. *Journal of Sport Behaviour* **28, 2:** 253–271.

Mason, D. S., and Duquette, G. H. (2005) Globalisation and the evolving player-agent relationship in professional sport. *International Journal of Sport Management and Marketing* **1:** 93–109.

Mason, D. S., and Slack, T. (2001) Industry Factors and the Changing Dynamics of the Player-Agent Relationship in Professional Ice Hockey. *Sport management Review* **4:** 165–191.

Mason, D. S., and Slack, T. (2003) Understanding Principal-Agent Relationships: Evidence from Professional Hockey. *Journal of Sport Management* **17:** 37–61.

Matheson, V., and Baade, R. (2008) Striking out: Estimating the economic impact of baseball's world series. *International Journal of Sport Management and Marketing* **3, 4:** 319–334.

Maxcy, J., and Mondello, M. (2006) The Impact of Free Agency on Competitive Balance in North American Team Professional Team Sports Leagues. *Journal of Sport Management* **20:** 345–365.

Medoff, M. (1976) On monopolistic exploitation in professional baseball. *Quarterly Review of Economics and Business* **16, 2:** 113–121.

Meehan, J., Nelson, R., and Richardson, T. (2007) Competitive balance and game attendance in major league baseball. *Journal of Sports Economics* **8:** 563–580.

Michie, J., and Oughton, C. (2004) *Competitive Balance in Football: Trends and Effects*. Football Governance Research Centre, Birkbeck College, University of London.

Mill, J. S. (1900) *Principles of Political Economy with some of their Applications to Social Philosophy*. G Routledge and Sons, London.

Mintel. (2005a) *Sports Goods Retailing – UK*. Mintel International Group Limited.

Mintel (2005b), Fitness Classes, http://academic.mintel.com.

Mintel (2005c) Sports Goods Retailing, http://academic.mintel.com.

Mintel (2006) Leisure Centres and Swimming Pools. http://academic.mintel.com.

Mintel (2007), Health and Fitness Clubs, http://academic.mintel.com.

Mitchel, H., and Stewart, F. (2007) A competitive index for international sport. *Applied Economics* **39:** 587–603.

Moorhouse, G. (1995) *The Official History of Rugby League*. Hodder and Stoughton, London.

Morley, B., and Thomas, D. (2005) An investigation of home advantage and other factors affecting outcomes in English one-day cricket matches. *Journal of Sports Sciences* **23, 3:** 261–268.

Morton, R. H. (2006) Home advantage in southern hemisphere rugby union: National and international. *Journal of Sports Sciences* **24, 5:** 495–499.

Musgrave, R. A., and Musgrave, P. B. (1973) *Public Finance in Theory and Practice*. McGraw-Hill Book Company, New York.

Musgrave, R. (1987) Merit goods. In: Eatwell, J., Milgate, M. and Newman, P. (eds). *The New Palgrave: A Dictionary of Economics*. Macmillan and Stockton, London and New York.

Neale, W. (1964) The peculiar economics of professional sport. *Quarterly Journal of Economics* **78, 1:** 1–14.

Nevill, A., Balmer, N., and Williams, M. (1999) Crowd influence on decisions in association football. *Lancet (letter)* **353:** 1416.

Nevill, A. M., and Holder, R. L. (1999) Home advantage in sport: An overview of studies on the advantage of playing at home. *Sports Medicine* **28:** 221–236.

Nichols, G. (2004) Pressures on Volunteers in the UK. In: Stebbins, R. and Graham, M. (eds). *Volunteering as Leisure/Leisure as volunteering: An International Assessment*. CABI Publishing, Wallingford.

Noll, R. (1974) *Government and the Sports Business*. Brookings Institution, Washington, DC.

NSW Treasury (1997) Economic Impact of the Sydney Olympic Games, http://www.treasury.nsw.gov.au/pubs/trp97_10/index.htm.

Oga, J. (1998) Business fluctuation and the sport industry in Japan: An analysis of the sport industry from 1986 to 1993. *Journal of Sport Management* **12, 1:** 63–75.

Owen, P., and Weatherston, C. (2004) Uncertainty of outcome and Super 12 rugby union attendances. *Journal of Sports Economics* **5, 4:** 347–370.

Page, L., and Page, K. (2007) The second leg home advantage: Evidence from European football cup competitions. *Journal of Sports Sciences* **25, 14:** 1547–1556.

Papanikos, G. (1999) *Tourism Impact of the 2004 Olympic Games*. Tourism Research Institute, Athens.

Pareto, V. (1906) Manual of Political Economy. Translated by A.S. Schwier (1971). New York Kelley.

Peel, D., and Thomas, D. (1988) Outcome uncertainty and the demand for football: An analysis of match attendances in the English football league. *Scottish Journal of Political Economy* **35, 3:** 242–249.

Peel, D., and Thomas, D. (1997) Handicaps, outcome uncertainty and attendance demand. *Applied Economics Letters* **4, 9:** 567–570.

Phlips, L. (1978) The demand for leisure and money. *Econometrica* **46, 5:** 1025–1043.

Pollard, R. (2006a) Worldwide regional variations in home advantage in association football. *Journal of Sports Sciences* **24, 3:** 231–240.

Pollard, R. (2006b) Home advantage in soccer. *Journal of Sport Behaviour* **29, 2:** 169–189.

Pollard, R., and Pollard, G. (2005) Long-term trends in home advantage in professional team sports in North America and England (1876–2003). *Journal of Sports Sciences* **23, 4:** 337–350.

Parro, N., Bizzaglia, G., and Conti, D. (1999) The Sports System and Sports Organisations in Italy. In: Heinemann, K. (ed). *Sports Clubs in Various European Countries.* Hofmann, Schorndorf.

Porter, P.K. (2007) The Paradox of Inelastic Sports Pricing Managerial and Decision Economics **28**: 157–158.

Preuss, H. (2004) *The Economics of Staging the Olympics. A Comparison of the Games 1972–2008.* Edward Elgar, Cheltenham.

Price, D., and Sen, K. (2003) The demand for game day attendance in college football: An analysis of the 1997 division 1-A season. *Managerial and Decision Economics* **24:** 35–46.

Price Waterhouse Coopers. (2005) *Olympic Games Impact Study, Final Report.* DCMS, London.

Primault, D., and Rouger, A. (1999) How relevant is North American experience for professional team sports in Europe? In: Jeanrenaud, C. and Kesenne, S. (eds). *Competition policy in professional sports: Europe after the Bosman case.* Standaard Editions, Antwerp.

Púig, N., Garcia, O., and Lopez, C. (1999) Sports Clubs in Spain. In: Heinemann, K. (ed). *Sports Clubs in Various European Countries.* Hofmann, Schorndorf.

Putnam, R. (2000) *Bowling Alone.* Simon and Schuster, New York.

Quirk, J., and El-Hodiri, M. (1974) The Economic Theory of a Professional Sports League. In: Noll, R. (ed). *Government and the Sports Business.* Brookings Institute, Washington, DC.

Quirk, J., and Fort, R. (1992) *Pay dirt: the business of professional team sports.* Princeton University Press, Princeton.

Rahmann, B., Weber, W., Groening, Y., Kurscheidt, M., Napp, H.-G., and Pauli, M. (1998) *Sozio-ökonomische analyse der fussball-welrmeisterschaft 2006 in Deutschland: Gesellschaftliche wirkungen, kosten-nutzenanalyse und finanzierungsmodelle einer sportgrossveranstaltung.* Sport un Buch Strauss, Cologne.

Rascher, D., and Solmes, J. (2007) Do fans want close contests? A test of the uncertainty of outcome hypothesis in the NBA. *International Journal of Sport Finance* **2, 3:** 130–141.

Rathke, A. and Woitek, U. (2007) Economics and Olympics: An efficiency analysis. Working Paper, Institute for Empirical Research in Economics, University of Zurich.

Research Centre for Sport in Canadian Society and Centre for Sport Policy Studies (2005) Volunteerism: Researching the Capacity of Canadian Sport. Sport Canada.

Robbins, L. (1940) *An Essay on the Nature and Significance of Economic Science.* Macmillan, London.

Roberts G., (2006) Accounting for achievement in Athens: a count data analysis of national Olympic performance, Economic Working Paper EWP0602, University of Victoria, department of Economics.

Robinson, J., and Godbey, G. (1997) *Time for life: the surprising ways Americans use their time*. Pennsylvania State University Press, University Park.

Robertson, R. (1995) Glocalisation: Time-space and homogeneity-heterogeneity. In: Featherstone, M., Lash, S. and Robertson, R. (eds). *Global Modernities*. Sage, London.

Roderick, M. (2001) The Role of Agents in Profesional Football in Singer and Friedlander Football Review: 2001–2002 Season.

Rodgers, B. (1977) *Rationalising Sports Policies; Sport in its Social Context: International Comparisons*. Council of Europe, Strasbourg.

Rodgers, B. (1978) *Rationalising Sports Policies; Sport in its Social Context: Technical Supplement*. Council of Europe, Strasbourg.

Rosen, S. (1981) The economics of superstars. *American Economic Review* **71, 5:** 845–858.

Rottenberg, S. (1956) The baseball players labour market. *Journal of Political Economy* **64, 3:** 243–258.

Russell, D. (1997) *Football and the English: A social history of Association football in England, 1863–1995*. Carnegie, Preston.

Sacks, J. (2002) The money trail, measuring your impact on the local economy using LM3. New Economics Foundation/Countryside Commission.

Salamon, L., and Anheier, H. (1997) *Defining the Nonprofit Sector: A Cross-national Analysis*. Manchester University Press, Manchester.

Samuelson, P. A. (1947) *Foundations of Economic Analysis*. Harvard University Press, Cambridge, MA.

Sanderson, A. R. (2002) The many dimensions of competitive balance. *Journal of Sports Economics* **3, 2:** 204–228.

Sanderson, A., and Siegfried, J. (1997) The implications of athlete freedom to contract: Lessons from North America. *Institute of Economic Affairs* **17, 3:** 7–13.

Sandler, T., and Tschirhart, J. (1997) Club theory: Thirty years later. *Public Choice* **93:** 335–355.

Sandy, R., Sloane, P., and Rosentraub, M. (2004) *The Economics of Sport: An International Perspective*. Palgrave Macmillan, Basingstoke.

Scheerder, J., Vanreusel, B., and Taks, M. (2005a) Stratification Patterns of Active Sport Involvement Among Adults. *International Review for the Sociology of Sport* **40:** 139–162.

Scheerder, J., Vanreusel, B., Taks, M., and Renson, R. (2005b) Social Changes in Youth Sports participation Styles 1969–1999: The case of Flanders: Belgium. *Sport, Education and Society* **10:** 321–341.

Schmidt, M., and Berri, D. (2001) Competitive balance and attendance: The case of major league baseball. *Journal of Sports Economics* **2, 2:** 145–167.

Schwartz, B., and Barsky, S. (1977) The home advantage. *Social Forces* **55:** 551–559.

Schwartz, J. T., Isaacs, J. P., and Carilli, A. M. (2007) To Race or to Place?: An Empirical Investigation of the Efficiency of the NASCAR Points Competition. *Journal of Sports Economics* **8:** 633–641.

Scitovsky, T. (1941) A note on welfare propositions in economics. *Review of Economic Studies* **9:** 77–88.

Scully, G. (1974) Pay and performance in major league baseball. *The American Economic Review* **64, 6:** 915–930.

Scully, G. (1994) Managerial efficiency and survivability in professional team sports. *Managerial and Decision Economics* **15:** 403–411.

Stamm H., and Lamprecht M. (2001) Sydney 2000 – The best Games ever? World sport and relationships of structural dependency, Paper presented at the 1st World Congress of the Sociology of Sport, July 2001, Seoul, South-Korea.

Semens, A.P. (2008) Player Representatives in the Football Industry, PhD Thesis University of Central Lancashire, UK.

Shropshire, K. L., and Davis, T. (2003) *The Business of Sports Agents*. University of Pennsylvania Press, Philadelphia.

Siegfried, J., and Zimbalist, A. (2000) The economics of sports facilities and their communities. *Journal of Economic Perspectives* **14, 3:** 95–114.

Simmons, R. (1996) The demand for English league football: A club level analysis. *Applied Economics* **28, 2:** 139–155.

Simmons, R. (1997) Implications of the Bosman Ruling for Football Transfer Markets's'in Sloane, P., (ed). *Institute of Economic Affairs* **17**:13–18.

SIRC (2005) Sport Market Forecasts 2005–2009, Sheffield.

Skille, E. A. (2005) Individuality or cultural reproduction. *International Review for the Sociology of Sport* **40, 3:** 307–320.

Skirstad, B. (1999) Norwegian Sport at the Crossroad. In: Heinemann, K. (ed). *Sports Clubs in Various European Countries*. Hofmann, Schorndorf.

Slack, T. (1999) An Outsider looking in or an Insider looking out? In: Heinemann, K. (ed). *Sports Clubs in Various European Countries*. Hofmann, Schorndorf.

Sloane, P. (1971) The economics of professional football: The football club as a utility maximiser. *Scottish Journal of Political Economy* **17, 2:** 121–146.

Sloane, P.J. and Campbell, A. (1997) The implication of the Bosman Case for Professional Football, University of Aberdeen Discussion Paper 02.

Solberg, E., and Wong, D. (1992) Family time use: Leisure, home production, market work and work related travel. *The Journal of Human Resources* **27, 3:** 485–510.

Sport England (1999a) Best Value Through Sport: The Value of Sport. London.

Sport England (1999b) Best Value Through Sport: Case Studies. London.

Sport England (2004a) The Framework for Sport in England.

Sport England (2004b) Driving up participation: The Challenge for Sport.

Sport England SouthWest (2006) Active Play and Informal Sport, Somerset.

Stamm, H., and Lampecht, M. (1999) Sports Organisations in Switzerland. In: Heinemann, K. (ed). *Sports Clubs in Various European Countries*. Hofmann, Schorndorf.

Staudohar, P. (1988) The football strike of 1987: The question of free agency. *Monthly Labour Review* **111, 8:** 26–31.

Stemple, C. (2005) Adult Participation in Sport as Cultural Capital. *International Review for the Sociology of Sport* **40:** 411–432.

Stratton, M., Conn, L., Liaw, C. and Connolly, L. (2005) Sport and Related Physical Activity: The Social Correlates of Participation and Non-Participation by Adults. Sport management Association of Australia and New Zealand, Conference, Canberra.

Sturgis, P., and Jackson, J. (2003) *Examining participation in sporting and cultural activities: Analysis of the UK 2000 Time Use Survey*. Department for Culture, Media and Sport, UK.

Sutter, M., and Kocher, M. (2004) Favoritism of agents – The case of referees' home bias. *Journal of Economic Psychology* **25, 4:** 461–469.

Szymanski, S. (2002) The economic impact of the world cup. *World Economics* **3, 1:** 169–177.

Szymanski S. (2003a) The economic design of sporting contests. *Journal of Economic Literature*, 41, December: 1137–1187.

Szymanski, S. (2003b) The assessment: The economics of sport. *Oxford Review of Economic Policy* **19, 4:** 467–477.

Szymanski, S. (2004) Professional team sports are only a game. *Journal of Sports Economics* **5, 2:** 111–126.

Szymanski, S. (2006a) A Theory of the Evolution of Modern Sport. International Association of Sports Economists, Working Paper, No 06-30.

Szymanski, S. (2006b) Why have Premium Sports Rights Migrated to Pay-TV in Europe but not in the US? In: Jeanrenaud, C. and Kesenne, S. (eds). *The Economics of Sport and the Media.* Edward Elgar, Cheltenham, UK.

Szymanski, S., and Kesenne, S. (2004) Competitive balance and gate revenue sharing in team sports. *Journal of Industrial Economics* **53:** 165–177.

Szymanski, S., and Kuypers, T. (1999) *Winners and losers, the business strategy of football.* Penguin Books, London.

Szymanski, S., and Zimbalist, A. (2005) *How Americans Play Baseball and the Rest of the World Plays Soccer.* The Brookings Institution, Washington, DC.

Taks, M., Renson, R., and Vanreusel, B. (1999) Consumer expenses in sport: A marketing tool for sports. *The European Journal for Sport Management* **6, 1:** 4–18.

Taks, M., and Kesenne, S. (2000) The economic significance of sport in Flanders. *Journal of Sports Management* **14, 4:** 342–365.

Taks, M., and Scheerder, J. (2006) Youth Sports Participation Styles and market Segmentation Profiles: Evidence and Applications. *European Sport Management Quarterly* **6:** 85–121.

Tcha, M., and Pershin, V. (2003) Reconsidering performance at the Summer Olympics and revealed comparative advantage. *Journal of Sports Economics* **4, 3:** 216–239.

The Conference Board of Canada (2005) Strengthening Canada: The Socio-economic benefits of sport participation in Canada. Ottawa.

Thrane, C. (2000) Men, women and leisure-time: Scandinavian evidence of gender inequality. *Leisure Sciences* **22:** 109–122.

Tidsell, C. (2006) Valuation of Tourisms' Natural Resources. In: Dwyer, L. and Forsyth, P. (eds). *International Handbook on the Economics of Tourism.* Edward Elgar, Cheltenham.

Tollison, R. (2001) Review of Rosentraub, M. (1999), Major League Losers: The Real Cost of Sports and Who's Paying For It. New York Basic Books. *Journal of Sports Economics* **2, 2:** 206–207.

Toohey, K., and Veal, A. (2000) *The Olympic Games: A social science perspective.* CABI publishing, New York.

Torkildsen, G. (1994) *Torkildsen's Guide to Leisure Management.* Longman, London.

Tullock, G. (1980) Efficient Rent Seeking. In: Buchannan, J., Tollison, R. and Tullock, G. (eds). *Toward a Theory of Rent Seeking Society.* A and M University Press, Texas.

United Nations (2001) International Year of the Volunteer 2001: International Symposium on Volunteering Final Report. International Symposium on Volunteering, 18 to 21 November 2001, Geneva, Switzerland. www.iyv2001.org.

U.S. Department of Health and Human Services, Centers for Disease Control and Prevention, National Center for Chronic Disease Prevention and Health Promotion, (1996) A Report of the Surgeon General, Atlanta, GA.

Utt, J., and Fort, R. (2002) Pitfalls to measuring Competitive Balance with Gini Coefficients. *Journal of Sports Economics* **3, 4:** 367–373.

Vamplew, W. (1988) *Pay Up and Play the Game: Professional Sport in Britain 1875–1914*. Cambridge University Press, Cambridge.

van Bottenburg, M., Rijnen, B., and van Sterkenburg, J. (2005) *Sports participation in the European Union: Trends and Differences*. W.J.H. Mulier Institute and Arko Sports Media, The Netherlands.

Verhaegen, D. (2006) *De verklarende factoren van de toeschouwersaantallen in de Belgische hoogste voetbalklasse, eindverhandeling handelswetenschappen*. Lessius Hogeschool, Antwerpen.

Veraros, N., Kasimati, E., and Dawson, P. (2004) The 2004 Olympic Games announcement and its effect of the Athens and Milan stock exchanges. *Applied Economic Letters* **11:** 749–753.

Von Allmen, P. (2001) Is the Reward System in NASCAR Efficient? *Journal of Sports Economics* **2:** 62–79.

Vrooman, J. (1995) A general theory of professional sports leagues. *Southern Economic Journal* **61:** 971–990.

Vrooman, J. (2007) Theory of the beautiful game: The unification of European football. *Scottish Journal of Political Economy* **54, 3:** 314–354.

Waylen, P., and Snook, A. (1990) Patterns of regional success in the football league, 1921 to 1987. *Area* **22:** 353–367.

Weed, M., Robinson, L., Downward, P., Green, M., Henry, I., Houlihan, B., and Argent, E. (2005) *Academic Review of the Role of Voluntary Sports Clubs*. Institute of Sport and Leisure Policy, Loughborough University.

Weisbrod, B. A. (1978) *The Voluntary Nonprofit Sector: An Economic Analysis*. Lexington Books, Lexington.

Weisbrod, B. A. (1988) *The Non-Profit Economy*. Heath, Lexington.

Weisbrod, B. A. (1998) *To Profit or not to Profit: The Commercial Transformation of the non profit sector*. Cambridge University Press, Cambridge.

Williams, G. (1994) *The Code War*. Yore Publications, Middlesex.

Williamson, O. (1969) Corporate Control and Economic Behaviour.

Williamson, O. (1971) Managerial Discretion, Organisation Form and the multi-Division Hypothesis. In: Marris, R. and Wood, A. (eds) (1971) The Corporate Economy, Growth, Competition and innovative Potential. London: Macmillan.

Williamson, O. (1975) *Markets and Hierarchies: Analysis and Antitrust Implications*. Free Press, New York.

Williamson, O. (1981) The modern corporation: Origins, evolution, attributes. *Journal of Economic Literature* **19:** 1537–1568.

Williamson, O. (1985) *The Economic Institutions of Capitalism: Firms, Markets, Relational Contracting*. Collier Macmillan, London.

Wilson, B. (2004) A Logistic Regression Model of the Decision of Volunteers to Enter a Sports Coach Education Programme. In: Stebbins, RA. and Graham, M. (eds). *Volunteering as Leisure/Leisure as volunteering: An International Assessment*. CABI Publishing, Wallingford.

Wilson, P., and Sim, B. (1995) The demand for semi-pro league football in Malaysia 1989–1991: A panel data approach. *Applied Economics* **27:** 131–138.

Winfree, J. and Fort, R. (2008) Fan substitution and the 2004-05 NHL lockout. Journal of Sports Economics, 10: 1-10. NOTE: The on-line version is not too clear about pagination, c f Brown and Link above!.

Winfree, J., McCluskey, J., Mittelhammer, R., and Fort, R. (2004) Location and attendance in major league baseball. *Applied Economics* **36:** 2117–2124.

Wolff, N., Weisbrod, B. and Bird, E. (1993) The supply of volunteer labor: The case of hospitals. *Nonprofit Management and Leadership* **14, 1:** 23–45.

Yu, M. (2004) *The Economic and Social Impacts of Hosting Selected International Games*. Research and Library Services Division Legislative Council Secretariat, Hong Kong.

Zuzanek, J. (1978) Social differences in leisure behaviour: Measurement and interpretation. *Leisure Sciences* **1, 3:** 271–293.

List of abbreviations

AC   Average costs
AFL   American Football League
AL   American League
AR   Average revenue
C   Total cost
CL   Champions League
ECB   England and Wales Cricket Board
EFL   English Football League
FA   Football Association
FIFA   Federation Internationale de Football Association
GAA   Gaelic Athletic Association
GLS   Generalized least squares
ICB   International Cricket Board
IOC   International Olympic Committee
IRB   International Rugby Board
MC   Marginal costs
ML   Maximum likelihood
MLB   Major League Baseball
MP   Marginal product
MPB   Marginal private benefit
MPC   Marginal private cost
mpc   Marginal propensity to consume
MPL   Marginal product of labour
MR   Marginal revenue
MRP   Marginal revenue product
MRS   Marginal rate of substitution
MRTS   Marginal rate of technical substitution
MSB   Marginal Social Benefit
MSC   Marginal Social Cost
NBA   National Basketball Association
NCAA   National Collegiate Athletic Association
NFL   National Football League
NHL   National Hockey League
NL   National League
OLS   Ordinary Least Squares
P   Price
PL   Premier League
Q   Output or Quantity
R   Total Revenue

RFL	Rugby Football League
RFU	Rugby Football Union
SL	Super League
UEFA	Union of European Football Associations

Index

411

ISBN: 978-0-7506-8354-8; PII: B978-0-7506-8354-8.00022-3; Author: Downward; Document ID: 00022; Chapter ID:

ISBN: 978-0-7506-8354-8; PII: B978-0-7506-8354-8.00022-3; Author: Downward; Document ID: 00022; Chapter ID: